Y0-BQA-396

The Popular Front in France

The Popular Front in France defending democracy, 1934-38

JULIAN JACKSON

Lecturer in History, University College, Swansea

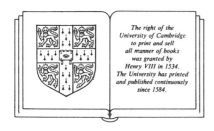

The right of the
University of Cambridge
to print and sell
all manner of books
was granted by
Henry VIII in 1534.
The University has printed
and published continuously
since 1584.

CAMBRIDGE UNIVERSITY PRESS

Cambridge

New York   New Rochelle   Melbourne   Sydney

Soc
DC
396
J335
1988

Published by the Press Syndicate of the University of Cambridge
The Pitt Building, Trumpington Street, Cambridge CB2 1RP
32 East 57th Street, New York, NY 10022, USA
10 Stamford Road, Oakleigh, Melbourne 3166, Australia

© Cambridge University Press 1988

First published 1988

Printed in Great Britain by The University Press, Cambridge

British Library cataloguing in publication data
Jackson, Julian
The Popular Front in France: defending democracy, 1934–1938.
1. Front populaire
I. Title
324.244'07   JN3007.F7

Library of Congress cataloguing in publication data
Jackson, Julian, 1954–
The Popular Front in France: defending democracy,
1934–1938/Julian Jackson.
        p.   cm.
Bibliography.
Includes index.
ISBN 0 521 32088 7
1. France – Politics and government – 1914–1940.
2. Popular fronts – France – History – 20th century.
3. Front populaire. I. Title.
DC396.J335   1987   944.081'5 – dc19   87-17204   CIP

ISBN 0 521 32088 7

ROBERT MANNING
STROZIER LIBRARY

FEB 21 1989

Tallahassee, Florida

CE

Contents

Illustrations

Preface

On 21 May 1981 François Mitterrand assumed the presidency of the Fifth Republic with the following words:

On this day when I take over the highest responsibilities, I think of those millions of men and women, leaven of our people, who have, over two centuries, in peace and in war, through their blood and their labour, shaped the history of France from which they have been excluded except through brief and glorious breaks (*fractures*) in the fabric of our society. It is . . . in their name that I speak . . . at this moment when, at the third stage of a long and arduous journey – after the Popular Front and the Liberation – the democratically expressed political majority in France has coincided with its sociological majority.

The Popular Front of 1936; the Liberation of 1944; the victory of the left in 1981: it is the first of Mitterrand's three 'stages' which forms the subject of this book. That Mitterrand should have sought historical legitimacy for his presidency in the Popular Front testifies to the resonance of the memory of that period in twentieth-century French history – however indisputably 'brief' and sometimes questionably 'glorious' a *fracture* it may have been. In 1936 France had her first ever Socialist Prime Minister, Léon Blum, and for the first time the Communists comprised part of the government's parliamentary majority (as they did again in 1944 and 1981 when contrary to 1936 they also participated in the government). The significance of these events is all the greater if it is remembered that in the seventy-six years between the founding of a unified French Socialist Party in 1905 and Mitterrand's victory in 1981 Socialists have headed governments for only five years (as opposed to twenty for the British Labour Party), and not always then at the head of recognizably left-wing governments.[1] Indeed as Mitterrand himself observed on another occasion, between the Revolution of 1789 and his victory in 1981, the left in France has been in power only three times. 1848, the Commune of 1871 and the Popular Front. Although other periods could be conceivably added to this list – for example 1924–6, 1944–7, 1956–8 – the very fact that their memory is too tarnished for the left today to be willing to claim them as part of its inheritance is sufficient to demonstrate the fragility of the left's historical achievement in France.

In this context it is not surprising that the memory of the Popular Front should loom so large.

The Popular Front was not an exclusively French phenomenon. The French Popular Front was only one national component of an anti-fascist strategy pursued by the Communist International (Comintern) in the 1930s. In 1928 the Comintern had defined fascism as simply one form of bourgeois domination in no way qualitatively different from bourgeois democracy: it was chronologically the final phase of capitalism and a necessary stage in the transition to Socialism. Fascists were therefore a less dangerous enemy than social democrats. The disastrous results of this policy in Germany led, gradually, to a revision of policy. Fascism was now defined as 'the open terroristic dictatorship of the most reactionary, most chauvinistic and most imperialist elements of finance capital'. Fighting fascism now became the first priority. This was the purpose of the Popular Front strategy which involved a postponement of revolutionary objectives in favour of a broad anti-fascist alliance with Socialist and liberal bourgeois parties. There were Popular Front governments in France, Spain and Chile, and Popular Front alliances in several other countries.

Although this book is a study exclusively of the French Popular Front, that history cannot be separated from its international context: for example, the attitude of the French government in 1936 importantly influenced the fate of the Spanish Popular Front and indeed of the Spanish Republic. In the 1930s, domestic political conflicts were throughout Europe placed by their protagonists in a wider international setting. As one of the leading intellectuals involved in the French Popular Front wrote in 1936: 'writers who have travelled to the United States or across Latin America, have been telling us how closely those peoples are following current events in France. On the success or failure of the French Popular Front may depend, they assure us, the political orientation of the world for the next fifty years.'[2] This was not entirely hyperbole. With the destruction of German Communism in 1933 Paris became the centre of the European anti-fascist movement and refugees from Hitler flocked to France. The Communist front organizer Willi Münzenburg transferred his operations from Berlin to Paris. The first official choice of the Left Book Club in Britain was Maurice Thorez's *France Today and the People's Front*.

Somewhat surprisingly there has been no general history of the Popular Front in English. And even in French there has been a curious lack of scholarly studies since the 1960s. The two most important books appeared around the time of the Popular Front's thirtieth anniversary. The first was George Lefranc's *Histoire du Front Populaire* (1965) and the second, published in 1967, was *Léon Blum, Chef de Gouvernement*, the proceedings of a colloquium on Blum's government held at the Fondation

Nationale des Sciences Politiques in 1965. Also useful is the little study by Jean Touchard and Louis Bodin, *Front populaire 1936* (1961), which contains many extracts from the contemporary press and provides a good picture of the heady atmosphere of 1936. And yet since these works were written there has been important new work on aspects of French history in the 1930s which any satisfactory overall view of the Popular Front needs to incorporate.[3]

Broadly speaking French histories of the Popular Front have fallen into three historiographical traditions each of which emerges from the politics of the period. First, there are what might be called the *gauchiste* works. These, whether Trotskyist, anarchist or left-Socialist, stress the importance of the Popular Front as a potentially revolutionary mass movement which was betrayed by the Blum government and by the political parties, especially the Communists. Representative of this view are the works of two members of the left wing of the Socialist Party in the 1930s, Colette Audry's *Léon Blum ou la politique du juste* (1956) and Daniel Guérin's *Révolution manquée* (1963), whose title is an argument in itself.[4]

Secondly, there is a tradition that could be characterized as Socialist. The most extreme example of this is Jules Moch's *Le Front populaire: grande éspérance* (1971). Moch, who died in 1985, was a young collaborator of Blum in the 1930s and a leading member of the Socialist Party after 1945. His book is written from a standpoint of almost totally uncritical adulation of Blum; the Popular Front is seen as a success. More reserved about Blum are the writings of Georges Lefranc especially his already mentioned history. Lefranc was in the 1930s a young Socialist intellectual and member of a group which tried to convert the party to 'planning' but was thwarted in this by the party hierarchy and by Blum himself; during the Popular Front period Lefranc transferred most of his activities to the trade union movement (CGT) where he was associated with the anti-Communist wing. In his historical writing he attempted to write with detachment rather than as an ex-participant, although his account betrays limited sympathy for Blum and sees the Popular Front as a missed opportunity to introduce the reforms advocated by the planners. Nonetheless Lefranc's history remains the best available, but it suffers from two drawbacks: first, he is much less familiar with, and interested in, the universe of the Communists than that of the Socialists and the CGT, and he tends therefore to underplay the Communists' role; secondly, although himself involved in the cultural life of the period (he and his wife ran the CGT's Workers Education Institute), he gives little space to the cultural upheaval which was such an important part of the experience of 1936.

The third tradition of writing about the Popular Front is that associated with the French Communist Party (PCF) – as for example in J. Chambaz *et al. Le Front populaire* (1972). Communist Party historiography has gradually evolved during the process of de-Stalinization and some of its more glaring distortions have been abandoned. But throughout it has been characterized by a desire to emphasize the crucial role played by the PCF in the creation of the Popular Front and to stress the autonomy of the French party and underplay its dependence on the Soviet Union. Communist historians have also tended to direct substantially more attention to the 'heroic' period of the formation of the Popular Front before 1936 (when the party's role was vital) than to the period of Blum's government (when its influence on affairs was more restricted): thus one of the most recent Communist rewritings devotes seventy-two pages to the period 1934–6 and only nineteen to the period 1936–8.[5]

Apart from these three historiographical traditions, the most prevalent image of the Popular Front in the French popular historical consciousness is of a moment of lyrical fraternity, a spring-time of *bonheur*. Blum's government is best remembered for having given paid holidays to the French working class. This is the Popular Front of the primary school text-book. Even those who lived through the period have a tendency to view it through this myth. Thus a recent poll which asked: 'What did the Popular Front mean to you?' received the following answer from an inhabitant of Marseilles: 'thanks to the Popular Front we were able to see the sea'.[6] But I have not approached the subject in a particularly revisionist spirit with the intention of debunking such myths or uncovering at what might now seem excesses of lyricism. Indeed, it would be wrong to do so precisely because the myth of the Popular Front was in an important sense its truth. It was lived as a myth, as a great revolutionary pageant, and what it said about itself is no less significant than what it achieved: its words were among its most important acts.

I have also endeavoured not to force the protean diversity of the Popular Front into the strait-jacket of a single interpretation, as well as trying to offer an account which is not too centred on Paris. And throughout I have sought to stress the Popular Front's triple character as a mass movement, political coalition, a government. Precisely because of this triple character it is impossible and unhelpful to attempt to date the end of the Popular Front with any precision. The unanimity of the left of which the Popular Front was the political expression came to an end in July 1936 with the outbreak of the Spanish Civil War; the political coalition in parliament suffered its first setback in December 1936 when the Communists abstained in a vote of confidence; Blum's government fell in June 1936; the Socialists withdrew from participation in government in January 1938; the working-class movement was crushed in the general strike of November 1938: these are the major milestones on the road to decline. But as David Thomson wrote many years ago, the Popular Front did not collapse: 'it was smothered by the looming clouds of international crisis'.[7] I have chosen therefore not to ascribe any definite terminal date to this book. It deals in most detail with the period from 1934 until the fall of Blum but I have allowed myself to stray as far as the end of 1938.

The book is not organized as a linear narrative history of the Popular Front because over such a short span of time a detailed narrative is not necessarily the best way of disentangling the various different themes; events crowd in upon each other too rapidly. But for those who know nothing of the period, I have started with a short narrative which provides a relatively neutral chronology and an introduction to the political background. During the course of the book I have therefore taken this background for granted and assumed that the reader will need no explanation of terms such as '6 February', 'the Matignon Agreement', 'the Pause' and so on. The body of the book is divided into a series of thematic chapters which I have tried as far as possible to centre around the main historical debates to which the Popular Front has given rise: what caused the change in the Communist Party's tactics in 1934? what were the origins of the strikes of 1936? why did the Communist Party refuse to participate in Blum's government? what were the effects of the 40 hour week on the French economy? why did Blum pursue a policy of non-intervention in Spain? and so on.

The book is divided into five parts. Part 1 examines the prelude to, and origins of, the Popular Front's election victory of 1936; Part 5 provides a short post-mortem. The three middle parts correspond roughly to the triple character of the Popular Front as a mass movement, government and political coalition: Part 2 examines the social and cultural upheaval of the Popular Front era; Part 3 examines the policies of Blum's government, and, more briefly, of the Popular Front governments which followed; Part 4 examines the tensions within the coalition (and also looks at the right-wing opposition to it). The divisions between these three parts should not be taken too seriously. There is no simple distinction between the Popular Front as coalition, mass movement or government: the three continuously interacted with, and acted upon, each other. Compartmentalization of this kind would have been absolutely antithetical to a political movement which aspired above all to break down the barriers between the different sections of a highly compartmentalized society.

Finally a note on terminology. In the title to this book I have used the term 'Popular Front' which is a translation of the French 'Front Populaire' and Spanish 'Frente Popular'. In fact up to 1936 two terms were in common use in France: 'Rassemblement Populaire' and 'Front Populaire'. The term 'Front' has more combative connotations suggesting a clear line between allies and opponents. 'Rassemblement', which roughly means a gathering together, is more ecumenical in tone: it defines not so much the enemies to be excluded as the friends to be included. The term 'Front' tended to be preferred by the Communists, and 'Rassemblement' by their bourgeois partners the Radicals (except by those who hoped to discredit the movement) but in fact the two terms were used at first more or less interchangeably. The great demonstration of 14 July 1935, sometimes seen as the official birth of the Popular Front, was officially known as the Rassemblement Populaire. The committee which drew up the programme of Blum's Popular Front government was technically called the Comité du Rassemblement Populaire. But in the end it was the term Front Populaire which caught on. The most accurate English translation would probably be 'People's Front', and this is indeed the expression that was used in England in the 1930s. Since the war, however, the translation 'Popular Front' has been more commonly used, and following this convention I have adopted the term here. Only when translating the names of the many organizations spawned by the Popular Front have I used the previous term: thus Fédération Musicale Populaire appears as People's Music Federation.

I should add in conclusion that I offer this book not as a piece of sustained original research on the Popular Front but rather as an attempt to provide the synthesis which is lacking. To a large extent, therefore, I have relied on the research of many other historians. I hope I have made my debt to them sufficiently clear in the footnotes; it is only thanks to their work that this book has been able to be written. I also owe a number of more personal debts: to the History Department of Swansea University, and especially to its head, Professor Richard Shannon, for respecting my (now sadly ended) 'new blood' status and leaving me time to work on this book; to Mrs Glennis Jones, also of the History Department, who with great forebearance typed the first draft of my text and used it as a somewhat abrupt initiation into the joys (and trials) of wordprocessing; to Dr Jeremy Jennings, of the Politics Department at Swansea, who not only read one or two sections of the text but, not less importantly, procured for us two summers running a flat in the fourteenth *arrondissement* of Paris (not really Popular Front terrain but very agreeable nonetheless) where I was able to do the bulk of research and writing; finally, to my friends Alun and Brig not so much for any specific help as for just, so to speak, being there.

Swansea, September 1986

Abbreviations

ADLP   Association pour le dévélopement de la lecture publique
AEAR   Association des écrivains et artistes révolutionnaires
APAM   Association populaire des amis des musées
BSP   Brevet sportif populaire
CAP   Comité administratif permanent
CASPE   Comité d'action socialiste pour l'Espagne
CCEO   Centre confédéral d'éducation ouvrière
CCN   Comité confédéral national
CGPF   Confédération générale de la production française (up to August 1936)
       Confédération générale du patronat français (after August 1936)
CGT   Confédération générale du travail
CLAJ   Centre laique des auberges de la jeunesse
CNRS   Centre national des recherches scientifiques
CPAS   Comité de prévoyance et d'action sociale
CSAG   Centre syndical d'action contre la guerre
CVIA   Comité de vigilance des intellectuels anti-fascistes
ECCI   Executive committee of the communist international
FMP   Fédération musicale populaire
FSGT   Fédération sportive et gymnique du travail
FTIF   Fédération des théâtres indépendants de France
FTOF   Fédération des théâtres ouvriers de France
m.   *milliard* (thousand million)
PCF   Parti communiste français
POI   Parti ouvrier internationaliste
PPF   Parti populaire français
PSF   Parti social français
PSOP   Parti socialiste ouvrier et paysan
SFIO   Section française de l'internationale ouvrière
UTS   Union des techniciens socialistes

Introduction

The Popular Front: a narrative

On 6 February 1934 Paris experienced its bloodiest night of political violence since the Commune of 1871. Right-wing demonstrators had gathered in the Place de la Concorde, on the opposite side of the river from the Palais Bourbon, seat of the lower chamber of the French parliament. Some of the demonstrators were protesting against the newly formed government of the Radical, Edouard Daladier, which was coming before the Chamber for the first time; others were expressing their resentment against the parliamentary regime itself. Many of them were members of the various right-wing 'Leagues' – extra-parliamentary, sometimes para-military organizations which had sprung up in the previous few years. Daladier's was the fifth government in twenty months and this ministerial instability at a time when France was experiencing the worst effects of the world slump had resulted in a surge of anti-parliamentary feeling. At the end of 1933 the situation had been exacerbated by the revelation of a financial scandal which revealed that the swindler Alexandre Stavisky had enjoyed the protection of leading politicians. As the police were trying to arrest Stavisky in January, he committed suicide. It was widely believed that he had been killed to prevent his disclosing information embarrassing to the government. On 27 January the government of the Radical Camille Chautemps was forced to resign because it had underestimated the strength of feeling about the Stavisky Affair. Chautemps' successor Daladier had considerable difficulty in forming a government. Determined to make an impact, he dismissed the Prefect of Police, Jean Chiappe, who was accused on the left of being far from even-handed in his treatment of right and left-wing demonstrators. The sacking of Chiappe only further antagonized the right.

On 6 February various right-wing organizations called on their supporters to demonstrate against Daladier. Most of these demonstrations were due to converge on the Place de la Concorde. The bridge which led to the Chamber was guarded by mounted guards and police. But as the Place started to fill up the police came under pressure from demonstrators trying

1

to cross the bridge. The crowd became increasingly violent. People threw marbles under the hooves of the horses; others carried canes to which were attached razors with which to slash the bellies of the horses; railings were torn from the Tuileries Gardens and used as missiles; a bus was set on fire. At around seven o'clock the first shots were fired, almost certainly by the rioters. Soon afterwards the police and guards began to panic and opened fire themselves. Not until the early hours of the morning were the rioters finally dispersed. During the course of the night there had been fifteen deaths (of which one policeman) and 1,435 wounded. While this was happening outside, Daladier was given a vote of confidence by the frightened deputies. But on the next day, fearing that he could no longer maintain order, he resigned. For the first time since the collapse of the Second Empire in 1870 a government had been brought down through street violence.

The French left had both contemporary and historical analogies through which to view these events. In contemporary terms it saw them as a failed fascist putsch. It was believed that the rioters had been attempting to storm parliament and end the Republic. Fascism had already destroyed democracy in Italy and Germany; France was the next target. In historical terms the left interpreted the events of 6 February as further proof that the French right had never fully accepted the existence of the Republic, or yet another of the assaults to which the French Third Republic had been subjected since its foundation in 1871.

After the short-lived experiments of the First and Second Republics (1792 to 1804 and 1848 to 1851), the politicians who set up the Third Republic had attempted to protect their fragile creation by rooting it in the hearts and minds of the French people. During the 1880s they had organized a system of compulsory education whose role was to inculcate Republican values. The primary school teacher (*instituteur*) became as it were the lay missionary of the Republic in every village of France. Republicanism was not only a political system but also a cultural atmosphere, a secular ritual with its own liturgy and symbolism. The Republic had its hymn (the Marseillaise), its festival (14 July) and its emblem (the *tricolore*). It was embodied in the allegorical female figure of Marianne (still to be seen on French coins and whose bust stands in every French town hall). In spite of these efforts the enemies of the Republic had not disappeared. In the first thirty years of its existence, the regime had at various times come under attack from the right – most importantly during the Dreyfus Affair of the early twentieth century.

Around the figure of Alfred Dreyfus, a Jewish army officer wrongly accused of having spied for the Germans, crystallized an epic struggle between right and left for the political soul of France. Out of the Dreyfus

Affair emerged two organizations still in existence in the 1930s: the League of the Rights of Man which assembled intellectuals of the left in defence of Dreyfus; and Action Française, a monarchist, anti-semitic organization, which used the case of Dreyfus to attack the republican regime. Supporters of Action Française, known as Camelots du Roi, were to be among the demonstrators on 6 February 1934, while the League of the Rights of Man was to play a significant role in the origins of the Popular Front. It was no coincidence, therefore, that in 1935 the Socialist leader Léon Blum published his *Memories of the Affair*. To the left, the events of February 1934 seemed only too familiar.

The left's traditional response to any threat to the Republic was unity. Thus during the Dreyfus Affair the forces of the left had swallowed their differences and combined to support a Ministry of Republican Defence headed by René Waldeck-Rousseau. But since the war unity had become an increasingly elusive goal. By the early 1930s the left was split into three main parties: the Radical Socialists, the Socialists and the Communists. The Radical Socialists (or Radicals as they were more commonly known) were in fact neither radical nor socialist. In the early twentieth century they had been the party most committed to the defence of the Republic. This made them stridently anti-clerical and situated them on the left. But their electoral support came especially from what the French call the *classes moyennes* – peasants, shopkeepers, small businessmen and so on. Since the war the social conservatism of this electorate had conflicted increasingly with the party's attempt to remain faithful to its origins on the left. A pattern developed in which the Radicals would ally with the Socialists at elections and then sooner or later break with them once in power over a matter of economic policy. This first occurred in 1924 when the *cartel des gauches* – an alliance of Radicals and Socialists – had won the elections. The Radicals had formed a government under their leader Edouard Herriot with Socialist support but in 1926 a serious financial crisis drove them into a government of so-called National Union headed by the conservative politician Raymond Poincaré. In effect, therefore, the Radicals had become a centrist party of government indispensable to the formation of almost any coalition of left or right.

The Radicals' political schizophrenia contributed greatly to the instability of French politics. But the Socialist Party (SFIO) also bore responsibility for this situation. Ever since its foundation in 1905, the SFIO had been unsure how far it could compromise its Marxist identity and collaborate in the bourgeois parliamentary system. Could Socialists ally with parties to their right such as the Radicals? Could they participate in governments headed by Radicals? In 1914, swallowing their reservations, the Socialists had joined the coalition government of so-called 'Sacred Union' formed to fight the war. But the bitter taste left by this experience had only increased the reluctance of many Socialists to participate in government again. Broadly speaking the governing organs of the party – the National Council and the Permanent Administrative Commission (CAP) – in which parliamentary deputies were in a minority, tended to be hostile to participation, while the party's parliamentarians tended to be more favourable. The different currents of opinion in the party were officially recognized in groups known as *tendances* which received representation on the National Council and CAP proportional to the number of votes their motions received at the annual congress which assembled delegates from the departmental federations into which the party was organized. On the right, the Vie Socialiste *tendance* was firmly participationist; on the left, the Bataille Socialiste was hostile to participation. In 1924, therefore, despite the wishes of many Socialist deputies, the party had refused to enter the government of Herriot. This certainly weakened Herriot's position.

The Socialists' readiness to compromise on this issue was restricted by the presence on their left of the Communists. The French Communist Party (PCF) had been born in 1920 out of a split in the SFIO at its Congress of Tours. During the late 1920s, the PCF, in accordance with the policy of the Comintern, had pursued increasingly extremist tactics, drawing no distinction between Socialists and the right-wing parties. One consequence of this policy was seen in the Communist behaviour at elections. French elections took place over two rounds. If no candidate received an overall majority at the first round, a second was held at which the candidate with a plurality of votes was elected. The usual practice at the second round was that the less well placed candidates of the left stood down in favour of the best placed in order to maximize the possibilities of a left-wing victory by avoiding a split vote (the same procedure was followed on the right). But in 1928 the Communists broke with convention and refused to stand down at the second round even if the result was to let in a candidate of the right. As a result of these divisive tactics the PCF had become an increasingly marginal parliamentary force (only ten deputies elected in 1932). The Socialists nonetheless remained vulnerable to Communist accusations that they were selling out to the right. This limited their freedom of manoeuvre. The divisions between Socialists and Communists were replicated in the trade union movement by a split between the Communist General Confederation of Unitary Labour (CGTU) and the General Confederation of Labour (CGT). As a further complicating factor, the CGT was quite independent of the SFIO and indeed at times highly suspicious of it.

The political deadlock which preceded the Stavisky Affair was a direct result of this disunity on the left. After the elections of 1932 the combined forces of the Radicals (157 deputies) and Socialists (131) had commanded a comfortable majority. But, as in 1924, the two parties could not agree on economic policy at a moment when the first effects of the Depression made action to revive the economy urgent. The Radicals' preferred remedy was a milder version of the deflation proposed by the right; the Socialists advocated reflation. The logical solution would have been for the Radicals to form a coalition with the right but they were prevented from doing this by their sentimental attachment to the left. Another logical solution would have been for the Socialists to oppose the Radicals systematically and force them to make a choice but this the Socialists were unwilling to do for fear of letting in the right. Instead the Radicals were permitted by the Socialists to retain power as long as they did nothing; if they attempted to present a comprehensive economic programme they were brought down. The results were five governments in less than two years, legislative paralysis, economic decline and the growth of anti-parliamentary feeling. Then came 6 February.

The response of the left was symptomatic of its disunity. The Radicals, traumatized by the riots, rallied to the right-wing National Union government of Doumergue which presented itself as the last bulwark against anarchy but seemed to others to be the first step towards fascism. The PCF called for a protest demonstration on 9 February and the CGT for a general strike on 12 February. The Socialists decided to hold a series of demonstrations on the same day. The Communist demonstration of 9 February resulted in bloody clashes with the police (6 deaths and 100 injured). At the last moment the Communists also decided to join the day of action called by the CGT for 12 February. The general strike of that day was an outstanding success, especially in the public sector. Demonstrations were held throughout France. In Paris the Socialists and Communists marched separately to the Place de la Nation. But no one knew what would happen when the two columns converged. In the words of Blum:

I was marching in the front row. The gap between the two columns narrowed from second to second and we all shared the same anxiety: would the meeting of the two columns be a collision? Was this *journée* going to degenerate into a conflict between two factions of the working class population of Paris? . . . Now the two columns were face to face and from all sides the same cry sprang up . . . People shook hands. The heads of the columns melted into each other. This was not a collision but a fraternization. By a sort of popular groundswell the people's will had imposed unity of action of the working class.[1]

Another participant remembered the occasion in similar terms:

after a silent, brief moment of anguish, to the astonishment of the party and union leaders, this encounter triggered off a delirious enthusiasm, an explosion of shouts of joy. Applause, chants, cries of 'Unity, Unity.' The Popular Front had just been born before our eyes.[2]

This was an overoptimistic view: it was many months before this moment of unity was transformed into durable political cooperation. Nonetheless the *journée* of 12 February rapidly achieved semi-mythical status as the left's answer to 6 February and proof that unity was possible if the will was there.

In the immediate aftermath of 12 February the PCF resumed its attacks on the Socialists. March saw the founding of the Committee of Vigilance of Anti-Fascist Intellectuals (CVIA) which aspired to rally intellectuals of all political colours in defence of democracy. The success of this venture was further evidence of a growing desire for left-wing unity which the political parties could ill ignore. At the end of June the political situation was transformed by a change in the attitude of the Communist Party which suddenly invited the Socialist leaders to collaborate with it in joint action. The Socialists were suspicious but could not easily refuse. On 27 July, therefore, the two parties signed a 'Unity Pact': on a limited range of issues they were to participate in joint demonstrations and they were to cease their attacks upon each other. At the local elections of October 1934 Communist and Socialist candidates stood down at the second ballot for whichever of them was likeliest to win.

By this time, however, the Communists were also hoping to extend the Unity Pact into a wider 'Popular Front' embracing the Radicals. Initially this strategy enjoyed no success. Certainly the Radicals were becoming somewhat restive in Doumergue's government which proved no more impressive than its predecessors. Its strongest member, the Foreign Minister Louis Barthou, who attempted to rebuild France's alliance system in Eastern Europe and even embarked on reviving the pre-war Russian alliance, was assassinated in the autumn. In the economic field the government used emergency decree powers to attempt the deflationary policy which had been politically impossible before 1934. In November Doumergue was replaced by another right-wing government under Pierre Flandin who had a somewhat more liberal image than his predecessor. For the moment the Radicals were happy.

In the municipal elections of May 1935 Socialist–Communist cooperation was seen to be paying off. There was a marked swing to the left at the expense of the Radicals. This development once again stoked up dissatisfaction among the Radicals. And when in June the government collapsed in a financial crisis, a number of Radicals in parliament flirted with the idea of rebuilding the left coalition. But negotiations to this end failed for lack of a common programme of the left and a new right-wing government was formed under Pierre Laval, with Radical participation.

The second half of 1935 was a uniquely complicated period. The Radicals, courted ever more assiduously by the Communists, remained trapped in a government of the right from which an increasing number wanted to escape. Thus when on 14 July a huge demonstration was organized by the left, the Radicals agreed to join even though one of the main purposes of the occasion was to protest against the government in which several Radicals sat! The 14 July demonstration was a huge success. In the morning, at the Buffalo Stadium in the suburbs of Paris, the political leaders of the left swore an oath to remain united:

We take the oath to remain united to defend democracy, to disarm and dissolve the Leagues, to put our liberties out of reach of the attack of fascism. We swear on this day, which relives the first victory of Republicanism, to defend the democratic liberties conquered by the people of France, to give bread to the workers, work to the young, and peace for humanity to the world.

By a curious coincidence, while the oath was being sworn, Alfred Dreyfus, ghost of a previous upsurge of Republican fervour, was being buried in the Montmartre Cemetry: the assembled delegates at the Buffalo Stadium stood in a minute's silence of respect. In the afternoon there was a march through Paris.

The date, 14 July 1935, marked the baptism of the Popular Front. The process of transforming the fraternity of the street into a functioning political alliance was aided by the unpopularity of Laval. Three aspects of his policy alienated the left. First, he launched the most vigorous effort at deflation hitherto undertaken: all government expenditure, including the income on bonds, was cut by 10 per cent. Laval seemed determined to become the French Brüning – with similar effects on his popularity. In fact there were signs of an economic recovery in the second half of 1935 but it was the cuts that people noticed. Secondly, although Laval had, as Flandin's Foreign Minister, signed a Franco-Soviet pact in May, this was a policy that he had inherited from Barthou and could not easily abandon. His heart lay in a *rapprochement* with Germany and Italy. Thus when Mussolini attacked Ethiopia in October Laval tried to resist the imposition of sanctions, thereby antagonizing a left which remained attached to the idea of collective security through the League of Nations. Thirdly, the summer of 1935 saw a revival in the activities of the Leagues, and it was believed, with justice, that Laval was doing little to curb them: democracy still seemed in danger and Laval its most lukewarm defender.

In the face of the mounting opposition to Laval, negotiations proceeded between Communists, Socialists and Radicals. A Popular Front programme was signed on 11 January 1936. The position of the Radicals in the government became untenable and a few days later they resigned, thus precipitating Laval's fall. There was, however, no question of forming a

Popular Front government to carry out a major programme of reform only three months before elections were due. Instead a caretaker government, enjoying Socialist support and Communist abstention, was formed under the Radical, Albert Sarraut. The dynamic of unity which affected the political left had even greater repercussions on the trade unions: at the beginning of 1936 the CGT and CGTU amalgamated into a single CGT.

In the early months of 1936 two events reminded the electorate of the threats to democracy and peace which the Popular Front had been formed to combat. In February Blum was set upon and beaten up by members of Action Française; in March Germany reoccupied the demilitarized Rhineland. The first event caused almost more of a sensation than the second perhaps because it created more surprise and elicited less ambiguous responses: there was a massive protest march through Paris, again demonstrating the mobilizing force of the left. Blum's convalescence freed him from the necessity of responding immediately to Hitler's *coup de force* which embarrassed a left opposed in equal measure to fascism (hence Hitler) and war (hence resisting Hitler).

The elections of May 1936 gave a clear victory to the Popular Front with the Socialists emerging as the largest party. The results were as follows:

	May 1932	Outgoing Chamber May 1936	June 1936	Change between 1932 and 1936
Left				
PCF	11	10	72	+61
SFIO	131	97	147	+16
Radicals	157	159	106	−51
Various left	37	78	51	+14
TOTAL	336	344	376	+40
Right				
Centre left	120	165	76	−44
Centre right	138	106	138	0
Independents	0	0	6	+6
TOTAL	258	271	220	−38

Note: The discrepancy between the figures in columns 1 and 2 was due to defections and changes of allegiance – for instance that of a group of dissident Socialists in October 1933.

Although the figures gave a clear majority to the Popular Front, it is important to remember that this potential majority had existed in the Chamber of 1932 and that, as in 1932, the new majority was dependent on the consistent allegiance of the Radicals. The second round of the elections had taken place on 3 May but according to constitutional practice the outgoing parliament remained in place for another month. Thus Sarraut stayed on as a caretaker with Blum in the role, as he put it, of 'uncrowned dauphin'. Some Socialists argued that he should have assumed power at once, but Blum preferred to respect constitutional convention. When the leftist Socialist, Marceau Pivert, observed that the Fascists would not have shown such scruples, Blum objected that this was precisely why the Socialists would do so. It may be that this constitutional hiatus, combined with the euphoria aroused by the election victory, contributed to the wave of strikes and factory occupations which broke out in mid-May and gathered pace at the end of the month. The employers urged the government to take action. Sarraut consulted with the Chief of Army Staff and the Paris Prefect of Police. It was decided to wait for Blum to take power. Meanwhile on 24 May, at the traditional march of the left to the Mur des Fédérés, where the last defenders of the Commune had fallen in 1871, the verdict of the ballot box was, as it were, confirmed in the street: according to some (probably exaggerated) estimates 600,000 people participated; there were cries of 'To work Blum.' Otherwise matters proceeded according to convention when the left took power: while Blum prepared his government there was a flight of capital. Given the Communists' refusal to participate in the cabinet – thus giving the Socialists a taste of the medicine they had inflicted on the Radicals in 1924 and 1932 – Blum's government consisted of 18 Socialists, 13 Radicals and 4 independent Socialists.

By the time that the government took office on 6 June, France was paralyzed by an almost total general strike, with thousands of factories occupied. On 7 June representatives of employers and the CGT met at the Hôtel Matignon, residence of the Prime Minister, at the invitation of Blum. When the employers' delegates heard of the wages paid to some workers, one of them is said to have muttered: 'How is such a thing possible? How could we have done this? We have failed our duty in allowing such things to happen.' Still, it was fear not guilt which motivated the employers to sign the Matignon Agreement on 7 June. The agreement provided for the immediate establishment of collective labour contracts; an increase in wages ranging from 15 per cent for the lowest paid to 7 per cent for the highest paid with the total increased wage bill of no single concern exceeding 12 per cent (exceptionally low wages were to be adjusted upward before the implementation of this measure); finally workers' delegates were to be elected in all factories employing over ten workers. Later Blum remarked of this period that the employers had viewed him as a 'saviour' who had ended the largest strike movement in French history. This was probably true but in fact the Matignon Agreement had little impact on the strikes. The bourgeoisie's real saviour was the Communist leader, Maurice Thorez, who declared on 11 June: 'It is necessary to know how to end a strike.' From this moment the movement receded. By the end of July it was largely over.

Three days after the Matignon meeting, the government, fulfilling promises Blum had made on that occasion to the CGT, presented three bills to parliament – the first instituting a two-week paid annual holiday to all workers, the second reducing the working week to forty hours, the third simplifying the procedure for drawing up collective contracts. The bills became law in just over a week. This was unprecedented speed for any legislation in the Third Republic; for measures of this scope it would have been inconceivable but for the 'Grande Peur' of June 1936. Even the traditionalist Senate swallowed its reservations. The first twelve weeks of Blum's government were indeed its most fertile legislative period. Before parliament rose for the summer twenty-four major reforms had been voted. Among these were the semi-nationalization of the Bank of France, the nationalization of the arms industries, a public works programme, the setting up of a Wheat Marketing Board, an extension of the school leaving age. Another early measure was the dissolution of the Leagues, but the most important of these – the Croix de Feu – simply turned itself into a party (the PSF) and became only more successful. On 14 July another Popular Front demonstration was held in Paris – this time to celebrate the election victory and the Matignon Agreement. This was the Popular Front's moment of apotheosis. The timing was providential: three days later a military revolt broke out in Spain.

With the outbreak of the Spanish Civil War the Popular Front's springtime of innocence had come to an end. Blum's instinctive desire was to send aid to the beleaguered Spanish Republic where a Popular Front government had been elected in February. After three weeks he succumbed to diplomatic and political pressures and applied a policy of nonintervention. This decision was bitterly attacked by the Communists; the first breaches appeared in the coalition. Another source of Communist criticism was the government's financial policy. The flight of capital, temporarily stemmed by the end of the strikes, resumed during August. In September the government, in spite of earlier reassurances, was forced to devalue. When the workers returned from their first ever paid holidays, they found that inflation had eaten away many of the gains of the summer: intermittent industrial conflict resumed in the factories. Symbolic of the new more tense political mood was the suicide in November of Roger Salengro, the Minister of the Interior, after a scurrilous right-wing press campaign accusing him of having deserted during the war. In December 1936 the Communists, stepping up their opposition to the government's non-intervention policy, abstained for the first time in a vote of confidence.

More immediately serious for the government's future was the deteriorating financial situation. The capital flight had resumed soon after devaluation and on 13 February Blum announced the need for a 'pause' in the implementation of further reforms. Given that there had been few reforms anyway since the summer this mattered mainly as a statement of intent designed to win financial confidence. At the beginning of March the pause was translated into policy: the government announced a cut in public expenditure and the appointment of a committee of three 'experts' to supervise the stabilization fund which had been set up to manage the exchange rate of the franc after devaluation. 'Experts' meant, as it usually does, conservatives – in this case, a banker, Paul Baudouin, and two orthodox economists, Charles Rist and Jacques Rueff.

While Blum tried unsuccessfully to appease the right, he found himself being estranged from the left. In March 1937 a left-wing demonstration took place in the Paris suburb of Clichy to protest against a meeting of the PSF which the government refused to ban. Clashes took place between the demonstrators and the police and in somewhat obscure circumstances the police opened fire and six demonstrators died; among the wounded was Blum's collaborator André Blumel who had rushed to the spot. Blum himself, who had been at the Opera, arrived in evening dress and top hat – a fact that the Communists did not overlook in later anti-Socialist polemics.

May 1937 saw the opening in Paris of the great International Exhibition which had been planned by Blum's predecessors but which it fell to Blum's government to organize. Much prestige was staked on making the Exhibition a glittering showpiece to the success of the Popular Front. But persistent industrial conflicts meant that, in spite of personal appeals to the building workers by Blum himself, when the Exhibition was finally opened – three weeks late – by the President of the Republic, elaborate strategies were required to hide the considerable amount of unfinished building work.

In June the capital flight, which had never properly ceased, threatened again the stability of the franc. The situation was aggravated by the sudden and dramatic resignation of the 'experts'. The government demanded emergency decree powers to put an end to the speculation. The Chamber granted this request by 346 votes to 247 but the decree bill was rejected by the Senate. The Chamber passed a modified version of the original bill which was again rejected by the Senate. The majorities in the Chamber had been substantial but probably only because a large number of Radicals who had become disaffected from the Popular Front knew that they could rely on the Senate to do their dirty work for them. It was no doubt partly for this reason that when the Senate rejected the bill a second time, Blum decided to resign. He had held office for 380 days.

The fall of Blum did not mean the end of the Popular Front as a political coalition, although as far as many Radicals were concerned, the politics of the next two years largely consisted in finding the most elegant means of extracting themselves from it. Blum was succeeded by the Radical Chautemps, who formed a government in which Socialists participated with Blum acting as Vice-Premier; the Communists now offered to participate but they were a year too late. Although the government relied on the same majority as its predecessor, it nonetheless marked a subtle shift to the right: the key post of finance minister passed from the Socialist, Vincent Auriol, to a conservative Radical, Georges Bonnet. The new government did very little except to devalue a second time, extend the pause and attempt even more unsuccessfully than Blum to put an end to the endemic labour unrest. In January 1938, Chautemps, in a speech in parliament, demanded greater loyalty from the working class. For this he was criticized by the Communists who announced that they would abstain in a vote of confidence. To general surprise Chautemps used this as an occasion to offer the Communists their 'freedom' outside the coalition, thereby effecting the next stage in the disintegration of the Popular Front coalition. The Socialists protested and the government fell. There followed a prolonged ministerial crisis during which Blum floated the idea of a government of national unity. The attempt foundered but that it could even be suggested was proof that the Popular Front formula was becoming increasingly hollow. Chautemps formed a new government without, on this occasion, Socialist participation.

The new government lasted only two months and resigned on 9 March two days before Hitler marched into Austria. Given the menacing international situation Blum made a more sustained attempt to form a government of national unity extending from the Communists to the far right. He took the unprecedented step of addressing the assembled deputies of the right. The idea was a noble one but the right lacked nobility and anyway knew that it could soon return to power on its terms not Blum's. Faced with the non-cooperation of the right, Blum formed another Popular Front government of Radicals and Socialists. No one, least of all Blum, had any illusions about the durability of this government. Its function was simply to prove that, in parliament at least, the Popular Front was dead, and to pave the way for other solutions. Blum's second government lasted in fact twenty-six days. Once again a demand for financial decree powers was rejected by the Senate and Blum resigned.

On 10 April 1938 Daladier, who had been one of the Radicals most associated with the Popular Front, formed a government. Five portfolios went to members of the centre-right, none to the Socialists. In August, Daladier, who had hesitated as to what labour policy he would pursue, announced the need to extend the 40-hour week, which the working class had come to view as its most precious acquisition in June 1936. His right-wing Finance Minister, Paul Reynaud, issued decrees to this effect in November. The inevitable and intended result was a clash with the CGT. The failure of a one-day general strike on 30 November, to which the government responded with uncompromising toughness, symbolized the end of the labour upheaval which had commenced in June 1936. The Popular Front, born out of the general strike of 12 February 1934, finally died in that of 30 November 1938. Ironically, the 12 February strike had initially been conceived to protest against the forced resignation of Daladier, and the strike of 30 November was called to protest against the labour policy of the same Daladier.

The Popular Front was dead in other ways as well. The problems it had been formed to solve had been replaced by new ones to which it had no answer. It had wanted peace but evaded the issue of whether this should be achieved by resisting Hitler or conciliating him. The Munich Agreement, signed by Daladier in September 1938, made such evasions impossible. Only the Communists opposed the agreement unanimously; the rest of the French political class was agonizingly divided: the line between supporters and opponents of the Popular Front no longer represented anything meaningful in French politics.

Munich did not of course avert war. In June 1940 hundreds of thousands of French citizens fled south from the invading German forces. This 'exodus' of the summer of 1940 seems like some hideously distorted mirror image of that no less famous exodus of the summer of 1936 when hundreds of thousands of workers departed on their first ever paid holidays. As if to underline the point, the same parliament (minus the PCF which had been outlawed on the outbreak of war) which had voted confidence in Blum on 6 June 1936 to save the Republic, voted full powers to Marshall Pétain on 10 July 1940 to destroy it.

Prelude to power

1 ∞ The origins of the Popular Front

A political phenomenon such as the Popular Front did not suddenly grow up like a mushroom out of two Sunday polling days. It was linked to, and was in large measure a product of, that which went before it.

I have already indicated the *raison d'être* of the Popular Front coalition: it was a reflex of instinctive defence against the dangers which threatened French Republican institutions, and liberty itself.

(Léon Blum, 1942)

On the evening of 6 February 1934 the trade union leader André Delmas ate his dinner in a Paris restaurant near the Gare de l'Est. At about half-past-eight the restaurant proprietor announced that people had been shot in the Place de la Concorde. Delmas was not inclined to take such lurid rumours seriously and returned home by bus. Next morning he woke up to a changed city: 'In a night, the social climate was transformed. Faces were tense but everyone endeavoured to look impassive . . . People observed each other covertly. I tried to categorise the people I passed on the pavement. In which camp did this one fit? . . . Others looked at me and asked themselves if I was friend or foe.' Another observer commented: 'in a night human relationships had been transformed'. Such reactions testify to the dramatic impact of the events of 6 February on the French left: at the headquarters of the CGT one union leader distributed revolvers to his colleagues.[1]

Any study of the origins of the Popular Front must begin on 6 February 1934. But at the same time we must not exaggerate the importance of the events of one night: no more than the Popular Front itself, was the *journée* of February born, like a mushroom, out of one Wednesday afternoon's discontents. The riots were merely a symptom of the crisis of French democracy, and their origin must be sought in the two or three years before 1934. Similarly, although 6 February may have transformed 'human relations', it did not immediately transform politics. Before this could happen there needed to be a modification in the political stance of the Communists. Having briefly examined the political situation before 1934, this chapter will therefore focus particularly on the political evolution of the PCF: the Communists did not create the Popular Front out of nothing; but without their initiatives it would have been inconceivable. Up to 1936 the other parties of the left were generally responding to the Communists rather than initiating policy themselves. Only after the election victory did this situation change.

Democracy in crisis: France 1929 to February 1934

Surveying the fifteen years since 1914 a French citizen in 1929 might have had little reason to doubt the durability of the existing political order. The Third Republic had brought France victorious through the First World War and successfully overcome the financial crisis of the 1920s. In 1929 the franc had never been stronger nor the economy more buoyant. In the 1920s industrial production in France had increased faster than anywhere else in Europe. This economic growth was accompanied by a process of industrial concentration and plant modernization. Around Paris especially, there had been a rapid expansion of the motor car and engineering industry. Symbols of this new world were the giant Renault plant at Boulogne–Billancourt and the Citroën factory at the Quai Javel. Paris suddenly became a major working-class centre; suburbs sprang up around the capital to accommodate the new industrial population. The appalling housing conditions and desolation of these suburbs were greatly to assist the implantation of the young Communist Party; the so-called 'red-belt' around Paris was to be a bastion of support for the Popular Front.

Throughout the later 1920s political power had rested with the right but here also changes were taking place. The pre-war generation was being replaced by younger men: Poincaré resigned from politics in July 1929. Among the new leaders was the energetic right-wing politician André Tardieu, France's dominant political figure between 1929 and 1932. Tardieu carried out a number of long overdue social reforms made possible by the prevailing prosperity; he made himself the spokesman of fashionable transatlantic ideas of rationalization and economic modernization.

But there was also another France in 1929 – a predominantly rural society with an almost static population. Between 1900 and 1939 the French population increased by 3 per cent (largely due to immigration) and that of Germany by 36 per cent. France was also an ageing society: no country in the world had a higher proportion of people over sixty. And as a result of the lack of births during the war the mid-1930s were to be the 'hollow years' when there would be almost half the number of 19 to 21-year-olds than would otherwise have been the case. The legacy of the war was felt in other ways as well: in the huge war cemeteries of Northern

France, in the presence of over one million war invalids and over 600,000 war widows, in the numerous war veterans associations – as a memory and a fear. War is often a mixer of social classes but France remained a highly compartmentalized society: a child who entered the primary school system and emerged at thirteen with the *certificat des études primaires* had no contact with the children of the privileged secondary schools; the industrial worker was often isolated by factory discipline from his workmates in the same factory or even the same workshop; the worker travelling third class knew nothing of the bourgeois travelling first. Politically the resistance to change in French society was most powerfully expressed in the indirectly elected Senate which enjoyed almost identical legislative rights to the Chamber. The minimum age requirement for election to the Senate was forty; the mode of election favoured the representation of rural and small town interests. Before the war the Senate had succeeded in blocking income tax for almost twenty years. After the war it played a similar role. Bills that it did not like were often buried in committee. This had been the fate of a bill introducing paid holidays which had passed the Chamber in 1931. It was left to the Popular Front to revive the issue.

These points need emphasis because the Popular Front was partially a revolt of the working class against a social order which excluded it from political power, partially a revolt of the young against a political order which seemed hidebound and unimaginative. *Jeunesse* was one of the keywords of the Popular Front. A dissatisfaction by the rising political generations with the existing political categories can be detected across the entire political spectrum well before 1934. In the late 1920s, within the Socialist Party a number of young intellectuals around Georges Lefranc expressed their frustration with the party's combination of electoral reformism and doctrinal intransigence. Among the party's parliamentary representatives various deputies, of whom the most important was Marcel Déat, chafed at the Socialist policy of refusing participation in government and articulated their impatience intellectually in a critique of Marxist orthodoxy.

In the Radical Party too the late 1920s saw the emergence of the so-called Young Turks consisting of pragmatists such as the journalist Emile Roche, left-wing intellectuals such as Jacques Kayser who wanted to reinvigorate Radicalism as a doctrine of the left, and iconoclastic young deputies like Pierre Cot, Gaston Bergery, Bertrand de Jouvenel, Jean Zay, and Pierre Mendès France. What the Young Turks shared was less an ideology than a style: they were united in their opposition to the lack of imagination of the party hierarchy and critical of the meagre achievements of Radicalism in power. Outside the framework of the existing political parties there was also, in the early 1930s, a flowering of political discussion groups and periodicals aspiring to transcend existing categories of right and left. Among the less ephemeral products of this effervescence was Emmanuel Mounier's periodical *Esprit* (founded in 1933) which attempted to detach Catholicism from its traditional links with the right.[2]

The 1930s were to lead these individuals in very different directions: Zay became the Popular Front government's youngest minister, Roche its most effective Radical opponent; Kayser became one of the drafters of the oath of 1935, de Jouvenel a member of the fascist Parti Populaire Français; Lefranc became a leading Popular Front activist, Déat eventually a fascist, and so on. To some extent such outcomes were the consequence of contingency: Déat, de Jouvenel and Bergery broke with 'the system' before the Popular Front provided new outlets for revolt and as a result they found themselves marginalized. But however divergent the trajectories they chose – or fate chose for them – they shared an initial set of common dissatisfactions and a presentiment that all was not well with the existing political order. The mid-1930s were to prove them correct.

At the beginning of 1931 France started to be affected by the Depression. The economic crisis had the effect both of reinforcing resistance to change in French society – setting in motion a reflex defence of the social status quo – and acting as a catalyst on the forces of change. The result was an institutional crisis – a crisis of the regime – which exploded in the riots of 6 February.

There are two facts to notice about the impact of the Depression on the French economy. First, although the slump hit France later than the rest of the world, it lasted much longer, partly owing to a stubborn refusal to devalue the franc. While most of the industrialized world was on the road to recovery by mid-1935, France was only just entering the trough of the Depression. Secondly, the Depression affected France not as a cataclysmic social collapse but rather as a slow paralysis; this made it possible to hope that it would be possible to sit the situation out. For example, at its peak in 1935 unemployment reached about one million (the official figure was never above 503,000) which, although considerable by French standards, was small by comparison with Germany or Britain. Leaving aside until later the impact of the slump on the working class in employment, we should note here that the social categories which suffered most, apart from the unemployed, were the *classes moyennes* – the peasantry (whose real incomes fell by some 30 per cent between 1930 and 1935) and shopkeepers and small businessmen (an 18 per cent fall). Those on fixed incomes benefited from the fall in prices, and the profits of large-scale industry were to some extent protected by cartel arrangements. The differential impact of the Depression resulted in conflicting political pressures: the peasantry required state intervention to raise agricultural prices; the unemployed on the other hand wanted cheap bread and adequate relief payments; small businessmen and shopkeepers demanded lower taxation and cuts in state spending, especially public sector salaries; the unions, strongest in the public sector, defended existing wage levels.

But for the newly elected chamber in 1932 the most immediate challenge posed by the Depression was the decline in tax revenues and the appearance of budget deficits. For the Radicals the solution was 'budgetary deflation', cutting the salaries of government employees (*fonctionnaires*). For the Socialists such action was socially retrograde, politically unacceptable (the *fonctionnaires* formed much of their electorate) and economically futile (since further depressing the economy through deflation would only increase the deficit). It was essentially this problem which had resulted in the fall of the Social Democratic government of Müller in Germany in 1930 and of MacDonald's Labour government in Britain in 1931. In both cases right-wing governments were formed to carry out the measures which Socialists refused to accept. In France this outcome, for reasons described already, was impossible. A political deadlock ensued and although a number of financial bills were passed they were too minor to have any significant effect on the economy. To an increasing number on the left the moral seemed only too clear. Déat and the participationist Socialists argued that their party must modify its intransigence. Their attitude reflected ambition but also a genuine fear (which the later political evolution of many of them should not obscure) that the paralysis of French democracy would pave the way for fascism. In Germany, after all, Müller had been succeeded first by Brüning and eventually, in January 1933, by Hitler. In October 1933 the conflict in the French Socialist Party came to a head and the dissidents seceded to form a new group, popularly known as the Neo-Socialists. Meanwhile the Socialist intellectuals around Lefranc became themselves increasingly estranged from the party hierarchy. Within the Radical party also there were rumblings of dissent. The Young Radical, Gaston Bergery, left the party to form in March 1933 a 'Common Front against Fascism.' The idea was to rally all individuals willing to oppose fascism irrespective of their party. Initially Bergery attracted the interest of one or two Communists and Socialists as well as a number of left-wing intellectuals, and his abortive Popular Front *avant la lettre* enjoyed brief notoriety in 1933 but foundered largely because it lacked the backing of any political party (in June 1933 the SFIO forbade its members to join). Another Young Radical dissenter, Bertrand de Jouvenel, also left the party at the end of 1933 in protest against deflation.

Meanwhile on the right, besides the growing popularity of various extra-parliamentary Leagues – the Jeunesses Patriotes, the Croix de Feu and so on – which demonstrated their anger against the regime in the street, several leading parliamentary figures, of whom Tardieu was the most vocal, announced the need for a strengthening of the power of the executive: to talk of a reform of the state had become respectable. Although the left castigated this as proto-fascism, it was true that throughout much of 1933 there was a virtual vacuum at the centre of French politics: the executive had more or less ceased to function. *Fonctionnaires* took to the streets to demonstrate against proposed cuts in pay; pressure groups representing the interests of small businessmen and shopkeepers organized shop closures and demonstrations; the Communists organized hunger marches; peasant protest became increasingly violent. In this sense the riots of 6 February demonstrated what the politics of 1933 should have made self-evident: governments could no longer govern; power was shifting to the street.

The immediate result of 6 February was to break the Socialist–Radical coalition and bring in a government of the right which attempted to impose its solution to the institutional crisis: Doumergue used decree powers and later attempted unsuccessfully to introduce a version of the constitutional reform advocated by Tardieu. The plan failed because the Radicals in the cabinet would not swallow it, thus precipitating Doumergue's fall in the autumn. This did not mean that the Radicals were prepared to return to the left, only that there were limits to how far they would follow the right. For the moment, the fate of the left lay in the hands of the Socialist and Communist Parties. They had been as startled by the potential for unity displayed on 12 February as by the 'fascist' danger revealed on 6 February. What lessons would they draw from these two experiences?

From 'Class against class' to 'United Front': 1928 to June 1934

On 24 January 1934 Thorez told the Central Committee of the PCF: 'we will in no circumstances pursue an agreement with the leadership of the Socialist Party which we consider . . . as an enemy . . . We want to organize a common struggle with the Socialist workers, in spite of and against, the Socialist leaders.' Six months later the 'unity pact' was signed between the leadership of the two parties, setting in motion the process which would end in the victory of the Popular Front. Between January and June, then, there had been a change in Communist policy. When did this take place, and why? Until recently Communist Party historians would have rejected the very validity of the first question. According to party historiography the 'turning point' (the *tournant* as it is known) occurred in 1931 when Maurice Thorez became party leader. If anything had changed in 1934 it was the attitude of the Socialist Party; to talk of a

Communist *tournant* in this year was anti-Communist. As for the second question – why did the *tournant* occur? – party historians, when they accept its validity at all, have tended to play down the influence of Moscow. Non-Communist historians, on the other hand, have stressed the radical nature of the change in the PCF's policy in 1934, and portrayed the party as subservient to the Comintern, and the Comintern as an instrument of Soviet domestic or foreign policy. In such accounts, the French Communists, and Thorez in particular, emerge as obtusely slow to grasp the transformation in the policies of the Comintern.

Recently, however, there has been a certain convergence between the two positions. The latest account produced by the PCF accepts the notion of a *tournant* in 1934 and imputes the decisive responsibility for it to Moscow. Communist historians fight a minor rearguard action by arguing that once Moscow had given the green light for change, Thorez was quick to seize his new opportunities. Since this does not entirely square with his demonstrable initial hesitation, they resort to oxymoronic descriptions of his 'measured boldness'.[3] Meanwhile non-Communist historians have become more sensitive to shifts in the PCF's policies before 1934 and to the diversity of opinion within the Comintern which was, at least up to 1935, far from being a monolithic body acting simply as a tool of Soviet diplomacy. It is now possible to present a more balanced picture.[4]

Since its foundations in 1920 the PCF had undergone a bewildering series of purges and doctrinal zig-zags. Sometimes these were the transposition, via the Comintern, of domestic Soviet power struggles on to the internal affairs of all other Communist parties; sometimes they derived from the Comintern's attempt to 'bolshevize' the French Communist Party, to create a new party owing nothing to previous French political traditions. The Comintern had various means of monitoring the policies of member parties: their leaders could be summoned to Moscow or special emissaries sent from Moscow. Regional secretariats conveyed and supervised changes in policy: France was under the Roman Secretariat. During the 1930s French affairs were followed especially closely by Dimitry Manuilsky who was the principal representative of the Russian Communist Party on the Comintern. By the mid 1930s he was in effect running the organization.

In 1927 the Comintern had imposed on the PCF the so called 'class against class' tactics prohibiting electoral alliances with other parties of the left. As a result, at the elections of 1928 the PCF's parliamentary representation fell from 26 seats to 14 because although its first round vote had increased by 188,000, only half of these voters obeyed the instructions to vote Communist at the second round. The 'class against class' policy is sometimes linked by historians to Stalin's shift to the left in order to isolate Bukharin. In fact it preceded it and was imposed with Bukharin's approval as a way of breaking the PCF's continued senti- mental attachment to the tradition of left-wing unity.[5]

But what started as a corrective to the reformist temptations of the PCF was soon transformed into a shift to the left throughout the Comintern, inaugurated in July 1928 at its Sixth World Congress, with the announcement of the so-called Third Period tactics. After periods of world revolution (1919–23) followed by a stabilization of capitalism (1923–8), it was argued that the world economy had entered a third period characterized by a crisis of capitalism and a consequent radicali- zation of the masses. The political corollary of this diagnosis was summed up in three formulae: 'class against class'; the labelling of social democrats as 'social fascists'; and the 'united front from below' which meant creating a united front of Communist and Socialist workers not by signing agreements 'at the summit' between party leaders but on the contrary by turning the Socialists against their leaders. Socialist parties were, in other words, to be treated as the principal enemies; bourgeois democracy was not to be distinguished from fascism. This radicalization of Comintern policy – which reflected the radicalization of Soviet domestic policies in the form of mass collectivization – completely ignored the realities of French politics: the masses had never seemed less radical, the Socialists rarely more strident in their opposition to the government. As a result the policy encountered considerable opposition within the PCF, especially from Jacques Doriot and Renaud Jean, both leading members of the party's ruling Politburo. Their opposition led in 1929 to another Comin- tern inspired change at the head of the party: Henri Barbé, Pierre Célor, Thorez and Benoît Frachon were promoted to be its collective leaders.

For the next five years the PCF faithfully executed the policies of the Third Period. But within this period there were subtle correctives to the Comintern line, resulting in further leadership purges. In May 1930 the French leaders were summoned to Moscow and criticized for underesti- mating the perils of excessive 'leftism'. The party had become too zealous in its sectarianism. This reprimand followed Stalin's famous 'dizzy with success' speech in March 1930 denouncing excesses in the collectivization campaign but it was also prompted by the parlous state to which sectarian tactics were reducing the French party. The PCF leaders answered these reproaches with a bout of self-criticism, but membership continued to fall, and a year later the party came under renewed attack from the Comintern. This time scapegoats had to be found: July 1931 saw the unmasking of the supposedly conspiratorial Barbé-Célor 'group' and Thorez's emergence at the head of the party. The so-called 'group', accused of having tried to sabotage the party by its sectarianism, had in fact suffered the consequences of failing to square the impossible circle of carrying out the Third Period policies and increasing the party's influence.

The ousting of the 'group' was supposed to inaugurate a new era of flexibility and free discussion in the party: 'let mouths open' wrote Thorez. It is on this episode that party historians once based the case for a *tournant* in 1931, of which the developments of June 1934 were, it is argued, only a logical extension. This is the attitude which informs, for example, Claude Willard's widely read text book on Socialism. A study written as late as 1981 spoke of the emergence of a party 'more organically linked to the masses'.[6] But such an account arose because Thorez's arrival at the head of the party needed retrospectively to be invested with historical significance.[7] In fact, at the level of policy, little had changed. At the Party's Seventh Congress in March 1932, Thorez spoke for four hours stigmatizing the Socialists as the most dangerous enemy; no dissent of any kind was expressed. As the Congress so well demonstrated, the real significance of the Barbé-Célor affair – the real *tournant* of 1931 if there was one – was that it represented the final stage in the process of Bolshevization: the definitive creation of a disciplined and Stalinized party. Far from mouths opening, they had closed for ever. In the pre-history of the Popular Front this period is of some importance because although the Popular Front years were substantially to change the party's image and increase its membership, its leadership had come to power in the 'class against class' years.[8] In 1931, however, there was no reason to suppose that Thorez would last longer than anyone before him. The Comintern hierarchy remained sceptical about the abilities of the French leadership, and Comintern control over the PCF was tightened in August by the arrival in France of a Comintern team headed by the Czech, Eugen Fried.

Meanwhile the party's decline continued: at the elections of 1932, where 'class against class' tactics were again applied, the party's first round vote fell from over one million in 1928 to 795,000; and at the second ballot the Communists lost 55 per cent of their first ballot vote. In 1933 membership fell to 30,000, its lowest ever figure. In many places the party was reduced to a mere rump. A Marseilles police report of January 1934 spoke of the party's thirty-four supposed cells as 'in fact non-existent: some only consist of one member who combines all the posts'; there was 'total indifference on the part of almost all the members' and most of the leaders.[9]

Having rejected the notion of any significant change in Communist policy or influence in 1931–2, one can nonetheless discern a modification of tone and practice which is important precisely because it is clear with hindsight that it prefigured the Popular Front. One sign of this was the Amsterdam–

Pleyel movement, an attempt to win over a broad spectrum of support around the theme of opposition to war and fascism. Although the scheme had probably been conceived by the Comintern's indefatigable front organizer, the German, Willi Münzenburg, the initiative was taken by the French party in 1932 and the idea publicly floated by its two leading intellectuals, the novelists Romain Rolland and Henri Barbusse. An international congress to launch the movement was held in Amsterdam in August 1932. Among the delegates, who numbered between 2,000 and 3,000, there were over 500 from France, including twenty members of the SFIO. Also present was Gaston Bergery. After the Congress, a French national committee was set up as well as a number of local French committees: by the end of 1932 these numbered 400 with, it was claimed, as many as 8,000 Socialist members. Three Socialist federations joined the movement.

In September 1932 the SFIO, fearful at seeing Socialist members inveigled into Communist front organizations, prohibited its members from joining the movement, and at a second Congress held at the Salle Pleyel in Paris there were only 199 Socialists out of a total attendance of over 3,000 (at the first there had been 291). After the Salle Pleyel gathering, the Amsterdam–Pleyel movement, as it was now known, lost momentum in France: 207 local committees were set up between January and June 1933, only 95 between July 1933 and February 1934, and many of these were pretty notional. This loss of momentum was due to the official hostility of the SFIO, to the new competition from Bergery's Common Front and to the continuing sectarianism of the Communists. But the limited success of the Amsterdam movement in attracting support for the Communists outside the narrow orbit of the party paved the way towards more supple political tactics that would be fully exploited in the Popular Front years.[10]

Another instance of some evolution in the party's attitudes was to be seen in its reassessment of the value of 'economist' non-revolutionary slogans. One aspect of the Barbé-Célor group's sectarianism was alleged to have been its neglect of the 'struggle for beefsteak' – for concrete material demands – in favour of abstract political slogans which failed to attract mass support. The PCF was therefore urged to emphasize 'limited demands' (*revendications partielles*) which would provide immediate relief to the working class. 'No demands', said Thorez, 'however insignificant can be ignored by the Party.' This meant articulating the grievances of all groups hit by the Depression in order to construct a broad coalition of the discontented. The strategy was distinguished from reformism because the function of *revendications partielles* was a mobilizing one: the party would translate these concrete material demands into political action. For the historian who has most carefully studied the PCF's conception of the role of strikes in its political strategy, this was a crucial theoretical adjustment which prefigured the party's attitude during the Popular Front period and beyond.[11] *Revendications partielles* could be the first link in a chain which took the Communists out of the ghetto and to the centre of the political stage.

In 1932 this change was primarily theoretical with little influence on practice, but at the local level the theory could already pay dividends. In Bagneux, a suburb of Paris, Communist activists successfully exploited the grievances of the residents of the new cheap housing developments who had been neglected by the municipal council. By taking over and reinvigorating the tenants' association in April 1933 the Communists helped the residents to express their views politically as well as organizing recreational activities for them. These efforts laid the bases of the Communists' Popular Front victory in the municipal elections of 1935.[12] The Communists also made a more sustained attempt than any other party to mobilize the unemployed. They organized committees of the unemployed to arrange hunger marches and demonstrations, and distribute unemployment relief. By the end of 1931 there were 85 such committees in the Paris region, incorporating some 12,000 unemployed. But greater success was limited by the sectarian language prescribed by the Comintern's political line.[13]

The year 1933 may, then, have witnessed the lowest ebb in the party's fortunes, but both the Amsterdam–Peyel movement and the theory of *revendications partielles* pointed towards new forms of action. For these to become fully effective, they needed to be harnessed to a more realistic political strategy. In 1932 and 1933 there were few signs that this would happen: the Comintern saw no reason to modify its line. It is worth noting that in Germany, the main focus of Comintern concern at this time, the tactic was, in terms of recruitment, not unsuccessful: membership of the KPD had risen from 170,000 (1930) to 360,000 (1932).[14] But Hitler's assumption of power in January 1933 revealed the consequences of the fratricidal disunity of German labour. In March, therefore, responding to an appeal from the Socialist International, the Comintern for the first time in years accepted the possibility of agreements between Social Democratic and Communist parties on joint anti-fascist action. The PCF seized upon the opportunity with enthusiasm and made overtures to the Socialists who, without proof of good intentions, remained suspicious. By April the Comintern had reverted to a hardline position and the PCF, not for the first time, was criticized for rightist opportunism. The path of rectitude was narrow indeed. The Thirteenth Plenum of the Comintern's Executive Committee (ECCI) in December, at which Thorez performed the ritual self-criticism, vigorously reaffirmed all the elements of the 'class against class' strategy. And Thorez's declaration to the Central Committee in

January 1934 faithfully reflected this line. This was the situation on the eve of 6 February.

The events of February took the party by surprise. On 3 February, in the face of mounting right-wing violence, a headline in *L'Humanité* read 'No panic'; on the 5th, refusing to differentiate between 'plague and cholera', the party called upon the workers to demonstrate both against the fascist demonstrators and the government. The instruction may have been clear enough in theory; its practical application was less so. When reviewing the events of 6 February some weeks later, two Communist leaders described 'painful scenes . . . of fraternisation between workers . . . and *Camelots du roi*', of workers 'mixed in with fascists'.[15] This is what 'class against class' tactics had led to.

In later years Blum apparently believed that the Communists had possibly planned a coup for the night of 9 February. The allegation is interesting for what it reveals of the murky atmosphere of those few days. But in truth the party would have been quite incapable of any such thing. In the aftermath of 6 February it was thrown into total disarray. Having resisted appeals for joint action from the Seine Federation of the SFIO, the PCF called for a demonstration on the 9th against *both* the fascists and 'the killers Daladier and Frot [Minister of the Interior]'. No distinction should be made between the defenders of the Republic and the 'fascists'. The demonstration went ahead despite a government ban. Meanwhile the CGT was planning a protest strike for 12 February. It held a meeting to which a number of left-wing organizations were invited, but not the Communists. The Socialists decided to plan a demonstration for the same day.

Would the Communists also participate? Again there was confusion. The Communist Berlioz later described the atmosphere in the party: 'I was at *L'Humanité* during all those days. One had to see all the orders and counter-orders that we received from every side, to such a point that one didn't know what to put in the paper the next day. One had the impression that there were several different leaderships . . . in the Party.'[16] Between 8 February and 11 February *L'Humanité*'s attitude to the CGT strike and the Socialist demonstration remained ambiguous. Not until a Politburo meeting on 10 February was the decision taken to participate in the demonstration, and this was announced in the second edition of *L'Humanité* on Sunday 11 February. It has been suggested that there was direct intervention from Moscow, possibly inspired by Kirov; or it may have been Fried who took responsibility for authorizing participation.[17] Whichever view is correct it is certain that no such decision could have been taken without the approval of Moscow in some form. This was the Communists' problem during the February days: a party leadership accustomed to await guidance from Moscow was required to respond rapidly to a highly fluid situation.

The strike and demonstration of 12 February was an indisputable success. The spectacular and spontaneous manifestation of unity in Paris was duplicated in the provinces: there were demonstrations in 346 towns (19 of which contained more than 5,000 participants); 161 of these involved both Socialists and Communists.[18] February 12 demonstrated that the reflexes of Republican solidarity were still powerful. In these circumstances what was the future of 'class against class tactics'?

In the weeks following 12 February all the efforts of the PCF were directed to a vigorous reassertion of that former policy. The Politburo meeting of 22 February declared that the party 'cannot . . . abandon its criticisms of the Socialist Party, the principal social support of the bourgeoisie'. Thorez's editorial of 19 April in *L'Humanité* was entitled: 'against the bloc with social fascism'. This line was pithily summed up by Paul Vaillant-Couturier: 'Defend the Republic says Blum? As if fascism were not still the Republic, as if the Republic were not already fascism.' In fact there had been a slight shift in the official party line. At the Politburo in February, Fried, clearly someone whose views carried weight, warned of the need to distinguish between different sections of the bourgeoisie, as Lenin had between Kornilov and Kerensky. The theme was expanded by Marcel Gitton at the Central Committee in March.[19] But such minor refinements made no practical difference as long as the Communists still pilloried the Socialists as 'social-democratic vomit'.

Why did the Communists seem so anxious to bury any memory of the unity of 12 February? One reason was no doubt the Doriot affair. Doriot had been in the 1920s one of the heroes of French Communism. He had been one of those opposed to the introduction of 'class against class' tactics in 1927 and although he recanted at the party's Sixth Congress in April 1929, he had in private become increasingly disillusioned about the party[20] and devoted himself primarily to nursing his electoral fief of St Denis. There was no love lost between him and Thorez. As extra-parliamentary right-wing violence grew in 1933 and the Socialists split over their attitude to the Radicals, Doriot resumed his criticism of Communist tactics: fascism was the principal danger; overtures should be made to the Socialists. These ideas were defeated in heated discussions at the Central Committee in January 1934. So far the dispute had been largely confined within the party, but after 6 February Doriot committed the cardinal sin – for Communists – of bringing it into the open. He refused to disband his local St Denis anti-fascist committee of Communists, Socialists and others which had been formed on 11 February; in March he called a meeting of the St Denis section which voted to support united action with the Socialists; and on 11 April he published an open letter to the Comintern putting his case for united action and attacking the party's attitude in February. As the leadership became embroiled in controversy with the dissident Doriot it was cornered into reaffirming its opposition to the policy he advocated.[21]

But there is little reason to believe that even without the problem of Doriot, the party would have revised its policy. The Comintern had given no new directives in spite of the permission to join the 12 February demonstrations. At the Thirteenth Plenum of the ECCI the PCF had been severely upbraided for its abortive negotiations with the Socialists earlier in the year. Thorez in particular had suffered considerable criticism. Never congenitally prone to take risks, it is not surprising that he was anxious not to burn his fingers again.

Whatever the wishes of the party leadership, it was increasingly clear that the fleeting unity of 12 February was not so easily forgotten. One sign of this was the founding of the CVIA. This was the initiative of a young civil servant, François Walter (employing the pseudonym of Pierre Gerôme), who succeeded in winning the support of three nationally known intellectuals: Paul Rivet, a distinguished ethnographer and a Socialist; the physicist Paul Langevin, known to be sympathetic to the Communists; and Émile Chartier (known as Alain) whom many considered as the philosopher of Radicalism. Alain in fact never attended meetings but his notional participation meant that the bureau of the CVIA contained representatives of the three main parties of the left.[22]

On 5 March the CVIA issued its first manifesto warning against 'fascist dictatorship' and a return to a 'new dark ages'. It quickly attracted a number of leading intellectual figures, but more significant than its national luminaries was the tissue of local anti-fascist vigilance committees which developed under its aegis or example. It cannot be stressed enough that the impact of 6 February was not restricted to Paris alone. Indeed the further one was from the capital, the more lurid the rumours could become: at Valence it was believed that bands of *Camelots du Roi* were planning to converge on the town and take control of the local arms depot.[23] The local reaction to such fears was, throughout France, an immediate reflex of Republican defence. By May 1934 the total membership of the CVIA was 2,300, by July 3,500. Not all the anti-fascist committees were necessarily linked to, or inspired by, the CVIA. Some, such as that in St Denis, were merely continuations of the committees set up by the Socialists, Communists and others to prepare the demonstration of 12 February. In the Loir-et-Cher it was the League of the Rights of Man which had on 11 February called for the setting up of a 'committee of defence of liberties and Republican institutions'; in March the local

Amsterdam Committee helped set up an anti-fascist committee at Vendôme including representatives of the CGTU, CGT, PCF and SFIO; then in July, at Romorantin, it was the Socialists who organized a committee which remained outside the orbit of the Amsterdam movement.[24]

This committee movement has hardly been studied and we do not even know how many committees there were. In the Languedoc alone forty-seven were formed between 12 February and 15 July; by May 1934 there were seventy-four in the single department of Lot et Garonne. Not all the committees were manifestations of left-wing unity. The committee set up in Nîmes in March included most groups from the Radicals and Neo-Socialists to the League of the Rights of Man, excluding the Communists; indeed it was probably set up as a rival to them.[25] But often these vigilance committees did include Communists and in these circumstances it became increasingly difficult for the Communist leadership to stick to its anti-Socialist policy. In many local instances Communists had decided to join the anti-fascist demonstrations of 12 February before this had been officially authorized by *L'Humanité* on 11 February.[26] At the Central Committee in March, Gitton admitted that many cells were calling for a common front of the left; and within the hierarchy other leading Communists such as Jean, André Vassart and André Ferrat added their voices, though not publicly, to Doriot's criticisms and advocated some cooperation with the Socialist leaders. In short, in the spring of 1934 the party was in a disastrous state: Ferrat, who later left it, claimed that without a change of policy many members would simply have quit the party by 'voting with their feet'.[27]

One hope might have been for the Communists to try and channel this anti-fascist sentiment into the Amsterdam movement. In some cases the Amsterdam movement did succeed in providing the local impulse to unity in spite of the official reservations of the Socialists. In the Basses-Alpes the local Amsterdam committee convened a meeting in May which some Socialists attended, including the Socialist mayor of St Tulle.[28] In the Languedoc the Amsterdam Committees, of which there were only eight before 6 February, played a secondary role in organizing the riposte of 12 February, but in the following weeks a number of Socialist sections joined them in spite of being forbidden to do so by their party. Generally, however, the CVIA seems to have been a more successful focus of anti-fascist activity in this period than the Amsterdam movement whose effectiveness was vitiated by the sectarianism of the PCF. The party implicitly recognized this fact when it allowed five intellectuals closely associated with it to join the CVIA's newly elected bureau in May. And after initial hesitations the Amsterdam movement allowed other organizations to join an anti-fascist rally it had organized in Paris in May: this was an admission of weakness more than an act of conciliation.[29]

The PCF, then, seemed in danger of being by-passed by a popular movement towards united anti-fascist action which the 'class against class' doctrine prevented it from exploiting. At this point the Comintern decided to intervene. As early as 1931 some figures in the Comintern, of whom Manuilsky was the most influential, had favoured a more flexible policy but the counsels of the hardliners – Bela Kun, Knorin, Lozovsky – had prevailed. And at least until January 1933 it could be convincingly argued that in Germany the policy was not unsuccessful. The softer line received an important boost in February 1934 with the arrival in Moscow of the Bulgarian-born Communist, George Dimitrov, who had acquired an international reputation after his acquittal in the Reichstag fire trial – the only success in an otherwise gloomy year for international Communism. Dimitrov, who had witnessed the *débâcle* of German Communism at first hand, became the leading advocate in Moscow of change in policy. In April he replaced Knorin at the head of the Comintern's Central European section – a significant promotion.

On 21 April Doriot and Thorez were summoned to Moscow. Thorez obeyed while Doriot refused. The fact that Thorez and the dissident Doriot had been summoned on terms of equality and that Doriot was extended the indulgence of two more invitations, was perhaps another indication that a shift in policy was on the cards. It has even been suggested that the Comintern was contemplating the replacement of Thorez by Doriot.[30] According to Vassart, the PCF's recently appointed representative to the Comintern, Thorez was treated with scant ceremony during his first two weeks in Moscow.[31] On 11 May he was seen by Dimitrov but the meeting seems to have made little impact – or Thorez was unsure what importance to attribute to it – because when he finally came before the Presidium on 16 May, he firmly reiterated the 'class against class' line. It was at this meeting, which witnessed heated arguments between opponents and advocates of the new line, that Manuilsky outlined a policy of serious negotiations with the Socialist leaders, addressing himself directly to Thorez: 'when you make . . . proposals . . . make sure they don't concern general issues but on the contrary concrete demands. Maurice, you understand, concrete! . . . You must pose conditions that the Socialists can accept.'[32] This time the signal for change was unequivocal. And on 31 May, a week after Thorez's return to France, the PCF's Central Committee offered talks to the Socialist leaders on a joint campaign for the release of the German Communist leader Thälmann.

The path towards united action with the Socialists was still not an entirely smooth one partly because of the PCF's hesitation in applying the new line. Negotiations between the two parties began on 11 June and on the same day the Comintern despatched a letter to all Communist parties reemphasizing the need for a united front. But an article by Thorez in the *Cahiers du bolchévisme* of 15 June (possibly written several weeks before) criticizing the Socialists led them to break off the negotiations. This was the situation when the Communists held their National Conference on 23–26 June. Thorez's opening speech on this occasion, although showing some signs of the recent modification of Comintern policy – he accepted that it might be desirable to defend bourgeoise democracy – remained highly ambiguous, not to say hostile, in its attitude to the Socialists. Once again the Comintern intervened: a telegram was sent from Moscow by Manuilsky instructing the party to show more enthusiasm for united action. As a result the Conference was prolonged for a day and Thorez's final speech declared the need for unity of action *at all costs*. And when on the next day the Central Committee decided to publish Thorez's two speeches, it expurgated various derogatory remarks about the Socialists contained in the first.[33] From this moment there were no further reservations on the part of the Communist leadership: on 25 June the party proposed the idea of a non-aggression pact with the Socialists. In the ensuing negotiations the Communists made the running and accepted the most concessions. The pact was signed on 27 July.

It is clear from this account that the decisive impulse towards united action came from the Comintern. As Renaud Jean, himself an early supporter of such a policy, told the June conference: 'the party has not even been consulted . . . our party is led without any consultation of the base'.[34] Far from resolutely seizing the opportunities opened up by the new Comintern line, as Communist historians claim, Thorez required much prodding from Moscow. But nor did he display the ineptitude which other accounts suggest. Thorez's caution was understandable given his unhappy experience in 1933, and the stormy Comintern debates which he witnessed in May 1934 must have led him to doubt how generally the new line had been accepted. Even Fried, whose role after all was to be in touch with Comintern thinking, was dressed down by Manuilsky in July for having failed to transmit the new policy to France with sufficient alacrity.[35] Indeed Manuilsky's urgency may well have derived from his knowledge of reservations about the new policy and the resulting need to produce results fast.

The hesitancy of the French leadership was also not perhaps as absurd as may appear in retrospect. For the past six years the party's policy had been predicated on the supposed radicalisation of the masses which would lead them to desert the Socialists. After February 1934 there was for the first time evidence that this was happening, even if not as yet to the Communists' advantage.[36] The Socialists had been affected no less than the Communists by the desire for unity at the base: the Seine Federation especially had urged unity of action with the Communists and at the Socialist Congress in May 1934 more than a third of the delegates had favoured joining the Amsterdam movement and a motion to send a delegation to Moscow to discuss unity of action had been narrowly passed. This disarray in the Socialist ranks was noted by Gitton at the Politburo of 25 May (after Thorez's return from Moscow).[37] And yet it was at this moment that the PCF was being instructed to give up its former strategy and talk to the Socialist leaders!

Why did the Comintern change its policy during the first half of 1934? Enough of the Comintern's archives have been released to permit a fairly full answer to this question. One argument, which views the Comintern primarily as an instrument of Soviet policy, is that the new line reflected a change in the international position of the Soviet Union. By the end of 1933 the Russians were losing hope of reaching any diplomatic accommodation with the new regime in Germany and in December the Soviet Politburo passed a resolution in favour of collective security (in other words finding allies in the West). Feelers were put out towards France and in April 1934 these received a favourable response from Barthou. This less hostile Soviet attitude to France, it is argued, was translated into a new policy of cooperation with the Socialists; an anti-German foreign policy by Russia implied that Communist parties give priority to anti-fascism. However plausible this view may seem as a deduction, there is, as J. Haslam has pointed out, no actual evidence for it.[38] And it does have flaws. Soviet diplomacy remained fluid until at least the end of 1934 – *rapprochement* with Germany was not ruled out – and given that in France the advocates of an anti-German foreign policy (and even in some cases of a Franco-Soviet *rapprochement*) tended to be on the centre–right, which had been returned to power after 6 February (Barthou was the most obvious example), any strategy which reinforced the strength of the anti-government left was hardly a necessary consequence of the Soviet Union's new diplomatic priorities. Many Radicals were certainly in favour of closer ties with the Soviet Union but they were after all in the government at this time, and anyway at this stage the united front policy did not extend to them.

The argument that the Soviet Union hoped to use the united front policy to bolster the strength of a potential diplomatic ally stands up no better because the strategy did not involve the Communists in giving up their anti-militarist propaganda. This did not occur until May 1935 when the link between Soviet diplomacy and Comintern policy became quite clear. That is not to say that no possible relationship between them existed before then. To the extent that the Soviet Union now had a clear interest in preventing France from succumbing to fascism it made sense to build up the strength of the anti-fascist French left, especially given that Doumergue's government was regarded by many as 'pre-fascist'. But Stalin is known to have had no interest in the Comintern – he viewed it with contempt – and it does not seem that the new line was imposed by him for diplomatic reasons. Indeed Manuilsky told Vassart that he was taking considerable risks in trying to win Stalin's acceptance of it. This had, it seems, been obtained by mid-May, no doubt partly because it could be shown to coincide fortuitously with new foreign policy objectives. But the fact that, as we shall see, opposition to the policy continued within the Comintern into 1935, does not suggest that Stalin's name was closely associated with it.

The success of Manuilsky and Dimitrov in converting the Comintern hierarchy probably lies – apart from the prestige of Dimitrov – in the disastrous state to which the tactics of the Third Period had reduced international Communism by 1934. When the Thirteenth Plenum of the ECCI met in December 1933, of 72 parties represented only 16 remained legal and 7 semi-legal. A few weeks later the situation had deteriorated further: the Austrian working class was bloodily crushed in February 1934; France seemed only narrowly to have escaped a coup a few days earlier. In short, the international Communist movement did not seem far from extinction, and the PCF, with the lowest membership in its history, had nonetheless become the largest party outside the Soviet Union. In April 1934 Manuilsky encouraged Vassart to speak to the Executive Committee of the Comintern about the disarray of French Communism and the desire for unity by the French working class. The Doriot Affair provided further evidence of this state of affairs. It may be, therefore, that in this way events in France, while not decisive in themselves, strengthened the hand of those within the Comintern who favoured a change in policy. And certainly it was to be the remarkable success of the policy in France which supplied Manuilsky and others with ammunition against those who remained nostalgic for 'class against class' tactics. In short, the *tournant* of June 1934, while clearly originating in Moscow, should be viewed as the result of a triple interaction between domestic French politics, debates within the Comintern and, finally, the new orientation of Soviet foreign policy.[39]

Concentrating exclusively on the PCF gives a slightly distorted picture of the politics of the first half of 1934. There were, after all, two signatories to the unity pact. But it is the Communist change which needs explanation. That is not to say that there was no significant opposition within the SFIO to allying with a party which had vilified it only a few weeks earlier. The National Council's almost unanimous decision to accept the unity pact far from reflected the full extent of this opposition. But once the Communists had adopted a more accommodating stance, it was impossible, given the more democratic structure of the Socialist Party, for the leadership to resist the popular pressure for unity of action. The force of this pressure had been strikingly demonstrated on 2 July when a meeting at the Bullier Hall in Paris organized jointly by the PCF and the Seine Federation of the SFIO – against the wishes of the party leadership – was so successful that a second overspill meeting had to be held in a neighbouring hall. Although many Socialist leaders accepted the unity pact with foreboding, they had little choice. As Blum wrote later, the masses would not have understood a Socialist refusal: the desire for unity was like an 'electric current'. Little can he have known in July 1934 how far it would lead.

From 'United Front' to 'Popular Front': June 1934 to July 1935

By the end of 1934 the unity pact was being applied through France, despite the hesitations of some Socialist federations. Differences arose partly over the interpretation of the pact: the Socialists attempted to restrict it specifically to anti-fascist demonstrations, the Communists hoped it could be broadened to cover a range of political and economic issues. At the Socialist National Council of March 1935 numerous speakers expressed criticisms of Communists for attempting to use the unity pact to extend their influence at the Socialists' expense.[40] Nevertheless the policy went on.

By this time, however, the Communists had dramatically transformed their original position by proposing that the Socialist–Communist pact be extended to include the Radicals. Once again discussion of this development in Communist policy has concerned the respective roles of the PCF and the Comintern. Whereas in the first half of 1934 Thorez was slow to read the signals from Moscow, it is generally agreed that from June onwards he applied the new line highly effectively. Indeed in the eyes of Communist historians he sometimes moved further and faster than the Comintern itself. And when the new strategy was formally ratified at the Comintern's Seventh World Congress in August 1935, the PCF, which had so often previously been singled out for blame, was praised for its bold initiatives. How fair was this assessment?

In May 1934 the Comintern had set up four Commissions to prepare its forthcoming World Congress and these became the centre of intense debate about future Comintern policy. Manuilsky and Dimitrov, who each presided over a commission, remained the firmest partisans of the new line, Piatnitsky, Kun and Knorin its main critics. At the beginning of July Dimitrov proposed that the categorization of social democrats as 'social fascists' and the designation of left socialists as the 'principal enemy' be abandoned. He also spoke of the important role of the *classes moyennes*. On 21 August the Comintern wrote to the PCF proposing an extension of the unity pact and suggesting an overture towards the *classes moyennes*. At the end of August Manuilsky argued that the Communist parties should start negotiations with petit-bourgeois parties, and representatives of social groups susceptible to fascist influence. This was the background to the PCF's initiatives in the autumn.[41]

At the meeting with the Socialists on 9 October Thorez suggested broadening the unity pact to include the *classes moyennes*; on the next day he called for a vast *rassemblement populaire*. The term Popular Front was first used in *L'Humanité* on 12 October when a speech by Thorez was published under the title: 'At All Costs Defeat Fascism: For a Wide Anti-fascist Popular Front.' The slogan was launched. But the Comintern seems to have become slightly alarmed at the speed of these developments. On 24 October Thorez was visited by a delegation of Comintern dignatories among whom was Palmiro Togliatti. Claiming to speak for Dimitrov and Manuilsky, Togliatti expressed reservations about French policy and attempted unsuccessfully to dissuade Thorez from making on the same day a planned public appeal to the Radical Party on the eve of its annual Congress. This episode is somewhat obscure. The three accounts we possess, all by members of the PCF, portray a bold Thorez ignoring the faint-heartedness of the Comintern. But it seems inconceivable that Thorez would have disobeyed a formal Comintern order, and anyway the French initiatives were broadly in line with Comintern thinking. The most probable explanation is that Togliatti's reservations were about the form of the PCF's policy rather than its basic orientation – he expressed similar reservations in a letter to Manuilsky in November – and that his intervention was purely personal, reflecting the continuation of divergences within the Comintern rather than an official view. Thorez therefore ignored the warning, probably with the support of Fried who had remained pointedly silent at the meeting.[42] On 24 October, then, Thorez made his famous speech at Nantes where the Radical Congress was to take place: he called for a broad Popular Front to fight fascism.

The purpose of the new strategy was clear enough. Once fascism was perceived as the principal threat, it was logical to appeal to the class seen as most susceptible to fascist influence. As Thorez put it: 'the race has begun for the conquest of the *classes moyennes*'. But what were the political implications of this policy? Did it mean broadening the unity pact to include the Radical Party or attracting Radical voters away from their party – that is a sort of 'united front at the base' applied this time to the Radicals?[43] Publicly the Communists talked of the formation of directly elected Popular Front committees throughout France, consisting of all people resolved to fight fascism irrespective of their party – an idea seemingly directed against the Radical Party and towards its members.

But at the same time secret overtures were made towards Radical leaders: Herriot was visited by Duclos and Frachon some time in the autumn; and Racamond of the CGTU visited Daladier in October.[44] Another possibility mooted by the Communists was to extend the Socialist–Communist unity pact by means of a 'popular front programme'. On 25 November they proposed to the Socialists a draft programme intended to rally the widest possible support. The document was extremely moderate in tone, so much so that the Socialists complained that it did not include 'a single measure of socialistic nature'. They proposed alternative measures which the Communists rejected, and the negotiations over this subject broke down in January.

In the autumn of 1934, then, it seems that the PCF was still experimenting with the Popular Front strategy and trying out several different approaches simultaneously: secret meetings with Radical leaders, directly elected Popular Front committees, a Popular Front programme. No doubt some leeway was still possible because the Comintern's exact line was still not fixed: one sign of this was the postponement for the second time of the Seventh Congress. At the ECCI Presidium in December 1934 the PCF's activities, defended in person by Thorez, were eventually approved after prolonged debate; Thorez even received the personal congratulations of Stalin. But, as it in contradiction to this, the Comintern newspaper at this time contained articles expressing suspicions of the new policy; one of them talked of the PCF's succumbing to the rightist danger.[45]

This was clearly a period of flux in Comintern policy when the success or failure of the PCF could weigh importantly in the debate in Moscow. And here the immediate results were not encouraging. Although at the cantonal elections in October the Radicals lost some seats to the Socialists and Communists whose candidates had stood down for each other at the second round, these electoral setbacks had no effect on the Radical attitude to the PCF. Those left-wing Radicals who had been critical of the National Union government and might have been responsive to Communist overtures were encouraged in November by Doumergue's replacement by Flandin. As for the idea of Popular Front committees, this had met with no greater success than the attempt to woo the Radicals. Given also that the Socialists were showing signs of restiveness, there seemed little to show for the Communist policy. Indeed it may be that in the spring of 1935 the Comintern was contemplating abandoning it: Vassart wrote a pamphlet (in the end unpublished) preparing the end of the unity pact by blaming its collapse on the Socialists;[46] Knorin and Piatnitsky continued to support the opponents of the new line. But it is not clear how strong this opposition was. Togliatti, for example, had overcome his earlier hesitations about the new policy.

In France, however, the situation was transformed in May by two events: the municipal elections and the signing of the Franco-Soviet pact (quickly followed by the PCF's abandonment of anti-militarism). The first showed the Radicals that their alliance with the right was increasingly unpopular; the second smoothed their path to an alliance with the PCF, by removing one of the most unacceptable planks in the Communists' political platform. The municipal elections revealed a marked swing to the left, especially to the Communists, who doubled the number of municipalities they controlled (from 150 to 297);[47] the Radicals fell back slightly. Even more significantly, many of the left's victories derived from local second ballot agreements between Radicals, Socialists and Communists. The most spectacular example of this Popular Front at the base, so to speak, occurred in the 5th *arrondissement* of Paris: at the second ballot all four left-wing candidates (PCF, Radical, SFIO and dissident Radical) stood down in favour of Paul Rivet of the CVIA who defeated a conservative candidate, a veteran of 6 February, who had been twenty-six votes short of an overall majority in the first round.

The signing of the Franco-Soviet pact on 2 May was stimulated by growing alarm in both countries at the German threat. The pact was ultimately of considerable importance for the arguments in the Comintern. Although Laval had been the French signatory, he was known to be lukewarm towards it and to favour *rapprochement* with Germany. And this was coming to be the attitude of an increasing proportion of the French right which saw in Germany a possible buffer against Bolshevism. Thus the Soviet Union was far from reassured by the signing of the Pact.[48] The Radicals – and especially Herriot – were at this stage seen as firm partisans of Franco-Soviet cooperation. Thus the Popular Front strategy of wooing the Radicals and breaking the National Union coalition now coincided more closely than ever with Soviet foreign policy. But more immediately important in France was Stalin's spectacular declaration approving France's national defence policy. Laval had secured this to embarrass the French Communists whose anti-militarism had not so far been affected by their new political line. Two months previously they had joined the Socialists in opposing the extension of military service; at a demonstration in November 1934 organized on the anniversary of the Armistice by the Amsterdam movement, demonstrators had torn down the tricolour.[49] But in fact, after initial hesitation, the Communists quickly adapted themselves to the new Soviet line. Far from being embarrassed, they were now free to use for the first time the language of the Republican patriotic tradition, the rhetoric of 1792, 1848, and 1871 which was to play such a crucial role in the appeal of the Popular Front. This was not an overnight conversion. Already Thorez had told the National Conference in June 1934: 'We love the great historic examples of 1789. We love the great battles of 1848, 1871, in which the proletariat already participated . . . that is why we love our country.'[50] Stalin's declaration removed the final obstacles to the full expression of such sentiments and allowed the French Communists to relaunch the Popular Front idea with real effectiveness.

At the end of May the Amsterdam movement, presumably at the behest of the party, proposed the holding of a mass anti-fascist demonstration on 14 July. After preliminary meetings in June, formal invitations were issued to the Radical and Socialist Parties. The date was a significant choice; 14 July, anniversary of the fall of the Bastille in 1789 and a national holiday since 1881, was one of the key dates in the Republican calendar. But since 1918 it had become appropriated by the nationalistic right and denounced by the left as a celebration of chauvinism. In choosing this date for an anti-fascist celebration the left was staking out for itself a claim to reappropriate the symbols of the Republic.

How would the Radicals react to an initiative which was obviously designed partly with them in mind? The Flandin government, very popular with them at first, had been discredited by its handling of the economy and fell in a financial crisis at the end of May. During the ensuing ministerial crisis the Communists had made parliamentary overtures to the Radicals, declaring themselves ready to support a Radical-led govern-ment. Whatever the PCF's earlier private contacts with Radical leaders, this open courting of the Radicals represented a new tactic no doubt stimulated by the Franco-Soviet pact. When Doumergue had fallen, the Communists had shown no interest in creating a new majority and had criticized Socialist attempts to do so at this stage.[51] The Communists' attempt in May 1935 to rebuild a cartel majority – now including Communists – was abortive because the Radicals and Socialists could not agree on a programme and the Communists were too small a parliamentary force to be able to impose their views. After prolonged negotiations, therefore, the Radicals found themselves participating in another National Union government, headed by Laval. But Laval was supported out of lassitude not enthusiasm: 72 Radicals voted for him, 7 against and 72 abstained.

This prolonged ministerial crisis showed that the idea of resuscitating the left-wing alliance had growing support among the Radicals. And Daladier, chief victim of the right's return to power, became increasingly associated with this tendency within the party. The most sensational manifestation of this was his appearance, in a purely personal capacity, on a common platform with Blum and Thorez at a meeting organized by the Popular Front of the 5th *Arrondissement*. In the provinces also, perhaps taking a lead from Daladier, there were unity demonstrations between Socialists, Communists and Radicals: at Chambéry Pierre Cot marched at the head of a Popular Front *cortège*, in spite of the hostility of the Radical mayor who resigned in protest.[52]

This, then, was the context in which the Radical Party's Executive Committee met on 3 July to consider if it should join the organizing committee for the 14 July demonstration. The committee decided almost unanimously to join. The mood of the meeting can be gauged by the reaction of Herriot, president of the party and member of the government against which any Popular Front demonstration was implicitly directed: he offered no opposition and merely expressed the wish that the Radicals continue to preserve their separate identity within the alliance.

Five Radicals were delegated to sit on the Comité du Rassemblement Populaire as the demonstration's organizing committee came to be known. Forty-eight organizations, including the CVIA and the League of the Rights of Man, finally took part in the demonstration. But most significant of all was the participation of the Radicals. The demonstration of 14 July was a spectacular success. After the meeting at the Buffalo Stadium in the morning, there was a massive march from the Place de la Bastille to the Place de la Nation. Some Communists still shouted 'All power to the Soviets' and there were red flags as well as tricolours (although the PCF had instructed its municipalities not to fly red flags). But the spirit of the occasion was summed up in the speech by the Nobel prize-winner Jean Perrin:

> they have taken Joan of Arc from us, this daughter of the people, abandoned by the king and rendered victorious by the elan of the people, then burnt by the priests who have since canonized her. They have tried to take from you the flag of '89, this noble tricolour flag of the Republican victories of Valmy and Jemappes . . . They have tried to take from us the Marseillaise, the revolutionary song which caused the thrones of Europe to tremble.

Speaking for the Communist Party, Duclos announced that the Communists could accept both the red flag and the tricolour, the Internationale and Marseillaise; a year earlier the Communist Aragon had written poems denouncing both tricolour and Marseillaise. Like the demonstration of 12 February 1934, the demonstration of 14 July 1935 was not merely a Parisian event. Demonstrations occurred throughout France. Many places witnessed their largest parades since the victory celebrations of 1918;[53] almost everywhere Radicals joined in demonstrations with Communists. July 14 symbolized the coming together of the popular movement born in the aftermath of 12 February with the official organizations of the left.

The lessons of 14 July and the successes of the PCF were not lost on the Comintern. The last suspicions towards the Popular Front disappeared. The historic Seventh Congress of the Comintern, which finally opened on

25 July in Moscow, was dominated by Dimitrov. He advocated a 'broad anti-fascist Popular Front' to defend democratic freedoms, and declared that Communists opposed 'national nihilism'; mention of revolution was largely absent from his report. Among foreign leaders, Thorez, who was especially praised by Dimitrov, had the privilege of presiding over the closing session. For the first time a Frenchman, André Marty, joined the executive committee of the Comintern. These favours were recognition of the fact that if the Popular Front had been conceived in Moscow, it was the French Communist Party which had shown that it could work.

From unity to victory: July 1935 to May 1936

The Seventh Congress was Thorez's moment of glory. But Dimitrov nonetheless urged the party to develop the Popular Front further by transforming it into a mass movement through the creation of elective committees. The idea of such committees had already been raised in 1934 without meeting much success. But it is far from the case that the Popular Front existed by mid-1935 merely as a pact between parties. It was only knowledge of the pressure for unity from below which had caused the Socialist and Radical leaders to overcome their suspicions of the Communists. What was the nature of this popular movement? Who participated in it? What were its aims? Why, in short, did hundreds of thousands of people demonstrate in the streets of France on 14 July 1935 and after?

The growth of the Popular Front as a popular mass movement was the result of a fusion of three phenomena: an anti-fascist reflex of Republican defence; a working-class movement of protest against the consequences of the Depression on working conditions; and opposition by *fonctionnaires* and elements of the *classes moyennes* to the economic policies of the government. The anti-fascist committee movement dates back, we have seen, to the aftermath of 6 February. Although in a sense the Socialist–Communist unity pact represented an attempt by the parties to take this movement in hand, the pact did not by any means put an end to it. In Narbonne the newly formed Socialist–Communist coordinating committee substituted itself for the existing anti-fascist committee. But in most cases such committees continued to exist in parallel with any organizations set up by the parties and were probably helped by the official end to the antagonism between Socialists and Communists. In the Loir-et-Cher the Amsterdam committee, the most active local anti-fascist organization, had 650 members in July, 900 in November 1934 and 2,300 in January 1936. And this was not merely a reflection of increased support for the Communist Party since the committee's size was greater than both the local number of party members (under 1,000 in 1936) and, in certain localities, even than the total of Communist votes in 1936.[54]

One feels that the Prefects whose task it was to report on their activities were themselves bewildered by the various 'anti-fascist vigilance committees', 'anti-fascist fronts', 'united anti-fascist fronts', 'anti-fascist common fronts' and so on, which mushroomed, flourished, mutated, amalgamated, or simply sank without trace during 1934. In the Paris region there were two groupings – the local Amsterdam Committee which brought together some thirty organizations, mostly Communist front organizations, and a 'Liaison Committee of anti-fascist forces' made up of a variety of non-Communist groups. By the end of 1934, the two movements cooperated on a 'Central Committee of Anti-fascist Action of the Parisian region' which comprised fifty-seven organizations including the CVIA.[55]

In spite of the diversity of nomenclature of these local committees, all were in fact variations on a single theme: anti-fascism. What was fascism? The CVIA addressed itself to the problem in a pamphlet. It defined fascism as a mystique of nationalism harnessed to the service of capitalism, 'a desperate attempt to stabilize degenerate capitalism by force.' In France the Leagues were viewed as 'fascist' even if they remained avowedly Republican.[56] But those who attended local anti-fascist demonstrations did not need definitions. 'Fascism' meant the sudden irruption of a Croix de Feu motorcade in the tranquillity of a provincial Sunday afternoon. It meant the holding of meetings addressed by right-wing orators such as Pierre Taittinger, Xavier Vallat or Philippe Henriot, a tireless apologist for the Leagues. These three were all members of the Fédération Républicaine, the most right-wing of the parliamentary parties. Although the Fédération, itself a traditionalist, Catholic and nationalist party, could in no sense be called fascist, the language of some of its more extreme members was becoming highly inflammatory. After February this was quite enough to be labelled as fascist. Thus in the Loir-et-Cher the local Amsterdam committee was set up as a direct response to a meeting addressed by Henriot at Blois in April 1934; in the village of Vineuil (1,810 inhabitants) in the same department, membership of the Amsterdam committee swelled from thirty to seventy-three members in the spring of 1936 after the holding of a Croix de Feu meeting. In the Ardèche, anti-fascist activity, which had died down after the impact of 6 February had worn off, revived in June after a speech at Privas by Henriot.[57] 'Fighting fascism' often meant merely preventing such meetings occurring or demonstrating against them. Claude Jamet, a *lycée* teacher (*professeur*), who has left us his local diary of a Popular Front activist, describes how on one occasion when de La Rocque failed to appear at an advertized meeting, he felt a momentary disappointment, 'like a football team whose adversary had scratched'.[58]

The local organizers of anti-fascist action were often, like Jamet, teachers or *fonctionnaires*. In the Loir-et-Cher the local Amsterdam committee was founded by the *instituteur* Bisault; the fifteen founders of the CVIA branch in Bourges were all *professeurs*. At a meeting held by the Basses-Alps anti-fascist committee in July 1934, one-third of those present were *instituteurs* or postmen.[59] Through such people anti-fascism was grafted on to a durable Republican tradition dating back to the nineteenth century. The following tract from the Seine-Inférieure makes this point clearly:

The bankers, the trusts, their ministers and their papers, have had only one idea since February 6th: to free themselves of any constraints and finish off their 40-year struggle . . . against universal suffrage and the REAL REPUBLIC.

This Coup was tried at the time of MacMahon [i.e. 1877], of Boulanger, of the Dreyfus Affair. Your forebears stopped it . . . This is the tactic of 1851, that which leads to a 2nd December [Louis Napoleon's coup of 1851], that is to say to personal power, DICTATORSHIP . . . and ALSO SEDAN![60]

By November 1934 the membership of the CVIA had reached over 5,200 (3,700 outside Paris). But, at this time the activities of the Leagues died down, partly because Flandin's government was known to be less sympathetic to them. It is no doubt for this reason that the Prefects' reports and the bulletin of the CVIA give the impression of a slackening of anti-fascist protest towards the end of the year. In the Languedoc, meetings held on 11 February 1935 attracted only half the numbers who had turned up six months before.[61] Then suddenly in June 1935 there was a recrudescence of Croix de Feu agitation with a spectacular meeting at Algiers. Throughout the autumn the left-wing press was full of stories of a possible Croix de Feu *putsch*; there were violent incidents at Limoges in November. The Laval government was believed to view such activities not unfavourably. This provided renewed impetus for the anti-fascist committees which were often now rechristened 'Popular Front committees.' In other cases the Popular Front committees were recent organizations, set up to organize the 14 July demonstration, after which they remained in existence. In many cases these committees differed from their predecessors in 1934 only by the inclusion of Radicals. The protest movement was widening.

This movement was fuelled in 1935 by the Depression and the unpopularity of government economic policies. But the relationship between the Depression, economic policy and the rise of the Popular Front is not straightforward. The response of the working class to the Depression will be examined in a later chapter treating the strikes of 1936. But one point can be noted here. Although there was a revival of factory-floor activism in 1935 – the strike explosion was not simply a result of the political victory of 1936 – it is not the case that the Depression necessarily promoted solidarity between public and private sector workers in opposition to deflation. Whereas all private sector workers had suffered wage cuts since 1930, *fonctionnaires* had successfully resisted cuts until 1934, and, given the fall in prices, they were viewed as a privileged class. In 1933 one Prefect noted that potential cuts in public sector salaries encountered 'indifference from manual wage-earners'. This diagnosis was borne out in 1934 when Doumergue's government introduced decrees to cut public sector pay. The left argued for solidarity between public and private sector workers: wage cuts in the public sector might be a signal for those in the private. Thus the Socialist–Communist unity pact provided for demonstrations against the deflation decrees. But in fact this campaign met with much less response than did the political demonstration of 12 February. And the traditional May Day action, to which the Communists had given particular importance in 1934 as a day of protest against the Doumergue decrees, was even less successful than in 1933. There were many reasons for this: the continuing polemics between Communist and Socialist trades unions; the fact that the Doumergue government was prepared to take disciplinary measures against striking *fonctionnaires*. But the *fonctionnaires* were also aware that their cause was not widely popular. The moral was clear: the unity of the left would result more easily from the reflexes of Republican solidarity than from opposition to an economic policy which affected the population differentially.

In spite of these setbacks the Communists pressed for vigorous action against deflation, developing the strategy of appealing to every social category affected by the Depression. In 1935 they abandoned their previous emphasis on the class struggle in the countryside and began to stress the interests of the peasantry as a whole. Thorez summed up the strategy in January 1936: 'we struggle on behalf of all the discontented'. This policy, we have seen, was rooted in the pre-Popular Front era; but only after 1934 did it really take off. It was not surprising that the peasantry should have been one target of the party's propaganda. By 1935 real peasant purchasing power had fallen by 30 per cent. Peasant protest began to pose a serious threat to public order. Among the beneficiaries of this was the rural demagogue Henri Dorgères who narrowly failed to be elected to the Radical stronghold of Blois in April 1935. As a result many Radicals became increasingly restive about deflation: this was reflected in their grudging acceptance of Laval's government in June.

The deflation decrees of the Laval government offered the possibility of widening the coalition of the discontented, and fusing it with the emerging Popular Front of Republican defence. With the Laval decrees public sector employees suffered their first cut in real pay since the start of the Depression. The opposition was on an altogether larger scale than against the Doumergue decrees. The first decrees were issued on 16 July, and meetings of protest occurred throughout the summer; there were riots at Brest and Toulon in which three demonstrators died. Demonstrating *fonctionnaires* were joined by landlords opposing rent reductions and small shopkeepers fearful about the depressive effects of further deflation: 'they no longer attack the *fonctionnaires* as they did previously' remarked one Prefect. Although not directly affected by the deflation measures, wheatgrowers from the centre of France and winegrowers from the south joined in the demonstrations.

The Laval decrees, then, radicalized the *fonctionnaires* and the *classes moyennes*, by bringing them into direct conflict with the state. But the decrees did not directly affect workers in the private sector except for a number of them reducing prices which Laval had introduced to sugar the pill. In fact retail prices began to rise before the end of the year but nonetheless the propaganda impact of the decrees on prices may have succeeded in driving a wedge between public and private sector workers. One Prefect noted that 'the struggle against fascism' was the leitmotiv of the demonstrations over the summer 'much more than the decree laws'.[62] That is not to say that there was no relationship between the recrudescence of conflict in the factories and the protest movement against the decrees. But it was anti-fascism, a term covering a multitude of sins – the Communists denounced deteriorating conditions in factories as 'fascism in the factory'[63] – which provided the unifying factor. From its origins the Popular Front was a negative coalition: in this lay the seeds of its disintegration.

The protest movement against the decrees raised important questions for the Radical Party. Having participated in the 14 July demonstration, did the party intend to remain a member of this new left-wing coalition which had, after all, so far achieved no more than the organization of a demonstration? And, if so, what was the nature of that coalition to be? Radical accounts of the 14 July demonstration usually referred to it as a *traditional* Republican celebration. The Radical Congress in October ratified the party's participation in the Popular Front but again stressed its traditional aspects. One speaker called it the 'mystique of the union of the left under a new name'. But if it was to avoid the fate of previous such alliances, a programme was necessary – both to define more clearly the objectives of the Popular Front and the Radicals' place within it.

After 14 July the task of drawing up a programme was assumed by the Comité du Rassemblement Populaire. The Comité's initial function had been to organize the demonstration of 14 July but after that date the ten most important participating organizations decided that it should remain in being. These were the PCF, SFIO, Radical Party, Independent Socialists, CGT, CGTU, CVIA, the Amsterdam Committee, the League of the Rights of Man and a collection of war veterans' associations. The Comité's deliberations lasted almost six months. There were two main areas of debate: first, the political structure of the Popular Front; secondly, the content of the programme.[64]

On the first issue the Radical delegates found themselves siding with the Socialists against the Communists who wanted the Popular Front to be organized into local committees which individuals could join directly rather than as representatives of organizations. This idea frightened both Socialists and Radicals who saw it as a Communist attempt to suborn their membership. In November, therefore, it was agreed that the Popular Front was 'neither a party, nor a super-party' but a 'centre of liaison' between organizations which would conserve their autonomy. It followed from this that the significance of any eventual programme would be limited. The Comité accepted the formulation of the Radical delegate Kayser that it was drafting 'neither an electoral programme, nor a programme of government' but merely a declaration noting points of argument. This removed the possibility of single Popular Front candidatures at the elections.

The negotiations over the content of the programme were more protracted. In this case the Radicals, trying to restrict the scope of the programme, tended to be supported by the Communists against the Socialists who were less inclined towards compromise. For the Communists the supreme priority was to reach an agreement with the Radicals. The main stumbling block to agreement was economic policy: should the deflation decrees be abrogated, and if so, how was the resulting deficit to be financed? Should a Popular Front government carry out a far-reaching programme, including nationalizations? Once again the more restrictive Radical view triumphed in the programme which emerged in January.

The programme was broadly divided into three areas: political liberties; foreign policy ('Defence of Peace'); and economic and financial demands. The first two caused no problems. 'Liberty' would be assured by the dissolution of the Leagues and a reform of the press; 'peace' by the League of Nations, collective security and progressive general disarmament. As for the economic section, nationalizations were almost entirely excluded. But the deflation policy was to be reversed: most of the decrees were to be abrogated and a public works programme was to be implemented. Although Radicals had participated in all the governments which attempted to implement deflation since 1932 – Laval's Finance Minister was himself a Radical – the repudiation of deflation marked not so much a concession to the Socialists and Communists as a shift of view within the Radical Party. There had always been a number of left-wing Radicals opposed to deflation but up to 1935 they had remained in a minority. Once the protest against deflation spread to its own electorate, the party became less enthusiastic about the policy. This did not involve any ideological conversion to a new policy – merely a recognition that the decrees were not a vote-winner.

The programme did not answer the question how the proposed reforms were to be financed: it included almost no figures. The reasons for this silence were made clear by Kayser: 'if there is nothing on the nature of the revenues to cover the immediate expenditure resulting from the application of the planned reforms, this is because, for the moment, each party has its own specific solutions'. The programme, then, was not a detailed blueprint for government. But it is not so unusual for political programmes to conceal more problems than they resolve. The preoccupations of the Popular Front programme lent themselves to being easily distilled into a simple slogan: 'bread, peace, liberty'. Its main importance was symbolic. After the débâcles of 1924 and 1932 the parties of the left had signed a common statement: this was an unprecedented political event.

As well as acquiring a programme, by the beginning of 1936 the Popular Front had also acquired a mystique – a political sensibility and rhetorical style. One feature of this was the theme of the 'two hundred families' launched by Daladier at the Radical Congress in October 1934. Daladier, whose speech was the success of the Congress, had attacked the families as representatives of a new 'financial feodality' controlling the French economy. The figure of the 200 derived from the fact that the Bank of France had 200 shareholders but its main virtue was its simplicity. The slogan caught on thanks to the role of the Bank of France in the financial crisis which brought down Flandin. The Bank of France was, in the words of one Socialist, 'the Bastille which provides the strongest resistance to popular sovreignty'. The economist Francis Delaisi wrote a pamphlet for the CVIA, *The Bank of France in the hands of the Two Hundred Families*. One of the major propaganda successes of the beginning of 1936 was an issue of *La Flèche* (the organ of Bergery's Common Front) entitled 'France, here are Your Masters' which claimed to expose the key controlling figures of the French economy. A few names recurred in all these *exposés*: the steel magnate Schneider, the banker Rothschild, and, most notoriously, François de Wendel, steel magnate, regent of the Bank of France, and senator of the Fédération Républicaine. *La Lumière* ran an article on France's six potential Fuhrers of whom de Wendel was one.[65]

The 'two hundred families' slogan was very much in the mould of the traditional Republican rhetoric of the *petit* against the *gros*, the little man against the powerful aristocrat. To a proletariat disoriented by the anonymity of modern capitalism it provided identifiable enemies. But its most important function was not so much to identify the enemy as to circumscribe and delimit it. The Popular Front would unite the people of France against a band of enemies no larger than the aristocratic *émigrés* of the counter-revolution: 'Today the bourgeoisie is preparing to destroy the work of the Revolution through the emigration of capital . . . Against the army of Coblentz the army of 14 July is preparing a new Valmy of liberty.'[66] De Wendel, de La Rocque and others were the new *émigrés* of a new counter-revolution; only united behind the Popular Front would the people of France defeat them. No party developed this theme of unity more insistently than the Communists. In a sensational election broadcast Thorez went as far as to offer an 'outstretched hand' (*main tendue*) to the Catholics, even to members of the Leagues, led astray by the propaganda of the 'two hundred families'.

In January 1936 the fall of Laval's government clearly marked a victory for the partisans of the Popular Front within the Radical Party. This did not mean that a majority existed in parliament to carry out the Popular Front programme published a few days before. No one on the left wanted a Popular Front government just before the elections. But the Sarraut cabinet which replaced Laval was a guarantee that the elections would be handled by a government sympathetic to the left. It is hard to imagine Thorez being permitted to broadcast under Laval's premiership. Just before the elections Auriol, on behalf of the Socialists, proposed that all candidates of the left be asked to subscribe to the Popular Front programme. The purpose behind this was to weed out the many anti-Popular Front Radicals who remained. But the Radicals refused to accept this infringement of their autonomy, and they were backed in this by the Communists intent above all on preserving the alliance.

May 1936 has been called 'the most important date in French electoral history since 1877'.[67] This may be true in retrospect but it is not necessarily how things appeared to contemporaries. In some places the campaign aroused less enthusiasm than that of 1924[68] and the impact of the Popular Front was variable. The *Manchester Guardian* journalist Alexander Werth, who toured France during April, did not find evidence of an especially vigorous campaign though he noted that the theme of the 'two hundred families' had caught on well.[69] The most novel feature was the use of the radio by all candidates (in 1932 it had been used by the Premier Tardieu alone).

The Radical campaign was particularly subdued. Among the leaders Herriot, Sarraut and Caillaux hardly spoke; Daladier, the Radical most associated with the Popular Front, rarely mentioned it. At the local level, of 106 Radicals elected, 77 (70.6 per cent) avoided taking any public position over the Popular Front, and this group included both supporters and adversaries. Of the 21 who openly supported it, most tended to avoid direct use of the name, preferring to talk of the 'union of the left' or 'republican discipline'. Only 10 candidates attacked it openly. Nor was the programme of the Popular Front widely reflected in the Radical manifestos: although 60 per cent advocated action against the Leagues and 51 per cent a modification of the deflation decrees, 33 per cent implicitly or explicitly supported deflation and only 10 per cent called for a shorter working week; 36 per cent demanded a reform of the Bank, a theme linked with the campaign against the 'two hundred families'. In short, the Radicals may have been members of the Popular Front but they preferred as far as possible to play the fact down for fear of offending part of their electorate.[70] The Socialists campaigned in the first round on a manifesto more far-reaching than that of the Popular Front, including the nationalizations which had been rejected by their partners. It was the Communists who most clearly identified themselves with the Popular Front, and launched a campaign of unprecedented vigour. They published nine pamphlets of which 7½ million were distributed around France, and a few days before the election every issue of *L'Humanité* contained a special booklet. The Communists called for a 'free, strong and happy France'.

The results of the first round of the election did not witness a marked overall swing from left to right.[71] The right's share of the vote fell from 37.35 per cent to 35.88 per cent (a loss of only 70,000 votes); the left's share rose from 44.48 per cent to 45.94 per cent (an extra 288,000). More important was the swing within the left: the Communist vote increased by 800,000 (6.78 to 12.45 per cent), the Radical vote decreased by 400,000 (15.88 to 11.88 per cent) and the Socialist by 30,000 (17.63 to 16.92 per cent). In the second round, Popular Front electoral discipline worked fairly well: only 6 seats were won by the right as a result of indiscipline on the left. When a Radical stood as a second round candidate of the left the total left vote was on average 3.7 per cent lower than in the first round; when a Socialist stood it was 7.8 per cent lower; and for a Communist 9.1 per cent lower. This testified to a certain reluctance among Radical voters to support Socialist and Communist candidates. But the Communists, benefiting for the first time from the working of the left-wing alliance, were the major beneficiaries of the election in terms of increased seats.

There are various points to note about the results. The Communists progressed in all but three departments but their most important gains were in industrial areas (the Paris region, the Nord, the industrial suburbs of Marseilles) as well as in a number of rural departments especially in the south-west. The Socialist figures are slightly misleading because they disguise large losses (of between 90 and 37 per cent) mainly to the Neo-Socialists in 12 rural departments, smaller losses (29 to 16 per cent) to the Communists in five industrial departments and large increases (60 per cent to 591 per cent) in a number of rural departments at the expense of the Radicals.[72] The 1936 election therefore confirmed a steady shift in the Socialists' electoral base from urban to rural France which had been taking place since at least 1919. It also demonstrated that the Socialists were under pressure from the Communists in industrial France.

The Radical vote fell in 66 departments. The Radicals lost electors on both the left, owing to their identification with conservative governments between February 1934 and January 1936, and on the right, owing to their new identification with the Popular Front. Centrist politics became increasingly untenable. Such signs of dynamism as the party did show came from the right. In the 18 departments in which the party's vote significantly increased, the local party federation was identified with hostility to the Popular Front. Thirteen per cent of Radical deputies owed their election to votes from the right as opposed to 5 per cent in 1932. If to these are added the 25 to 30 known anti-Popular Front candidates elected thanks to the Popular Front alliance, this meant that although the party had been returned as part of a victorious left-wing coalition, the right ring had emerged stronger than before. Hardly a propitious omen for the future of the alliance.

The victory of the left was not a surprise. The form it took was: few had predicted the massive increase in Communist support, and Blum, like many others, had believed that the Radicals would emerge as the largest party. But he was quick to announce, on 5 May, that the Socialists were ready to lead the new government. For the first time France was to have a Socialist Prime Minister.

2 ✎ The leaders

A few days after the elections Blum appealed to the Communists and to Léon Jouhaux of the CGT to participate in this government. Both offers were promptly rejected although both the CGT and the Communists promised Blum their support. This was a curious position for Blum to find himself in. On various occasions in the previous decade the Socialists had themselves been solicited to join governments and always refused; now Blum found himself in the opposite role. The significance of this situation was greater than may at first seem the case. Since the beginning of the century French Socialists had been haunted by the problem of power: was it legitimate for them to join or form governments within a system they were dedicated to destroying? If they did participate, what could they hope to achieve? Before the war this debate had been overshadowed by the 'Millerand case.' In 1899 Alexandre Millerand, one of the leading Socialists of the day, had joined the government of Waldeck-Rousseau, an action which divided French Socialists into two camps. Millerand's gradual evolution to the right (after the war he ended up as a right-wing President) seemed to vindicate those who argued that participating in the system was to betray Socialism. When a unified Socialist party was formed in 1905 a compromise was reached: Socialists would not participate in governments except under (non-specified) extraordinary circumstances. With the outbreak of war, this condition seemed to have been attained and a number of Socialists joined the coalition government of so-called 'Sacred Union.' As feeling against the war grew, the legitimacy of participation again came into question, and the Socialists withdrew from government in 1917. But at the level of theory nothing had been resolved and the issue continued to agitate the Socialists throughout the interwar years.

The Communist Party, which had partly been born out of revulsion against Socialist collaboration in the war effort, viewed the issue of power through the precepts of Leninism: there could be no question of integration into the bourgeois state. But the Popular Front tactic posed new questions not covered by Leninist doctrine: was participation not the logical consequence of the new policy? As for the CGT, before the war it had viewed the bourgeois state with hostility. Although since 1918 this position had been modified, the organization continued to prize its independence of political parties. Only the Radicals had no doubts: when power was offered they would always take it.

In this chapter, therefore, we shall examine, through the personalities of the leaders of the four principal organization of the Popular Front – the SFIO, the PCF, the Radical Party and the CGT – what they expected of the Popular Front in power and how they defined their relationship to it as a government. The four men could hardly have been more different in character, background or education and there was little personal sympathy between them. But what united them was no less important than what divided them: in French terms they stood on the 'left'. They were all steeped in a common historical heritage which derived its points of reference from the Revolution and the Republican tradition. All were keen readers of Victor Hugo. It was this legacy, as much as the threat of fascism, which made the Popular Front possible.

Léon Blum: moralist in politics

In a battle like this, a leader is needed: command must be exercised under your permanent control but with full powers vested in me. I have never used this sort of language before. You know that whatever standing I possess with you, with the party, I owe on the contrary to a constant effort of conciliation and persuasion. Today something else is required. In the face of new circumstances a new man must emerge. I do not know if I have the qualities of a leader for so difficult a battle; I cannot know it, any more than any of you. You will put me to the test and I shall put myself to the test. But there is something that I will never lack: resolution, courage and fidelity . . . I do not come to you saying 'take away this chalice, I did not want this, I did not ask for this'. Yes, I did want it, I did ask for it, because it is the victory of our party as part of a Republican victory.

This public expression of self-doubt, extraordinary in a man about to assume the head of his country's government, was made by Blum to the National Council of the SFIO six days after the elections of 1936. Far from heralding the emergence of a 'new man', the confessional style, the public self-examination, the personal appeal, are characteristic of the whole of Blum's political career. Indeed in spite of Blum's transformation from *fin de siècle* aesthete to engaged Socialist, his life is striking for its consistency of moral purpose. But when he prepared to accept the 'chalice' in 1936, the challenge facing Blum was more than a personal one. In the years before 1936 he had reflected at length on the Socialists' relationship to political power within the bourgeois parliamentary system. It was the results of this meditation, and indeed the wider moral vision of rationalist Socialism with which Blum had identified himself, which were to be put to the test in 1936.

Blum was born in the Rue St Denis, Paris, in 1872, two years after the Republic in whose defence he spent much of his life, and one year after the suppression of the Commune, which always loomed for him as an example of the folly of premature revolution.[1] The Rue St Denis was in a crowded quarter of small traders amongst whom, Blum recalled, the memory of 1789 and 1848 was deeply embedded. Blum's father was the head of a thriving haberdashery business and the family was raised in bourgeois comfort, though not in the luxury alleged by later right-wing propaganda. Equally false were the rumours of his Bulgarian Jewish origins. In fact Blum's parents were of Alsatian Jewish descent. He was brought up in a fairly Orthodox milieu, but, having left home, he abandoned the Jewish faith. In the face of anti-semitic attacks Blum would always affirm his Jewishness with pride, but, as he declared in his homage to Weizmann, he had been 'born in France, of a long line of French ancestors, speaking only the language of my country, nurtured predominantly on its culture'.[2] A Jewish Frenchman not a French Jew, as Colette Audry, has put it.

This does not mean that Blum's Jewishness was without implications for his politics. In the first place it linked him to the French revolutionary tradition to which the Jews owed their emancipation. He also believed that it linked him to Socialism. In Blum's words: Judaism was 'the religion of justice . . . Only the idea of an inevitable Justice has sustained . . . the Jews in their long tribulations . . . The ancient Jews did not believe in the immortality of the soul . . . It is the world which must someday order itself according to the rule of reason.' His mother, he remembered, took a concern with fairness to the point of melancholy. It was no coincidence, he believed, that Marx and Lassalle were Jews.

Having been an outstandingly brilliant schoolboy, Blum was admitted to the Ecole Normale Supérieure (one of the elite educational institutions of France) in 1890. But, finding the strict discipline uncongenial, he left without regrets after one year. He then enrolled at the Sorbonne, took a law degree and in 1895 passed the arduous entry exam to the Conseil d'Etat, France's highest court of administrative law, where he served with distinction until entering parliament in 1919. But law was primarily a means of support. Blum's main interests were artistic and he quickly began to make a reputation in literary circles. In 1892 he started a nine-year collaboration with the recently founded *Revue Blanche*, an influential *fin de siècle* literary periodical whose contributors included Gide, Proust, France, and Mallarmé. Blum's articles were mainly on literary and philosophical subjects; in 1896 he became principal book reviewer until succeeded by Gide in 1901.

Blum's literary taste ranged widely from the seventeenth-century French classicists to Hugo, Stendhal, Jane Austen, Tolstoy, Disraeli. What attracted him especially were subtlety of psychological perception and clarity of thought and style. At the age of twenty-two he wrote for the *Revue blanche* a panegyric on 'classical taste' – on the search for precision of expression. Throughout his life Blum attempted to emulate such qualities and as a result his political oratory and journalism have worn much better than the more florid performances of many of his contemporaries. Blum's training as a jurist accentuated this trait: his skills were analytical, of dissection rather than creation (he quickly abandoned his youthful forays into poetry). Blum always preferred to proceed by argument: *Les Nouvelles conversations avec Eckermann*, the book in which he outlined his political and philosophical beliefs in 1901, was cast in the form of a Socratic dialogue. When he was put on trial by the Vichy regime at Riom in 1942, his judges were astonished at the dialectical skill of their 70-year-old defendant,

Blum once wrote that his revolt against injustice was as old as his conscience. But it was a chance meeting in 1893 with Lucien Herr which directed these feelings towards Socialism. Herr, the librarian of the Ecole Normale Supérieure, had served as mentor to generations of *normaliens* many of whom, including the Socialist leader Jean Jaurès, he had converted to Socialism. Initially, however, Blum's commitment to Socialism remained largely theoretical: his interests and friendships, apart from that of Herr, were literary. The young Blum charmed himself effortlessly into the literary salons of Paris. He was an accomplished dancer and fencer, a witty conversationalist, elegant, almost dandyish, in appearance. Two events transformed this glittering ascension: the Dreyfus Affair and Jean Jaurès. The affair catapulted him into active politics; Jaurès, whom he came to know in 1897, when the affair was breaking, was the 'symphonic genius' to whom he owed 'all I believe and all that I am'. Between 1897 and 1905 Blum became closely involved with the Dreyfusard cause and with Jaurès' efforts to create a unified Socialist movement.

But once the Dreyfusards had triumphed and Socialist unity been achieved, Blum, though remaining close to Herr and Jaurès, returned to his former existence. He worked at the Conseil d'Etat as well as becoming the leading drama critic of his day. In these years he also published two books which reflect admirably the nature of his moral vision. His study of Stendhal, *Stendhal et le Beylisme* (1914), admires not the detached analyst of emotion but the poet of disinterested and noble passions: Julien Sorel's hyprocrisy for Blum was the only defence of a vulnerable sensibillity against a hostile world. *Du mariage* (1907) advocated a period of sexual experimentation for women preliminary to marriage. The book was not an apologia for free sex but a plea for honesty and equality in human relationships. Blum's three marriages – his first two wives died – were all happy.

Why Blum retired from politics in these years in unclear. Possibly he felt overawed by Jaurès who tried twice to persuade him to stand for parliament. Possibly he felt uneasy in a Socialist Party increasingly tempted by unconditional anti-militarism. Once again Blum's tranquility was shattered by external events. On 31 July 1914 Jaurès was assassinated; two days later France was at war. The Socialists joined the government and Blum became *chef de cabinet* to Maurice Sembat, the Socialist Minister of Public Works: he was never to leave the fray again.

The war gave Blum his first experience of administration, in which, as in everything, he excelled; it also propelled him into the politics of the Socialist Party. In the void left by Jaurès he emerged as a leading figure. As the Socialists became rent by divisions over the war, Blum, although aligned with the advocates of national defence, attempted to conciliate between the different factions. In 1919 he was elected to the Chamber. When, at the Congress of Tours, a split in the party became inevitable, Blum outlined more lucidly than anyone else the implications of joining the Comintern.

After the split Blum became effectively the leader of the Party although the head of the party organization and possibly its most popular figure, was the secretary general, Paul Faure. Blum never held any official party post beyond that of secretary, later president, of the parliamentary group, and political director of the party paper *Le Populaire*. But his ascendancy was unchallenged. In Lefranc's words, Faure was the party's heart, Blum its head. Blum owed his position to his overwhelming intellectual superiority. Although never classed as a great orator – his voice was weak – Blum's speeches, and his regular leaders in *Le Populaire*, had extraordinary effectiveness deriving from their combination of compelling sincerity and controlled argument. Blum never talked down to his audience: he appealed to their intelligence. As the opening quotation illustrates, Blum saw his role in the party as that of conciliator and persuader. This passion to persuade permeated both his public utterances and his private conversation: the trade unionist René Belin noted how Blum's phrases would often end with an interrogative 'Non?', as if continuously seeking the complicity of his interlocutor.[3]

At times Blum's ceaseless quest for approval became a sort of reflex of self-justification, public baring of the soul a weapon in his armoury of persuasion. 'There are two things that I can never be reproached with: lack of courage and lack of fidelity' (September 1936); 'I am a man who, if I felt I had failed, would accuse myself before you – all the more as my greatest concern would be that my faults or mistakes be concentrated on me and not on the Party' (June 1938): such phrases recur throughout Blum's speeches. Blum's need for esteem and reassurance formed an important element in his character. This trait was possibly accentuated by the fact that Blum was always partly an outsider within his own party and within the working-class movement. Although a man of personal warmth he never had the popular touch of a Jaurès or the professional camaraderie of a Laval; he did not readily use the familiar *tu* form, and his elegance and fastidiousness of manner struck some in his own party as affectation.[4] As premier he would receive workers' delegations in the library of his Ile St Louis apartment at eleven o'clock in the morning, still dressed in slippers and dressing-gown. For Jouhaux, he was always 'M. le Conseiller d'Etat.' Delmas and Belin noted how, faced with a working-class union interlocutor, he often seemed disarmed.[5]

Colette Audry's verdict is even less charitable: she depicts Blum as Sartre's *salaud*, refusing to dirty his hands in the cause of the revolution. His only concern was to be universlly loved as the 'just' man, to preserve the purity of his liberal conscience: his personal innocence was his political guilt.[6] It is true that Blum always displayed considerable legalistic scrupulousness. In 1936 he was concerned that the Popular Front government assume power in 'the most normal, the most legal way'. On another occasion he wrote: 'for a Socialist party the way in which it quits office is more important than the way in which it occupies it'. But Audry's attack misfires because for Blum the invocation of some higher 'revolutionary morality' – the dirtying of hands, so to speak – would have been to betray his vision of Socialism and his rationalist conception of mankind. In criticizing the propaganda techniques of the Communists Blum quoted the Socialist, Jules Guesde: 'how will we construct the new society if, on the day of victory, you have corrupted the human materials out of which it is to be built'. In his *Nouvelles conversations avec Eckermann*, Blum, in the role of Goethe (a revealing choice!) imagines the possibility of a *Faust* Part III in which Faust (alias Jaurès) will be a Socialist who converts men to Socialism through persuasion and education and refuses to appeal to man's baser instincts.

Throughout his life Blum attempted to be faithful to the example of Jaurès. Jaurès had provided 'a new human gospel . . . a faith'. Socialism for Jaurès was a 'living synthesis of all that has value of truth, art or morality in humanity'.[7] Like Jaurès, Blum viewed Socialism as inseparable from the Republican idea, as the culmination of the French Revolution and indeed the whole tradition of Western humanism. In spite of some youthful snipes at Marx, Blum also inheritied Jaurès' synthesis of Marxism and French Socialism. Jaurès had, he wrote, 'moralized, idealized necessity (that of Karl Marx) or at least he endowed the moral ideal with . . . the force of its necessity and inevitable victory'. Both these elements are vital to the understanding of Blum's Socialism. On one occasion he described Socialism as 'a morality and almost a religion as much as a doctrine'.[8] It was the highest manifestation of the universal instinct towards human solidarity. But as a Marxist he also believed that capitalism was condemned by its contradictions, that revolution was inevitable and that it would be carried out by the proletariat.

Blum would therefore always have refused the label of reformist, or rather, following Jaurès, he rejected the antithesis between reforms and revolution. The Bolsheviks (as he preferred to call them) had committed the Blanquist error of confusing the political seizure of power with the social revolution. The social revolution was a substitution of the capitalist system of property relations by a collectivist one, and it could only occur at the requisite state of capitalist development. To seize political power before this would either result in failure (as in the Commune) or in dictatorial terror (as in Russia). Until the economic conditions were mature, then, the role of Socialists was to secure the maximum of progress compatible with the present social order, and prepare people's minds for the collectivist society. This was the sense in which every reform contributed to revolution by preparing the 'foundations of socialist order' on which the new society would one day be built. In this view even Millerand's participation could be described by Blum at the time – he later retracted the judgement – as 'a form of revolutionary act' because it 'anticipated the regular course of human evolution'.

But although Blum scorned any romantic nineteenth-century association of revolution with barricades and argued against the idea of a total rupture with the past, he rejected the notion of a transition to socialism by means of a series of 'almost imperceptible gradations'. At the final stage there would be a qualitative change from one regime to another, possibly involving violence. This moment of transition would almost (sic) always involve a rupture of legality and a transitional dictatorship of the proletariat. But Blum emptied this notion of the connotations which it had acquired in Russia: the dictatorship would be provisional and democratic; it was the necessary passage from one form of legality to another rather as the provisional government had led from the Second Empire to the Third Republic.

Most commentators rightly observe that Blum's stress on the Socialists' 'preparatory' and pedagogic function, his fear of 'premature' action, seemed to push the revolution into an infinitely receding future.[9] But Blum was not a social democrat: he never abandoned the idea of the Revolution and he opposed the revisionist doctrines of the Belgian Socialist, Henri de Man. One reason for this was his susceptibility to criticism from the Communists: the Socialists must preserve their 'originality' and not become a 'party like others'. The split at Tours therefore had the paradoxical effect of strengthening the Socialists' allegiance to Marxist doctrine.[10] But as they became an increasingly important electoral force, this raised an acute problem of political tactics: what attitude should Socialists take to non-Socialist left-wing governments? Could the party participate in Herriot's government in 1924? Could it accept an offer of participation from Daladier in October 1929?

All Blum's talents as a conciliator were necessary to prevent this issue from splitting the party. The problem partly derived from the conflict between the party machine and the parliamentary representatives who felt responsible to the wider constituency of their electorate: in 1929 the parliamentary group had accepted Daladier's offer only to be disavowed by the National Council. In what he considered his most significant doctrinal contribution to the Socialist Party, Blum attempted in 1926 to clarify this debate. He drew a distinction between the 'conquest' and the 'exercise' of power. The former was the socialist revolution which would only occur when economic conditions were ripe: political power was a necessary but not sufficient condition of revolution. The exercise of power, on the other hand, occurred *within* capitalist institutions and respected the legality of those institutions: to attempt to use it to move to the conquest of power before the economic conditions were ready would be a betrayal of trust, a 'swindle' (*escroquerie*). Although the exercise of power would be a painful experience, once the Socialists had decided to take part in the parliamentary system, its possibility could not be avoided. But it should not be undertaken unless the Socialists were the largest party in the coalition. In any other circumstances, participation would involve all the disadvantages of power with none of its advantages. For this reason Blum supported the Socialist decision to reject participation in 1924 and 1929, and to pose unacceptable conditions for participation in 1932.

The distinction between exercise and conquest of power served the double function of reminding the right of the party in 1926 that the SFIO remained committed to revolution and the left in 1936 that participation in government need not imply revolution.[11] It also guarded against what Blum called 'revolutionary disappointment' by those expecting too much from a Socialist government. Cynics might say that it provided an alibi in advance for failure. The doctrine was always seen as very much personal to Blum and his actions in 1936 are incomprehensible without it: even if there was a 'revolutionary situation' in 1936, for Blum it would have been an *escroquerie* to try and exploit it.

Blum's efforts to keep the party out of power before 1936 have often been viewed as excessively doctrinaire but they were probably the only means available to Blum for holding the party together.[12] It is certainly true that this contributed to the weakness of the parliamentary system. But unless one argues – implausibly, given the nature of Third Republic politics – that by entering government the Socialists might have successfully anchored the Radicals on the left, Blum, who could remember the precedent of Millerand, can be credited with having prevented the Socialists being sucked into the quicksands of centrist politics and having preserved them intact for the Popular Front experiment. But perhaps as a result expectations were all the greater, and the trauma of office more dramatic.

It should be noted, however, that for Blum the conditions of the Popular Front government were different even from those of the 'exercise' of power. When formulating his doctrine in 1926 he had accepted the possibility in exceptional situations of joining non-Socialist governments, if the Republic was in danger. What was a hypothesis in 1926 became a reality in 1934. On the morning after the 6 February riots Blum told Daladier that the Socialists would be prepared to join the cabinet. In 1935 he refined his theory by inventing a third category: the 'occupation of power'. In this case the Socialists would accept the responsibilities of government not in order to transform the capitalist system (as in the conquest) nor to prepare its transformation (as in the exercise) but merely to defend it against fascism. This did not imply a purely negative posture: fascism could only be defeated by acting resolutely against the economic crisis which had engendered it. On these grounds Blum was prepared to participate in a Radical cabinet.

When, to general surprise, the 1936 elections put the Socialists in first place, thus conforming to the conditions for the 'exercise' of power, Blum felt constrained by the Popular Front programme (which went much less far than the Socialist programme). This was a point he repeated many times:

the country has not given a majority to the Socialist Party. It has not even given a majority to the parties of the working class. It has given a majority to the Popular Front . . . Our aim is not to transform the social system, it is not even to apply the specific programme of the Socialist Party, it is to execute the programme of the Popular Front.

The Socialists had a contractual obligation to go no further than this. The Blum government of 1936 was, then, to adopt Blum's terminology, situated somewhere between the 'exercise' and the 'occupation' of power. Within these strict limits the object was not to transform the system but to 'learn if from this social system it is possible to extract the maximum of order, welfare, security and justice for all who work and produce'. This statement defined Blum's conception of the limits and possibilities of his government in 1936.

Few politicians, as James Joll remarks, 'have discussed and explained the reasons for their political actions as publicly and as freely' as Blum.[13] But how can we judge him as a political leader? Behind the tall, slightly frail figure lay great reserves of personal courage as he demonstrated in February 1934, and again in 1940. But his self-doubts were no posture. He genuinely questioned whether he had the qualities of a man of action. The verdict of one critical ex-Socialist was that he was 'disarmed by his very intellectual superiority as Hamlet by his conscience'.[14] But Blum was no Hamlet. Those who worked closely with him testify that, unlike the vacillating Daladier, once he had made up his mind he was difficult to sway.[15] Blum's political hesitations stemmed not from indecisiveness but on the contrary from the constancy of his legal and moral scrupulousness. He was not a major Socialist theorist but he had a powerful intelligence. His collaborators in 1936 were amazed at the rapidity with which he mastered the most complex technical dossiers: 'the man knew everything' commented one of his ministers.[16] Blum's personal moral stature is unassailable: Gide's final judgement, after many barbed comments along the way, was that he had rarely met such 'personal disinterestedness and nobility'. Even four years of wartime incarceration did not dim his optimism. In his last article for *Le Populaire* in 1950, on the day before his death, he wrote a sentence that could stand as his epitaph: 'I hope it and I believe it. I believe it because I hope it.' Perhaps the major irony of Blum's career was that having spent the first half of his political life preserving the Socialists from the temptations of power and stressing its limitations, once called upon to assume office in 1936, he felt himself morally bound by a programme of government which fell below even the minimum expectations of his party. Would his allies be equally scrupulous?

Maurice Thorez: Stalinist Jacobin

In the 1949 edition of his autobiography, *Fils du peuple* [Son of the People], Thorez tells of the 'strong impression' made upon him during his first visit to Moscow in 1925 by the 'simple and profound' contributions of Stalin at a Comintern meeting. In fact, as has been pointed out by Thorez's biographer, Philippe Robrieux, Stalin did not speak on this occasion, and even if he had done, the young Thorez would hardly have noticed him among the constellation of revolutionary figures whom he was seeing for the first time. The memoirs of André Ferrat give a more plausible account of the paltry impact made by Stalin on the French delegation during this visit. The anecdote is nonetheless instructive as a demonstration of the somewhat elastic notion of truth in the different versions of Thorez's autobiography. It also highlights a parallel between the ascent of Thorez and that of Stalin with whom he was to be so closely linked: neither would in 1925 have appeared as a future party leader; both owed their success to opportune inconspicuousness, to application not brilliance.[17]

In 1925 the rising figure of French Communism was not Thorez but Doriot, hero of the party's anti-colonial campaign and veteran of countless skirmishes with the police. Even in February 1934, when he had probably decided to break with the Party, it was Doriot who fought alongside the demonstrators in the street battle of 9 February. Thorez, on the other hand, had never been a man for street heroics. Six years earlier, at a clandestine meeting of the Central Committee which was raided by the police, he was found with his feet protruding beneath the door of the cupboard in which he had taken refuge. In *Fils du peuple* he alleged that he had been betrayed, but the truth seems to be that whereas the two other leading Communists present, Duclos and Benoît Frachon, had followed a prearranged contingency plan and escaped through the garden, Thorez had lost his nerve. Thorez's temperamental lack of combativity verged on submissiveness – submissiveness to the teachers at his primary school where he was a model pupil, to his forceful second wife Jeanette Veermeersch, to the envoys of the Comintern. According to Ferrat, Thorez once broke down and cried when he came under criticism at a Comintern meeting in 1932. Manuilsky is once said to have complained of his 'servility'.

These characteristics combined with considerable native intelligence made him an ideal leader for the disciplined party of the Stalinist era. Thorez had served his political apprenticeship in the tough school of Communist politics in the 1920s where survival depended on scenting the abrupt changes in Comintern tactics. He learnt his lesson the hard way. In 1923, one of the leading figures of the PCF, Boris Souvarine, had been attacked as a Trotskyist. This was part of a power struggle taking place in the Soviet Union, a fact of which probably Souvarine himself was hardly aware, and certainly not the young Thorez who wrote to offer his support: 'I consider as arbitrary the classifications of "right" "centre" and "left" applied to party members . . . I do not accept that we should argue . . . over texts and speeches, displacing commas, distorting ideas.' Eleven years later, having lived down this 'Trotskyist' temptation, Thorez had become a master of arcane distinctions between 'right opportunists' and 'left deviationists'. By artfully selective quotation he even argued in June 1934 that Doriot had opposed united action with the Socialists.

Thorez had come to realize where the real source of power lay: Moscow. By the end of the 1920s he was, with Barbé, the French Communist leader who had most visited Moscow. Once, in his cups, he told Vassart that success depended on retaining the confidence of the Soviet party, and above all Stalin. This knowledge he applied effectively. In 1932, at a Comintern meeting where the French leadership had been criticized for the poor showing of the party in the elections, Doriot had escaped lightly owing to his personal electoral success in St Denis. But while Doriot, basking in this praise, left Moscow immediately after the meeting, Thorez stayed behind and secured a decentralization of Communist regional organization in France, thus weakening Doriot's hold over the Paris region.

Political life in the French Communist Party was conducive neither to confidences nor unguarded friendships and there is much about Thorez's personality that remains elusive. Solitary walks were his main recreation. As a young man he could be jovial in company (though never humorous): he enjoyed singing with a group of comrades. But such promiscuous conviviality is precisely the kind which requires no self-exposure. His autobiography was merely a contribution to party mythology. Was Thorez aware of any sense of betrayal in his transformation from eager defender of Souvarine in 1923 to the docile casuist of the 1930s? Did his visits to the Soviet Union ever inspire any inner doubts in his faith in Soviet Communism? Answering such questions is impossible. Thorez's biographer has a hard enough task merely to sift the basic facts of his life from the functional half-truths of party hagiography.

Thorez was born in 1900 in a mining village of the Nord. He was the illegitimate son of a grocer but his mother had married a miner, Louis Thorez, when Maurice was three. The dominant figure of his childhood was his maternal grandfather, Clément, a miner and an ardent Socialist. As a diligent and intelligent pupil he came top in his *certificat d'études primaires*, and having left school, he started work not down the mines, but, helped by the patronage of his *instituteur*, in a clerical post for one of the mining companies. This peaceful existence was cut short by the outbreak of war in 1914 when he and his grandfather were evacuated to the Creuse where he encountered a new form of pacifist, peasant Socialism different from the Jacobin Socialist tradition in which he had been brought up. By 1919, after his return to the Nord, he had joined the Socialist Party and become a supporter of the revolutionary wing which advocated joining the Third International. Exactly how this decision was reached we do not know, but given the influences of his background it was a natural evolution.

If, then, the first sentence of *Fils du peuple* – 'son and grandson of miners' – is not absolutely accurate, it is not far from the truth. While the milieu of the young Blum recalls that of Proust's Swann, Thorez's background was nearer the world of Zola's *Germinal*. But although *Fils du peuple* is concerned to stress Thorez's authentic proletarian roots, he was only briefly a worker himself. On his return to the Nord, having lost his clerical post, Thorez embarked on a variety of jobs – miner, baker's boy, labourer, painter – none held for very long. As Robrieux points out, Thorez had no qualification, no trade, no fixed workplace: the party quickly became his life, his workplace, his mode of social advancement. There was a revealing exchange between Thorez and Ferrat when the latter refused a summons to Moscow realizing that to do so meant expulsion from the party: 'but what will you do?' exclaimed a horrified Thorez no longer able to contemplate life outside the party. Blum and Daladier also deeply identified with their parties but in addition they had a position in the world outside them. This was not true of Thorez who thrived on his success as he rose in the Communist hierarchy. In 1926 the Cominterm envoy Jules Humbert-Droz wrote: 'Thorez is quickly getting spoilt . . . [he] contents himself with easy oratorical successes and with a growing popularity which goes to his head.' Vassart has a malicious description of Thorez's 'beaming smile' on his election to parliament in 1932, and his 'childish delight' at showing bus drivers his parliamentary deputy's identity card which entitled him to be taken on as an extra passenger. The details of his rise to power are not important. Elected to the Central Committee in 1924, appointed as one of the collective ruling Secretariat in 1929, and then selected by the Comintern to denounce the 'group' in 1931, Thorez had emerged as the leading figure in the party by 1932. The success seems rapid but the PCF was at this time a party in which the young could rise fast. And also fall: as we have seen, Thorez's position was possibly still precarious in early 1934. Not until the party's Eighth Congress in January 1936 did Thorez become general secretary (a post which had originally been suppressed in 1929 but now had the added glory of being that held by Stalin).

Thorez's speech to the Congress lasted four hours and ran to 128 pages. This was significant: in the etiquette of Stalinism length was power. Indeed by 1937 one can see the beginnings of the personality cult which was to reach such grotesque proportions after the war. The publication in 1937 of *Fils du peuple* is one example of this trend. The decision to build up national leaders was part of Communist policy in the Popular Front years and mirrored the growth of the Stalinist personality cult in Russia. *Fils du peuple*, which was largely ghosted by a somewhat louche Communist journalist, appeared in a fanfare of publicity: 100,000 copies were sold in a few days. At a meeting at the Renault plant in January 1937 Thorez was presented with gifts by young girls.

Although much of this adulation was manipulated, it is also true that in the Popular Front years Thorez grew in political stature and personal confidence. The new policy may have owed much to Dimitrov, Manuilsky and, later, the exigencies of Soviet diplomacy, but it was one which probably responded to Thorez's deepest instincts: in 1927 he had argued in Moscow against the imposition of 'class against class' tactics, although faithfully carrying out the policy once it had been decided on; in 1930 he had privately admitted to Vassart his personal sympathy with the latter's advocacy of a united front with the Socialist leaders; he had strongly supported the Amsterdam movement even when the Soviet Union expressed reservations; in 1933 he had, we have seen, attempted overtures towards the Socialist leaders and it was because of being reprimanded for this that he was slow to adapt in 1934. But once the new policy was under way, Thorez applied it with panache and audacity. He rediscovered the Republican teachings of his *instituteur*, and his revered grandfather, the tradition also of Victor Hugo from whose books he loved to read to his son. In the 1936 election campaign a bourgeoisie reared on the myth of Communism as 'the man with the dagger between his teeth' were startled by the siren tones of the boyish, blue-eyed, reassuring figure of Thorez: 'a tender and bleating voice, more persuasive than that of Philomela' wrote the novelist Mauriac. Photographs of the period show Blum standing to acknowledge the applause, his fist clenched in defiance, and next to him, a smiling Maurice Thorez, tricolour sash across his chest, hand stretched out fraternally to the crowd below.

Thorez's increased authority owed much also to the presence of Eugen Fried who, it will be remembered, had been sent out in 1931 to supervise the French leadership. Fried was a Central European intellectual deeply imbued with French history. Between Fried and Thorez a close relationship developed and in the dark days of 1932–4 Thorez may have owed his political survival to him. As an autodidact with a voracious intellectual appetite but aware of the gaps in his culture, Thorez appreciated the company of intellectuals,[18] but his relationship with Fried went deeper than this. Indeed Fried was possibly his closest ever friend. By 1934 Thorez's first marriage to Aurore Memboeuf had broken up and he had started to live with Jeanette Vermeersch, a party activist, while Fried moved in with Aurore and became a second father to Thorez's eight-year-old son, Maurice. On one occasion Maurice junior remembered being scolded by Fried for having spoken slightingly of the revolutionary leader Brissot, a revealing illustration of Fried's love of French history. The two *ménages* spent much time together; Fried took as his party pseudonym the name Clément, possibly a tribute by Thorez to his grandfather. In the development of the Popular Front policy it is therefore impossible to distinguish between the contributions of Thorez and Fried who worked in total intellectual symbiosis. Fried's existence was unknown to most people but it was quite probably he who invented the term Popular Front and conceived the idea of the *main tendue* broadcast.[19]

Thorez's deepest instincts may have inclined him away from the party's sectarian tendencies but this does not mean that there was any affection between him and Blum. In 1940, when the PCF was again in a political ghetto, an article appeared, signed by Thorez, attacking Blum with extraordinary venom. A few extracts convey the tone: 'the repugnant character'; 'his hands with long, hooked fingers', 'repugnant reptile'; 'haunted, like Lady Macbeth by his inumerable victims'. Even if this was written by the Soviet propaganda services, as Robrieux, who is not indulgent to Thorez, believes, it is nonetheless true, as Annie Kriegel observes, that even at the height of Popular Front euphoria, it is hard to find Thorez naming Blum with warmth – 'our comrade Blum' was his most effusive effort – let alone praising him.[20] There were no doubt many reasons for this: between the 64-year-old Jewish intellectual Blum and the 36-year-old somewhat callow Thorez, yawned a gulf of generation, background, education and experience. And it was Blum who had at Tours so vigorously stated the case against Bolshevism. But when Blum offered the Communists places in his government in 1936 it was not lack of personal sympathy which prompted Thorez's refusal. The PCF's response was determined by the requirements of Popular Front tactics.

The Communists' reflection on political power in the bourgeois state was dominated by a single historical experience: that of Lenin between February and October 1917.[21] In these nine months Lenin had developed the 'dual power' strategy: the role of the Bolsheviks was to mobilize the revolutionary potential of the masses as an alternative focus of power to that of the bourgeois state. But when the bourgeois provisional government of Kerensky came under a right-wing threat from Kornilov the Bolsheviks rallied to its temporary defence. Similarly in 1936 the PCF rallied to the defence of the bourgeois Republic while at the same time remaining outside it. In Kriegel's formula, the Communists tried to be both 'within' and 'without' the existing socio-economic and political system.

The Popular Front policy temporarily subordinated the ultimate revolutionary objectives of the party to the immediate struggle against fascism. This meant fighting 'fascism' within France, defending France against Nazi Germany and strengthening the Franco-Soviet pact. The three objectives were linked: the 'fascist' forces within France were anti-Soviet and most likely to attempt *rapprochement* with Hitler's Germany. Hence Duclos, speaking to the Comintern in January 1936, defined Laval as doubly dangerous because of 'the support he gives the fascist leagues and . . . his anti-Soviet foreign policy'.[22] The Radicals were courted for the same two reasons: as the party which represented that class which might be most tempted by the Leagues; and because many of their leaders had defended a pro-Soviet foreign policy and were more reliable than the Socialists on national defence.

But the Popular Front tactic raised two problems. First, were there limits to the collaboration with bourgeois and social democratic parties which that tactic prescribed? Secondly, what was the relationship between that tactic and the party's longer term revolutionary strategy? Both these issues were considered by Dimitrov at the Seventh Congress. Participation in a Popular Front government was in theory permitted depending on the concrete situation: it was not a doctrinal question. But the nature of an authentically Popular Front government was narrowly defined. Three conditions had to be met: a paralysis of the apparatus of the bourgeois state; the mass of workers had to be ready to act violently against fascism; a considerable proportion of the other organizations participating in the Popular Front had to be ready to apply, with the Communists, 'merciless' measures against fascism. A Popular Front government would not be a revolutionary government of proletarian dictatorship but it might be 'one of the main forms of transition' towards such a government. Although this was an unprecedented admission that the transition to revolution could occur by other than violent means, the revolution did not of course necessarily imply a Popular Front for its realization; nor, conversely, would the Popular Front necessarily lead to revolution.

This analysis was expounded by the PCF in the months leading up to the elections. At one stage in the autumn of 1935 it seemed as if Thorez had widened the criteria of participation but after rectifications by various members of the Comintern, he fell back on the more restrictive Seventh Congress line. As Duclos told the Comintern in January to the satisfaction of Manuilsky: 'we will clarify all these stories about a Popular Front government ... so that it is clearly understood that there are no embryonic ministers in the PCF'.[23] An authentic Popular Front government would, Thorez told the Party Congress in January, be 'the preparation for a total capture of power by the working class, in short a government which is the preface to armed insurrection for the dictatorship of the proletariat'. It would be quite different from a simple government of the left in the style of the cartel, a 'vulgar policy of collaboration'. The Communists, then, were prepared, according to the circumstances, to envisage participation in a Popular Front government – but a Popular Front government 'as we conceive it'.

This could be read either as an advance explanation of why, if the Communists did participate, this would by definition be different from 'vulgar ministerialism' – as it were, preparing the ground for an eventual participation – or an attempt to stake out the limits of collaboration with bourgeois democracy, to check any temptation towards further integration. The latter seems more likely since the whole thrust of the Communists' comments pointed to a refusal to participate in any Popular Front government. And when in January 1936 suggestions were made that the Socialists might join a Radical cabinet after the elections this was attacked as 'neo-millerandism'.[24] When, therefore, after the left's electoral victory, the Communists refused Blum's invitation to join his government, this should have caused no surprise. As Thorez said on 6 May 'we will not participate in government; we have said and repeated it very loyally in the course of our election campaign'.[25] On the other hand, neither the emergence of the Socialists as the largest party nor the scale of the Communist vote had been predicted by the PCF which had anticipated a Radical government. Did this unexpected situation make participation possible after all?

In the 1960 edition of *Fils du peuple* – but not those of 1937 or 1949 – Thorez claimed that after the election he had been in favour of participation but that the Politburo had been against. Duclos confirmed this in 1966, but he had said previously that the situation was not discussed since it had been settled by the Seventh Congress. Two members of the Central Committee – Billoux and Cerretti – claim that the issue was not discussed by the Politburo; Auguste Lecoeur, a member of the party who was not present at the time, had later heard it said that Thorez had inclined against and Duclos and Frachon for.[26] Whatever the truth, it seems inconceivable that if Thorez, with the weight of Fried behind him, had officially advocated participation, it would have been refused. And why, if he had, did he and Duclos not say so before the 1960s? But these conflicting accounts suggest that the party was thrown into some confusion by the election result. Its official argument against participation was that it did not want to provide the enemies of the Popular Front with the pretext to set off a panic, and at the same time it promised the government its 'loyal support'.

Kriegel has not been convinced by this explanation, arguing that by remaining outside the government the Communists were more likely to alarm Blum than to reassure him, and she sees the decision, in line with the resolutions of the Seventh Congress, as the PCF's means of avoiding excessive integration into the system. But perhaps the party's explanation should not be entirely discounted. Communist participation might have alarmed the *classes moyennes* more than participation would have reassured Blum. On the other hand, Kriegel's view is supported by the fact that a few days after his party had promised 'loyal support', the Communist Vaillant-Couturier announced, in a celebrated phrase, that the Communists would form a 'ministry of the masses' outside the government. On 15 June Duclos provided Blum with a gloss on this statement: 'we are going to give you our votes, but outside the walls of this assembly there is an entire population which wants its legally expressed wishes to be respected'. Far from being reassuring, this sounded like a threat. The most recent view of party historians is that the Communists, taken unawares by the unexpected election result, were slow to perceive the dual possibilities offered by both participating in the government and mobilizing popular support in the country.[27]

We do not possess sufficient information to arrive at a definitive answer – it does not seem that there was direct Comintern intervention – but a provisional conclusion is necessary if we are to understand the Communists' attitude towards the government in the coming year. The resolutions of the Seventh Congress limited Communist participation to what was in effect a pre-revolutionary situation, and if these resolutions were a deciding factor, it is not surprising that the PCF refused to participate since it did not see – or want to see – 1936 as a revolutionary situation: the priority was anti-fascism. But the conditions prescribed by the Seventh Congress were circular – by joining a government the Communists by definition turned it into a Popular Front government 'as we conceive it' – and vague enough for it to be argued that they had been met in 1936. This does still not answer the question why the Communists claimed that they had not been met.

Some light is thrown on the issue by a report by Dimitrov to the Comintern, approving the PCF's decision not to participate. First, he stressed again that the issue of participation was not a matter of principle but had to be judged according to political opportuneness. Secondly, the Communist and Socialist victory had not, he argued, been substantial enough to allow a frontal assault on fascism in parliament. This presumably meant that the fact that the Radicals held the balance of power in parliament limited what the Communists could expect to achieve as members of the government. Thirdly, Dimitrov saw a danger that participation would give rise to attacks on the Popular Front (this gives some credence to the Communists' public pretext for not participating). The Communists had therefore to do all in their power to develop their influence and that of the Popular Front throughout the country – among the peasantry, in the army and so on.[28]

Before the elections Duclos had written that political parties had more flexibility to influence policy from outside the government than within it,[29] and Dimitrov's report shows that in June 1936 the Communists remained a prisoner of this view. As Thorez told the Central Committee a few days after announcing the decision not to participate: 'our votes will decide nothing, but the presence of the masses throughout the country will count . . . The essential issue is not that of a few Communist ministers but the action and organization of the masses, and this has already been our experience.'[30] This was indeed true: the Communists' success in creating the Popular Front had been carried out from an almost non-existent parliamentary base – from outside parliament – and this is how they continued to see their role: mobilizing the masses both to increase their own support and to influence the course of policy.[31] It is undoubtedly the case, therefore, that in 1936 the Communists underestimated what could be achieved from within parliament or the government: for example, they could much more effectively have opposed non-intervention if there had been Communist ministers. The Comintern soon came to realize this: in September 1936 the Spanish Communists were authorized to enter the Socialist government of Largo Caballero. And in June 1937 the PCF offered to participate in the government of Chautemps, but its participation was no longer desired. The Communists had missed their chance, and on those issues where the Socialists might have benefited from Communist support in the cabinet against their Radical partners, they were forced to face the Radicals alone.

Edouard Daladier: Radical Robespierre?

On 3 July, 1935 at the meeting of the Radical Party's executive committee which decided to permit participation in the 14 July demonstration, the party president Herriot announced that he would not stand again when the post came up for re-election. In making this declaration Herriot, recognizing the growing support for the Popular Front in the party, was in effect handing power over to his rival Daladier. And in January 1936 Daladier was elected president of the party.

No one seemed more appropriate than Daladier to lead the Radicals into the Popular Front. He had a double reputation as being of the left and as being a man of action and determination. As a party activist wrote to him after 6 February: 'I had hope in you and I took you for a true Jacobin, inheritor of the tradition of our great ancestors. When I learnt the news of the repression of the Paris riots, I admired your defence of the regime. There, I said, is a true Jacobin. But now you resign to avoid bloodshed. That I don't understand.'[32] As this disappointed supporter discovered, and as his colleagues already knew, Daladier's Jacobin reputation – the Robespierre of Radicalism as Herriot was its Danton – concealed a more complex reality.

Daladier, the son of a baker, was born in 1884 near Avignon. His early career was similar to that of many bright children from modest backgrounds: he obtained a scholarship, attended the *Lycée* at Lyons, and eventually himself became a *professeur*. Unlike Blum, who was too shortsighted, and Thorez, who was too young, Daladier fought in the war, emerging as a sergeant. Elected to the chamber in 1919, he served his political apprenticeship as a follower of Herriot, serving as a junior minister in this 1924 government. The break with Herriot came when the latter joined Poincaré's National Union government in 1926: Daladier was among the forty-nine Radical deputies who abstained in the government's first vote of confidence. From this moment he established himself on the left of the party.

In 1927 Herriot's opponents in the party built up Daladier because they needed a member of the rising generation as a figurehead in their campaign against Herriot. Daladier, hitherto a second rank figure, was persuaded to stand as president. He was presented as 'an active, energetic man, capable of crystallizing around himself all the forces which are young in mind and body'. The Daladier myth was launched. And as party president between 1927 and 1931, Daladier consolidated it by becoming the patron of many Young Turks. After the withdrawal of the Radicals from the National Union government in 1928, Daladier started to court the Socialists and in October 1929 he attempted to form a left-wing government by offering them participation. The offer, we know, was rejected. This rebuff eroded his authority and in 1931 Herriot, whose star was again rising, replaced him as president. But the Socialists' intransigence had left Daladier's left-wing reputation intact (after all, he had offered them power), and when he became Premier in 1933 hopes on the left were high. Although the Socialists did not participate in his government, Daladier managed to hold the cartel majority together for eight months until brought down by the Socialists in October 1933.

If this brief biography is examined more closely, it becomes clear that neither element in the Daladier myth bears much relation to the truth. Daladier had certainly entered politics on the left but the rejection of his offer to the Socialists in 1929 scarred him and he never trusted them again. In May 1930 he was rumoured to be secretly negotiating with Tardieu to form a right-of-centre government. When he offered participation to the Socialists in January 1933 Daladier had neither expected nor wanted them to accept: the key financial posts had already been promised to two conservative Radicals. After the Socialists finally toppled his government, in spite of a number of concessions made to them, the normally phlegmatic Daladier exploded into rage against Blum. The two men were barely on speaking terms for several weeks and Daladier drew the following conclusion:

watch out for the difficulties of governing with the Socialists. I was one of those who made the greatest sacrifices for the union of the left . . . no one went further than me, who had a reputation for firmness, down the road of concessions. And yet it is to me that M. Léon Blum said no.[33]

Nor must Daladier's flirtation with the Young Radicals be taken too seriously. It was a relationship of convenience which did not reflect any fundamental convergence of view. For the Young Radicals, Daladier was a useful figurehead in their assault upon the old party *notables*; for Daladier their support made it possible to perfect the image of youthful innovation upon which his rise to power was based. In mid-1933 there were rumours in political circles that Daladier was planning to break with the Young Radicals. Blum, on the other hand, believed that Daladier was planning to split the Socialists,[34] a strategy which implied building a majority around a convergence between the Young Radicals, the left of the Radical Party, and the right wing of the Socialists. That such divergent interpretations could flourish was a symptom of the speciousness of Daladier's left-wing posture: if Daladier often appeared to be on the left, it was because usually Herriot appeared to be on the right. Daladier's career was in fact marked by extraordinary ideological versatility: in the week before 6 February he had tried three different types of ministerial combination.

Daladier's versatility disguised weakness. His allegedly Napoleonic decisiveness – the 'Bull of Vaucluse' was one of his nicknames – was spurious, although Daladier may have come to believe in it himself. The only feature he shared with Napoleon was premature baldness. The reputation for firmness was nourished by his manner: where Herriot was expansive, Daladier, belying the meridional stereotype, was taciturn to the point of rudeness. In the photographs of the Popular Front meeting of 14 July 1936, which show a radiant Thorez and a smiling Blum, Daladier is grim-faced, looking indeed, as Fabre-Luce once said of him, as if he were the chief mourner at France's funeral. The taciturnity disguised not firmness of purpose but irresolution. Daladier's ministerial colleagues were exasperated by his indecisiveness and his tendency to change his mind according to the last visit received.[35] Daladier's political practice was, in short, no different from that of any average Radical politician for whom the supreme political virtue was compromise.

Where Daladier's 'Jacobin' reputation did contain some truth was in his capacity for organization and predilection for party discipline. On becoming party president in 1927 he at once set about invigorating the party organization and trying to impose voting discipline on the parliamentary group. This concern with organization possibly reflected the early precariousness of his position within the party and also a certain authoritarianism in his temperament: as Premier in 1938 he quickly reduced the party hierarchy to a cipher. But Daladier was in private a modest and unassuming man who disliked ceremony. René Belin found his manner 'unaffected and cordial'. On occasion he would cycle to important dinner parties.[36] His only personal indulgence was possibly a tendency to drink. Perhaps his political authoritarianism stemmed indeed from personal insecurity. If there was a moral centre to Daladier's political identity, it lay in a deep Republican patriotism. After June 1936 he was continuously Minister of National Defence, a position which he enjoyed and in which he was respected by the military.

In public, the Daladier myth remained intact until 1939 and made him popular among party activists and unpopular with his colleagues. Thus

Daladier came to view the base of the party as the source of his strength. Paradoxically his resignation on 7 February may in the long run have helped him: he was the man who had resisted the rioters on 6 February and his resignation could, with some justice, be blamed on the desertion of his Radical colleagues. After a short period in the wilderness Daladier was therefore ideally placed to lead the Radical opposition to the National Union government. The Congress of Nantes in October 1934 was his political comeback: the startling success of his speech attacking the 'two hundred families' encouraged him to develop his opposition to the government. In May 1935 he attacked the government's deflation policy, although as Premier in 1933 he had attempted the same policy himself. On 28 May 1935 he took the plunge and appeared on a common platform with Blum and Thorez.

Once again Daladier had climbed to power as a leader of the left. But, as we have seen, the extent of his commitment to the left was limited. More importantly, he remained sensitive to the mood of the Radical rank and file and his loyalty to the Popular Front would not survive any shift to the right at the base. Finally it is worth noting that although Daladier was the Radical most associated with the Popular Front, the Communists were in fact slightly suspicious of his reputed lukewarmness towards the Soviet Union, and they were consistently more sympathetic to Herriot owing to his known pro-Soviet views and in spite of his reservations about the Popular Front.[37]

The Radicals, whose political function was to hold office, were not interested in the debates of the Socialists and Communists about what to do with power: their concern was how to retain it. Daladier's conception of the Popular Front was, like that of most Radicals, a very traditional one (though it had for him the personal gratification of a revenge for 6 February): he defined it as the 'alliance of the 3rd estate and the proletariat'. And as we have already seen most Radicals interpreted it simply as a new version of the traditional union of the left. In the view of one Radical partisan of the Popular Front, the alliance with the Communists, which did seem to represent something new, was not a lurch to the left: 'the Communists are now much more Radical than we will ever be Communist'.[38] The Radical conception of the Popular Front was, then, a highly restrictive one. But should the Communists prove not to be Radicals, there was every likelihood that many Radicals would turn against them. Daladier was not the man to stand in their way.

Léon Jouhaux: from syndicalism to planism

Of the figures discussed in this chapter, none had dominated their organization longer than Léon Jouhaux. Having been elected General

Secretary of the CGT in 1909 at the age of thirty, he had held the post ever since. By 1936 he had become an institution: in CGT circles he was known familiarly as 'The General' or 'The Pope'. No doubt it would be an exaggeration to say that Jouhaux was the CGT – although he had been heard to remark on more than one occasion 'la CGT c'est moi' – but certainly no one had done more to guide the organization away from its pre-war revolutionism towards its reformist stance of the 1930s.[39] Little of this could have been predicted in 1909. Jouhaux had been elected at a time when increasing tension within the CGT was threatening to split the organization. He was chosen because he was too unknown a figure to be closely associated with either side in the conflict.

There had been little remarkable about Jouhaux's career up to that point. Born in 1879 in Paris he had been brought up in the working-class suburb of Aubervilliers; his mother was a cook, his father a cigarette worker. His grandfather had been shot during the June days of 1848, his father involved in the Commune. Like Thorez, Jouhaux was forced to give up a promising education in order to earn a living. In 1895 he entered the Aubervilliers cigarette factory, and joined his local union. Given this background, Jouhaux gravitated naturally enough into the anarchist circles whose political culture was that which impregnated the CGT at this time. But it was precisely whether this was the direction that the CGT should continue to take which was dividing the organization when Jouhaux took over.

Officially the CGT had been committed since its foundation to the doctrine of revolutionary syndicalism which believed in the absolute autonomy of the labour movement: workers must carry out their own emancipation by direct action – the culmination of which would be a general strike – not by relying on political parties. Politicians, even Socialists, were viewed with suspicion, the state with distaste. Revolutionary syndicalism owed its success within the CGT to the organization's federal structure. A union (*syndicat*) did not join the CGT directly but had to affiliate to its trade federation. The CGT was therefore a confederation of federations which were each represented equally on its governing National Confederal Committee (CCN) irrespective of their size. At the biennial annual congress each *syndicat* had one vote – also irrespective of its size. Thus policy was controlled by a number of small unions which were able to outvote the larger reformist unions. This confederal structure reflected the syndicalists' abhorrence of centralization and their preference for trade unionism as the activity of an ideological working-class elite which would lead the rest of the working class towards revolution rather than for the mass unionism which existed in Britain and Germany: in 1912 the CGT accounted for only some 7 per cent of the French working class. Jouhaux became Secretary General at a time of growing demands for a more flexible policy to increase the organization's effectiveness, although even the most convinced 'reformists' opposed formal links with parliamentary Socialism.

Jouhaux's joint biographers demonstrate convincingly that, having become Secretary General, he had begun to steer the CGT on a more reformist course before 1914. Nevertheless the turning point in his career was provided by the war when he discovered the Nation and the State. In July 1914 the CGT, faced with the undeniable nationalism of the French working class, was forced to abandon its anti-militarism overnight. In his speech at the funeral of Jaurès, Jouhaux employed the language of Republican patriotism, presenting 1914 as a replay of Year II: to defend France was to defend Liberty. But as the war dragged on this optimism was dented and many trade-unionists emerged more deeply pacifist than they had been before. Of more durable importance to the CGT was its new attitude to the state. In all kinds of ways the organization was drawn into the war effort. Jouhaux sat on various government committees; for the first time he formed links with politicians. When Clemenceau came to power in 1917 he even offered Jouhaux a post in his government. Although the offer was refused, it was a striking recognition of the transformed status of an organization which in 1913 had been on the verge of illegality.

The role of the CGT during the war supplied Jouhaux with a reformist model to which he remained faithful throughout his life. He defined his new outlook in the following way: 'we must give up the policy of the clenched fist and adopt a *politique de présence* in the affairs of the nation'. The *politique de présence* meant that the representatives of the workers should be present at every public arena in which the interests of the workers were discussed; they should be willing to negotiate with governments and employers to advance the interests of their members. The policy was given concrete form in the CGT's first postwar programme which proposed the setting up of a National Economic Council uniting representatives of government, trades unions and employers, and the nationalization of a number of key industries.

The new direction taken by the CGT did not go unchallenged and the organization again moved towards a schism. The conflict paralleled that taking place in the Socialist Party at the same time. At its origin was the growth of opposition to the war and the CGT's support for it, but this initial division became overlaid by the problems raised by the Russian Revolution: was there now a revolutionary situation in France? At the end of the war the CGT had been swelled by hundreds of thousands of new members with little previous union experience but full of millennarian enthusiasm, and Jouhaux was increasingly unable to resist pressure for militant action. In 1920 he was faced, in spite of his best efforts, with the *fait accompli* of a railway strike by the Railway Union Federation. To support the railway workers the CGT launched the idea of a staggered wave of strikes, industry by industry. The government responded firmly, the tactic failed and the strikes were called off. For the revolutionary wing of the CGT Jouhaux had betrayed the workers; for Jouhaux the labour movement had been saved from total annihilation. In 1921 the inevitable split occurred. The revolutionary minority decided to hold a separate congress, was expelled from the CGT and founded the CGTU.

The issues dividing the two organizations were not a simple replica of those dividing the CGT before the war. The conciliatory policies pursued by the postwar CGT did not mean that Jouhaux had sacrificed its independence of political parties. The CGTU, on the other hand, although claiming to be the authentic inheritor of the pre-war tradition, became quickly subordinate to the PCF.

In the years after 1921 Jouhaux painfully reconstructed the CGT whose suddenly inflated membership had suffered both from the split and from the repression which followed the failed strikes. The federal structure of the organization was maintained but an element of proportionality was introduced into the representation of unions at the Congresses. How far the *politique de présence* brought results is questionable. In 1919 the government had, under union pressure, passed laws legalizing collective contracts and introducing an 8-hour day. But during the 1920s the CGT was powerless to prevent employers from by-passing this legislation. The CGT offered itself as a responsible partner but found itself rarely accepted as such by employers whose attitude towards labour remained autocratic and hostile. The CGT could all the more easily be ignored since its membership recovered only slowly from the traumas of 1920–1. By 1930 it had climbed from 480,700 immediately after the schism to 580,000 – the best figure until 1936. It was also the case that an increasing proportion of the CGT's membership was made up of tertiary sector workers – a development which worried Jouhaux. The only comfort for him was that in the same period the CGTU's membership had declined – in tandem with the PCF – to 323,000.

Whatever the weaknesses of the CGT as an organization, Jouhaux himself had by the mid-1920s become a figure of stature on the French political scene. Much of his time was spent at Geneva representing French labour on the various international bodies which had been set up after the war: he was French representative at the League of Nations between 1924 and 1938. There is no doubt that Jouhaux enjoyed the prestige that these gatherings brought him and found it difficult to tear himself away from them: between 9 June and 16 June 1936, during some of the tensest days of the strikes of that year, Jouhaux was in Geneva attending a conference of the International Labour Organization (ILO). He came to acquire a strong sense of his own indispensability, and was quickly suspicious of possible rivals. In the mid 1930s one of the principal victims of this jealousy was René Belin who was in 1933 promoted to be one of the secretaries of the CGT and rapidly became seen by many as Jouhaux's *dauphin*. As a result Belin's account of Jouhaux in his memoirs must be treated with caution. For Belin, Jouhaux was a man who had become accustomed to the sleepy routines of the CGT and complacent about its low level of membership; his main concern was to strut on the European stage.[40] Perhaps there is some truth in this but the differences between the two men were partly of style and temperament. While Belin was relentlessly hardworking, a good journalist and an avid reader, Jouhaux hated all paperwork and found it difficult even to write a letter. Most of his articles were ghosted by his collaborator Maurice Harmel. The spoken word was Jouhaux's forte. At meetings, with his bulky figure slumped back in his chair and his eyes closed, Jouhaux often appeared to observers to be asleep. But in fact he always listened carefully, and once he rose to speak he was a powerful orator in the lyrical mode. At times, such as his famous speech at Jaurès' funeral, he become carried away by his own rhetoric. For Delmas, Jouhaux without his voice was like Samson bald.[41] Consequently his speeches do not read well today.

Jouhaux's dislike of paperwork was perhaps a habit which remained from his anarchist days. It was not the only one. Although he had come to form close relationships with one or two politicians, Jouhaux never overcame his distrust of politicians as a breed and his relationships with them were personal rather than political. He always used the *tu* form with Pierre Laval ('Pierrot') who had also started his days on the pacifist extreme left. But to be a member of the SFIO – the 'Socialos' as he called them contemptuously – was no recommendation for Jouhaux's approval. When the CGT called its general strike on 12 February Jouhaux was careful to detach the CGT from responsibility for the demonstration organized by the Socialists on the same day. Between Blum and Jouhaux there was no warmth (they would never have used the *tu* form). Blum was much too fastidious a figure for the more earthy Jouhaux; he, for his part, found Jouhaux somewhat uncouth. Such a judgement was unfair. Jouhaux had developed genuine interests in the arts, especially in painting; on the other hand he despised the theatre – one of Blum's loves – as superficial.

Jouhaux had lived through a lot since 1909 and Belin may be right that by the 1930s he was a man with no illusions left. Certainly he had few friends or confidantes. In spite of his florid oratory he was brusque in private conversation. The lyricism of his Geneva performances concealed a definite pessimism born of many tribulations. His attitude to the calling of the general strike of 12 February is a good example of this. The principle of the strike had been decided on the morning of 7 February as a means of offering support to the beleaguered Daladier. But when Jouhaux arrived at Daladier's office to transmit the decision, Daladier informed him that he was resigning. The purpose of the strike was now redundant. Jouhaux, haunted by the memory of 1920, was reluctant to go ahead with strike action. Having been overruled by his colleagues he warned them that if the strike failed he would resign. In this case Jouhaux's pessimism was not vindicated. But on each of the three occasions during the Popular Front years when the CGT was confronted with the possibility of a general strike – 12 February, March 1937 (after the Clichy incident) and November 1938 – Jouhaux argued for caution.

A similar caution pervaded Jouhaux's attitude to the prospect of reunification with the CGTU – understandably given that for years he had been villified by it as a class traitor. As long as possible he resisted negotiations. But the CGTU bombarded the CGT with invitations for joint action and these could not be ignored indefinitely. When negotiations began in October 1934 Jouhaux did not participate in them, whereas the CGTU sent its leading figures. After a year of discussion the procedures for reunification were decided. Unions and federations were to carry out their own unification and elect new leaderships. This process was crowned at the national level in March 1936 by the reunification Congress of Toulouse which was to decide upon the statutes of the new CGT. Because the ex-*confédérés* were considerably more numerous at this stage than the ex-*unitaires*, the views of the former prevailed entirely. The CGT retained its federal structure: the leadership was not elected by the Congress, as the Communists wanted, but composed of representatives of the federations. Formal independence from parties was maintained and the Communist union leaders had to resign from the PCF's Central Committee. The composition of the new CCN reflected the predominance of the ex-*confédérés*. But Jouhaux was not much reassured. At the last meeting of the old CCN in January he gloomily counselled his colleagues to read Souvarine's fiercely critical biography of Stalin which had just appeared. A few days earlier he had written to a friend; 'unity is taking place. Will it be viable? One must hope so, without harbouring illusions about those who have learnt nothing and whose mentality has not changed.'[42]

Once unity had taken place, however, Belin and others who more than shared Jouhaux's suspicion of the Communists were astonished how little he did to assist their efforts to block Communist penetration of the CGT. But leaving aside the fact that, as we shall see, on foreign policy Jouhaux often found himself in closer agreement with the Communists than with his former colleagues, his attitude is not so surprising. Jouhaux was temperamentally averse to doctrinal squabbles: he was essentially a pragmatist. Where Belin forced issues Jouhaux preferred to fudge. Having already lived through one split, he wanted at all costs to avoid another.

What were Jouhaux's attitude to, and expectations of, the Popular Front? In the early stages, we have seen, he inclined towards caution. That is not to say that he was blind to the dangers of fascism. Like most of the left he was stunned by the events of 6 February. His solution was to take up the doctrine of 'planism'. It is necessary to say something about planism here because to many on the left it represented the alternative anti-fascist strategy to that proposed by the Popular Front. And for a while Jouhaux hoped that the Popular Front could be converted to it.[43]

The inventor of planism was the Belgian Socialist, Henri de Man. He argued that fascism could only be resisted by uniting the proletariat and the *classes moyennes*. Once it might have been possible to do this around a platform of social demands. But economic crisis proved that capitalism was in decline and incapable of fulfilling such demands. Instead of obtaining larger slices from a diminishing cake by 'redistributional reforms', it was necessary to increase the size of the cake – revive the economy – by 'structural reforms'. This could be done by a plan which envisaged nationalizations of key industries and banks. Large sectors of the economy would remain in private hands but state control of key sectors would both free the rest of the economy from dependence on monopoly capital (thus winning over the *classes moyennes*) and enable the government to expand the economy. The Plan, then, was both the blueprint of a mixed economy and an instrument of propaganda through which to rally the forces of anti-capitalism. It was the means to its own end.

Jouhaux's conversion to planism at the start of 1934 was consistent with his outlook since the war. The practical reformism envisaged by the planists was similar to the CGT's programme of 1918. Jouhaux also liked to see the CGT taking its own initiatives independently of the SFIO. In the spring of 1934, he set up a brains trust to draw up a plan for France; on it sat many Socialists disillusioned by their own party's rejection of planism. A draft of the Plan was published in September 1934 and a definitive version a year later. Once the Comité du Rassemblement Populaire started work on a Popular Front programme in 1935 Jouhaux hoped that the CGT representatives would be able to swing it into adopting the Plan as its programme. But this was not to be and the Popular Front programme, which contained almost no 'structural reforms', was a grave disappointment to the CGT.

The reasons for the rejection of planism are simple enough. The attitude of the Socialists will be considered in a later chapter.[44] But the opposition of the Radicals and Communists was sufficient to bury the idea. For the

Radicals the Plan was too far-reaching a project. The Communists'
objection was a dual one: on one hand they viewed planism as a reformist
strategy to shore up capitalism; on the other, they opposed it as too radical
and liable to frighten the *classes moyennes*. The irony is that planism had
been devised precisely as a means of winning over the *classes moyennes* by
offering them a revitalized capitalism.

Planism's economics was rudimentary and it was not the economic
panacea that its advocates believed. But the planists' greatest weakness
was political. They offered the Plan as a kind of mobilizing mystique
against fascism but even among the rank and file of the CGT it never
aroused much enthusiasm. The myths of the Popular Front proved to be
more effective. The Plan appealed for an overhaul of the 'system'; the
Popular Front's rhetoric offered an attack on individuals: the 'two
hundred families', 'let the rich pay' and so on.

The defeat of the planists on the Comité du Rassemblement Populaire
did not entirely end their hopes. At the Congress of Toulouse the
ex-*unitaires* defended the Popular Front programme and the ex-
confédérés the Plan. Given that the latter were in a majority, Jouhaux
could have persuaded the new CGT to reaffirm its support for the Plan.
But he did not wish to find himself disavowing the Popular Front. A
compromise was reached: the Congress voted to support both the Plan
and the programme. As Jouhaux cunningly pointed out, this was no
different from the political parties of the Popular Front all of whom were
going into the elections under their own manifestos while also supporting
the Popular Front programme.

On 13 May, after Blum's invitation to Jouhaux to participate in the
government, the CGT transmitted its refusal of a ministerial post but
promised to collaborate with the government in realizing the 'immediate
demands contained within the Plan of the CGT' and in a 'massive' public
works programme (itself part of the Plan). Thus in Jouhaux's eyes the Plan
remained on the agenda. As for the offer of participation, according to
Belin, Jouhaux was tempted to accept. But at a secret meeting to discuss
the issue (to which the ex-*unitaires* were not invited) he was overruled.[45]
Whatever Jouhaux's personal inclination – and other accounts are less
definitive than Belin's – the arrangement finally reached with Blum cannot
greatly have disappointed Jouhaux since it corresponded perfectly to the
role that he had been trying to win for the CGT since 1919: recognition,
collaboration and independence. At a meeting with Blum on 29 May it
was decided to set up a small team, including Blum and Jouhaux, to
collaborate on the application of the government's programme. As to
when this machinery should be set in motion, Jouhaux noted, in the
memorandum which he drew up after the meeting, Blum's reply that
'however speedily the government acts, the issue certainly won't arise

before July'.[46] All this planning was to no avail. The team was never set up. No more than Blum had Jouhaux predicted the explosion of strikes that was about to transform the political climate. The CGT was suddenly presented with the greatest challenge and the greatest opportunity in its history. Jouhaux, who preferred a quiet life, was plunged into the storm.

PART 2

The explosion

3 ✍ The social explosion

Our workers have adapted to these American methods without any difficulty
. . .They are enchanted with this type of work, which is less tiring, less of a strain
and more remunerative.

(André Citroën, October 1927)

When I first entered the main workshop of the Citroën factory at St Ouen, I was
terrified. As I made my way through the appalling racket, I thought: 'you're not
going to like it here, my boy' . . . Even more than the urgings of the bosses, it was
the huge drum-beat of the machines that speeded your movements . . . When I left
the factory, it followed me, it had entered into me. In my dreams I was a machine.
The whole earth was nothing but an immense factory.

(Georges Navel, *Travaux*)

On taking power in June 1936 Blum's government was confronted with
the most massive strike movement in the history of the Third Republic. In
the history of France only the strikes of 1968 were on a yet larger scale.
According to the official statistics there were 12,142 strikes and
1,830,938 strikers in June 1936 alone; the previous highest *annual* total
of strikers, in 1920, was 1,316,559. And given the suddenness and
rapidity of the June strikes, these figures certainly underestimate the truth.
Those who experienced the days of June 1936 had no doubt that
something momentous had occurred. The progressive industrialist, Jean
Coutrot, described the events with a lyricism worthy of Michelet: 'we
have lived through prodigious days, days without precedent in the already
lengthy history of the human race. In the future the *journées* of June 1936
will be known to little children as historic days, the first of a new era
without any relation to the years before.' After the Matignon Agreement,
Jouhaux also saw the beginning of a 'new era': 'for the first time in the
history of the world, a whole class has obtained at the same moment an
improvement in its conditions of existence'.

It was not only the scale of the movement which impressed contemporaries but also its form: over three-quarters of the June strikes (8,941)
consisted of factory occupations. Alexander Werth described the extraordinary sight of the Paris suburbs during June 1936: 'building after

85

building – small factories and large factories, even comparatively small workshops – were flying red, or red and tricolour flags – with pickets in front of the closed gates'.[1] The occupations were generally organized and disciplined, there was little damage to property; machinery and stocks were looked after with jealous care by the striking workers. But, as Blum pointed out at the Riom trial, it was precisely this 'tranquility, this sort of majesty' which inspired such terror in the bourgeoisie. Were the workers intending to take over the factories themselves?

In the political history of the Popular Front the strike movement was of vital importance; it provided the incoming government with an initial momentum which could not be resisted even by the Senate. But the strikes also restricted the government's freedom of manoeuvre; at Riom Blum described them with some ambivalence as a 'social explosion' which 'struck the government in the face' as soon as it took power. Most commentators on Blum's economic policy have criticized the introduction of the 40-hour week; but it is worth remembering that in June 1936 he had little alternative.

Debate over the strike movement has centred around two issues. First, its origins: were the strikes a 'spontaneous' release after five years of depression and falling wages, and was their rapid spread attributable to 'contagion', simple imitation? Or were they organized by the PCF or other groups whether as a preliminary to a seizure of power, as a means of pushing Blum into action or as a means of discrediting the Socialist government by forcing it to turn against the workers? The second debate concerns the significance of the strike wave: did it create a 'revolutionary situation'? Did the government and the political parties betray the revolution in 1936? Was it true that, in the words of Pivert, 'everything is possible'?

Discussion of these issues has led to an over-concentration on the spectacular events of June 1936 and a neglect of the industrial conflict of the following eighteen months. At stake in this struggle were the material gains of June, and whether the pattern of industrial relations inaugurated by the Matignon Agreement could be institutionalized, or whether, once the balance of power had shifted back to the employers, labour would again be consigned to its ghetto of oblivion.

These are the three principal questions which will be considered in the three sections of this chapter. But it must be remembered that in the end any generalization about the strikes of 1936 is extremely hazardous owing to France's highly diversified industrial structure. The strikes spared almost no sector of industry from Renault's huge Billancourt plant with its 32,000 workers to tiny workshops in which the employer was hardly distinguishable from his workers, from the relatively highly unionized

coalminers and dockers to the totally un-unionized employees of department stores. Much of what follows is based on the precious accounts
gathered from participants either by contemporary journalists such as
Werth or by historians such as Georges Lefranc. But we are better
informed about the strike at the Renault plant than in some small
provincial workshop; we hear more from union activists than from simple
workers. Yet all these experiences will have differed. The worker with a
memory stretching back to the strikes of 1920–1 will have lived the events
of 1936 differently from the young workers knowing only the 1930 world
of depression and repression. The strikes will have represented different
kinds of experience for a Polish immigrant worker in the Nord or a
woman employee of the big department stores where most of the
workforce was female.

June 1936: conspiracy or spontaneity?

About the basic chronology of the strike movement there is little dispute.[2]
It can broadly speaking be divided into three stages. Although the strikes
first became politically important when they spread to the Paris region,
their origin is usually traced back to the Bréguet aviation factory at Le
Havre. Protesting at the dismissal of two workers who had failed to turn
up on 1 May, the workforce occupied the factory on 11 May; after a night
of occupation, the two workers were reinstated. A similar strike – for
identical reasons – broke out at the Latécoére factory in Toulouse on 13
May. Slightly different was a strike, also with occupation, at the Bloch
aviation factory at Courbevoie on 14 May: in this case the workers
demanded a wage increase; again they were speedily successful. On 26
May strikes occurred in two more engineering factories near Paris.

During the next three days the strikes spread throughout the heavy
engineering industry of the Paris suburbs; on 28 May the Renault plant at
Billancourt was affected. By the end of the week some 70,000 workers
were on strike in the Paris area. On 29 and 30 May local agreements
between employers and workers were signed in most strike-affected
factories, and it was agreed that negotiations would begin over a collective
contract to cover the entire Paris metallurgical industry. By 1 June the
strikes seemed largely to have ended: only 5,000–10,000 workers were
still on strike. But this respite was due largely to the beginning of the
three-day Whitsun holiday weekend: the workers wanted to enjoy the
holiday at home rather than in the factory; they could always strike again
once work resumed.

This was indeed what occurred on 2 June when a new rash of strikes
occurred. The first stage of the strike movement had been largely
restricted to the metallurgical industry of the Paris region; the second was

to be vaster both in the geographical area and the type of industry affected. In the Paris region strikes spread to the most diverse industries – chocolate factories, printing works, building sites, locksmiths – as well as to those engineering factories previously untouched. And in many factories, such as Renault, where agreement had been reached before the weekend, strikes broke out again. On 5 and 6 June, the employees of the large Parisian department stores in their turn went on strike; on 8 June they were followed by employees of insurance companies, and then by hotels and restaurants. In the Nord the first important strike occurred on 2 June; two days later 94 factories were occupied and over 36,000 workers on strike; by 9 June the figures were respectively 1,144 and over 254,500. In Le Havre all important factories had been occupied by 4 June; in Caen the strikers reached their greatest intensity between 8 June and 11 June.[3] Only three departments were left untouched.

The arrival of Blum's government and the signing of the Matignon Agreement did nothing to stem the movement which reached a peak on 11 June. Even the British Ambassador, who had taken a fairly sanguine view of events, now began to panic when confronted by 'hungry Bob Cecil clamouring for coffee and eggs' at the Embassy because the staff of the Hotel Bristol were on strike; the situation seemed reminiscent of Russia in 1917 with Blum in the role of Kerensky.[4] The atmosphere in Paris on 11 June was indeed tense; there were rumours of a descent of rural workers into the city or even of a Communist or fascist coup. Salengro moved mobile guards into the capital.

On 11 June Thorez made his famous speech on the need to know how to end a strike. 'To seize power now', he added 'is out of the question.' The third – and declining – stage of the strike movement dates from this moment. The decline started where the movement had first developed on a large scale: in the metallurgical factories of the Paris region where an agreement was signed between employers and unions on 12 June. By 15 June most textile, mining and engineering workers were back at work. But the move back to work was irregular: in the Rhône there were still 25,000 strikers on 25 June; in the Nord 20,000 on 11 July.[5] In some cases the strikes went on into August.

Of the two competing theories about the causes of the strikes, neither will stand in its crudest form. The contemporary right-wing publicist Jacques Bardoux popularized a conspiracy theory: the strikes had been a Communist plot to seize power which was abandoned at the last moment. Although widely accredited in the conservative press, Bardoux's theory, which contained such implausibilities as a collusion between Stalin and Trotsky, was totally unconvincing.[6] On the left some blamed German *agents provocateurs*. Other contemporary observers stressed the role of extreme non-Communist leftist groups. One of the most clear-headed contemporary studies blamed 'leaders from outside the factory' often with dubious accents.[7] But whatever the role of leftist activists in prolonging certain strikes, they did not have the factory-based influence to play any part in their outbreak. And they were powerless to prevent their end.

The most convincing argument for the thesis of 'spontaneity' is that there was an almost inverse correlation between levels of unionization and strike activity. To quote A. Prost:

> the railway-men, post-men, public-services and teachers who contained a large percentage of union-members (respectively 22, 44, 36 and 35%) remained perfectly calm. Yet metal engineering, textiles and food processing where the level of unionisation was tiny (respectively 4, 5 and 3%) went on strike. The extreme example is that of the department stores where there was no union section but where there was a spectacular strike.[8]

Not surprisingly, then, the CGT was totally unprepared for the strikes: 'we do not know how this movement originated' declared Jouhaux. As for the theory of a Communist plot, in the one industry with relatively high union membership in which important strikes did occur – coalmining – the ex-*unitaires* were comparatively weak.

But the argument for 'spontaneity' with its attendant view that the spread of the strikes was due to 'contagion', is, in its simplest form, no more satisfactory than the conspiracy version. Certainly the strikers were not merely passive fodder to be manipulated by 'agitators'; nor were they all political innocents who mysteriously erupt on to the political stage with no history of struggle behind them. The relationship between the 'base' and the union leaders was complex; figures of official union membership can, we shall see, be misleading. In the Bréguet factory, often seen as the origin of the movement, the strike which broke out on 11 May had been carefully planned during the previous week by the Communist, Eudier, secretary of the local metalworkers union, as a riposte to the sacking of two union members who had stopped work on 1 May. And the 1 May stoppage was itself the result of several weeks of propaganda by the ex-*unitaires*.[9] There was, in other words, a prehistory to the strikes of 1936, a prehistory in which union activists – often Communists – played an important part.

This is particularly clear from Bernard Badie's study of the strike at Renault's Billancourt plant which, inasmuch as it was unionized at all, was, like most of the engineering sector, a Communist preserve.[10] Even so, the number of CGTU members in 1934 was only 120, and the PCF cell a similar size. But these figures mean little in the unfavourable conditions of the 1930s when CGTU membership was forbidden; an unsuccessful strike in February 1932 had enabled the management to purge 'undesirable' elements from the workforce. More significant was the existence of what Badie calls 'quasi unionists' – those who had lived through previous periods of union activism, such as the strike of 1926, when union membership rose to 1000.

In the early 1930s, CGTU propaganda in the factory aroused little response. The catalyst for a revival of action was 12 February 1934. Management attempts to prevent the workers from demonstrating led to clashes with the police in which two workers died. This event was not forgotten. In the course of 1934 and 1935 the union (responding to the new Communist emphasis on *revendications partielles*) began to pay more serious attention to the concrete complaints of the workforce; it started a system of rolling strikes in different workshops. But, once again, given the general political situation, this policy was only a partial success: the planned stoppage on 1 May 1935 was a fiasco. The first round of the 1936 election acted as a new catalyst and the union propaganda for a strike on 1 May was this time successful: 85 per cent of the workers failed to turn up for work.

When strikes broke out in the Paris region at the end of May, the Renault factory was not among the first affected, but the Renault workers soon found themselves surrounded by a sea of striking factories and were quickly appealed to for support by the strike committees at the neighbouring Hotchkiss and Farmann plants. But the strike which broke out at the Renault factory on the morning of 28 May was not the result of 'spontaneous' imitation: the signal was given in the artillery workshop, that which was mostly tightly controlled by the PCF section. Then, after the arrival of leading Communist union leaders – Costes, the deputy for Boulogne Billancourt, J-P. Timbaud, Frachon, Eugène Hénaff – the strike spread rapidly throughout the factory. A young vaguely Socialist striker, 'Jacques', described to Alexander Werth his arrival in the factory on 28 May: he had known nothing about the coming strike but was told by a Communist in his workshop that a strike would start at 9 a.m. Early in the morning Communists came round to encourage the workers to strike: 'Now, I must say that between 9 and 11 many of us did not know what to do ... But as everybody else stopped work we naturally did the same.'[11] Once the strike had started the Communists attempted to retain their control: party members were elected to the strike committees.

In the coalmines of the Nord and Pas de Calais the story was similar.[12] At 26 per cent in 1935 the level of unionization was relatively high with the CGT (29,000) outnumbering the CGTU (7,300). But once again we should be wary of the significance of these figures: in the elections to choose delegates responsible for safety the Communists were extremely successful. In early 1936 there were signs of new militancy and union membership began to increase: by March it stood at 65,000 (43 per cent of the workforce). In mid-April, after various meetings with the employers to negotiate improved wages and conditions, the union decided to call an unlimited general strike from 1 May if its demands were not met. In reaching this decision, the ex-*unitaires* played an important part. Police reports claimed that although few rank-and-file miners had been eager to strike, most were ready to follow their leaders if necessary. In fact no strike was needed and a convention was signed with the employers. When breaches of this convention took place the ex-*unitaires* were the most vociferous in calling for the workers to take action, and the strikes which broke out at the end of May concerned the application of the April convention. On 4 and 5 June when more strikes broke out in a number of pits, local Communist activists again took a leading role: for example, in the strike at the Couchy company on 6 June, the first pit to come out was controlled by the Communists; not until the afternoon did the ex-*confédéré* pits stop work. In order to control the escalating movement, the CGT declared a general strike from 8 June.

In Marseilles the turning point in working-class mobilization was a dock strike in December 1935 called by the *unitaires* in protest against a wage reduction accepted by the *confédérés*.[13] The success of this action had great local impact: union membership in the docks rose from 100 in April to 3,000 after the strike. Following the dockers' example there was a successful one-day strike by tram-drivers protesting against a 10 per cent wage cut imposed by the Laval decrees. The first factory occupation occurred at the Coder engineering plant, a longstanding target of Communist propaganda. The strike, which broke out on 29 May was carefully prepared by the factory's Communist union activists in close collaboration with the party and the local Popular Front committee. The signal for work to stop was the sounding of the factory siren at 10 a.m. By midday the factory was like a fortress; the strike committee was dominated by Communists. This pattern was repeated in several strikes which followed.

There are various interesting features about these examples. First, whatever the influence of the Paris example on the rest of France, it is also clear that in the Nord and in Marseilles the strikes had their distinct prehistories which are obscured by theories of 'contagion': the non-application of the April convention was an important issue in the Nord; the impact of the dockers' strike was important in Marseilles. Secondly, in all the cases discussed, the Communists played a central role both in preparing the ground by longstanding propaganda and in the timing and organization of the strikes which broke out at the end of May. That is not to say that they were applying any carefully laid Communist plan. It does not seem that the party leadership had given any particularly clear, or new, instructions. Most probably the ex-*unitaires* were acting much as they had been instructed to do during the last four years. As Henaff told the PCF's Central Committee, the organization of the strikes had unfolded 'on the basis of methods developed for fifteen years by the CGTU'.[14] What had changed was the reaction to the workforce. The party leadership which had previously felt that its success in organizing strikes was lagging behind the more specifically political mobilization of the Popular Front[15] was as surprised as anyone else by this. But in the early stages it was not displeased: providing the movement could be controlled it gave substance to the notion of the 'ministry of the masses'. A Communist newsheet to the Marseilles dockers in June announced that the government opened up 'immense possibilities' but these would only be realized 'to the extent that our wishes are demonstrated in mass action obliging the deputies and government to fulfil their promises'.[16] The strikes offered the prospect of doing this.

Why, after a long period of social quiescence, were the workers prepared to follow the calls to strike in 1936? There were various reasons. First, the transformed political situation made action seem possible. It is no coincidence that the Popular Front victories in the first round of the election were followed by the most successful 1 May strikes for many years: at the Renault factory a great stir was created by the election of Costes, a former Renault worker, to the Boulogne–Billancourt seat.[17] Also important were the municipal victories of the Popular Front candidates in May 1935. In many strikes sympathetic municipal councils provided free provisions to the occupiers of the factories. Doriot's St Denis municipality produced 130,000 free meals in fifteen days.[18] The political and social movements were, then, from the outset closely linked. They made each other possible: as we have seen, the new militancy at the Renault factory dated from 12 February 1934.

A second factor conducive to strike action was the end of the fratricidal struggle between CGT and CGTU. A rise in union membership had begun once reunification came into view. This increase, which is difficult to quantify, was not on the vast scale of the summer, but it testified to a new mood of confidence.[19] The reunification, at least at the beginning, also helped to reinvigorate the old CGT: it conferred new respectability on the ex-*unitaires* who had previously been shunned by many workers; it infused the former reformist leaders with the energy of the ex-*unitaires* who tended to be younger and more accustomed to taking risks. Thirdly, the slight upturn in the economy at the end of 1935 may have increased confidence: at Renault the end of cuts in the workforce in 1933 immediately preceded the militancy of 1934. Generally the heavy engineering sector in which the first strikes occurred was one of the main beneficiaries of the economic recovery.

It was not only ex-Communists who played a role in the organization of the strikes. The situation varied depending on the balance of influence from factory to factory. Ex-*confédérés* were not necessarily a moderating force: at the Sautter Harlé factory where a score of activists decided in April to stop work on 1 May, it was an ex-*confédéré* of anarcho-syndicalist views who pushed for a strike and the ex-*unitaires* who preached caution.[20] Among the various strike activists whose recollections have been gathered by Lefranc we find the most varied political backgrounds ranging from Socialist planists to dissident Communists.[21] Often these local activists had encouraged a strike in spite of the scepticism of the union leadership: Marcel Brient, who participated in the Samaritaine strike, recalled the 'clear desire to halt the movement' by the leaders of his union, appalled at the unlikely chance of a strike in the department stores; the strike went ahead nonetheless – and with great success.[22]

Even when the strikes broke out suddenly, and without, as far as can be seen, any organization, the ground had often been prepared by the surreptitious work of a few local activists. This was perhaps 'spontaneity' if anything was; but it did not come from nowhere. On the other hand it is also clear that in its second phase the strike movement acquired a momentum of its own: strikes broke out in factories with no previous tradition of labour organization. Such was the case described by the Socialist, Daniel Mayer. In the central court of his residence was a small artisanal workshop whose workers appealed to him for help: 'Naturally we are going to stop work like everyone else. Would you be able to help us draw up a list of demands.'[23] On 12 June at the Magasins Réunis department store in Paris when most other department stores had been on strike for several days, 'something indefinable was in the air' but it was too dangerous for the employees to talk to each other let alone discuss the possibility of a strike. By the afternoon, however, several notes had independently reached the desk of the only employee to be known to be a CGT member: 'You can count on me'; 'do you want my help?'; and so on.[24] In such cases certainly the strike was spreading 'spontaneously' and 'contagiously' providing that by contagion we mean that the proliferation of strikes revealed the potential for collective action and that by spontaneity we imply not that the grievances of 1936 had not previously existed, but that suddenly it seemed conceivable that they might be expressed. In many cases workers struck first and prepared their list of demands afterwards. If they lacked political sophistication, they possessed intuition of the highest order: the chance might not come again.

In all the cases we have discussed, the strikers turned not surprisingly to any known union activists in the factory to run the strikes. But often, where no union members existed, the strikes threw up their own leaders. The relationship between these new strike leaders, the mass of strikers and the official union leaders was far from easy: the workers wanted 'their' strike; the national CGT leaders – whether ex-*confédérés* or ex-*unitaires* – wanted to take control of the movement; the factory leaders found themselves caught in between. Often at negotiations the strikers preferred to be accompanied by a sympathetic local councillor than by a union official.[25] Jules Moch has told of his experience on being despatched with a Communist union leader to obtain fuel from occupied factories for the bakeries of Paris (the transporters were all on strike): the first factory would not let them in and seemed to contain no unionists; the second agreed to do so but only because there happened to be a Socialist Party member who recognized Moch.[26]

The Renault strike provides a good example of this precarious relationship between strikers, strike delegates and union leadership. The Billancourt plant had been evacuated on 29 May – after one night of occupation – when an agreement was signed by the leaders of the Paris metallurgical workers union. But when work resumed after the Whitsun holiday the union was confronted with revolt by the workers and possibly some of the strike delegates: strikes broke out in various workshops; when Costes intervened to calm the situation, rumours spread that he was in the pay of Renault. To stifle this incipient dissent the Communist union leaders held a meeting of strike delegates from all the engineering factories which was intended to express confidence in the union leadership; the Renault delegate was very recalcitrant. The resumption of the strike, then, was due largely to pressure from the base: the union leaders, if they wanted to keep control of the movement, had no choice but to legitimize this situation. The strike delegates were trapped in between but seem in this case to have been closer to the base than the union leadership. Similarly, the generous agreement reached on 9 June between the miners' union leaders and the mining companies was initially rejected in several parts of the Pas de Calais. It took strong intervention by union leaders to bring the reluctant workers to accept the agreement a day later.[27]

To explain these events both the Communists and the official authorities tended to talk of 'irresponsible' elements or 'Trotskyists'. But the Trotskyists had a very weak factory base in 1936: at Renault there is no evidence that they had any group at all; not until 1938 did they play any serious role in the factory. In the Pas de Calais the opposition to the 9 June agreement was encouraged not by 'Trotskyists' but by Communist activists such as, for example, one Henri Jacquin at No. 4 pit at Lens, who was later reproached for this 'irresponsibility' by the party. The truth is that it was easier to start a strike movement than to end one. In different sectors there were often particular grievances which were not covered by general agreements – as, for example, at the Samaritaine where the strike lasted two days longer than in the other department stores. In other cases the strikes threw up delegates who lacked understanding of the economic realities: in the Hautes Pyrénées various workers demanded that wages rise to Parisian levels in spite of the fact that local prices were much lower.[28]

As for the over-zealous attitude of local Communist union activists, such as Jacquin, they may have been genuinely confused about the party's attitude, and continued to behave as they had before 1936. To take the example of Marseilles: in June 1936 the party had opposed the calling of a butchers' strike which risked being unpopular with the public. But two Communist activists who were booed at a meeting of butchers for opposing the strike were criticized by a Communist Congress in July: 'when one cannot prevent a strike it is necessary to know how to call it at the right moment and finish it as soon as possible. The instructions of the Party must not be taken too literally. One must show psychological understanding and know how to manoeuvre without making oneself unpopular.'[29] It is easy to see how local activists might become confused.

The Renault strike perfectly illustrates the party's dilemma: having encouraged, or at least not prevented its activists encouraging, strike action as a means of extending the party's influence, it then found difficulty in containing the movement without cutting itself off from its popular base. But nor did it want to jeopardize its Popular Front strategy of courting the *classes moyennes*. Hence the fluctuations in the party's attitude. By the second week in June, however, the leadership had clearly become alarmed by the extension of the strikes and decided upon the firmer stance outlined in Thorez's famous speech. On 14 June *L'Humanité*'s headline read: 'The Communist Party is Order!'. In those sectors where the Communists were most influential the new tactics fairly swiftly brought an end to the strikes. And if in other cases the return to work was slower, the tide had definitely turned.

But was ending a strike equivalent to betraying a revolution? Was 1936 a dress rehearsal for the 'betrayal' of 1968? What, in short, was the deeper significance of the strikes of 1936?

June 1936: festival or revolution?

The view that the revolution was betrayed in 1936 has come especially from former members of the Gauche Révolutionnaire – Daniel Guérin, Colette Audry, Maurice Jaquier.[30] It is worth noting that this judgement is largely retrospective. The Gauche Révolutionnaire was too weakly implanted in the factories to have played a role in the strikes. Pivert's article 'Everything is possible' (answered by an article in *L'Humanité* entitled 'Everything is not possible') meant by 'everything' merely an increase in wages and the election of workers' delegates. And the Gauche

Révolutionnaire hailed the Matignon Agreement as the most that was feasible in the circumstances.[31] Only the Trotskyists resolutely defended a revolutionary position.

Most observers of the strike movement have, on the contrary, emphasized the limited nature of the strikers' demands and their lack of political radicalism and sophistication. In the second stage of the movement workers struck without any clear idea of what they wanted. We have already mentioned the example quoted by Mayer; Lefranc tells of frequent arrivals in his office at the CGT of strikers who wanted to know what to demand now that they had decided to strike because 'everywhere people are going on strike'.[32] It might be argued that it was precisely this *disponibilité* which did make the situation potentially revolutionary in 1936: a movement whose aims were so nebulous could all the more easily have been channeled in any direction by a determined revolutionary party. Revolutions are not necessarily started by conscious revolutionaries. Annie Kriegel has therefore preferred to talk not of a 'revolutionary situation' in 1936 but of a revolutionary 'élan': whatever the subjective aims of the strikers, their mass irruption into the political arena completely transformed the conditions of politics.[33]

But there is another factor to consider. Almost all accounts of the strikes of 1936 describe the ostensible lack of class hatred, the prevalent atmosphere of 'joy'. The strikes, in this view, were an explosion of fraternity, a collective celebration, as much as a battle in the class war. Michel Collinet, an ex-member of the Gauche Révolutionnaire, has eloquent pages comparing the strike movement to the 'mysterious *fête*' in Fournier's novel *Le Grand Meaulnes*: in the strike 'time was abolished'.[34] Unlike the Paris metalworkers of 1919 the strikers did not demand power for the CGT; they sang and celebrated. The most vivid photographic images which have come down to us from 1936 are of improvised dances in factory courtyards; makeshift orchestras playing to groups of workers on hastily erected stages; laughing workers perched on factory gates waving to the street below; food parcels being hoisted up to the strikers by their wives while passers-by look on with sheepishly amused complicity: in short, the strike movement as a sort of collective truancy, an escape from the daily round. At the 1965 Colloquium on Blum's government two words recur constantly in the discussion of the strike movement: 'joy' and 'festival' (*fête*). The classic text of this nature comes from a contemporary article by Simone Weil who had herself worked in a factory in 1934–5:

Pure joy. Unadulterated joy ... Joy at entering the factory with the smiling authorisation of a worker who guards the entrance ... Joy at freely passing through these workshops where, when I worked there, everyone felt so alone at their machine, joy at forming groups, chatting, eating together. Joy at hearing, instead of the pitiless din of the machines – music, singing, laughter. Jokes were cracked and people laughed just for the pleasure of hearing themselves laugh. There was no unpleasantness. Certainly people were happy to let the bosses know that they were not all powerful . . . But people were not cruel. They were too happy.

Most of these judgements of the strikers' mood tend, however, to come from observers not participants. The case of Simone Weil is slightly different and her account must be taken seriously. But as an intellectual with anarchist sympathies she no doubt lived the events of June 1936 somewhat differently from the mass of the strikers.[35] There is perhaps another side to the story. As well as joy there was fear; as well as celebration, struggle; as well as friends, enemies. The photographs also show us clenched fists and red flags; grim faces as well as smiling ones. And anyway people do tend to smile and wave at cameras.

To understand the mood of the strikers we must begin with the five years before 1936. Owing to the inadequacies of French statistics the repercussions of the Depression on real wages are hard to establish. All workers suffered cuts in money wages but these were often considerably less than the fall in prices which took place in the same period. According to the economist, Alfred Sauvy, average *real* hourly industrial wages actually rose by 27 per cent between 1930 and 1935, and average weekly wages (taking account of short-time work) by 18 per cent. But these average figures disguise considerable local differences: at the Renault factory average real wages slightly increased; in the mines they fell by up to 20 per cent. Taking account of wage cuts, short-time work and full unemployment, one historian has estimated the total fall in workers' real income between 1930 and 1935 at 15 per cent. The differential effects of the Depression therefore ranged from an increase in real wages at one extreme to a severe decline at the other (worst affected being the unemployed).[36] But even if some workers were financially better off, it must be remembered, first, that it was the nominal wage level of which they were most conscious, and, secondly, that every cut in money wages represents an exercise of arbitrary power against the workforce: the revolt of 1936 was as much about this as about wage levels. Indeed the Depression's major impact was not so much on real wage levels as conditions in the factories. Unemployment in France may not have reached the levels of Germany or America but it provided employers with a powerful weapon: no worker was irreplaceable. Employers exploited this situation to crush union activism, enforce tighter factory discipline and impose a crude form of rationalization in order to halt the decline in profits. In the mines of the Nord rationalization was introduced in the form of the 'Bedeaux system' in which workers were paid according to new, supposedly scientifically determined, production targets, and wages were docked if these were not met. One result of the effort to meet these targets was an increase in serious and fatal accidents which rose from 48 per 10,000 workers in 1932 to 79 in 1935. A report by a chief mining engineer in 1933 pithily summarized the effects of the new system: 'harder work by the workers obtained by means of stricter discipline'.[37]

It would be hard to exaggerate the severity of the conditions in French industry whether large-scale or small. The Renault factory which had a particularly sinister reputation was popularly known as the *bagne* (penal colony) and the Ile Seguin, where part of the factory was located, as Devils Island. Smoking was forbidden; arrival two minutes late could result in dismissal; foremen acted as petty dictators; cloakrooms were searched to discover copies of *L'Humanité*; the presence of informers (*mouchards*) sustained an atmosphere of suspicion; legendary tales circulated about the rarely seen ever feared 'Seigneur', Louis Renault himself. 'Rationalization' in the eyes of the workers came to represent an aggravation of all these tendencies. It meant an acceleration of production schedules (a speeding up of assembly lines and increased surveillance by time keepers – the hated *chronométreurs*), deteriorating sanitary conditions (some workers would quench their thirst from the lavatory bowl), more accidents, tighter discipline (fingerprints and photographs of all new workers) and arbitrary fines.[38] Georges Navel, whose first impressions of the Citroën factory have already been quoted in the epigraph to this chapter, also described his experiences at his previous factory where the Taylor system had been applied in all its rigour:[39] 'works police in peaked caps . . . patrolled the factory, even opening the doors of the WCs or peeping over their partitions to make sure that the squatting workers were not smoking'. Once again Simone Weil provides the most eloquent testimony. She describes the petty tyranny, the fantastical production schedules, the jealousies among workers: 'there are two factors in this slavery: speed and orders . . . One must, when putting oneself in front of the machine, kill one's soul eight hours a day, one's thoughts, one's feelings, everything.'[40] Perhaps worst of all were the conditions in the large Paris department stores where wages were minimal and hours long; where even possession of the Radical paper *L'Oeuvre* was pounced on; where unions were unthinkable and working conditions little better than the situation described in Zola's *Au Bonheur des Dames*.[41]

The workplace was not only a hostile universe but also often an incomprehensible one: workers viewed their payslips according to one observer, as 'an unintelligible scribble' after innumerable subtractions for fines and additions for mysterious bonuses.[42] In one Renault workshop in 1931 out of forty-eight unskilled workers none received the same wages (again demonstrating the difficulty of estimating the impact of the Depression on wages). The divisiveness which this situation induced was aggravated by the competitive atmosphere encouraged by rationalization: 'we no longer help each other; egoism has free reign . . . each works for himself', complained the Anzin miners.[43] In the Renault factory, workers hid their payslips from each other. Because of the fear of *mouchards* it took months for a new Renault worker to gain the confidence of his fellows. Pierre Sauvage, a worker in a Paris electrical factory, described his workmates as 'uncommunicative, distant from each other'.[44] What might be called this psychological isolation was reinforced by physical isolation. In the Renault plant workers from one workshop were forbidden entry to another. In the Citroën factory management showed films about the firm to its workforce: their perception of the factory as space was controlled and reordered for them by the management.[45]

In these circumstances it is not surprising that the resurgence of industrial conflict at the beginning of 1936 should have been initially more about material conditions, and to some extent union rights, than pay. In the mines of the Nord protest centred especially around the effects of rationalization: the unrealistically high production quotas, the bullying foremen, the fines, the deskilling of labour.[46] At Renault the workers' demands in 1935 ranged from the right to elect delegates to the construction of a garage for bicycles. Communist union activists became skilled in applying the Party's strategy of using these minor grievances as a springboard to lead the workers on to more general issues such as the demand for collective contracts. The first strikes in 1936 were about dismissals of workers rather than about wages. Once the strikers became conscious of their strength their demands became more ambitious and included wage rises. A pattern emerged, which was reflected in the Matignon Agreement: wage rises and the recognition of union rights became the major points of contention between union negotiators and employers. But even when, at a national level, the unions had successfully negotiated an agreement, at factory level strikers insisted on the redressment of local grievances: at the Samaritaine the workforce held out for two extra days to obtain the abolition of the Bedeaux system. Such grievances, however petty they may seem, were not trivial precisely because any attempt to air them previously would have been considered almost subversive: in Sauvage's electrical factory, before 1936 workers had had to queue outside, whatever the weather, when receiving their pay; someone had the idea of a petition to protest against this situation; but no one dared to sign first for fear of being sacked as a ringleader – until the workers hit upon the scheme of signing 'in the round'. What more telling example could there be of the universe of the French factory before 1936?

In this context the occupation of the factories in 1936 clearly represented an important symbolic gesture: the reappropriation of an alien space, the domestication of the workplace – indeed the *discovery* of the workplace and of fellow workers. Werth's 'Jacques' said of the first day of the Renault occupation: 'the workers that day felt very much *at home*'. Maurice Lime, whose novel *Les Belles Journées* described a strike at Montrouge, wrote that the strikers 'joined in each others conservations. They got to know each other as a family'.[47] Another witness told how, on the election of Costes on 3 May, workers at the Renault factory suddenly 'conversed without knowing each other'. This instantaneous fraternity was not restricted to the factories: Gide reported to Martin du Gard the atmosphere of Paris in June 1936: 'People come up to each other in the street; passers-by stop and join in the discussion; a large group forms under the bemused eye of the police'.[48] But given the previous atmosphere of mutual suspicion within the factory, this sudden fraternity meant that one *dared* to speak to one's neighbour. It involved discoveries which fear had hitherto obscured – that a work comrade had long been a union member; that the factory concierge had always hated the boss.[49]

To this extent, then, the 'joy' of 1936 is undeniable. And it gives the strike movement its distinctive and almost unreal quality. Unreal precisely because the strikers accepted the provisional status of their action. Let us listen again to Werth's 'Jacques': 'it is strange to think that in a few days everything may go back to "normal" and Renault will come into his own again. And the posters and flags and wireless sets will have gone. Again the engines will start turning and again the foreman will be able to order you about and glare.' Simone Weil noticed this phenomenon when she described the mood of the strikers as that of 'soldiers on leave'. The strikers, that is, wanted not so much to transform the world as to escape temporarily from it. The fact of occupying the factories was not, as in the Italian sit-down strikes of 1920, intended as a prelude to expropriation. Wider political aims were almost totally absent.

This was not always the case. M. Jaquier remembered a speech in a Montrouge factory – 'we are living a revolutionary situation . . . we want to socialize, not just nationalize, key industries . . . *All power to the Soviets*' – which was 'frenetically applauded' except by a few Communists.[50] At a meeting of strike delegates from the Paris metallurgical factories on 6 June, the representative from Citroën–Javel announced that 'our comrades would be quite able to organize production without the employers'; and other claims of this kind were made.[51] But these seem to have been viewed more as threats to cow the employers into conceding wage demands than as objectives in themselves. It is the case of the Delespaul Havez chocolate factory in the Nord which has attracted the greatest attention from historians: the occupation began on 4 June; on 3 July the strikers decided to distribute stocks free. But this was a special case: the strike had lasted a month and the stocks were perishable. The running of the factory was undertaken to force the employers to capitulate, not as an end in itself. And the affair had no influence: it was conspicuously ignored by almost all the press.[52] Much more general was the attitude encountered by Moch where the workers guarded stocks which they viewed not as their property – but that of their employer.

But there is, we have suggested, another side to the picture. Occupying factories may have had a symbolically liberating value; it was also an important gesture of defiance. For Eudier, the Bréguet occupation placed an important security in the hands of the strikers. Faced with the prospect of police intervention they threatened to destroy the prototype plane which was in the factory, and the employers asked the police to withdraw. There has been some debate about where the strikers derived the idea of sit-down strikes. The novelty of the phenomenon in France was betrayed by uncertainty about how it should be described: the employers preferred to talk of 'occupations', Blum of 'installations' and Coutrot of 'habitations', the latter terms avoiding the notion that the workers had broken in from outside. '*Grève sur le tas*' (sit-down strikes) was the most neutral term. The tactic had been advocated in February in an article by René Lefeuvre of the Gauche Révolutionnaire but it is unlikely that this had any influence. On 24 May, on the day of the *Mur des Fédérés* demonstration, *L'Humanité* carried an article celebrating the successful factory occupations at Le Havre and Toulouse; it has been suggested that this issue, passed around at the demonstration, contributed to popularizing the idea, but this seems improbable about an unobtrusive article on page five. No doubt the practice of *grèves sur le tas* had by the beginning of June developed its own momentum but, as with the strike movement generally, there is no need to look for a single model. The phenomenon was not completely unknown in France: there had been a sit-in at Citroën in 1933. The best known foreign examples had occurred in various Polish coalmines from 1931; indeed occupations had come to be known in France as 'Polish strikes'. A spectacular two day *grève sur le tas* in 1934 at a mine in the Pas de Calais had led to the expulsion of 180 Polish miners. And in the sit-down strikes of the Nord minefield it may be that the influence of Polish workers, who formed a large proportion of the workforce, was as important in June 1936 as the example of the Paris metallurgical factories.[53] In Le Havre, Eudier claimed to have studied the experience of sit-down strikes at Lodz and Sofia.

If the exact origins of the occupations were diverse, their logic was clear enough: to prevent employers sacking their labour force and taking on unemployed workers. As a Renault striker told a journalist: 'our tactic is to occupy, to hold out at any cost, as in a besieged city . . . Outside the factory we would be nothing more than unemployed, incapable of maintaining our unity against the company unions and fascists.'[54] For the Communists the occupations had the important secondary consequence that they assembled the workers in one place and provided a captive audience for political education, for the dissemination of the party's propaganda: in the Renault factory copies of the Communist press were distributed free to every striker.

Occupation, then, was born partly of fear; 'joy' could often disguise nervous tension. Emmanuel d'Astier, present in the Renault factory on the night of the first strike, noted: 'In spite of the laughter . . . and the jokes, nerves are on edge . . . One feels the people are oppressed by the apparent lack of any resistance from outside, on the look out for some mysterious provocation, for an implacable enemy.' On the first night of the second strike there were sudden rumours that the police were about to charge.[55]

One reason why the image of joy should have predominated in descriptions of the strikes was the speed with which many of them were concluded: a strike which lasted one or two days might well seem more like a picnic than a struggle. Over time the atmosphere could change: at a factory at Mondeville in Calvados the initial mood was celebratory; but tempers quickly frayed: there were moves to lock foremen in the factory and violent incidents took place with non-strikers.[56] Where strikes dragged on, boredom set in – one striker at the Galeries Lafayette recalled that she had never done so much knitting – and entertainments had to be devised to revive flagging morale. The dancing and games were all genuine enough but as time passed they became less a spontaneous outburst than a strategy. In the words of one strike leader: 'we took the necessary precautions to avoid the workers becoming bored during the factory occupation'. One of the Renault strike leaders told Badie that 'we needed to keep the men in the factory . . . and this climate of festival was an excellent way of doing so'. And his factory was visited by variety artists, professional boxers, and so on. Werth's 'Jacques' commented: 'our fellows certainly don't lack imagination in trying to keep the strikers from being bored.'[57]

This was all the more necessary because the factory occupations required a degree of discipline. The first Renault strike had been utterly chaotic (one reason why the PCF was not unhappy to bring it rapidly to an end): some workers had become drunk, there had been fights over women; people slept in the brand new cars. But in the more prolonged second occupation the strike committee imposed a strict discipline: alcohol was forbidden; women and minors were forbidden to stay the night; sub-committees were set up with responsibility for security, food, entertainment and so on; rotas of pickets monitored all arrivals and departures; strikers were only allowed to leave the factory for short periods. As 'Jacques' admitted to Werth: 'It's a bit like being in a prison' – a remark redolent with irony given the factory's previous nickname of the 'bagne'. This imposition of discipline led to tension between the strike delegates and the rank-and-file workers, a situation exacerbated by the fact that the strike committee kept the workers in almost total ignorance of the course of negotiations with the management (perhaps because they themselves were unsure about what line would ultimately be followed by the PCF leadership). The result was, as Simone Weil wrote, that 'the workers know nothing about the negotiations . . . there is an atmosphere of mistrust and suspicion.' This feature was probably less pronounced in small factories but it reminds us that if for the organizers and union activists the strikes offered the excitement of new responsibilities, for some ordinary workers they might partly have come to present the substitution of one discipline for another. Three rank-and-file Citroën workers interviewed by Sylvie Schweitzer, remembered the CGT in 1936 as an irksome constraint.[58]

Tensions also existed between strikers and employers or their representatives on the factory floor. Although many lurid rumours that managers had been locked up in their factories turned out to be false, and although employers were usually allowed to enter and leave the factory freely, the strikers by no means always displayed the benevolent indifference to their employers described in the accounts by Weil and Coutrot. On the first day of the Renault sit-in the strikers processed to the Ile Seguin shouting 'Down with the Seigneur'; there were simulated funerals of suspected Croix de Feu members with strikers mimicking nuns and priests; effigies of foremen were hung from beams. After the occupation Renault was able to claim 161,200 f. to cover damage committed during the strike. And there were reports of a 'mean spirit' in the Renault factory by 11 June.[59] In the Anzin mines the workers' hatred was especially directed against supervisors (*porions*) and sometimes engineers: unpopular ones were searched out in their homes: some *porions* were forced to march at the head of processions carrying red flags while insults were hurled at them. At the Samaritaine one supervisor was locked in his office for days and, once discovered, was escorted out by members of the strike committee while spat upon by the assembled crowd.[60]

The theatrical form which this class conflict took – the burning of dummies, the mock trials, the simulated funerals – was very much part of the 'spirit of 1936': of processions and marches, of popular theatre. At the end of the Renault strike, the victorious workers marched out of the factory in procession, ceremoniously accompanied by a number of floats containing elaborate *tableaux vivants* symbolizing aspects of the Popular Front. Theatrical imagery came naturally to observers and participants: Coutrot felt as if he were living in a Pirandellian dream world;[61] the organizers of the strike in the Magasins Réunis suddenly felt, as they were about to present their grievances to the management, that 'we were beginning to play a role; we wanted it to be a good premier role. We threw ourselves into it.'

In all the attempts to create a people's theatre in the Popular Front years, none was to be more successful than the performance that was enacted by the masses themselves in June and July 1936: their role was to play 'the masters'. In the short account by 'Jacques', one phrase recurs: today 'we are the masters'; 'that day M. Renault's no-smoking regulations were overlooked with a vengeance. We were the masters'; 'at present we are the masters'; 'I had a pleasant feeling of being one of the lords and masters of Renault's.' And this, we know, is the account of a simple rank-and-file striker who felt somewhat alienated from the strike leadership. One of the strike delegates at the Magasins Réunis described how, when presenting their demands, 'we received our Directors'; for once it was not the directors who received the workers. Much more than a conventional strike, then, the occupations represented a complete inversion of the traditional hierarchy of authority in the factory: in this perhaps lay their deepest significance.

The irony is that a strike movement as total as anything dreamed of by the pre-war revolutionary syndicalists should have resulted in a victory for the kind of reformist solutions advocated by Jouhaux since 1919. The judgement whether or not there was a 'revolutionary situation' in 1936 must depend on our view of a number of political factors – the internal cohesion of the Popular Front, the attitude of other social classes, of the police and army, the international situation – and these are subjects that will be treated in following chapters. But if we are considering the mood of the strikers alone, it is far from the case that the Matignon Agreement was the only possible outcome to the labour conflict of June 1936. The strikers may not have always had a very clear notion of their objectives; but their movement was much more potentially menacing to the social order than many people have, for different reasons, been willing to admit.

The guerilla war: June 1936 to November 1938

In the history of the Popular Front two peaks of labour conflict dominate the landscape: June 1936 and 30 November, 1938. But it was between these two dates that the most important conflicts were fought out. The spectacular political victory of the Popular Front had given rise to the strikes of June; its slow decline took place against a continuous background of industrial conflict. Factory occupations became commonplace. But if the form of the occupations had become a ritual – election of a strike committee, distribution of food tickets, departure of women workers at night, accordeon players in factory courtyards – their mood became progressively more bitter. The joyous element of the June strikes was increasingly absent from the strikes which followed. The imagery of celebration gives way to that of war: Prost talks of a prolonged period of 'social guerilla warfare'; Simone Weil described November 1938 as the employers' 'battle of the Marne'.[62] The strike and occupation at the Renault factory in November 1938 took on a semi-insurrectory character. This change in mood between June 1936 and November 1938 had developed quickly. At the Sautter-Harlé armaments factory where a strike had already occurred in June a new one broke out in September, lasting thirty-five days: this time the atmosphere was tense; strikers armed themselves with missiles and iron bars against a possible police assault.[63]

In this confused period of constant labour unrest four moments of intensified conflict can be singled out. First, the autumn of 1936: in September the number of strikers was higher than in any month except June and July. Worst affected was the Nord: in September, over 100 textile factories were occupied by 33,000 workers, and in November and December, some 15,000 metallurgical workers occupied their plants for 53 days. The second major resurgence of labour unrest took place at the end of 1937. In this case the scale of the strikes was less important (the numerical peak for 1937 was reached in April) than their spectacular nature: in December a strike broke out at the Goodrich tyre factory near Paris and the workers occupied the factory. On the morning of 23 December the Minister of the Interior, having resolved to make an example of the incident, surrounded the factory with 600 mobile guards. The strikers sounded sirens to arouse workers from neighbouring factories and by the end of the day the factory had been encircled by 30,000 workers. To avoid a clash the government withdrew its troops and a peaceful evacuation took place a few days later. At Christmas an even more dramatic event occurred: a sudden strike of the public services of the Seine region. On 29 December Paris was without transport, gas or electricity. For the first time the public service sector, which had been largely unaffected by the events of June 1936, struck against a Popular Front government. Thirdly, in March and April 1938 there was a vast strike, affecting some 150,000 workers, in the Paris metallurgical industry. This was the most extensive strike movement since June 1936. Finally, in November 1938 wildcat strikes against the application of the Reynaud decrees on the 40-hour week broke out all over the country: the culmination – and death-knell – of this movement was the general strike of 30 November.

Understanding this period of strike activity is complicated by the changing political context: as governments moved further to the right the significance of strike action changed. The increasing bitterness of social conflict was partly a reflection of political disillusion and partly a reaction to a tougher government stance. Although the police had evacuated a small Paris chocolate factory in September 1936, Blum's government had hesitated to take action against factory occupations; Chautemps risked a conflict with the Goodrich workers but then climbed down; Daladier evacuated the Renault factory in November 1938 with 3,000 mobile guards, 1,500 police and tear gas.

Without neglecting the changing political situation, one can suggest some general reasons why the 'Matignon era' celebrated by Jouhaux failed to inaugurate social peace. First, prices began to rise steeply from August 1936. The causes of this increase – the wage rises of the summer, the successive devaluations, production bottlenecks – are best considered in a later chapter. What concerns us here are its social effects: workers struck to preserve living standards. In the Paris metallurgical industry four wage increases were granted in 1937 resulting in a total increase since Matignon of between 21 per cent and 30 per cent depending on the category of worker; in the same period retail prices in Paris had risen (at the lowest estimate) by 38 per cent. The Matignon gains had been more than wiped out. Taking account of the 40-hour week, hourly wages had increased by between 48 and 56 per cent but for the worker already employed full-time before the introduction of the 40-hour week this did not represent any increase in weekly take-home pay.[64]

At the same time as fighting to preserve real wages, workers had to confront an increasingly aggressive attitude on the part of employers who were organizing their own revenge for the humiliation of June 1936 both on the factory floor and at the national level. We shall examine the employers' counteroffensive in a later chapter[65] but here it is necessary only to note that the employers' grievances were not altogether unfounded. They were partly reacting against what one historian has described as a 'revolt against work', in the factories after June 1936.[66] In the coalmines of the Pas de Calais innumerable short strikes broke out over trivial issues. And in September 1936, one of the local CGT leaders, an ex-*unitaire*, spoke of 'multiple strikes . . . sparked off for futile and unimportant reasons' and appealed for 'discipline and confidence in the union organization'. Four months later the local union issued a similar warning: the workers were helping the employers 'to sabotage the present experiment'.[67] In the Renault factory workers' resistance took the form of absenteeism, lateness, production slowdowns and violence against non-union workers. Here again union officials were moved to protest. In April 1937 the CGT paper *L'Unité* referred to 'an unusual number of absences on trivial or non-existent grounds . . . everyone should respect the work schedule set up by the management and accepted by us. We implore you to obey our union's discipline, for in no way should we lay ourselves open to the enemy.'[68]

Such examples could be easily multiplied. The previous structures of authority had been irremediably undermined by the experience of June 1936; it was not clear what new ones were to be created in their place. The problem was perceived by Simone Weil who visited the Nord in the autumn of 1936 and returned worried: 'before June there was in the factories a certain order, a certain discipline founded on slavery. The slavery has largely disappeared; the order linked to the slavery has disappeared at the same time. One can only welcome this. But industry cannot survive without order.'[69] In many cases the void was filled by the newly created post of workers' delegates elected to supervize the application of the new social laws but who in fact became the most powerful figures on the factory floor. Weil described the situation in a factory at Maubeuge whose delegates controlled production quite arbitrarily and called strikes at the slightest pretext, without consulting the union. Much of their militancy was directed against foremen who, having been accustomed to unquestioning obedience, found themselves caught between the conflicting demands of workers and management and were drawn into an increasingly anti-labour stance. At the Renault factory in March 1937 the foremen went on strike against 'union tyranny'.[70]

It is too simple to stigmatize the delegates and workers for irresponsibility or abuse of power. There were serious issues at stake: the attempt to lower production quotas was part of the struggle against the excesses of rationalization, and with unemployment still high it was logical for the construction workers of the 1937 Exhibition to delay completion as long as possible. The workers' delegates were dealing with specific local situations. Given the systematic repression which had occurred in the years before 1936 it is not surprising that they lacked experience or wider political vision. There was also a difference of perception between the unions and the workers about the purposes of the strike movement of 1936. In the mines of the Nord and Pas de Calais, the union argued that abolishing the *chronométreurs* would increase productivity: 'it would restore to the miner 'the love of his job that the bullying has made him lose . . . The men work better when left in peace.' To prove that this was true the unions urged the workers to work harder. The maintenance of production was a 'precondition of the success of the Popular Front'. At Marles the union even created vigilance committees to monitor productivity. But this productivist rhetoric fell on deaf ears.[71]

The political and union leaders of the Popular Front were well aware of the danger of provoking an employers' backlash but they were no more able to control the workers than were the local officials. The CGT which had played such a limited part in the outbreak of the June strikes had been their main beneficiary. In one year membership rose from about 778,000 to a peak of 3,966,600 in March 1937. In factories which had contained almost no unionist, suddenly every worker belonged to a union. But the CGT had only limited influence over these new recruits. In September 1936 the CGT mooted the idea of factory 'neutralization' as a way of preventing occupations: when a majority of workers voted to strike, the factory would be closed under government supervision until an agreement was negotiated. But this idea, although applied in some cases, failed either to appease employers or prevent workers taking over the factory in the first place. In April 1937 Jouhaux warned to no effect that 'strikes must not be called at every moment'.

If the CGT was unable to influence the workforce, could the PCF do any better – or did it want to? The attitude of the Communists has been a matter of some controversy with most commentators only agreed that the party played a central role. Critics from the left accuse the party of stifling the working-class protest in deference to the diplomatic requirements of Moscow; critics from the right blame it for undermining the Popular Front: Moch and Auriol, for example, saw a sinister coincidence in the fact that the important metalworkers' strike of March 1938 coincided almost exactly with the period of Blum's second ministry.[72] The strike, that is, was a manoeuvre directed against Blum by the Communists. The American historian Daniel Brower suggests that the strikes came to an end once the PCF had obtained guarantees about foreign policy from Blum's successor, Daladier. It is, therefore, worth considering this strike in some detail not only for its political importance but also as an exemplary study of the limits of Communist influence even in one of the strongholds of their power.[73]

The strike broke out ostensibly over the renewal of the collective contract which had expired at the end of February. It began at the Citroën factory on 24 March. By the next day 30,000 workers were affected. Although Communist activists may have instigated the strike – possibly to contain the growing discontent of the workers – Communist leaders joined with the Socialists in trying to prevent its spread. Doury and Timbaud, Communist leaders of the metalworkers' union, warned the workers that the Blum government would fall if the union made the strike official; when Jouhaux was booed by the strikers at a public meeting this was deplored by Gitton in *L'Humanité*. As the strikes spread the Communist leaders denounced 'Trotskyist *agents provocateurs*.' Meanwhile Blum, whose second government was largely taken up with this dispute, invited representatives of employers and unions to Matignon. The negotiations in the automobile industry got nowhere; in the aviation industry he proposed on 30 March a settlement which was accepted by the metalworkers' union but rejected by the employers: this had involved a 7 per cent wage rise and a 45-hour week in factories working for national defence. When the government fell on 8 April the Communists no longer made any effort to hold back the strike wave: the Renault workers came out and by 13 April there were some 150,000 strikers. It seems, then, that the Communists had tried to contain the strike movement; the employers had sabotaged the negotiations; and only *after* Blum's fall were the Communists no longer prepared to run the risk of being outflanked on the left. In short, the obsession with the supposedly ubiquitous role of the Communists is quite misplaced: as in June 1936, torn between preserving a revolutionary identity and loyalty to the Popular Front, they were following events as much as making them.

Certainly the party did on occasion use strikes for political ends: in September 1936 there was a one-hour strike in the Parisian metallurgical factories to protest against the policy of non-intervention in Spain. But even in this case the strike was for 'bread and Spain' because the party was unsure if it could mobilize a strike over a purely political issue.[74] Such cases of the party directly provoking a strike are exceptional. The opposite was more common. At the Goodrich factory in January 1938 it was the Communist leaders of the chemical workers' union who, in the face of considerable opposition, persuaded the workers to accept a settlement which entirely failed to meet their original demands. In April, once they had taken control of the Paris metalworkers' strike, the Communist union leaders quickly brought it to a conclusion despite the protests of many workers. The result was increasing disaffection from the official union organizations: the metalworkers union lost some 80,000 workers in the next few months. There is evidence that extreme leftist groups were now acquiring some influence in the engineering factories of the Paris region: the Trotskyist scarecrow had become a reality. At the Renault factory Communists took a leading part in organizing the strike which broke out against the Reynaud decrees on 24 November 1938 but the local Communist leaders were unable to persuade the workers to evacuate the factory and avoid violence; the result was a bloody confrontation which left forty-six police and at least twenty-four strikers badly injured.

Faced with the powerlessness of the CGT and the PCF to influence the workers, it fell to the government to try and impose some kind of order into industrial relations as a way of consolidating the gains of June 1936. The Blum government, partly in deference to the Radical wing of the coalition, became increasingly critical of the labour unrest. But Blum's appeals were no more successful than Jouhaux's. The most poignant example of this was his failure to persuade the workers on the site of the 1937 Exposition to end their wildcat strikes and accept temporary longer hours so that the Exposition, which was intended to be the Popular Front's showcase to the world, could start on time.

Where persuasion failed, could the law work? Already the collective bargaining act passed after Matignon had introduced a modicum of order into the *laissez-faire* world of French industrial relations. The effects of the new law were rapid: the average number of collective contracts signed annually between 1930 and 1935 was 22; between June and December 1936 the number rose to 2,336. But disputes often arose in the interpretation of these agreements. In the autumn of 1936, Blum therefore brought together representatives of the CGT and CGPF to work out a new Matignon Agreement on conciliation procedures. Although initially these negotiations proceeded quite smoothly, the employers broke them off in November. At the end of 1936 the government therefore introduced a compulsory arbitration bill requiring all industrial disputes to be submitted to newly created arbitration procedures. Given that originally the law had been introduced as an expedient and contained no sanctions for disobedience, it worked relatively well: of 9,631 conflicts reported to prefects between January 1937 and March 1938, 6,199 were submitted to the machinery set up by the law, and of these 2,610 (27 per cent) were settled in four days by departmental arbitration commissions and 3,589 (37 per cent) by more lengthy conciliation procedures. The relative industrial peace of 1937 probably owed something to the working of the law. But for major industrial disputes such as the strikes in the metallurgical industry in March 1938 government intervention still proved to be necessary.[75]

The arbitration law had only been designed to run for six months. It was extended for another six in July 1937. When it came up for renewal at the beginning of 1938 Chautemps' government attempted to integrate it into a wide-ranging 'Modern Labour Code' intended to create a whole new machinery of conciliation for French industrial relations. This ambitious project sank with Chautemps' ministry and instead a revised version of the Compulsory Arbitration Law was passed in March 1938. Like Blum in the autumn of 1936, Chautemps had hoped that employers and unions could negotiate an agreement. But the intransigence of the employers had wrecked the negotiations. The truth is that the whole dream of a 'new Matignon' was based on the false premise that the original Matignon Agreement had been a negotiation between equals rather than a capitulation by the employers. By 1938 the employers felt strong enough to offer no concessions. Thus the whole issue of compulsory arbitration became largely irrelevant. The employers were now ready for a confrontation that they could win.

By 1938 the conflict had come to centre around the 40-hour week. The issue was as much symbolic as economic. For the Daladier (and the second Blum) government, the main priority was to increase rearmament production. For the employers the objective was to exploit this situation in order to destroy the 40-hour week, reimpose factory discipline and restore profit margins. For many union leaders there was no theoretical objection to accepting longer hours to meet rearmament needs providing that this did not become a means of reducing hourly pay. Thus the metalworkers' union had accepted Blum's proposed arbitration award for the aircraft industry in March 1938 and later swallowed even the arbitration award in which work in excess of 40-hours was not to be payed at a higher rate but the basic wage rate was to be increased. For many workers, however, any extension of the 40-hour week was unthinkable, particularly in the conditions of 1938 when all the victories of the previous two years seemed to be crumbling and unemployment remained. When in July Daladier attempted to obtain longer hours in various engineering factories working for national defence, he at first received a cautiously encouraging reply from Antoine Croizat, the Communist head of the metalworkers' union. But in August the union resoundingly rejected the idea almost certainly because it feared that the workforce could not be persuaded. Daladier was therefore pushed into a more aggressive policy which culminated in the Reynaud decrees.

The decrees were used by the employers as a means of provoking a conflict with labour. In many cases, when applying the decrees, they chose the arrangement of hours most likely to antagonize a workforce for whom the conquest of the weekend was one of the major victories of 1936. Thus the Hutchinson factory at Puteaux fixed the new work schedules at seven hours on weekdays and nine on Saturdays; at the Farmann factory at Puteaux workers were told that they would henceforth be working a six-day week: on Saturday no one appeared for work and the entire workforce was sacked. The strikes and occupations which greeted the decrees were ruthlessly suppressed by employers and police. Factories were forcibly evacuated and known activists sacked.[76] At the Renault factory, once the strike was over the management used the end of the strike as a pretext to carry out cuts in the workforce which had been planned since July.[77]

The CGT, pushed especially by the Communists, decided upon a one-day general strike for 30 November 1938. But it was not clear what such action could achieve. By the time it occurred, the spontaneous strikes provoked by the decrees had been crushed. Not surprisingly the strike of 30 November was a failure. In calling it the leaders of the CGT remembered the success of 12 February 1934. But history did not repeat itself. The Popular Front had lived by symbols, processions and theatricality. In November these weapons were turned against it. At the end of the Renault strike there was a sinister inversion of the celebration which had marked the end of the factory occupation in June 1936. The defeated workers were forced by the police to march out of the factory making the fascist salute to cries of, 'Long live the police', while a policeman banged an iron bar, shouting 'one for Blum, one for Timbaud, one for Jouhaux'.[78] By failing to provide any convincing new structures of authority in the factory or to set up an effective arbitration machinery, the leaders of the Popular Front had left the victories of 1936 dangerously exposed to the counter-attack of the employers. By November 1938 all that effectively remained of those victories were the paid holidays. June 1936 passed into memory – and myth.

4 ∾ The cultural explosion

In 1936 . . . we were 20 years old. But everyone was 20 years old in 1936.

(J.-P. Le Chanois, 1955)

Parallel to the great popular and social movement of the Popular Front, or rather forming merely one aspect of it, a vast cultural movement is unfolding in France. Its motto could be this: open up the gates of culture. Break down the barriers which surround, like a beautiful park forbidden to the poor, a culture reserved to a privileged elite.

(Jacques Soustelle, June 1936)

In its first manifesto the CVIA announced it would be putting itself 'at the disposition of the workers' organizations'; in the following year, marching in the demonstration of 14 July 1935, the playright Henri-René Lenormand heard the crowd cry: 'Long live intellectuals! Long live science! . . . Long live the professors! May they never die!.'[1] Neither this commitment by intellectuals to politics nor the touching popular respect for the virtues of intellectuals were new in France. They date back to at least the Dreyfus Affair when the term intellectual was coined. During the Popular Front, however, the phenomenon reached one of its moments of periodic intensity. In the 1930s, this was not an exclusively French development: the Seventh Congress of the Comintern had explicitly urged Communist parties to increase their recruitment among intellectuals. If, as Dimitrov urged, a weapon in the struggle against fascism was history – to rescue history from 'fascist falsifiers' who 'pose as the heirs and continuators of all that is exalted and heroic in [a nation's] past'[2] – the role of intellectuals became central. Through organizations such as the CVIA and Amsterdam–Pleyel intellectuals entered the public arena. They marched, signed manifestos, wrote articles, attended congresses. Some distinguished names appear repeatedly – André Malraux, Paul Langevin, Romain Rolland – but it was the commitment of hundreds of lesser known individuals which gave the phenomenon its impact.

As much as being a political and social movement, then, the Popular Front was also a major cultural upheaval. A total of ninety-eight organizations were officially affiliated to the Comité du Rassemblement Populaire, ranging from the Naturist Union of France to the Workers' Gymnastic and Sporting Federation, from Youth Hostel Associations to the Committee for the Fiftieth Anniversary of Victor Hugo. Even if such grandiose titles often disguised Communist front organizations, the heterogeneity of the list gives a flavour of the diversity of the Popular Front.

The cultural and social explosions were interdependent. The social laws – the 40-hour week and the paid holidays – brought to the forefront the 'problem of leisure'. How were the workers to occupy themselves during the newly acquired leisure time to which we have seen they were deeply attached? This may have been perceived as a problem but also as an opportunity for those intellectuals who aspired to build bridges between the 'people' and 'culture' (necessary if culture was to be defended from fascism). In the words of the People's Music Federation (FMP), one of the cultural organizations which grew out of the Popular Front: 'it is not enough for the intellectuals to go to the people; the people must come to the intellectuals'.[3] Perhaps the new leisure at last made this possible.

Defining the relationship between art, politics and leisure was far from peripheral to the ambitions of the Popular Front. It was widely accepted by contemporaries that through the 'organization of leisure', as the contemporary phrase had it, Fascist Italy and Nazi Germany, with their Dopolavoro and Strength through Joy programmes, had been outstandingly successful in mobilizing mass consent. If the Popular Front aimed to reinvigorate republicanism in France, it had to show that democracy could accommodate the imperatives of mass politics no less successfully than totalitarianism: culture and leisure lay at the heart of this endeavour.

Intellectuals and masses: defining a cultural policy

Valliant-Couturier's phrase 'the ministry of the masses' summed up one of the most important aspects of the Popular Front: the entry of the masses into politics. The Popular Front's most glorious moments were lived in the street – in demonstrations, rallies, marches. The nature of these demonstrations varied. In the earlier stages they were acts of protest – against fascism, against the decrees – which could result in violence (9 February, the Toulon demonstrations). But gradually there was a transition from demonstration as protest to demonstration as celebration. Demonstrations became family outings: the number of women and children participants increased. The working class inhabited the street as it was to inhabit the factories – as much to assert a presence as to make specific demands. Politics became a pageant.[4]

The most famous of these popular *journées* took place in Paris. Estimates of the number of participants vary but there is no doubting the orders of magnitude:

12 February 1934: between 30,000 and 100,000 marched from the Porte de Vincennes to the Place de la Nation;

14 July 1935: between 100,000 and 500,000 marched from the Bastille to the Nation;

16 February 1936: over 500,000 marched from the Pantheon to the Bastille to protest against the attack on Blum;

24 May 1936: possibly 600,000 marched to the Mur des Fédérés.

None of these occasions was more spectacular than the demonstration of 14 July 1936. It was, comments Werth, 'the most immense procession Paris had ever seen' with possibly over one million participants. Two columns of marchers set off separately to converge for the first time in the Place de la Bastille where the July Column was decorated with a huge tricolour and flags of the provinces of France. The two cortèges then set off by different routes to meet again in the Place de la Nation where they were addressed by Blum, Thorez and others. The speeches started at 5 p.m. but when they finished at 7 p.m. there were still demonstrators at the starting point. Many of the demonstrators dressed in costumes of the Revolution; they built floats depicting events of the Revolution. This popular creativity was mirrored by the contribution of professional artists who contributed gigantic portraits of revolutionary heroes – Robespierre, Voltaire, Marat, Rouget de Lisle (author of the Marseillaise), Hugo – which were set up at the base of the July column. Politics, history and art were fused into a massive popular celebration. As the Radical, Albert Bayet, enthused: 'on July 14 1936 something as momentous has occurred as on July 14 1789'.[5]

The whole of France experienced a similar descent into the street. In the provinces the Comité du Rassemblement Populaire decided to celebrate the election victory on 14 June: on that day, in the Languedoc, there were processions in Nîmes (10,000), Narbonne (7,000), Carcassonne (3,000) and Perpignan (15–40,000) and in numerous smaller towns. All these demonstrations were more than political gatherings: there were also festivals and celebrations. In the Loir-et-Cher the festival organized by the Amsterdam committee on 14 July began with bands and sporting competitions; in the afternoon there were fairground games, including a coconut shy with effigies of 'fascists' as targets; in the evening there were fireworks.[6]

In her memoirs Simone de Beauvoir describes herself and Sartre watching the 14 July demonstration in Paris with detached sympathy. But for most intellectuals of the left in this period detachment was impossible: the Popular Front was lived as a great festival of fraternity. The following three passages provide characteristic examples of the mood. The first is an editorial from the pro-Popular Front periodical *Vendredi*:

14 July 1936! Overcome with exhaustion, we know that we will not succeed in explaining what this day has meant for us. In front of the blank page our heads are still spinning. Our feet are still tapping the rhythm of our long march, our ears ringing with songs whose echo refuses to die away . . . We marched, we sang with our comrades. Our voices were perhaps a little out of tune, but we had with us a youthful generation that sang loudly, and sang in tune, our common hopes . . . Marching between the banks of the crowd, under windows where flags were flapping, we looked at the faces. And if we are so joyous this evening, it is perhaps because of a fraternal spirit that came from the smiles and friendly glances from men and women we did not know . . . Suddenly a whole immense crowd revealed itself as more friendly even than the best of our friends. . . . St Just used to say that happiness (*bonheur*) was a new idea. Today we have breathed in the streets of Paris the newness and youth of that idea.

The second extract is from a journalist who wrote for a variety of left-wing papers:

14 July Nineteen Thirty Six. A huge crowd takes me by the elbow, and I plunge further into the mass of welcoming bodies. Six hours I have been on my feet in the Faubourg St Antoine . . . Never have I been loved in this way: loved by unknown people, because I am with them, because I am one of them . . . Around us all, in us all, there is one absolute conviction: 'that's it, we are going to be happy'.

The third is a description of 14 July 1935 at Nîmes from a local paper:

The children of the Revolution have grouped together . . . Their faith is so sincere that they have rediscovered that sense of expansiveness which turns an unknown neighbour into a brother and creates a feeling of total communion. Happy moments, unforgettable moments for those who have lived through them.[7]

In such passages certain themes recur: solidarity, fraternity, communion; youth; joy, hope, happiness. This vocabulary of lyricism no doubt obeyed certain conventions. It contained a degree of self-consciousness: Claude Jamet, from whose diary we have already quoted, felt as if he were one of the heroes of Jules Romains' novel *Les Hommes de bonne volonté*. Life and history had meaning again: he was living in what Péguy called an epoch. But the lyricism was more than a literary conceit: the fraternity of the street was also, as another participant remembered, a revenge for the isolation which many people felt on the morning of 7 February.[8]

Nowhere was the lyrical mood better conveyed than in the pages of *Vendredi*, and particularly by one of its editors, Jules Guéhenno. *Vendredi* was a literary periodical founded in November 1935 to provide a forum for intellectuals who supported the Popular Front. Its editors were the journalist Andrée Viollis who had Communist sympathies; the novelist André Chamson, close to the Radicals; and Guéhenno whose closest admiration among Popular Front political leaders was for Blum. Guéhenno and Chamson had with Jacques Kayser drafted the Oath of 14

July 1935. Guéhenno had risen from a modest background to become a well-known academic figure and literary essayist. Since 1929 he had been editor of the left-wing literary periodical *Europe* from which he resigned in February 1936 when he feared that his editorial independence was coming under threat from the Communists: 'I did not want to choose between parties or sects.' *Vendredi* was to be the perfect instrument of his political ecumenicalism. Guéhenno's ideal was a humanistic one: the Popular Front was about happiness and restoring human dignity. Eight years earlier he had worried that he would become estranged from his origins: 'I tried with all my force to recover the unity of my plebian soul.' The Popular Front offered a prospect of achieving this. When he looked back on his experience in the Popular Front, 'fraternity' was the word that appeared most frequently. But the unity of the soul was never entirely regained and there was always something self conscious in Guéhenno's experiencing of the fraternity of 1936. In his *Journal d'une 'Révolution'* he wrote: 'it sometimes seemed to me that we were playacting the Revolution . . . Our excuse was our faith. None of us thought that the great show of revolution in which we were the actors was the revolution itself.' Guéhenno's good faith, his political innocence, his humanism, his generosity, were all part of the spirit of 1936. He wrote of his unease in demonstrations when it was necessary to raise a clenched fist, and he only did so twice with real anger; he worried that for most people the gesture was an empty ritual, not an act of faith.[9]

In 1937 Guéhenno became embroiled in a controversy with André Gide which poignantly illustrated the dilemmas confronting intellectuals in politics in the 1930s. In 1932, at the age of sixty-three, Gide, having hitherto remained aloof from politics, announced his sympathy with Communism and, although not joining the party, he became its greatest catch since Rolland. But, in November 1936 he published his *Retour de l'URSS*, a disillusioned account of a visit to Russia earlier in the year, and became the target of a Communist attack. In November 1937, Gide, who had frequently contributed to *Vendredi*, asked it to publish an article of his refuting an attack on him in *Izvestia*. Guéhenno refused because he did not want to accentuate the growing divisions in the Popular Front. An angry public correspondence ensued between the two men. Guéhenno accused Gide of being a political dilettante: 'you have used politics as one uses literature – for self-discovery'; Gide accused Guéhenno of sentimental blindness in his attitude to unpleasant political truths. But Guéhenno's position was more complex than Gide allowed. Manès Sperber, a German refugee in France, and active in anti-fascist intellectual circles, shared Gide's doubts about the Soviet Union but still questioned the opportuneness of publishing them at this time. Guéhenno had himself been disturbed by the news of the show trials in Russia and wrote two

critical articles in *Vendredi* (for which he was criticized by the Communists), and *Vendredi* had published extracts from *Retour de l'URSS* in
1936. The problem for Guéhenno was that 'we are free ... but also
engaged'. Where did engagement become a forfeiting of freedom? In
November 1938 *Vendredi* was to fold under the strain of this dilemma.
Its existence had been almost exactly coeval with that of the Popular
Front – testimony to the lyrical illusions of 1936 and to the disappointments of 1938.[10]

In defining the relationship between intellectuals and masses, culture and
politics, the central role was taken by the Communist Party. No party
made greater efforts to woo the intellectuals, and to the extent that we
can talk of a Popular Front cultural doctrine, it was largely the creation of
the Communist Party. In the 1920s the Communists lacked a coherent
cultural policy.[11] Various intellectuals had been drawn to the party out of
anti-militarism or general anti-conformism; most left quickly, finding its
conformities as irksome as those they were fleeing. The most recent
example were the Surrealists who had joined in 1927, and, with the
exception of Louis Aragon, been excluded in 1933. Aragon put his
Surrealism behind him and became one of the party's leading cultural
spokesmen. One of the party's most illustrious intellectual recruits was
Barbusse who joined in 1923, and remained a member until his death in
1935. Barbusse was no Marxist – he had joined through pacifism – but
his prestige allowed him to pursue his own literary line without interference.

In the late 1920s the Soviet Communist Party developed a theory of
proletarian literature which corresponded with its left-ward shift in
economic policy. Literary activity was taken in hand by a new Association of Proletarian Writers (RAPP); literature was put at the service of
the social transformation; workers were exhorted to write pieces celebrating the joys of constructing a Socialist society. This experiment was
shortlived and unsuccessful: the RAPP was dissolved in April 1932. In
France the policy had never been applied with much enthusiasm. Barbusse, editor of *Monde*, a literary journal founded in 1928 to apply the
new cultural line, continued an eclectic editorial policy for which he was
criticized by the Russians. But the French leadership showed reluctance to
take sanctions against their most celebrated intellectual. In short, the PCF
fluctuated uneasily between literary traditionalism (Barbusse), the avant-
garde (the Surrealists) and a theoretical espousal of proletarian literature.
But the RAPP period was important for showing that it was possible for
the Communists to aspire to the organization of cultural activity and the
definition of a cultural line. Out of this period emerged a cultural organization which was to become, after a profound metamorphosis, the instru-

ment of the PCF's Popular Front cultural policy. This was the Association of Revolutionary Artists and Writers (AEAR).

The AEAR was founded at the beginning of 1932 with the aim of gathering together, under the vague aegis of the party, all intellectuals opposed to 'fascism'.[12] In July 1933 it started to produce a monthly journal, *Commune*. The AEAR was not entirely unsuccessful in its ambition of creating a broad cultural front against fascism: its manifesto protesting against German fascism in March 1933 was signed by, among others, Gide, Guéhenno and Malraux, none members of the party; and Gide agreed to sit on the editorial board of *Commune*. In February 1934, Paul Vaillant-Couturier, one of the originators of the AEAR and increasingly the party's official spokesman on cultural matters, declared that the AEAR would welcome 'fraternally and without exclusivity all intellectuals whatever your hesitations and objections' who wanted to join the 'cultural combat'. Was this, then, a cultural Popular Front *avant la lettre*? Did the PCF's cultural *tournant* precede its political *tournant* in June 1934? This was only true up to a point. Those non-Communist intellectuals who rallied to the AEAR before 1934 did so more because they had come to fear fascism than because the party had changed its cultural line. *Commune* still defined itself as 'against bourgeois culture; for revolutionary proletarian culture'.[13]

The real change came in mid-1934 when the emphasis of the AEAR shifted from a commitment to 'revolutionary' culture to a general defence of what Aragon described in April 1936 as an 'indivisible' culture. 'We do not insist on a certificate of Marxist faith', Vaillant-Couturier told a meeting of intellectuals in October 1934, 'a vague sympathy for the Soviet Union and a horror of war would in themselves be enough for us to stretch out our hand fraternally to you.'[14] This cultural *main tendue* was strikingly illustrated by a major International Writers Congress for the Defence of Culture organised by the PCF (with help and funds from Münzenburg) in Paris in June 1935; among the foreign speakers were E.M. Forster and Robert Musil; Gide and Malraux presided over the first session. From August 1936 *Commune* appeared not as the review of the AEAR but as a 'French literary review for the defence of culture'. The conversion was complete.[15]

What culture was being defended? In the first place, as Aragon had said, it was indivisible. In the words of the novelist René Blech: 'there are not two cultures . . . but one alone, to which the labouring masses have a right as much as the intellectuals'.[16] This was the culture of Heine, Kant, Wagner, Mann, Dante, Petrarch.[17] But, more specifically, the Communists presented themselves as defenders of *French* culture, a development which paralleled their rehabilitation of French history. The function of this strategy was to stress both the Frenchness of the Communists – their

rootedness in the French tradition – and the foreignness of the so-called
Nationalists. Comparing the Leagues to the émigrés of the Revolution, the
'army of Coblentz', became the standard attack in the Communist
arsenal. Thus Aragon's 'Defence of the French Novel': 'I deny the quality
of *Frenchness* to the prose of Coblentz, to the prose of the Versaillais [the
army that suppressed the Commune in 1871], to the prose of the seditious
elements in 1935. *Our French novel* is French because it expresses the
profound spirit of the French people . . . It is the arm of the true French
against the 200 families who run the banks, the gaming houses and the
brothels.'[18] The triple struggle of the Popular Front for liberty, bread and
peace was also a triple defence of culture against book-burners, speculators and barbarians (the 'Huns of the twentieth century').

No one expressed the reconciliation between Communism and French
culture more lyrically than Vaillant-Couturier. The Communists 'do not
polemic with history' he wrote in October 1936; they recognized the
creative spirit in all its manifestations from Descartes to Pasteur. Vaillant-
Couturier saw the genius of 'eternal France' in 'the sweetness of her
climate . . . the fortunate disposition of her plateaux', in the tradition of
French *politesse*, in the prehistoric cave paintings of the Dordogne. In
short: 'we are continuing France . . . our party workers are deeply rooted
in her soil. Their names have the savour of her countryside.' French, said
Duclos, was the 'universal language of intelligence'.[19]

This invocation of history and the French tradition developed gradually: the first favourable article on Victor Hugo appeared in May 1935;
the celebration of France's Christian heritage, the cathedrals, in 1937.[20]
As the unity of the Popular Front turned to recrimination in 1938 the
Communists' obsession with history became increasingly frenetic, culminating in the campaign for the celebration of the 150th anniversary of the
revolution which dominated the party's activity in 1938 and 1939.[21]
Duclos devotes forty-six tedious pages of his memoirs to this subject
describing his campaign to have a metro station named after Robespierre.
A more substantial achievement was the setting up (at the suggestion of
the Fried) of the Museum of the French Revolution at Montreuil. In June
1939 the party held a huge festival to celebrate the Revolution at the
Buffalo Stadium: after a procession of choirs, 600 liberty trees were
planted by 600 children dressed in white and in Phrygian bonnets.[21]

By 1939 these were the tactics of desperation – an attempt to retrieve
through history the consensus that had been lost in politics. But between
1935 and the end of 1937 the PCF's ecumenical cultural line made it
highly successful in attracting a large number of intellectuals: among
those who joined the AEAR in 1934 were Malraux and the pacifist
novelist Jean Giono; in 1935 Guéhenno, Chamson and Julien Benda.
None of these were members of the PCF. In 1935 the AEAR started to set

up so-called Maisons de Culture which were intended to become local cultural centres and extend the appeal of the organization by means of lectures, discussion groups and staging of artistic events. The Paris Maison de Culture was run by Aragon. By 1937 the Maisons de Culture had around 70,000 members, by 1938, 90,000.[22] *Commune* repeatedly stressed that the Maisons de Culture must exclude all 'political' issues:[23] nothing must stand in the way of the widest possible alliance to defend the widest possible cultural heritage.

The cultural objective of the Popular Front, as defined by the Communists, was, then, to reunite the people with 'their' culture, 'their' history, 'their' nation, to bring together intellectuals and masses in common defence of a national cultural patrimony. To what extent was this objective reflected and realized in the artistic effervescence which followed Blum's victory – in the cultural explosion of 1936?

Breaking down the barriers: art and the people

Just as we have seen that the social explosion of June 1936 had a pre-history, so too did the cultural explosion. At the root of both was the Depression: the unemployed worker, who marched in the street demanding a job or hung around street corners waiting for a job, suddenly became visible. The implications in the artistic field were twofold: a new preoccupation by some intellectuals with the world of the worker; and a heightened preoccupation by working-class organizations with the cultural requirements of their members. The most striking example of the former phenomenon was the development of an agit-prop theatre influenced by the example of Germany. The aim of these agit-prop groups was to put themselves 'at the service of the proletariat', to take theatre to the street and factory. Great stress was put on spoken choruses which allowed large-scale participation of those without theatrical training. Much was done by Vaillant-Couturier to encourage these groups and put them in touch with each other. An important step in this direction was the setting up in 1931, under the aegis of PCF, of the Federation of Workers' Theatres of France (FTOF). This both provided a loose and tolerant coordinating organization – belying any over-simplistic sectarian image of the PCF during this pre-Popular Front period – which existing theatrical groups could join and stimulated the creation of new ones. By 1935 there were over 200, concentrated especially in the Paris region.

Many of these groups are now merely names; their existence was often ephemeral and local. The most celebrated, and that about which we are best informed, was the October Group, born in 1932.[24] Its central figure, and author of most of its pieces, was the young anti-conformist poet Jacques Prévert. The October Group was affiliated to the FTOF but retained its independence (it contained a Trotskyist among its members). The spirit of the enterprise was defined by another member, Raymond Buissières: 'what interested us was not at all the theatre but the revolution'. What mattered was to be topical: within twenty-four hours of Hitler's accession to power Prévert had written a spoken chorus which was performed on 31 January 1933 (another advantage of spoken choruses was their flexibility). For the Citroën strike of 1933 Prévert wrote a chorus (performed outside the factory gates) the end of which admirably sums up the tone of the group:

> There he is leaving the Casino at Cannes
> there he is at Nice strutting along the Promenade des Anglais
> in his white jacket . . .
> There he is strolling . . . taking the air
> Taking the air of the workers
> taking their air, their time, their life
> and when one of them coughs up his lungs in the workshop
> his lungs wrecked by sand and acid,
> he refuses him a bottle of milk.
> What the hell does he care about bottles of milk?
> He is not a milkman . . . He is Citroën . . .
>
> And if his sales start to fall
> he only needs to speed up production and lower
> the workers' wages
> LOWER WAGES
> But those who have been too long shaved
> like puppy dogs
> they still have their wolves' teeth
> to bite
> to defend themselves
> to go on strike
> Strike . . . strike
> LONG LIVE THE STRIKE

At the same time that the theatre was moving towards the factory, the CGT and PCF were organizing new educational structures for their members. In 1931 the CGT set up its Centre for Workers' Education (CCEO). Courses were given on literature, history, economics; the emphasis was on providing a broad general education not in any sense a proletarian culture, however that might be defined. At the end of 1932 the PCF founded its Workers' Institute which, while different from its special training schools for future party officials, was nonetheless designed to offer specifically Marxist training. But in both cases the courses were run by intellectuals: in the former case the Socialist *normalien* Georges Lefranc; in the latter the Communist *normalien* Georges Cogniot.[25]

These theatrical and educational developments were not without precedent. The Dreyfus Affair, that previous great political and intellectual upheaval, had given rise to two not entirely undissimilar experiments: the shortlived Popular Universities in which intellectuals had attempted to bring education to the workers; and the development of a 'People's Theatre,' in which a central role had been played by Romain Rolland.[26] The number of workers affected by the FTOF or by the educational efforts of the CGT and PCF in the early 1930s was tiny, and we must not exaggerate the importance of the Maisons de Culture before 1936. Although there were signs of a cultural effervescence which paralleled the political growth of the Popular Front, the key event, as in the outbreak of strikes, was the election victory of 1936.

Blum's government had several implications for cultural activity.[27] First, as we have seen, the new social laws raised the 'problem of leisure'. The problem had been prefigured in the factory occupations when, as we have seen, the workers organized their own distractions as well as inviting popular entertainers and agit-prop groups to perform in the factories. Secondly, the end of deflation affected spending on the arts and education: the credits of the Ministry of Fine Arts were raised by 38 million f., those of the Education Ministry by 705 million f. Thirdly, the new government energetically promoted cultural activity in the widest sense. Given his background, it is not surprising that on several occasions Blum himself intervened personally in the cultural field. He also created two new ministerial portfolios: an 'Undersecretary of State for the Organization of Sport and Leisure' confided to the Socialist, Léo Lagrange, and an Undersecretary of State for Scientific Research, confided first to Irène Joliot-Curie and later to the physicist Jean Perrin.

The government's interest in culture was incarnated in the efforts of two of its most energetic ministers, Léo Lagrange, and Jean Zay, the Radical Minister for Education. Both were young – Zay was thirty, Lagrange thirty-six – resourceful and dynamic. They intervened in the widest possible range of cultural activities – sport, tourism, theatre, music, scientific research, cinema – as well as in the areas more specifically under their influence. Zay was involved in a fundamental, if abortive, reform of the education system, in setting up a scientific research institute (the CNRS), in a plan to reform the cinema, in introducing legislation to protect the right of authors against exploitation by publishers, in reorganizing state theatre, and so on; Lagrange's activities were no less wide-ranging. Both remained in office until Daladier came to power, and although their most important work was done in the first year their continued presence in government carried over some of the earliest objectives of the Popular Front into its declining stages. Finally, Blum's government inherited the great International Exhibition – L'Exposition –

planned for 1937. Although this had been conceived several years before, its detailed preparation largely fell to the Popular Front: the Exposition became a major international showpiece of the cultural aspirations of the new government.

As Pascal Ory, the most illuminating writer on this subject, has argued, the cultural achievements of the Popular Front were the result of a fruitful interaction between the initiatives of the government, the political parties and numerous cultural organizations which had grown up alongside, or in the wake of, the Popular Front. After the election victory the Socialists had established their own cultural association – Mai 36 – and *Vendredi* started to set up cultural groups (the *Savoir* groups), which would organize cultural activities bringing together intellectuals and workers. The role of the Communists was vital, not only through their Maisons de Culture and through the indefatigable activity of Vaillant-Couturier, but also in parliament where two Communists took on key responsibilities: Cogniot as *rapporteur* of the education budget and Joanny Berlioz as *rapporteur* of the arts budget.

The theatre provides one example of this interaction between government and Popular Front organizations. In April 1936 the FTOF was transmuted into the Federation of Independent Theatres of France (FTIF). The dropping of the word 'Worker' was symbolic, the tone of the new organization was less militant and corresponded better to the PCF's ecumenical line; this was the occasion when Aragon talked of the indivisibility of culture. Agit-prop was no longer the order of the day. (At more or less the same period in Britain the Communist Workers' Theatre Movement became the Unity Theatre.) After the election victory three new theatrical associations were set up: the CGT's Theatre of the People, the theatrical section of Mai 36, and the theatre collective *Art et Travail*. The FTIF pressed for the setting up of a network of national and regional popular theatres.

Meanwhile the government took a number of initiatives of its own. In the area directly under his authority, the state theatre, Zay, immediately took steps to reinvigorate the atrophied Comédie Française by appointing a new director, the dramatist Edouard Bourdet, flanked by an advisory board of four assistants, Jacques Copeau, Charles Dullin, Louis Jouvet, Georges Baty, who were the leading figures of the Paris contemporary theatre, and all variously concerned with extending the theatre's appeal. Zay also subsidized one or two large-scale theatrical productions – such as a staging in July 1936, at reduced prices, of Rolland's play *July 14* – and provided subsidies for a number of experimental theatre companies. Lagrange also showed interest in the theatre: he gave official support to the CGT's Theatre of the People, organized a spectacular production of

Rolland's play *Danton* in July 1936 in Paris, arranged cheap seats for working-class organizations at some state theatres and provided financial aid to new theatre groups, such as the travelling theatre company of Jean Dasté. Zay and Lagrange were ultimately only able to offer limited assistance but that they tried at all was indicative of a changed attitude. Zay relates in his memoirs the reaction of one seasoned politician: 'why are you bothering yourself with the theatre? . . . A minister of education shouldn't bother about the theatre. What's the theatre after all?'[28]

Although the government's intervention fell short of the ambitions of the FTIF, cultural organizations and government were united by a common aim which underlay the whole cultural endeavour of the Popular Front and is summarized in the quotation by Soustelle in the epigraph to this chapter. The quotation continues: 'in every area the people of France is becoming aware of its historic task: it does not want to be excluded from the cultural treasures accumulated by the nation'. Or, as Berlioz put it more pithily, 'culture must become "republican" in the etymological sense of the word'.[29]

Several organizations set up in the spring of 1936 attempted, in liaison with the state, to translate this doctrine into action. Among these was the People's Association for the Friends of Museums (APAM), founded on the initiative of Soustelle. Its aim was to 'establish a close communion between the masses, the great mass of workers, and museums': to bring the people to the museum and the museum to the people.[30] APAM, which affiliated to the Paris Maison de Culture, organized cultural visits for groups of workers in conjunction with working-class organizations. Within the first year 25,000 people had participated in these trips. It mounted exhibitions in factories and well as lobbying for museums to open longer and employ more attractive techniques of display. The government supported these initiatives: June 1936 saw the beginning of night opening at the Louvre and February 1937 of cheap nightly opening once a week when prices were lowered for workers and the young. In 1938 APAM held a popular festival; painters offered works as prizes at a tombola: a worker from Vitry won a Matisse.[31]

A second organization concerned with the popularization of culture was the Association for the Development of Public Reading (ADLP), founded in July 1936. Presided over by the labour historian Edouard Dolléans (director of Lagrange's *cabinet*), and enjoying the active support of Julien Cain, administrator of the Bibliothèque Nationale and a close friend of Blum – this web of relationships is a good illustration of the collaborative interaction referred to above – its aim was, as it were, to break down the barriers between the people and the libraries. Its most important achievement was to set up the first official travelling library – Bibliobus – in the Marne, an idea which had first been attempted by the

Socialist, Georges Monnet, in the Soissons region. Within two years the Bibliobus had reached a wider audience than all the previous libraries of the *département* in their existence.[32] Under the inspiration of Lagrange a model library was set up at the Exposition embodying many of the ideas of the ADLP.[33]

In the realm of music, the state's role was relatively limited – Zay attempted a not entirely successful reorganization of the State Opera – and the most important initiatives were taken by the FMP, the musical branch of the Maisons de Culture, presided over by the composer Roussel. During the summer of 1936 the FMP, in which the majority of contemporary composers participated, succeeded in setting up a network of 140 music groups. Its activities ranged from laying on music courses for working-class audiences to providing the music for Popular Front festivals. *Commune* set itself the objective of setting up a popular choral group in every locality of France.[34]

The Popular Front, it should now be clear, was concerned less with creating new cultural forms, with the *content* of artistic creation, than with the democratization of an existing, traditional culture which it hesitated to call into question. The key word in 1936 was not the restrictive 'proletarian' but the all-embracing 'populaire'. This cultural ecumenicalism could go to surprising lengths. One cites the example of the 'Green Book,' compiled at Blum's own request. This was a catalogue of those books suitable for purchase by French libraries abroad, for which government financial aid was increased by 20 million f. The list included works by both Blum and Maurras. One of the most successful events of the Exposition – and also an idea of Blum's – was a massive retrospective exhibition of the history of French art. In both these cases the objective was to extend knowledge of a cultural patrimony defined as generously as possible. It is hardly surprising that the October Group, which shared the objective of bringing art to the people but had a political conception of the nature of that art, should have fallen apart in 1936. In Prévert's words: 'I gave up . . . when in working-class circles it became good form to replace the Internationale with the Marseillaise.'

A striking example of the Popular Front's relative lack of interest in creation was the fact that its greatest theatrical success should have been the staging of Rolland's *Juillet 14*, a play written in 1902 during the first experiment of popular theatre in France and not performed since. The 1936 production mounted by the Paris Maison de Culture ran for two months. It was a collective effort designed to implement the Popular Front's cultural principles: the curtain was designed by Picasso; the music composed by Auric, Milhaud, Honegger, Ibert, Roussel and others (all members of the FMP); the actors were from the Comédie Française and from some of the FTIF groups with walk-on parts played by members of the CGT. There were no programmes, star billing of particular actors was avoided, the 40-hour week was strictly observed. At the end of the first performance actors and audience joined together to sing the Marseillaise and the Internationale. Two contemporary reviews convey the atmosphere:

Between the stage and the audience there was a current so intense and continuous that it seemed that . . . there were no longer actors playing a role but that Marat, Desmoulins, Hoche . . . were themselves speaking to the people of 1789, to the people in the auditorium. Everything contributed to creating this atmosphere of collective warmth: the day, the subject, the mood. The Bastille *really* was taken on this evening in 1936. And when at the end actors and audience sung together the Marseillaise and the Internationale there was no longer anyone *watching* or *listening*, there were no longer actors playing roles. (*Vendredi* 24 July 1936)

On some evenings, towards the end of the final act, the public, drunk with eloquence and enthusiasm, sung the Marseillaise with the actors themselves, fists raised. This was in keeping with the subject of the play: Rolland had himself hoped for a sort of final communion between stage and auditorium . . . Does this not show that there is today a theatre-going public which is not only interested in attending plays but also in communing with their neighbour so as to feel closer to them, so as to feel carried away, with the rest of the audience, by a shared *élan* of unanimity which expresses the collective preoccupations of the moment. (*La Lumière* 15 August 1936)[35]

In these accounts what matters is less the content of the play than the fervour of the audience, less the nature of the art than the relationship between the audience and the spectacle. This was not political theatre but theatre as a continuation of politics by other means, and politics as a form of theatre, entirely appropriate to a period when so often politics had become theatre and its protagonists aware of themselves as actors in a sort of historical epic. The reactions of the audience here were dependent less on the nature of the play than the exaltation of the moment. As one reviewer wrote of the performance of Rolland's *Danton* in the same month: 'to analyse the play would be to betray the spectacle'; what mattered was the audience.[36] This was a fragile basis for a new art.[37]

The possibility of a conflict between encouragement of avant-garde culture and the objective of breaking down the barriers between the masses and art was not seriously confronted. The composer Charles Koechlin (a leading member of the FMP) argued that 'it is not necessarily the case that the masses will not comprehend our music until it contains concessions to them . . . The absence of musical culture by the masses is, on the contrary, a guarantee of their comprehension.'[38] In the field of painting Fernand Léger sidestepped the problem in the same way: the education system had imposed false artistic values, inherited from the Renaissance; children's natural creativity should be allowed to express itself. Le Corbusier's Pavilion of Modern Times at the Exposition contained huge blow-ups of paintings done by children.[39]

It was in the visual arts that the most vigorous debate occurred over the relationship between the avant-garde and mass culture. The issue was raised in a debate at the Paris Maison de Culture, the proceedings of which were published as a book entitled *The Problem of Realism*.[40] Léger rejected a return to the 'subject' in art and argued that it was possible to build a bridge between the masses and modern art by incorporating the images of industrial technology – whose products were made by the people and could be appreciated by them – into the vocabulary of the artist. This 'new realism' would not need to sacrifice the language of post-impressionism on the altar of popularity. But other artists proposed a revival of figurative art – of the subject, or even the 'social subject' – as for example in Boris Taslitzky's *Hommage to Villemin* (a 14-year-old boy killed on 9 February). For the painters Lhote and Goerg this return to social realism was not only desirable but inevitable: it was impossible to paint in the same way before 6 February and after. The dialectically skilful Aragon attempted a middle position between Socialist realism, which was being institutionalized in the Soviet Union, and the French tradition which the Communists were simultaneously rehabilitating in France. Instead of Léger's 'new realism' he proposed a 'French realism': the only road to Socialist realism was for the artist to steep himself in the reality he knew best – the nation. The practical importance of his debate should not be exaggerated: the most famous work of art to emerge from the French Popular Front, Picasso's *Guernica*, exhibited at the Spanish Pavilion of the Exposition, owed nothing to these discussions and made no concessions to realism of any kind. In the end, however, the divergences in the debate were less important than the underlying consensus. Whatever their disagreement about the means, Aragon, Léger and others would all have agreed with the painter Ozenfant that art could only reinvigorate itself by 'drawing its sap from the masses'.[41] This was the aspiration of the age.

Although the cultural priorities of the Popular Front concerned popularization rather than innovation, the two cannot always be separated. One means towards the former was to impregnate 'traditional' art with popular values. Artistic life would be reinvigorated and dignity restored to the artist by an audience for whom art was more than a distraction; existing cultural forms would not emerge unaffected from their confrontation with a mass audience. But in what ways would this occur? The notion of the indivisibility of culture and the very eclecticism of the Popular Front's artistic vision excluded the drawing of boundaries between 'bourgeois' and 'popular' art: 'there is no such thing' declared Vaillant-Couturier 'as an art for the people, something subordinate that one manufactures for them'.[42] But this did not exclude the drawing of *some* boundaries. The workers must be rescued from the most degraded forms of 'popular' culture – the songs of the popular singer Tino Rossi, American gangster films and so on – which were not authentically popular at all but imposed by the bourgeoisie on the worker 'the better to humiliate him, debase him, lull him to sleep'. Koechlin attempted to distinguish between 'light popular music' and a real people's music, 'expression of the people'.[43]

One route to this end was to rehabilitate an authentically popular art form of which the left had hitherto been suspicious: folklore. 'Folklore, treasure of the people, does not belong to the enemies of the people' declared Aragon.[44] An international folklore conference was held in Paris under the patronage of Zay and Lagrange. The most significant achievement in this field was the setting up of the Musée des Arts et Traditions Populaires. Cultural popularization also involved the search for new aesthetic forms appropriate to mass audiences. The quantitative could, as it were, become qualitative. This was especially true in the theatre where there was a fashion for grandiose spectacles which extended the bounds of the traditional theatre. The most striking example was J.-R. Bloch's massive spectacle *Birth of a City* which attempted to recreate in October 1937 the success of Rolland's *Quatorze Juillet* in the previous year. The theme of the piece was the revolt of man against the alienation of city and factory life. The scenery was by Léger, the music by Milhaud and Honegger; there were up to 700 people on stage including acrobats, cyclists, spoken choruses, mimes and dancers. At the moment of liberation the blue overalls of the workers were transformed into multi-coloured pullovers – a symbol of joy. Perhaps this might have worked in 1936; but in 1937 it was not a success. The fascist writer Robert Brasillach commented that this was the only play he had attended at which the cast was larger than the audience.[45]

In the visual arts the Popular Front coincided with, and reinvigorated, certain artistic trends which had preceded it. In his Pavilion of Modern Times which only went ahead thanks to the personal intervention of Blum, overriding the veto of the Paris municipal council, Le Corbusier presented his projects for the new urbanism for which he had argued for years, including a projected 'cartesian skyscraper' and an immense national centre of popular leisure with a 100,000 seat amphitheatre and an area for parades. Since 1925 Léger, Delaunay and others had proselytized for mural art – a collective popular modern art which heralded the end of post-Renaissance individualism and prefigured the fraternity of the future. The Popular Front, and especially the Exposition, presented them with their opportunity. Dufy did a huge mural on the history of electricity for the Pavilion of Light, Léger a mural for the Palace of Discovery. The whole notion of the artist as individual was called into question. *L'Humanité* drew attention to the significance of the fact that seven of France's leading composers had collaborated on the music for Rolland's *Juillet Quatorze*: although the quality of their contributions might have differed, what mattered was this 'effort at collective musical art . . . without which a real people's music cannot develop'.[46] In 1937, Mai 36 mounted *Liberté*, a piece written collectively by various dramatists and portraying the history of France largely as a prelude to the Popular Front. The play was not a success.[47]

Another route towards the elaboration of new cultural forms was outlined by Dolléans: 'the new culture is not a luxury. It is within reach of the humblest and the most distant; it is a bond . . . Synthesis of vision, sound and silence, the cinema, records, radio and photographs have all powerfully contributed to the formation of the new culture, the culture of the total individual.'[48] These relatively new but rapidly expanding cultural forms received more attention from the Popular Front government than from any of its predecessors. Ory remarks that Blum's was the first government to have had a policy towards the radio. The radio waves were opened to labour organizations; the CCEO was allowed to broadcast twice weekly.

In harmony with the seriousness with which it treated the most recent forms of cultural expression, was the status which the Popular Front accorded to science. The most successful event of the Exposition was Perrin's Palace of Discovery (Palais de la Découverte), a museum devoted to all aspects of scientific, mathematical and astronomical discovery combining the Popular Front's concern for popular pedagogy with the importance it gave to science as a vital component of France's cultural patrimony. Zay's education reforms were intended to increase the importance of science within the school curriculum as part of the general project of breaking down barriers between all areas of human endeavour (the reform would also have broken down the final barriers between the primary and secondary education systems). The aim, as Dolléans said, was the 'culture of the total individual'.

One idea, then, runs like a leitmotiv through every aspect of the Popular Front's cultural experiments: 'break down the barriers' – the barriers between people and culture, between different forms of cultural expression, between audience and performer, between creator and cultural consumer, between past and present, between science and art. This aspiration could lead in contradictory directions – embracing the avant-garde or reaffirming traditional cultural values. But these were not perceived as contradictions precisely because the Popular Front's cultural eclecticism, its defence of the widest possible cultural front, allowed cultural diversity (even if, in the process, some, such as the October Group or the Surrealists, felt by-passed or betrayed).

It is difficult to assess the real impact of the Popular Front on the cultural experience of the French people, to judge the profundity of this 'brief and ardent liaison between People and Culture' (Lacouture). Certainly the activities of organizations like APAM and ADLP did not affect a substantial audience. The CGT newspaper commented that, in entertainments organized by unions for their members, popular comedians had often been replaced by serious artistic spectacles.[49] But Léger relates that when he offered himself as a popular lecturer on art at Lille, he encountered an audience of 100 professionals and not one worker. At a festival organized by the Seine Federation of the Socialist Party, Tino Rossi was the star performer. Cheap nightly opening of the Louvre was abandoned owing to lack of demand. Opening the doors of culture to the people did not guarantee that they would select the culture being offered. Hence perhaps, the slightly wistful comments in 1938 by Georges Vidalenc, one of the lecturers at the CCEO, about the way that the workers were employing their new leisure: 'it is sad to see the preoccupation of workers with the commercialistic Tour de France . . . Our comrades have better things to do'; he lamented that young workers seemed above all to enjoy reading *L'Auto*.[50] Perhaps then the real cultural significance of the Popular Front was to open the way to the mass cultural consumerism of the postwar era. For most people the art of the Popular Front period meant probably not *Guernica* or the murals of Léger but advertising or film posters, not the music of Honegger and Roussel, but the popular songs of Maurice Chevalier or Charles Trénet which reflect curiously little the political preoccupations of the time.[51] After all, had not Aragon himself proclaimed in one of his more dithyrambic moments: 'I greet you my France, for that light in your eyes which saw the Bastille fall . . . for Racine and for Diderot, . . . and for Maurice Chevalier . . . for Jeanne from Lorraine [i.e. Joan of Arc] and for Babeuf.'[52] Who was to say that Chevalier would not be preferred to Racine?

Breaking down the barriers: leisure and the people

If culturally the Popular Front was a precursor of the 1960s, so also the first departures to the sea in 1936, the first *congés payés*, prefigure the massive summer migrations, *les grands départs*, of contemporary France. To treat the Popular Front's attitude towards sport and tourism separately from its general cultural vision is to accept a compartmentalization absolutely alien to its view of the world. Concern with the 'total individual' meant that the physical was not to be separated from the intellectual, culture from sport (the Buffalo sports stadium was the stage of Bloch's *Birth of a City*). Zay tried to introduce physical education into schools. The Maisons de Culture organized 'camping and culture' sections in which outdoor activities could be combined with historical visits.

If, then, we will here consider sport and tourism separately, this is partly for convenience and partly because of the special place which the *congés payés* hold in the popular memory of the Popular Front: they are the achievement for which it is best and most fondly remembered. The image of working-class couples on tandems departing to the countryside is as closely associated with 1936 as the barricade with 1968: the number of bicycles in France rose from 7 million in 1936 to almost 9 million in 1938.[53] Blum himself referred to his achievements in this field in a celebrated passage of his defence at Riom:

I did not often leave my ministerial office during the period of my government, but each time that I did, I crossed the huge Paris suburbs and saw the roads covered by streams of 'old bangers', motorbikes, and tandems with working-class couples dressed in matching pull-overs . . . All this gave me the feeling that, through the organization of work and of leisure, I had . . . brought a ray of beauty (*une espèce d'embellie*), of light, into dark and difficult lives . . . that we had not only made it easier for them and their families to live but that we had opened up a vision of the future and given them hope

J.-P. Chabrol's novel on the Popular Front is called *L'Embellie*. But this is a subject which can be treated in more than merely sentimental terms. It is worth examining in more detail the Popular Front's discourse on leisure, if we may use the phrase.

The 'problem of leisure' was not new in 1936. It arose from the belief, expressed on the right – where Lagrange was dubbed the 'Minister of Idleness' – but quietly shared on the left, that without guidance workers would dissipate their leisure in drink. Sporadic efforts to organize the leisure activities of the workers had been made both by paternalistically-minded employers and by some trades unions. But the social reforms of 1936 raised the need for more adventurous policies.[54] Apart from setting up Lagrange's ministry, Blum's government had started with no very clear policy towards leisure. The new post was first attached to the Ministry of Health; then, after the fall of Blum's government, it was, at the behest of Zay and Lagrange, transferred to the Ministry of Education. This reflected the emergence of a clearer view about the role of leisure. In defining this view an important part was played by Lagrange.[55] Lagrange had not been notable for any previous interest in popular culture or sport, but he and his collaborators were activated by an enthusiasm which compensated for their exiguous financial resources. One of them, Etienne Bécart, describes how he and other members of Lagrange's team would go and meet groups of workers returning to Paris from their first paid holidays; through bad planning some of the younger workers returned without even having enough money for the *Métro*; as a result Bécart took to arriving with a pocket of small change to help them out.[56] The anecdote perfectly illustrates the atmosphere of amateurishness, informality and enthusiasm (not to say the good public relations) of Lagrange's team.

Improvization was all the more necessary because, at least as regards the *congés payés*, there was little time for preparation. In 1936 *congés payés* had figured neither in the programme of the Popular Front nor even in the demands of the first strikes. This does not mean that they had not been a longstanding demand of working-class organizations – the CGT had officially demanded them since 1925 – but union activists had not found them to be a successful theme of propaganda among the workers for whom the idea seemed an impossible dream.[57] The *congés payés*, then, emerged suddenly out of the strike movement of June – when the impossible became realizable.

Within days of the passing of the new law, Lagrange had succeeded in persuading the railway companies to provide cheap holiday tickets for workers (a 40 per cent reduction). The main destinations were the beaches, especially of the South: Menton, primarily a winter resort, had 1,400 French tourists in August 1935, 3,400 in August 1936, 4,900 in August 1937. The age of mass tourism had dawned. A second major area of Lagrange's activity was the promotion of sport. He attempted to remedy the inadequate provision of public sports facilities such as playing fields and swimming pools: a scheme to provide a 50 per cent state subsidy for the building of sports facilities was started in three departments: 25 million f. was spent in 1936. Although financial constraints in 1937 prevented any important extension of this programme, by the end of that year 400 projects had been undertaken. Lagrange officially encouraged participation in sport by introducing, in 1937, the Brevet Sportif Populaire (BSP), a certificate of aptitude in a number of easily accessible sports – running, swimming, climbing. In 1937, 600,000 children took the test, and 420,000 passed.

In outlining his *politique des loisirs* (policy for leisure) Lagrange reiterated four themes. First, to 'allow the youth of France to discover joy and health through the practice of sport'. 'Joy', 'dignity', 'youth', *bonheur*, 'health' are words which recur insistently in Lagrange's speeches. The *bonheur* was to be both spiritual – restoring the sense of joy which the factory had destroyed – and physical, improving the health of the French people. The former consideration embodied what contemporaries perceived as a fundamental aspiration of the strikers in 1936; the latter expressed the fears of an ageing society aware of the threat across the

Rhine. The emphasis on youth was intended to show that democracy as well as fascism could harness the revolt of youth.

Secondly, Lagrange aimed to create 'moral unity'. He wanted, 'to bring together the different elements of French youth'. He advocated the setting up in every locality of leisure clubs through which people would organize their own leisure activities. The clubs would also create an arena for people 'to exchange, without inhibitions, the fruits of their different experiences: the miner, the artisan, the mason, the clerk, the peasant, the *instituteur*, will gradually understand . . . the unity of human labour'. Few such clubs were set up in Lagrange's time but he saw a version of his vision realized in the youth hostel movement which he supported enthusiastically: he saw youth hostels as the 'prefiguration of a fraternal society'. This was leisure as an expression of the Popular Front's ambition to *rassemblement*, a version of the *main tendue.*

Thirdly, the aim was to generalize participation in tourism ('the Riviera for all') and sport (not sporting records but 'the participation in sport of the greatest numbers') and to democratize elite sports such as skiing or tennis (a game 'without brutality . . . worthy of being popularized'). In sport also the barriers had to come down. The most striking example of this kind was the development of 'people's aviation' clubs which were promoted by Pierre Cot, Minister of Air, with the enthusiastic support of the PCF. Finally, while aware of the impressive achievements of the fascist states in the field of leisure activities, Lagrange wanted to prove that it was possible also for a democracy to 'create a vast organization of sport and leisure'. Encouraging different elements of the population to meet each other in recreation would develop the 'attitude of mutual sympathy, respect and fair-play' on which democracy was built.

Joy and youth, unity and *rassemblement*, participation and democratization, democracy and liberty: these are four classic Popular Front themes. And in the domain of recreation, as in that of culture, there was a convergence of views between the government and the Popular Front organizations: the organizations could rely on the government to support their activities; the government could rely on them to carry out some of the enterprises for which it lacked the resources. One of these organizations, to which Lagrange devoted special interest, was the youth hostel movement. The first youth hostel was set up in France in 1930 by the Christian Democrat, Marc Sangnier, who at the same time founded the French Youth Hostel League. In 1933 a rival organization, the Secular Youth Hostel Centre (CLAJ), was set up under the patronage of various left-wing organizations. There was also a third movement inspired by Giono. But it was in 1936 that the youth hostel movement really took off. The number of youth hostels leapt from 250 in June 1936 to 400 by the end of the year. This expansion (largely to the benefit of the CLAJ) was encouraged by Lagrange who visited existing hostels and opened new ones; he was sometimes described as the 'minister of the youth hostels'.

The sudden success of the youth hostel movement obviously owed something to the demand for cheap holiday accommodation but also to the fact that it propagated an ideology sharing many of the values of the Popular Front. Youth hostelling was to express a new attitude to life. In the words of the *Cri des Auberges*, journal of the CLAJ, each hostel must be a 'veritable miniature Republic of the Young' which 'united young intellectuals, workers and peasants'. Youth-hostelling dealt a blow to the 'snobbism of the privileged'. Another theme was the celebration of the countryside, of escape from the unhealthy environment of the town and factory. This was expressed in the song *Au devant de la vie* which became the anthem of the youth hostel movement (and indeed of the Popular Front: it provided the theme tune to the CCEO's radio broadcasts):

> *Ma blonde*, do you hear in the city
> The shrieking of the factories and the trains?
> Let us go and meet the breeze
> Let us go and meet the morning.

Songs and folklore were an important part of youth hostel culture: the *Cri des Auberges* exhorted its readers to revive 'songs of the provinces, old songs of former days' as a way of 'penetrating the popular soul'.

At times the popular soul was resistant to penetration. There were incidents between youth hostellers and peasants, shocked at seeing young girls in shorts; conversely the *Cri des Auberges* was shocked that on Sundays peasants sought out the bistro or the cinema: they must be taught to love nature. There was also friction between hostellers from middle-class and those from working-class backgrounds. But, in spite of attempts to attract the working class, the large majority of hostellers were teachers or students. *Rassemblement* was not so easy to achieve. The more libertarian aspects of the movement – the early poems of Prévert were avidly read in the youth hostels – offended against the Popular Front's quest for cultural and political consensus, and its pacifist internationalism conflicted with the Communists' recently acquired Jacobin nationalism. But the optimism, the anti-elitism, the call to fraternity and solidarity, the idea of escape, were integral elements of the vision of both the hostelling movement and of the Popular Front. As Chamson wrote in *Vendredi*: 'if we had to give a face to the Popular Front, as artists have given one to liberty, it would be that of a young man, bronzed by the sun, muscular, used to walking and to the open air, his soul innocent and yet not naïve, singing "Allons au devant de la vie." '[58]

Another organization on which Lagrange could rely to supplement his activities was the Labour Sporting and Gymnastic Federation (FSGT) formed in December 1934 from a fusion of the Socialist and Communist Sporting federations (the early date showing how the dynamic of unity proceeded at an uneven pace). At this time the organization had 515 clubs with 18,000 members; by 1938 the figure had risen to 1,687 clubs with 102,694 members.[59]

A role was also played by the CGT. In most factories of the Paris region sporting clubs were set up as well as Recreation Committees (*Comités des loisirs*) which organized festivals and excursions. Often these were clubs formerly run by the employers and now taken over by the workers. In 1937 the CGT set up a Bureau of Tourism which gathered information about cheap hotels and organized a weekly saving scheme to help workers pay for their holidays, as well as laying on excursions. The CCEO arranged courses on the history, architecture and geography of Paris to provide basic information for CGT guides who had volunteered to show visiting workers and peasants around the capital.[60]

This was an important point: tourism was not only a distraction it was also a discovery of France and French history. In a letter to a CGT newspaper, a rural postman described how before 1936 his only previous visits to parts of France outside his home province had come during his military service and in war; he had never seen the mountains or the Côte d'Azur; now thanks to the Popular Front the working class could 'at last know France, our country, other than simply through geography and the cinema'.[61] Seeing France, turning the abstract 'hexagon' of the class-room into reality was another way of creating 'moral unity'. Lagrange organized a weekend visit to Paris for a group of young workers: they were given a guided tour of the city's monuments. The Communist historian Jean Bruhat lectured to groups of workers visiting St Malo on a trip organized by *L'Humanité*. He also had the idea in 1939 of writing a series of articles in *L'Humanité*, in conjunction with the Tour de France, about the impact of the Revolution in each region visited by the cycle race.[62] This neatly fused travel, sport and history as well as showing how far the PCF had moved since 1933 when it not only showed little interest in France's history but also condemned the commercialism of the Tour de France.

This discovery of France can be placed in a tradition dating back to the early years of the Third Republic. In his *Peasants into Frenchmen* Eugen Weber has described how the French peasantry was integrated into the national community through conscription, road building and compulsory education. In the same period the most successful school manual of Republican propaganda had been the *Tour de France par deux enfants* describing the journey round France of two school-children from Alsace. The *congés payés* were put in the same tradition: having reappropriated the space of their factories in June 1936, the workers of France would take possession of their country in August.

We must not exaggerate the degree to which the population was able to make use of the new opportunities for leisure. The 40-hour week did not become general before March 1937 and was under attack by the beginning of 1938. As for the *congés payés* they remained for most workers an impossible luxury in spite of the 'Lagrange tickets': almost 550,000 were bought in 1936, 907,000 in 1937, 1.5 million in 1938. These figures are not insignificant but still only represent a small proportion of the eligible population. Holidays did not overnight become a feature of French working-class life.[63]

Nor do we know how the first paid holidays were lived by their beneficiaries. Workers at the Renault factory described their experiences in the union newspaper. Some wrote through the prism of schoolbook platitudes – 'the smiling villages of the Alps' – others in the idiom of the Popular Front – it was necessary to 'strengthen the fraternal links which bind us to ... our peasant brothers' – but others were suddenly confronted with a France whose existence they had not suspected: Brittany seemed to be in 'the Middle Ages'. One concluded: 'we are marching towards a better world: there must be no laggards'.[64]

The Popular Front was not of course the only government to confront the problem of mass leisure and mass culture in the 1930s. 'Many participants and few spectators'; bringing 'the masses into the state'; reaching the masses 'not seeking champions or grooming exceptional athletes to break records'; encouraging cycling to promote fraternity among workers 'divided by ... provincialism': these phrases came not from Lagrange but from Mussolini and his *dopolavoro* organization.[65] Mussolini also introduced the 40-hour week, an equivalent of the BSP, cheap holidays trains for workers, a travelling theatre company and a bibliobus. But we should beware of simplistic assimilations. In many ways the *dopolavoro* policy was quite different from the Popular Front – in the emphasis on military prowess, the preference for collective activities over individual ones, most importantly, the attempt to subsume all activities under the aegis of the state. In Germany, where the youth hostel movement was altogether vaster than in France, it was taken over by the Hitler Youth; in France three youth hostel movements coexisted. Mussolini would not have talked about 'fairplay' and mutual respect.

On the other hand some of the themes of the Popular Front were to recur hauntingly in France of Vichy: the obsession with the young (*jeunesse* one of Lagrange's favourite words, was also one of Pétain's),[66] the celebration of the countryside and of folklore, and indeed the search for 'moral unity'. Vichy too introduced its certificate of aptitude in sports but it was a Brevet National not a Brevet Populaire. It may be, paradoxically, that the Popular Front, that supremely political movement, contributed unwittingly, in its search for consensus and fraternity, to a process of depoliticization, or at least that it did not link its conception of leisure and culture clearly enough to the Republican vision that it was defending. Apoliticism had been the motto of the Maisons de Culture (and of the CLAJ). The rationale of this strategy was political *rassemblement*; perhaps depoliticization was one of the results. This problem was perceived by some of the Popular Front's defenders. Three lecturers at the CCEO wrote in 1938 about the dangers of an excessive concentration on the young to the detriment of the old, and on physical activity – 'the religion of muscle' – over intellectual. They worried about a 'certain indifference . . . towards social, economic and political questions'. The youth hostel movement had been very successful in central Europe where 'this physical liberation of the individual has not prevented social and political servitude; it is even possible that it has up to a point helped it. The joy of walking together carries the risk that people will walk together *with joy* in any direction whatever.'[67] These words were not unprescient.

'Give back the cinema to the people of France' (Renoir): cinema and the people

There are various reasons why the cinema provides an ideal case-study of the Popular Front's cultural achievements – quite apart from the fact that the 1930s is often seen, to quote the title of a recent book, as 'The Golden Age of the French Cinema.'[68] In the first place, cinema had the attraction of being a collectively produced art form. Secondly, as the most popular and rapidly expanding form of mass entertainment, the cinema was of central importance for a movement concerned with the problem of mass culture. As Lagrange said, cinema was ideally suited to be an 'instrument of popular culture' and to 'improve the intellectual and moral education of the masses'.

Thirdly, cinema is unique in being an art that is also an industry, and therefore more directly dependent than other art forms on the economic environment. French cinema was severely hit by the slump: between 1933 and 1934 capital investment in the industry fell from 70 million f. to 17.3 million. The collapse of the huge Gaumont and Pathé companies, which dominated production until 1935, had the beneficial side-effect of providing more openings for experimental film-makers.[69] The cinema was also directly affected by the social upheaval of June 1936: film studios and cinemas were occupied by strikers. Like any other workers, film technicians and artists won collective contracts giving improved working conditions and providing directors with greater autonomy from production companies.

But, however closely the cinema may have been involved in the political turmoil of the 1930s, there are pitfalls in using particular films as historical evidence. It is not necessarily true that the most celebrated films, those which survive to mould our retrospective vision, were the most successful or representative films of their day. Although it is indeed true that Jean Renoir's *La Grande Illusion*, the most famous film of the period, was the box-office hit of 1937, it shared this privilege with the now forgotten *Ignace*, a military vaudeville starring the comedian Fernandel. Of the fifteen most popular films shown in France in 1936, none was what would now be considered one of the classic Popular Front films (of these fifteen the one which most reflected certain Popular Front themes was . . . *Modern Times*!).[70] Also, while it is tempting to single out films which seem to reflect perfectly certain contemporary themes, there is a danger in attributing spuriously symbolic importance to particular films. In 1936, Julien Duvivier directed *La Belle Equipe*, the story of five unemployed workers who win a lottery and set up collectively a small café-cum-dancehall. Although their enterprise ends badly, the themes of the film – the cooperative effort of the workers and the tender depiction of popular pleasures by the banks of the Marne – are often seen as expressing the mood of 1936. Yet in the same year Duvivier also made *L'Homme du Jour*, the story of an electrician (Maurice Chevalier) who achieves sudden fame by saving the life of an actress, but, finding himself unable to cope with his exposure to the life of the rich, goes back to his former existence. The moral of the film, summed up by Chevalier in the phrase 'the place of the electrician is not in front of the projector', is that everyone should know their place in society. Hardly a 'frontist' theme.

To select certain films is valid to the extent that some directors, influenced by the Popular Front, did for a while believe that they could transform the cinema just as, more generally, the Popular Front would transform the world. In the field of the cinema we can observe the same converging process already noted in the case of the other arts: a greater interest by film-makers in social issues; and a new concern with the cinema by the political organizations. One sign of the former process was that many film-makers and film critics joined the AEAR. But as early as 1930 Jean Vigo had called for a 'social cinema'; and a year later the young Marcel Carné exhorted film-makers to take their cameras into the street. None was to do this more convincingly than Renoir in *Toni* (1935). Set in the world of Italian immigrant workers in the south of France, the film broke with convention both in being shot on location and in using non-profess-ional actors. But this bleak film about the lives of individuals crushed by fatality looks forward more to postwar neo-realism than to the Popular Front's optimistic vision of a world that can be changed. *Toni* was not liked by Communist critics.[71]

It was Renoir's next film, *The Crime of M. Lange*, released in January 1936, which was the first to express the Popular Front's ideology in the cinema. The script was by Prévert, and many other members of the October group participated in its making. Lange, a dreamer who spends his nights writing a novel, *Arizona Jim*, is the exploited employee of a small printing business. The firm goes bankrupt and its evil owner, Batala, flees his creditors and is wrongly thought to have been killed in a crash. The workers set up a cooperative which flourishes, thanks to the sales of *Arizona Jim*, until Batala returns to claim his property. Lange, who cannot bear to see the workers divested of their achievement, shoots him and escapes. At the Belgian border he is recognized and apprehended, but when the group of workers into whose hands he has fallen hear his story – which the film tells in flashback – they let him free.

There is hardly any need to underline the ways in which this film reflects the themes of 1935: the unity of intellectuals and workers (Lange and the printers), the solidarity of a small cooperative successfully triumphing over the incompetence of the unscrupulous capitalist. The feeling of solidarity is powerfully accentuated both by setting the whole film around the sociable community of the small courtyard in which the factory is located and by Renoir's fluid use of the camera, the most famous example of this being the 360 degree pan which sweeps around to take in the whole cooperative just before Lange shoots Batala. In his memoirs Renoir describes how his aim was to move away from the fragmented editing of the Hollywood cinema and display the unity between his characters and their environment and between each other. *The Crime of M. Lange* uses a new cinematic language in the service of a new political vision.[72]

In the second process mentioned above – interest in the cinema by political organizations – the pioneer was Marceau Pivert who set up in 1936 a cinematographic section of the Seine Federation of the SFIO which made short propaganda films: the first was a documentary about the rally at the Mur des Fédérés in May 1935, another about the attack on Blum in February 1936. But although the section made at least a dozen films, its activities petered out in 1937.

The efforts of the Communist Party were more ambitious. At the end of 1935 it invited Renoir, on the strength of *Le Crime de M. Lange*, to make a propaganda film for the elections. The film was to be a collective enterprise in which Renoir would have overall direction. The film, with the very 'frontist' title *La Vie est à nous*, was an explicit presentation of the Popular Front's ideology as conceived by the Communist Party; Vaillant-Couturier supervized its conception. It opens with a series of images celebrating the natural and historical wealth of France as recounted to a classroom of children by an *instituteur*. The children wonder why, if France is so rich, they are so poor. A spoken chorus (incorporating a practice popularized by the FTOF) gives the answer:

> France does not belong to the French
> But to two hundred families.
> France does not belong to the French.

Later we see an album of portraits of France's leading capitalists, including Renault and de Wendel. After newsreels of Hitler, Mussolini and the French Leagues, there are three short sketches illustrating the evils of contemporary France: the story of an ageing worker sacked because he cannot meet the new production targets (supervized by an unsympathetic *chronométreur*) and then reinstated after a successful protest strike; a peasant who resists eviction for indebtedness thanks to the solidarity of his neighbours; a young unemployed engineer who is rescued on the verge of starvation by two young Communists: they take him to a party meeting where another spoken chorus tells him:

> Comrade you are not alone.
> In the depths of your distress
> You are not alone.

The film ends, after speeches by leading Communists, with a massive demonstration in which the people take physical possession of that France which at the beginning of the film had not been theirs. The 'two hundred families', the celebration of the beauties of France, the appeal to the *classes moyennes* (the peasant and the young engineer), the attack on factory conditions, the call to solidarity ('you are not alone') – all the Popular Front themes are there.[73]

After the election victory, the Popular Front hopes for the cinema came to be invested in the organization *Ciné-Liberté*.[74] Founded in the spring of 1936, *Ciné-Liberté* was initially an outgrowth of the cinematic section of the Paris Maison de Culture. It was one of those innumerable cultural associations which sprung up in the early months of 1936, often at the instigation of the PCF, but attracting a far wider audience. The name was a conscious imitation of *Radio-Liberté*, an organization started slightly earlier by Vaillant-Couturier to press for a reform of the radio. *Ciné-Liberté* was organized as a cooperative, an idea much in the spirit of the Popular Front. Its members included directors, critics and actors, as well as simple cinema enthusiasts; by the autumn of 1936 it claimed 12,000 members. Among its leading figures were Renoir, who had acquired semi-official status as *the* Popular Front director, and the film critic and script-writer Henri Jeanson who edited its shortlived newspaper, also called *Ciné-Liberté*.

The organization agitated for a reform of the French film industry. 'We must give the cinema back to the people of France' declared Renoir 'and ... prise it from the hands of profiteers and crooked businessmen.' Bankrupt studios should be nationalized and handed over to the CGT. Another target was state censorship. In neither of these objectives was *Ciné-Liberté* successful. It failed to achieve the lifting of the ban on Vigo's *Zéro de Conduite* (a film about a school rebellion) or even on *La Vie est à nous* which could at this time be openly seen in America.

The most significant aspect of *Ciné-Liberté*'s activities was the making of films to provide an alternative to the commercial cinema. The first of these was a documentary on the factory occupations of June. By the autumn of 1936 seven short documentaries had been made. In 1937 there followed films on the Exposition, on Spain and on Popular Front meetings. Under the aegis of *Ciné-Liberté* two feature films were also made for the PCF and two for trade unions: *Sur les Routes d'Acier* for the rail union and *Les Bâtisseurs* for the builders' union. In *Les Bâtisseurs*, two builders – played by two unemployed workers – are seen restoring Chartres Cathedral; later Le Corbusier expounds his vision of modern urbanism and the film ends with a hymn to work by Honneger.

But the main *Ciné-Liberté* production, and the one which came to swallow up its entire activity and resources, was Renoir's film about the French revolution, *La Marseillaise*. This was to be a film by the people, for the people and about the people. By the people because the 3 million francs needed to finance it were to be raised by public subscription – by 'the people of France' and not by 'the trusts'. For the people because it was to be *the* cinema showcase of the Popular Front: the idea was launched to the public in May 1937 at a meeting presided over by Zay, at which Lagrange, Pivert, Jeanson and Renoir all spoke. About the people because it was to be a history of the Revolution from below, the Revolution as lived by the common people not the revolutionary heroes. It tells the story of a group of 'patriots' from Marseilles who march to defend the Revolution in Paris where they participate in the downfall of the monarchy in August 1792.

The political importance attached to the film was shown by the large number of interviews and articles devoted to it before its appearance, including an exhibition mounted at the Paris Maison de Culture. The revolution had been chosen as the subject of the film, Renoir explained, because it was 'the epoch which offered the greatest similarity with our own'. Contemporary parallels were always at the forefront: the film ends with Valmy where, according to Renoir, the defenders of France were joined by an 'international brigade' (his phrase) of Belgians, Russians and

Germans. Renoir's insistently repeated intention was to destroy the myth of the revolutionaries as 'wild-eyed, irrational, criminal types on the fringes of society' (just as the Communist was portrayed by the right as 'the man with the knife between his teeth'); on the contrary, they were 'people as clean and decent as you and me'. Although Renoir offered his film as an attack on 'the aristocratic spirit which today we call fascist', his revolution is a reassuringly good-humoured one: hardly a drop of blood is shed. Even Louis XVI, played by Renoir's brother Pierre, is depicted with gentle irony, as someone whom the march of history has rendered redundant.

The fundamental theme of the film, however, is not revolution but the development of national consciousness, the birth of a nation: as the Marseilles patriots move across France they are, as it were, taking possession of their country, like the first workers during the *congés payés* of 1936. The Marseillaise, the song of their march, becomes the palpable expression of their new-found unity. The only real villains in the film, as Ory points out, are foreigners or Frenchmen on foreign soil: Marie Antoinette, the *émigrés* at Coblentz, the Swiss guards of the Tuileries. In short, the film was a celebration of national reconciliation, a film of the *main tendue* – 'why should a man wearing a cassock necessarily be a reactionary' says one of the revolutionaries – in which the enemy is reduced to a small handful of irreducible opponents. The theme would have been familiar to any spectator in 1936, and if it were not, a Communist critic underlined the point: 'the scene of the Coblentz *émigrés* could have taken place in a Parisian salon of June 1936'.

But at the very moment that the film was being made, the Frontist vision that it articulated was in reality disintegrating. Already in May 1937 much of the previous year's enthusiasm had died down: it proved impossible to raise the necessary funds by popular subscription and the final financing had to be provided by the CGT. At the same time the *Ciné-Liberté* cooperative became a limited company controlled by the CGT. When the film came out at the beginning of 1938 the cultural unanimity of which it was an expression no longer existed. It received a lukewarm critical reception even from circles once sympathetic to the Popular Front. Jeanson wrote a scathing review. A few months later he contrasted the 'real Renoir full of good humour, openness and simplicity' with the 'false Renoir . . . of the *Marseillaise* and the party of cells and dungeons'.[75] It had been hoped that *La Marseillaise* would be the first of a long line of *Ciné-Liberté* films; in fact it proved to be the last. And *Ciné-Liberté*, having started as a radical project to transform film-making in France, ended as a conventional cinema club.

Having looked at the way in which certain film-makers explicitly attempted to translate Frontist ideology on to the screen, it is worth

returning to the question of how generally these themes were taken up by
the commercial cinema. In 1931 the critic, Georges Altmann, summed up
the role of 'the working man' in French cinema: 'he opens doors. He
carries the baggage. He says "Mme. is served." He says thank you for the
tip. He shouts "Vive la France" in the newsreels.'[76] To what extent had
the Popular Front affected this situation? According to one recent study,
the predominant themes of the French cinema in 1936–7 were unchanged
– military farces, vaudeville comedies, melodramatic costume dramas –
and the prevailing mood was cynicism.[77] Another recent book finds only
nine films in which the proletariat figure to some extent between 1936 and
1939. And of these, three were made by Renoir and two by Marcel
Carné.[78] Even here we cannot always strictly talk of the proletariat: the
world of M. Lange, one of the nine films, is that of the traditional
workshop not the large-scale factory. Although the modern industrial
proletariat irrupted into French politics in 1936, it remained largely
absent from the cinema screen. Another of these nine films was the
comedy *Choc en Retour* (1936), which, although depicting the inside of a
factory, inverts the Popular Front's conception of the world: it shows an
employer successfully manipulating his credulous workers into a strike for
his own ends. At best, then, the Popular Front only affected a very small
sector of French cinematic production. The case of Renoir is the most
striking. In the period of his honeymoon with the PCF, Renoir made six
films, including those discussed above.[79] Although it would be crass to
circumscribe Renoir's vision within any simple formula, all these films
show a humanism and generosity which is certainly an ingredient of the
mood of 1936. The theme is always one of reconciliation: in his
adaptation of Gorky's *Les Bas Fonds* (1936), the reconciliation between
aristocrat and criminal; in *La Grande Illusion*, between aristocrat and
proletarian, German and Frenchman, Jew and Frenchman. Renoir's
motto was 'everyone has their reasons'. But although as a result of the
Popular Front Renoir was drawn to subjects which he might not otherwise have treated, it is perhaps less the case that his vision of the world was
transformed by the politics of the Popular Front than that, like say
Guéhenno, he found in the Popular Front a politics which seemed to have
transformed its vision of the world to his.

Carné is altogether different. The universe of his films is a highly
stylized urban decor of fog-laden ports, lights reflected in sinister wet
streets, trains shrieking in the night. Certainly he treats the world of the
working man, sometimes the proletariat, but the vision is a bleak one: 'I
paint the drowned man beneath the swimmer', says the artist in *Quai des
Brumes* (1938). The vision is also that of Prévert, who never collaborated
with Renoir again after *The Crime of M. Lange*, but went on to write the
scripts of three of Carné's pre-1940 films: his view of the world was too

astringent and his spirit too rebellious ever to accept the cosy generosity of the Popular Front's official ideology. *Quai des Brumes* (Carné/Prévert), set in the mists of Le Havre, describes the doomed brief love of an army deserter (Jean Gabin) and a girl who is in the clutches of her depraved guardian; at the end Gabin is gunned down in the back by a vicious local mobster. Carné has described how Prévert and Renoir almost came to blows after Renoir had described the film's black view of humanity as fascist.[80] The incident is significant as yet another example of the decline of the cultural fraternity of 1936 when Renoir and Prévert had worked together.

Jean Gabin, the doomed hero of *Quai des Brumes* and of so many other films of the 1930s, might seem at first an archetypal Popular Front figure: his face is that of the man who has suffered, worked and struggled; he is quick to anger but his surly exterior, his gruffness, hides vulnerability and frustrated tenderness. With Gabin the worker wins his place on the screen. And yet, Gabin is also a loner, set apart from humanity – a deserter (*Quai des Brumes*), a fugitive from the police (*Le Jour se lève*), a vagabond (*Les Bas Fonds*), a worker isolated from his fellows by mental illness (*La Bête Humaine*) – in short, a fugitive from his own destiny. Nothing could be further removed from the *camaraderie* of the Popular Front.

In no film is this more clear than in Carné's last pre-war film, *Le Jour se lève* (Carné/Prevert (1939)). It opens and finishes in a small bedroom at the top of a strange, high isolated block where Gabin, the factory worker, is on the run from the police for having murdered his boss to protect the love which had briefly salvaged his grim existence. At the end of the film, as dawn rises, Gabin shoots himself to escape arrest, just before the alarm goes off to call him to the factory or, in this case, to prison (in René Clair's *A nous la liberté* (1931) they are virtually equivalent). The era which opened with the warm and protective solidarity of the courtyard in *The Crime of M. Lange* ends, ten weeks before the outbreak of war, with the worker-as-individual, defenceless and cut off from the crowd below which watches, and waits for the inevitably tragic denouement. The workers shout 'François, we will help you' – but they are charged and dispersed by the police.

Carné's films, then, are a testimony to the pessimism of 1938 and 1939 – after the hopes of 1936. As Arletty says in *Hôtel du Nord* (Carné/ Jeanson 1938), as she is trying to sleep through the celebrations of 14 July, a day so central to the mythology of the Popular Front: 'they may have taken the Bastille 150 years ago, but they haven't got rid of black marias'.

PART 3

The exercise of power: peace, bread and liberty

5 ∜ 'Liberty': defending democracy

One of the most common criticisms made of Blum is that he was excessively prone to caution. There is some truth in this. We have already noted his exchange with Pivert in May 1936 about whether or not to assume power immediately. On 4 June Blum presented his list of ministers to President Lebrun, but not until the government appeared before parliament on 6 June would he officially become Premier. The outbreak of strikes had however created a dramatic situation, and it was Lebrun who insisted that the Ministers of the Interior and Labour take power at once and urged Blum to broadcast to the nation on the next day. Blum agreed, having first pointed out the irregularity of this procedure from a constitutional point of view.

Although it is worth remembering that our knowledge of Blum's motives during this period comes from his defence at the Riom trial when he was, for obvious reasons, concerned to stress the strict constitutionalism of his behaviour, his words at Riom probably did represent his attitude fairly accurately. Blum's careful observance of the forms in 1936 derived not only from temperamental caution and the habits of a legal training, but also from his conception of the purpose of the Popular Front. Five times in his Ministerial Declaration, Blum spoke of the need for 'Republican defence.' A year earlier he had written in *Le Populaire*: 'parliamentary institutions, as they function today, and whatever judgement we have of them, are one of the lines of defence of parliament against the fascist threat, and our duty is therefore to maintain them and bolster their capacity for resistance'.[1] Blum's caution in 1936 had, then, a political purpose: the 'fascist' attack on liberty involved an attack on existing parliamentary institutions; and defenders of liberty were consequently cornered into a defence of the constitutional status quo. This was a different view from that of many Socialist planists who were less sentimental about the Third Republic (the difference was partly one of generation: Blum had been born with the Third Republic and his first political action had been to rally to its defence during the Dreyfus Affair). In these circumstances it is not surprising that the institutions of government were among the areas least affected by the upheavals of 1936. The whole point of Blum's notion of the occupation of power was that the presence of the friends of democracy in government guaranteed that democratic institutions could not be subverted from within by their enemies. Of the Popular Front triptych of bread, peace and liberty, liberty could best be defended not so much by reforming political institutions directly as by providing bread – overcoming the depression – and preserving peace.

That is not to say that Blum's government offered no institutional changes. Eighteen years earlier in his *Letters on Government Reform* (reissued in 1936), Blum had suggested a number of administrative changes likely to increase the efficiency of the government. Such reforms were all the more necessary in 1936 for a government that intended to carry out a far-reaching social programme and expected that its policies might encounter resistance from the higher officials within the administration itself. At the National Council on 10 May Blum promised his party that a *souffle républicain* (a breath of Republicanism) would sweep through the civil service to ensure loyal collaborators for the new government. How successful was he in these objectives?

Defending liberty 1: administrative reform and *Souffle Républicain*

In his *Letters on Government Reform* Blum argued that the *Président du Conseil* should be the 'inspirer, guide and arbitrator' of government policy. He likened his conception of the premier's role to that of a 'captain of industry'. His other main model for efficient government was the war cabinet of Lloyd George: the short work is stuffed with admiring references to the British example.[2] In 1936 Blum introduced three innovations based on ideas outlined in the *Letters*. First, as *Président du Conseil* he broke with convention and took no other ministerial portfolios so as to retain a better overall view of his government's strategy. Secondly, he set up a 'General Secretariat', headed by Jules Moch, to coordinate government policy. This body consisted of a staff of about fifteen people specializing in different areas corresponding to a ministerial department. All proposed legislation likely to affect the overall shape of government policy was to be examined by the Secretariat before being submitted to Blum. Thirdly, Blum organized his ministers into six groupings, each headed by one minister who would coordinate between them. For example, Salengro, Minister of the Interior, headed a grouping entitled General Administration, which included the Ministries of the Interior, Education and Justice.[3]

The intention of these three reforms was clearly to improve the coherence of government policy. But their importance must not be exaggerated. The grouping of ministries proved to be largely theoretical owing to the reluctance of individual ministers to sacrifice their authority. The head of each committee was himself a minister which probably only accentuated such rivalries. Only in the case of the National Defence grouping under Daladier (uniting the War, Air and Navy Ministries) did the new organization of the government have any concrete effect. The idea of having a *Président du Conseil* without portfolio had already been tried by Doumergue and Flandin but was given up by their successors. The practice was continued by Chautemps after Blum's fall but abandoned by Blum himself in his second government when he took the Treasury portfolio (though in effect he devolved his responsibility to Pierre Mendès France). The most original feature of Blum's government was certainly the Secretariat which worked relatively well, at least according to Moch. But, as we shall see, it was not always successful in providing the government with a viewpoint independent of the official administration.

What probably contributed more to the coherence of Blum's government than any organizational changes were, firstly, Blum's own impressive powers of assimilation which allowed him to remain abreast of the activities of most of his ministers, and secondly, his close working relationship with a few trusted collaborators – especially Jules Moch and André Blumel, his *chef de cabinet*. Indeed their closeness to Blum caused some jealousy within the Socialist Party. At the Socialist Congress of May 1936 Blumel, Moch and Georges Monnet, also close to Blum, lost their seats on the CAP thanks to a manoeuvre by Paul Faure. In fact places were finally found for them but the incident revealed residual suspicion within the party at the Socialists' entry into government.[4] If we are to believe General de Gaulle, Blum was only partially successful in turning himself into the 'inspirer, guide and arbitrator' that he had hoped. In his War Memoirs de Gaulle described visiting Blum to convert him to his ideas on army reform. During the conversation the telephone rang ten times distracting Blum's attention towards minor administrative and political questions. As de Gaulle was leaving, Blum observed with a gesture of weariness: 'you see how difficult it is for a head of government to hold to the plan you have outlined when he cannot remain five minutes with the same idea'. But de Gaulle did have his reasons for presenting such a picture.[5]

There were one or two other novel features of Blum's government: the appointment of a Secretary of State for Leisure and the setting up of a department with responsibility for scientific research. Also unprecedented was the presence for the first time of three women as under-secretaries of state (at a time when women were still deprived of the vote): Cécile Brunschwicg at the Ministry of Education; Suzanne Lacore at the Ministry of Health, with special responsibility for the protection of children; and Irène Joliot-Curie as Undersecretary of State for scientific research. The appointments were largely symbolic in their importance. As Blum wrote to Lacore when urging her to accept his offer: 'your mere presence will signify a great deal'. Apart from these changes there was nothing particularly unusual about Blum's cabinet (besides of course the very presence of the Socialists). The government was large: twenty-one ministers and fourteen undersecretaries of state. Of these, eighteen were Socialists, fourteen Radicals and four Independent Socialists. The participation of so many Radicals, many of whom had served in previous governments, provided familiarity: Daladier was Vice-Premier. On important issues Radical and Socialist ministers gathered separately to work out their position – though opinion did not always divide on party lines. All the members of the government were deputies or senators except for the three women (and later Perrin) and Paul Faure who sat as a Minister of State without portfolio representing the SFIO. Some historians have suggested that Blum might have shown more imagination by calling on various extra-parliamentary figures associated with the Popular Front – for example Paul Rivet or Guéhenno. Among contemporaries André Delmas was bitterly disappointed: 'we had hoped for a sort of committee of public safety, a small group of men possessing vast powers. Instead we had a huge cabinet of 35 ministers organized into groups'; the choices had been made in the traditional way according to the influence of different 'groups, sub-groups and factions'.[6]

For most supporters of the Popular Front, however, the real test of Blum's government would be its attitude towards the civil service. The need for a purge was one of the favourite subjects of the Socialist press.[7] Disbanding the Leagues was one of the government's first actions but it was from the higher echelons of the administration that the most insidious opposition was feared on the left. And the government's caution in this area came under continuous criticism from the Socialist Party, the PCF and the CVIA.[8] Possibly Blum was once again held back by scruple. Thus he waited until September before replacing the unpopular Peyrouton as Resident-General in Morocco partly because he was reluctant to appear to be settling a score with someone whom he had personally attacked while in opposition (Peyrouton was protected by his influential father-in-law, the Radical Malvy). A certain number of high officials were removed: Emile Labeyrie replaced Jean Tannery as Governor of the Bank of France in June; Pierre Guimier, administrator of the Havas press agency and also director of a right-wing newspaper, was forced out of the former position in November; the assistant commissioner of the Exposition was dismissed for writing a public letter of sympathy to Maurras.

In some cases the government went beyond changes at the top. Before the demonstration of 14 July 1936 there was a purge of the Paris municipal police including the removal of Paul Guichard, its head since

1918. In the armed forces Pierre Cot, the Air Minister, ousted seven generals of division and made 170 changes in the lower ranks within six weeks. But overall the famous *souffle républicain* failed to occur. This was most striking with regard to the Prefects – the main representatives of the government in each department – who were less affected by the arrival of Blum's government than they had been by Herriot's in 1924. Whereas Herriot had shifted one-third of the Prefects laterally and transferred eight of them out of the corps in August, Blum waited until September to shift seventeen laterally and transfer five. The judiciary, which had often treated street demonstrations of the right with greater leniency than those of the left, was protected by legal immovability. In June 1936 the government introduced a bill allowing it to modify the retirement ages of government personnel, but this measure, drafted with the judiciary in mind, was emasculated by the Senate. Another long-term possibility was to democratize the recruitment of the higher civil service, most of whose members came from bourgeois backgrounds and were trained at the private Ecole Nationale des Sciences Politiques. This was the aim of Zay's bill to organize a National School of Administration. But the proposal met with fierce resistance. It did not pass the Chamber until 1939 and lapsed with the outbreak of war.

Whether the success of Blum's government was importantly affected by its failure to carry out a more extensive purge is less easy to show than the fact that this was believed by the Socialist Party. As in any government, a vigorous minister like Cot or Zay was able to achieve much irrespective of bureaucratic apathy or hostility. Very few officials were as overtly partisan as the ambassador to Madrid, Jean Herbette, whose sympathies in the Spanish Civil War were firmly pro-Franco. At the colloquium on Blum's government held in 1965, former collaborators of Blum provided somewhat conflicting evidence on the attitude of civil servants. Blumel claimed that apart from those in the colonial service and, possibly, the Foreign Ministry, they were by no means hostile; as for Prefects, they were very obedient. Moch and André Julien (responsible for North African affairs in the General Secretariat) spoke of resistance from Prefects and from officials at the Ministry of Finance; Cot encountered the same at the Air Ministry. A recent examination of opinion in the army suggests that although the officer corps was stridently anti-Communist it was not irreducibly opposed to a government of the left. Much of the credit for this went to the very Republican Chief of Staff Georges Gamelin and to the reassuring presence of Daladier as Minister of War. On the other hand, the discovery in 1937 of two clandestine right-wing networks in the army testified to the existence of considerable suspicion.[9]

It is most probably the case that throughout the French bureaucracy, hostility to the Popular Front, where it did exist, was tempered by the belief that the coalition would break up sooner rather than later. Rather than actively sabotage the government the safest strategy was probably to ride out the storm. Blum did not have time on his side – and no one knew this better than his civil servants.

Defending democracy 2: France overseas: a test case

The study of the colonial policy of the Popular Front provides an interesting test case of the limitations of power – the gap between aspirations and achievement, and the reasons for it. Responsibility for policy towards France's overseas territories was divided between three different ministries: Algeria, as a department of France, came under the Ministry of the Interior; the North African protectorates (Morocco and Tunisia) and the middle-eastern mandates (Syria and Lebanon) under the Ministry of Foreign Affairs; and finally, the colonies properly speaking (Indo-China and Central and West Africa) under the Ministry of Colonies. Some attempt at coordination had been made with the setting up in 1935 of the High Committee of the Mediterranean and North Africa, but this body, which anyway enjoyed no jurisdiction over West Africa or Indo-China, had only a very notional existence.

The Popular Front lacked a clear colonial policy.[10] Its programme envisaged the setting up of a commission of enquiry into the situation in the overseas territories, particularly North Africa and Indo-China. This vagueness concealed differences of view between the constituent organizations. The Radicals were broadly in favour of the colonial status quo. The Socialists in the 1920s viewed colonization as a preparation for self-government. The right was criticized for having failed to create a colonial elite capable one day of assuming power. The PCF, actively anti-colonialist since its foundation, had since 1935 come to subordinate anti-colonialism to anti-fascism: France must in no way be weakened. As Thorez put it in 1937: 'the right to divorce does not signify the obligation to divorce'.[11]

Blum delegated the main responsibility for colonial policy to four individuals all of whom had reputations as advocates of reform. The Socialist, Marius Moutet, Minister of Colonies, was a longstanding critic of colonial oppression and had campaigned against the use of forced labour in Indo-China. Maurice Viollette, who had been a liberal governor of Algeria between 1925 and 1928, was appointed by Blum to a Ministry without Portfolio with a brief to concern himself with Algeria. (Violette's freedom of manoeuvre was limited by the need to take account of the Radical, Raoul Aubaud, Under-Secretary of State at the Ministry of the Interior with special reference to Algeria.) Pierre Viénot, an independent Socialist appointed Under-Secretary of State at the Ministry of Foreign Affairs, was given responsibility for the North African protectorates and

Middle Eastern Mandates. Finally, Charles-André Julien – colonial historian and anti-colonial activist – was made Secretary General of the High Committee of the Mediterranean. In this capacity he was attached to Blum's Secretariat. His brief was to turn the committee into a genuine instrument of coordination and information, providing Blum with an independent comprehensive view of North African affairs.[12] Julien had expressed his views on colonial policy in an article in *Vendredi* in May 1936. He denounced the 'seigneurs' who ran the French colonies, demanded an immediate purge of those higher civil servants 'most responsible for the policy of repression': the only justification for colonization was 'sincerely to prepare the independence of the indigenous peoples'.

Whatever the previous commitment of the Socialists to ultimate self-government, this was not at any stage the objective of Blum's government nor of any of the ministers concerned with colonial policy. The militant anti-colonial Socialist, R.-J. Longuet, who turned down a post in Viénot's *cabinet*, was startled to be told by him of the 'benefits' of French civilization in the colonies.[13] Moutet was hardly less affirmative: 'colonialism being a fact whose sudden disappearance at the present would bring about more dangers than advantages, can only be morally justified for Socialists to the extent that it brings positive benefits to the natives'.[14] In evaluating the results of the Popular Front's colonial policy we should therefore always remember the strictly limited nature of its objectives. Why had the Socialists renounced – at least temporarily – their earlier commitment to self-government? The major reason was the weakened international position of France. In Indo-China Moutet's explicit aim was to develop the colony as a market for a French economy suffering badly from the Depression. Thus the first priority was to alleviate the severe agricultural crisis prevailing in Indo-China: a socially progressive policy in Indo-China was in the best interests of the French economy. There was also a military consideration: 'our army' declared Moutet 'will only find healthy recruits from a reinvigorated indigenous peasantry . . . We will not be able to find reliable troops from a sickly peasantry.'[15] In other words France's vulnerable international position dictated that she exploit the colonies more fully. For this reason political reforms took second place to economic and social reforms. That is not to say that the Popular Front did not propose a certain measure of political liberalization, particularly in North Africa, but its ambition in this field should not be exaggerated.

Nonetheless in the overseas territories themselves expectations were high. The Algerian, Fernand Abbas, talked of 'an explosion of joy: never had the Algerian people been so unanimous in their hopes'. The same was true in Indo-China and Morocco.[16] The government's first acts did indeed suggest that changes were on the way: eighteen out of thirty colonial governors were transferred or replaced. In some cases the new men had decidedly liberal reputations. Marcel de Coppet, a Socialist and friend of André Gide, with long experience of Africa, became Governor of West Africa. In Morocco the unpopular Peyrouton was replaced, after some delay, by General Noguès. There was also a change in style. In a radio broadcast in Tunis in March 1937, Viénot scandalized the European settlers – which was not difficult – by calling for profound reforms.

In fact the hopes aroused in the colonies by the arrival of Blum's government were not to be fulfilled, as can be demonstrated by the study of a few examples. In Algeria, the so-called Blum–Violette bill, unveiled at the end of 1936, would have extended the franchise to between 20,000 and 25,000 Algerians. These proposals aroused an immediate storm of protest from the French settlers in Algeria. Their opposition was taken up in France by the colonial lobby. The attitude of Blum's Radical partners ranged from outright hostility to cautious disapproval. Aubaud himself was far from enthusiastic. Blum could have introduced the proposals by decree, but, in the words of Julien, the caution of the *conseiller d'état* prevailed over the politician. The bill was buried for several months in committee. When it emerged for a final vote in March 1938, 320 Algerian mayors resigned in protest. But with the Popular Front entering its terminal stages there was no longer any strong government backing for the reforms. And the Blum–Violette bill was finally buried by the Senate with the tacit complicity of the Daladier government.

A similar fate awaited the treaty signed with the Syrian nationalists in December 1936 by Viénot who had had to overcome the reservations of Defence Ministry and Foreign Ministry officials. According to the treaty, after a probationary period of three years, Syria would become independent but remain linked to France by a political and military alliance. Once again the treaty was obstructed in the Chamber, opposed in December 1938 by a Senate Committee and eventually never presented for ratification by the Daladier government which bowed to the pressure against it. In Senegal the new Governor, de Coppet, applied a number of social laws (relating to accidents at work, protection of women and children and so on) which had long been enforced in France but never in the colonies.[17] Unions were permitted under strict conditions. A school building programme was announced. De Coppet not only met with resistance from local French employers but also from within his own administration. He became an increasingly isolated figure and as the political pendulum in France moved to the right he lost all government backing for his policy of prudent reforms. Finally, after a strike of railway workers in September 1938, he was dismissed by Georges Mandel, Colonial Minister in Daladier's government.

In Indo-China Moutet introduced a number of important agricultural reforms – an anti-famine plan, a reorganization of agricultural credit – but his proposed colonial investment fund for a public works programme (to be carried out by paid workers not, as in the past, forced labour) was blocked by the Senate. The only political reform carried out was a partial amnesty of political prisoners; the government also displayed a more tolerant attitude towards the press. But the Commission of Enquiry set up in January 1937 (in accordance with the Popular Front programme) to examine colonial problems was a totally ineffective body. It never even reached Indo-China for fear that its arrival would encourage the nationalist movement. (After Blum's fall the Senate put an end to its funding.) When in October 1936 the nationalist leaders in Indo-China, who were predominantly but not exclusively Marxist, started a local campaign to consult the population on the grievances that could be presented to the commission, Moutet authorized their arrest.[18]

What conclusions can we draw about the achievements of the Popular Front's colonial policy? Certainly they fell far short of the expectations of the local populations. At one time it used to be argued that the Popular Front's generous aspirations in this field were sabotaged by the various forces of opposition. But in fact, as we have seen, Blum's government had no intention of breaking dramatically with past policy. Indeed the historian of Popular Front policy in Indo-China argues that Moutet was merely offering a more flexible and intelligent colonialism than that of his conservative predecessors: the objectives were similar.[19] Having conceded, however, that the Popular Front's original objectives in colonial policy were strictly limited, we still need to ask why even these were far from achieved. From the sabotaging of the Blum–Violette reforms to the blocking of Moutet's colonial investment fund, the government was on several occasions thwarted in its aims.

Resistance by local vested interests was very important, especially in Algeria where the proportion of European settlers was high. This resistance was reinforced in France by a powerful colonial lobby, particularly influential in the Radical Party and the Senate. Nor could the government or the colonial governors always rely on the loyalty of their local officials who were often opposed to reform. At the beginning of 1937 a number of civil servants in Morocco were reprimanded for attending a meeting devoted to the 'struggle against communism and democracy'.[20] In Senegal, de Coppet's hopes of introducing educational reforms were checked by the local education officer Charton. In Indo-China the local colonial authorities dragged their feet in applying even the political amnesty. The only *souffle républicain* which took place in Indo-China was the appointment of a new governor general. Generally continuity prevailed. Gaston Joseph, the powerful director of political affairs at the Ministry of

Colonies since 1929, was retained by Moutet and remained in place until
1943: after each meeting of Moutet's *cabinet* (which he did not attend) he
and the minister would revise the decisions taken by Moutet's Socialist
collaborators.[21]

Apart from these obstacles the government faced a more fundamental
problem of ignorance about what was actually happening overseas. The
case of Morocco is instructive.[22] In spite of the hopes it raised, the
replacement of Peyrouton by Noguès made no difference: the Moroccan
nationalist movement, the Comité d'Action Marocaine, was repressed and
its leaders arrested. Noguès countered possible left-wing criticism of his
rule by presenting the nationalist movement as pan-Islamic, anti-semitic,
insurrectionary and sympathetic to Franco. According to the most recent
historian of Moroccan nationalism none of these claims were true. But
Julien's attempts to obtain independent and accurate information from the
High Committee of the Mediterranean were unsuccessful. He was forced
to rely entirely on the services of the Ministry of the Interior, the Ministry of
War and the Quai d'Orsay. In August 1936 he wrote to Moch: 'nowhere
are there properly constituted dossiers allowing the minister to reach a
personal conclusion. Ministers are informed in the most haphazard way;
they are at the mercy of circumstances.' His attempts to set up coordinated
sources of information were supported only by Moutet. But the Ministry of
War blocked his suggestion that its overseas services section should be
attached to the Premier's office. As a result, Julien, brought in as an
'expert', was himself at the mercy of his experts. A meeting of the High
Committee of the Mediterranean in March 1937 discussed the pan-
Islamism of the Nationalists; Noguès accused them of being agitators who
rejected any reforms short of the total exclusion of all Frenchmen. This was
false but no one present raised any objection.

The General Secretariat, on which Blum laid such store, proved, then, in
the colonial field at least, to be inadequate both as an instrument of
coordination and a source of independent information. But we should be
wary of generalizing too hastily from this example. In the first place, the
fact of their distance from Paris made it more difficult to implement new
policies in the colonies. Secondly, colonial policy was not a priority for the
Popular Front. Julien believed that Blum should have made the Algerian
reforms a question of confidence in parliament, but Blum had no intention
of risking his government's future on so marginal an issue. The failure of
Blum's colonial policy certainly demonstrated the difficulties of overcoming resistance from a wide range of interests including elements within the
administration and the coalition. Could such resistance be overcome in
the more central area of economic and financial policy. Even to the limited
extent of its ambitions, the Popular Front had not brought 'liberty' to the
colonies. Could it bring 'bread' to France?

6 ✦ 'Bread': the Blum New Deal

Blum came personally to express his congratulations. That is unheard of . . . He entered the front door, leaped the three steps to the point where I was standing, seized me and kissed me violently! . . . Having been kissed by Stalin, I am now immune to any form of osculation, and I listened to as genuine an outpouring of enthusiasm as I have ever heard . . . Blum himself said to me that he felt his position had been greatly strengthened because he is attempting in his way to do what you have done in America. (William Bullitt, American Ambassador in Paris, reporting to Franklin Roosevelt in November 1936 after the latter's re-election as President)[1]

Du pain et du travail: bread and work: such was the cry of innumerable demonstrations in the streets of France during the 1930s. If 'fascism' was the child of Depression, and war of fascism, bringing bread and work to the people of France was the fundamental objective of Blum's exercise of power. It was fundamental also because the Socialists argued that the financial crises which had brought down at least five governments since 1932 were simply the result of the Depression. If this were correct, Blum's political survival depended on economic recovery: the fate of Mac-Donald's Labour government provided a recent lesson in the political consequences of economic failure. So also did the fates of the left-wing coalitions elected in France in 1924 and 1932: in both cases financial crisis had led to political nemesis. As a result, the theme of the 'wall of money' – the French equivalent of the bankers' ramp – had entered into the demonology of the French left.

Before considering the Popular Front's response to this challenge, it is necessary to say something about the deflationary policies of their predecessors. Deflation meant two things: cutting government expenditure to eliminate the budget deficit and encouraging prices to fall. The policy had various purposes. First, it was feared that deficits would lead to price inflation. Secondly, it was argued that business confidence was a function of financial stability. Thirdly, since the devaluations of sterling (1931) and the dollar (1933), French prices had become uncompetitive. Unless French prices fell devaluation was inevitable. But this solution was denounced by the French political establishment as inflationary and immoral. The issue was debated in the most hysterical terms: Paul Reynaud, the leading advocate of devaluation, even received death threats.

Ironically, the Laval government, under which deflation supposedly reached a culmination, succeeded in exactly the opposite of its aim. The government had tried to cut government expenditure and reduce prices. But further reducing the budget deficit proved impossible, especially since it proved necessary to start increasing arms expenditure. Thus, in spite of the cuts, the deficit increased, and the government was only able to survive financially because the Bank of Finance secretly agreed to rediscount Treasury Bills. By May 1936 the number of these Bills in circulation had reached 20.8m f. (in May 1932 the figure had been 4.2m). On the other hand this monetary inflation did act to stimulate the economy and there were signs of economic recovery towards the end of 1935. One result of this was to push prices up and further undermine the franc. In short, the government whose main priority was financial stability and the defence of the franc bequeathed to its successors a slightly improving economic situation, an untenable franc parity (the Bank of France lost 16m f. of gold in 1935) and an imminent financial crisis which was only averted by disguised monetary inflation.

Defining the doctrine: *la politique du pouvoir d'achat*

Blum strongly believed that every political party needed specialists. Nowhere was this more urgent than in economic and financial policy where the left felt itself to be especially vulnerable: the standard left-wing view of Herriot's 1932 government was that it had been swallowed up by the bureaucrats of the Finance Ministry, the 'experts of right-wing governments, the Rueffs, the Rists'.[2] Rist was France's leading liberal economist; Rueff, a high official at the Finance Ministry, was a prominent liberal economist and a life-long scourge of Keynes, notorious in the inter-war years for his theory that the high level of British unemployment was caused by unemployment relief.

A particular target of left-wing suspicion were the Finance Inspectors (Rueff was one) who staffed the highest echelons of the French bureaucracy, especially the Finance Ministry itself. Recruited largely from the upper bourgeoisie and trained at the private Ecole Libre des Sciences Politiques, they were seen as representatives of the purest *laissez-faire* liberalism, ready to sacrifice the economy to financial orthodoxy. In fact there was more diversity among the inspectors than appeared from outside.[3] In the late 1930s some of them began to take considerable interest in Keynes' *General Theory* and one of them embarked on a translation in his spare time.[4] But the left-wing caricature was not entirely a myth. Ever since the beginning of the Depression the Finance Ministry officials had discouraged all expenditure programmes,[5] and they were far from sympathetic to the incoming Socialist ministers in 1936. When the government was forced to devalue in September 1936, the Ministry of Finance officials drew up a bill whose preface blamed the Socialists' financial mismanagement rather than recognizing that they had inherited an untenable franc parity. Once this document was seen by Auriol's advisers, they threatened to resign collectively in protest. In the end a crisis was avoided by the drafting of a new document. The incident showed that the incoming Socialist ministers had reason to be wary of their civil servants.[6]

Blum's concern that the Socialists should have their own experts did not go unfulfilled. In a country where economics was a poor relation of the education system and the economic expertise of most politicians was minimal, the Socialists' record was not discreditable. Blum himself had no formal training in economics but he tried as far as possible to remedy this deficiency, and at least half his leaders in Le Populaire treated economic issues in a consciously didactic spirit. Blum's economic knowledge, was certainly no more rudimentary than Roosevelt's, and like Roosevelt he sought out intelligent and unorthodox advice wherever it could be found. In 1934 he offered the editorship of the economic page of Le Populaire to the 24-year-old Robert Marjolin, one of the fathers of French planning after 1945. Recently returned from a year in Roosevelt's America, Marjolin had started to turn himself into an economist by ignoring such French economics as existed and assimilating the work of Keynes and other English-speaking economists. Among Blum's confidants was the journalist Georges Boris who held a number of heterodox opinions – he was among the earliest advocates of devaluation in France – and later became one of The General Theory's first readers in France.[7] Among professional economists in the party were the Austrian-born Marxist Lucien Laurat and the future deputy André Philip. Blum also enjoyed good relations with the Jewish banker Horace Finaly, director of the powerful Banque de Paris et des Paysbas (Paribas). Finaly was one of those shadowy but influential figures at the intersection of politics, finance and journalism. His sympathies were with the left, reminding us that even if the 'wall of money' did exist, it had cracks. The Socialists needed such friends badly.

To further improve the Socialist Party's technical expertise, Jules Moch set up a sort of Socialist think-tank, the Union of Socialist Technicians (UTS), which was recruited especially from Socialist polytechniciens, among whom was Moch himself. The UTS later provided several members of the government's Secretariat. Although it met with suspicion from the party hierarchy, the UTS had the personal support of Blum

himself. The party's official spokesman on financial affairs was Vincent
Auriol, a close friend of Blum. Auriol was a fiery speaker but a maker of
phrases rather than policy. This made him popular with the party rank
and file but for François Bloch-Lainé, at that time a very young Finance
Inspector with sympathies on the left (he had voted Socialist in 1936), he
could 'not be taken seriously'.[8]

According to the Socialist diagnosis, the economic crisis was not, as
pundits of the right believed, due to overproduction or overindustriali-
zation but to underconsumption. Socialist economic policy was, to quote
Blum, 'guided by one overriding idea: to use the power of the State to
increase the purchasing power of the masses'. This was the purpose of the
celebrated purchasing power policy (*politique du pouvoir d'achat*). What
were the origins of this analysis? Some historians have mentioned the
example of Roosevelt. Certainly Blum viewed the course of the New Deal
with interest, and Boris, Marjolin and Philip all wrote studies of the
American experience. But the Socialist position had in fact already been
largely worked out by 1933, before Roosevelt became President, and at
least in the early stages of the New Deal, Blum was sceptical as much as
sympathetic: 'we are not lying in wait for his failure', he wrote of
Roosevelt in 1933, 'but nor do we want to stake our reputation on his
success'. By 1936, as the epigraph to this chapter shows, he had become
more enthusiastic. In short, the New Deal gave heart to Blum in 1936, but
it was not the original inspiration of his policy. In Blum's view, the flaw in
Roosevelt's approach was that it derived merely from inspired empiricism
– something he came to appreciate only later – not from a Marxist
analysis. For the Socialists the underconsumption at the root of the
Depression was an inevitable result of the contradictions of capitalism and
could only be ultimately resolved by Socialism. The party's analysis, then,
remained firmly within a Marxist framework, and this is important to
remember when considering its attitude to such solutions as planism.

To state the impossibility, within capitalism, of eliminating the causes
of the Depression, was a somewhat negative stance for a party after all
constrained to work within that system. Thus the rationale of the
politique du pouvoir d'achat was that, even if the ultimate causes of the
Depression could not be cured, it was possible to provide temporary relief.
To raise purchasing power, the Socialists proposed a whole range of
measures: unemployment insurance, agricultural marketing boards,
public works, and a reduced working week at unchanged weekly wages.
The details of these proposals were modified between the onset of the
crisis in 1932 and Blum's election victory. This was especially the case
regarding the shorter working week – probably the central plank in the
programme. The Socialists had originally seized on the figure of forty

hours largely for reasons of euphony.[9] But by 1936 more realistic counsels had prevailed and the Socialist manifesto of that year specified no particular figure. Although little research had been carried out on the economic implications of shortening the working week, Moch proposed that the reduction should vary depending on the sector involved. The policy had a double purpose: to mop up unemployment by redistributing the available jobs and to stimulate the economy by raising aggregate demand. To objections that the resulting increase in production costs would aggravate the Depression by driving more businesses to bankruptcy, the Socialists argued the contrary: as a result of rationalization labour had become a less important factor of production than fixed capital costs; unit costs could be reduced not by wage reductions but by spreading fixed costs over increased output, that is, by stimulating demand. If, then, the details of the *politique du pouvoir d'achat* were susceptible to modification, its broad aim was constant: to offer an alternative to deflation.

What was the Socialists' attitude to the two other major subjects of economic debate before 1936 – the budget deficit and devaluation? It was vital that the Socialists develop a view on these issues because public finance and foreign exchange crises had scuppered the left in 1924–6 and 1932–4. On the first issue the Socialists argued that it was futile to subordinate economic policy to budgetary orthodoxy because the deficit was a consequence of the crisis. This was not an argument for the deliberate creation of a deficit, rather an assertion that only Socialists could restore balanced budgets. But the implication was that a provisional deficit might be unavoidable. The Socialists also advocated a less narrow conception of accounting: when yet another budget balancing measure was drafted in 1933, they proposed instead a six-year programme of capital expenditure to be financed by borrowing; spending of this kind should not be included in the annual budget.

But this did not explain how the government would survive if it could not borrow the necessary funds, a prospect which had loomed on several occasions between 1932 and 1936 when even governments of the right had found the banks reluctant to take too much government paper. When, in 1935, it seemed likely that a Popular Front government might take power, the financial question became more pressing. The Communist solution was a capital levy and increased taxation. But the Socialists opposed major tax increases during a Depression. Blum's solution was therefore different. Before the new economic policy had had its beneficial effects on the financial situation, the government would meet its obligations as the right had done: by rediscounting Treasury Bills at the Bank of France; and if the Bank refused this facility to a government of the left, the government would simply not meet its payments, and appeal to the patience of the *fonctionnaires* until the resistance had been overcome. This unreassuring idea was largely a means of avoiding the issue: the truth was that the Socialists had no financial policy beyond hoping that success on the economic front would obviate the need for one.

On the subject of devaluation Blum attempted to introduce some rationality into a dangerously passionate debate. His concern was less to present a case for or against devaluation than to demistify the issue. From the moment that Roosevelt had devalued in 1933 Blum questioned publicly if it would be possible to maintain the franc parity indefinitely. The corollary of this view was the need to 'prepare public opinion which still lacks a sense of reality'. In April 1934 he tentatively suggested that devaluation might be desirable, arguing that it was at the origin of Britain's recovery. These statements seem cautious but in the atmosphere of the day they were at the limits of political respectability. A year later Blum had moved away from this position: devaluation was psychologically difficult in countries, such as France, which had experienced important inflation in the 1920s. And the Socialists fought the elections on the unrealistic platform of 'neither devaluation nor deflation'. As devaluation became economically more urgent it had become politically more sensitive. Blum admitted to the Socialist Party Congress in 1935 that he felt 'ill at ease' in discussing the issue publicly. Marjolin who made favourable remarks about devaluation in *Le Populaire* received a mailbag of angry letters from party members. Thus Blum was forced into a constrained silence. But he was not the only Socialist to have his doubts: Marjolin, Auriol, Moch, Laurat and Philip were all to different degrees convinced of the need to devalue. This was an area where the Socialists displayed considerably more lucidity than most in the face of national hysteria.

A third topic of economic debate within the party was planism. Planism was taken up by two *tendances* within the party: Révolution Constructive, a group of young Socialist intellectuals, including Georges Lefranc, who were disillusioned with the previous performances of Socialism in government; and a group run by Laurat which presented planism not as a strategy for stabilizing capitalism but as a transition from capitalism to Socialism – a sort of French NEP. As well as these two groups, a number of individuals such as Moch and Philip were also won over. The success of planism within the party was not, however, helped by the fact that it had also been immediately taken up by the dissident Neo-Socialists who found in it a radical gloss for their political reformism.

Planism was debated at the Socialist Party Congress of 1934 with a mixture of incomprehension and hostility. For the Party hierarchy any tampering with Marxist shibboleths was sacrilege. But it was Blum who offered the most careful reflections. In his attack on the Neo-Socialists, Blum had already warned that they were hoping to fight fascism by using its own weapons. He saw both their renunciation of internationalist Socialism (in favour of . . . national Socialism?) and their preoccupation with the *classes moyennes* (turning 'Socialism, a class party, into a party of *déclassés*') as signs of this. By implication Blum detected similar dangers in planism. He also predicted that the mixed economy proposed by the planists would become permanent: the market sector would be consolidated. Socialists could not accept such restrictions on their action: the task was to 'maintain Socialist doctrine in its integrity, its purity'. For Blum, then, whose thought was confined within the polarities of capitalism or Socialism, exercise of power or conquest of power, de Man's distinction between structural and redistributional reforms was fictional within capitalism: the only meaningful structural transformation was the total socialization of the means of production. Retaining this eschatological belief in the idea of the revolution saved the Socialists from revisionist temptations.[10] It was no coincidence that planist circles in France were to be among the most receptive to Keynesianism. Blum was also astute enough to see the germs of fascism in planist thinking: it has recently been argued by Zeev Sternhell that planism laid the bases in France of a nationalist, authoritarian, anti-Marxist, anti-parliamentary 'Socialism' which attempted to appeal to all classes.[11] And it is indeed the case that many planists gravitated towards fascism (but many did not). On the other hand, although planism was probably not the economic panacea that its advocates believed, it did at least offer, at the theoretical level, a more logical position than that of Blum, who was in 1936 to take on the task of applying what he believed to be palliatives to a system he believed to be doomed.

Even if planism was officially defeated within the Socialist Party, it remained influential: many planists were to hold important positions within Blum's administration. Various disaffected Socialist planists, such as Laurat and Lefranc, joined Jouhaux's brains trust. Generally the planists pushed the party into thinking more seriously about economic policy. They also stimulated it to revalue its attitude towards nationalizations. For the planists nationalization was crucial. The Socialists were less convinced. Although some nationalizations had been included in the party's 1932 election manifesto, at this time they played only a peripheral role in the party's anti-Depression strategy. But in August 1935 Blum devoted a series of articles to the problem of nationalization. He first established a distinction between 'socializations' which involved expropriation without compensation, and 'nationalizations', which could be carried out by a non-Socialist government within the framework of capitalism. In short: 'nationalization is to socialization what the exercise of power is to the conquest of power'. Having thereby deflated the planist claim that nationalizations represented a 'structural' transformation, Blum went on to show how they could contribute to fighting the Depression by giving the government direct control over vital sectors of the economy.

Thus a limited tactical convergence between planist and Socialist views occurred at the moment that negotiations were beginning over the Popular Front programme. The Socialist negotiators joined with those from the CGT in advocating nationalizations. But they were unable to overcome the hostility of the Radicals and Communists. The programme did include the nationalization of the armaments industry but this was on political not economic grounds. It also demanded greater state control over the Bank of France. This did not mean that there was any intention – as there certainly was by the planists – to use the Bank as the instrument of a planned credit policy. The Bank was a target because of the political role it was believed to play in undermining governments of which it disapproved. It was the citadel of the 'two hundred families'.

The programme of the Popular Front contained, then, only the crudest lineaments of an economic policy inspired loosely by the *politique du pouvoir d'achat*. It proposed a series of measures to increase purchasing policy: a national unemployment fund; a Wheat Marketing Board to increase agricultural incomes; a reduced working week (no figure specified) at unchanged wages. On details the programme was silent: no figures, for example, were given for the proposed public works plan. Most serious of all, it was not clear how the measures were to be financed. The Communists' solution was 'to make the rich pay'. This was because they viewed the programme less as a solution to the crisis than as a means of political mobilization. The programme should therefore ideally be a list of demands: 'demands unite, theories divide'.[12] Blum was sceptical of how much could be expected from the Communist tax proposals, and the CGT planists attacked them as demagogic. The Popular Front programme did include some mention of tax increases and suppression of tax fraud, but the fundamental problems of finance were avoided. Devaluation, which would have been one solution to the problem, was not mentioned, being opposed by both the Communists and the Radicals. To prevent it the programme envisaged the possibility of exchange controls. In short, the programme left many questions unanswered. But it was a more far-reaching document than the Radicals could have been persuaded to sign four years earlier, and unequivocally condemned the deflation which most Radicals had supported since 1932. Many conservative Radicals remained unconvinced by the new policy, but the balance of power in the party had shifted away from them. Daladier, who was totally ignorant about economics, had emerged as a leading opponent of deflation. The Popular Front programme may then have been a vague and incomplete document, deserving all the criticisms which have been made against it, but it clearly committed any incoming government of the left to a radical reversal of the economic policies which had been followed in France since the beginning of the Depression.

Applying the doctrine: the Blum experiment

The importance that Blum attached to economic affairs was reflected in the fact that all the major portfolios in this field went to Socialists. As his Finance Minister, Blum made the predictable choice of Auriol. But in spite of the Socialist efforts to build up a team of economic specialists, André Delmas was shocked to discover that even a few days before taking over his post, Auriol had still not selected his advisers.[13] This state of unpreparedness probably reflected the Socialists' surprise at winning the election, but it was hardly encouraging if the government hoped to resist the orthodoxy of the Finance Ministry officials. To coordinate economic policy and provide an alternative to the Finance Ministry, Blum set up a National Economic Ministry. An under-secretary for the national economy had existed since 1930 but this had been a post without political influence or staff. To head the new ministry Blum appointed Charles Spinasse, a Socialist sympathetic to planism. Attached to the General Secretariat was a section responsible for coordinating public works expenditure, a symbol of the importance that the government hoped to attribute to this area of policy. Within the Secretariat as a whole, responsibility for economic policy fell to the Socialist deputy E. Antonelli who had been a member of Jouhaux's brains trust. Among planist sympathisers who held influential positions were Gaston Cusin, a CGT planist from the Civil Servants union, who became a member of Auriol's *cabinet*, and Georges Soulès of the Révolution Constructive group, a *polytechnicien* and member of the UTS, who served both in the public works section of the Secretariat and on the staff of the National Economic Ministry. Also at the Ministry were Jacques Branger and Jean Coutrot, both industrialists and *polytechniciens*, and although not Socialists, both advocates of a neo-liberal version of planning; Coutrot was involved in innumerable planning groups.

These attempts to improve the quality of economic policy-making gave Blum's government a somewhat technocratic air, but they were ultimately ineffective. Spinasse's ministry lacked weight and staff: Alfred Sauvy, who worked for Spinasse, described him as a 'minister without a ministry'.[14] In the autumn of 1936 the ministry drafted a planning project which was ignored by the government.[15] Soulès's contribution was to produce a report showing how the employers were sabotaging many of the Popular Front's reforms. The public works section of the Secretariat was confronted with the hostility of the Ministry of Finance and in December 1936 its three leading members resigned in frustration. Power remained with the Finance Ministry. Soulès became quickly disillusioned: the government seemed to be living from day to day.[16] This is certainly true of the early and most productive days of the government: planning of any kind was impossible when the most important priority was to end the strikes. *None* of the measures promised by Blum at the Matignon negotiations had been included in the Popular Front programme, even if the purchasing power theory made it easy to accept them theoretically. As Jules Moch remarked pertinently to later critics of Blum's economic management: in June 1936 policy was not made in a laboratory.[17]

The economic policy of Blum's first government falls into three phases.[18] The first, from June to September 1936, was the period of reflation without devaluation, faithful to the election slogan 'neither devaluation nor deflation'. This period saw a whole series of policies intended to stimulate demand: the Matignon wage increases, the 40-hour week at unchanged weekly wages (applied on an industry-by-industry basis between September 1936 and March 1937), the setting up of the Wheat Marketing Board, the repeal of various deflation decrees, and a public works programme. Of the measures in the Popular Front programme designed to raise purchasing power, only two had not been carried out by the end of the year (and were not to be so): the setting up of a national unemployment fund and of a comprehensive pensions scheme.

Although Blum called the public works scheme 'a capital element' in his economic strategy,[19] even in this first period his public spending plans were hardly more adventurous than those of his predecessors. Jouhaux, meeting Blum in June 1936, was worried by the timidity of his ideas on public works.[20] The spending bill passed in August 1936 proposed 20m f. of new expenditure over three years of which 4m f. was to be started in 1936. But only 1m f. were actually allocated for 1936, and the distribution of the expenditure was dictated more by political bargaining than economic criteria: rural interests received 29 per cent of the spending for 1936. Even before the plans for 1937 were amputated by the 'pause', then, the public works programme had played a subordinate role in Blum's economic policy.[21]

The second phase of policy was inaugurated by the devaluation of September 1936. The government did not renounce its commitment to reflation but the emphasis of the policy changed: it was argued that devaluation, besides stimulating exports, would attract capital back into France, reduce interest rates and encourage business confidence and investment. The third phase, beginning with the announcement of the pause in February 1937, was one of budgetary retrenchment. This reversal of policy occurred as a result of a treasury and exchange crisis and did not represent an economic conversion. But it was given an economic rationale: to win back the confidence of investors and allow the country to digest the reforms already carried out.

These three phases of policy were characterized by one important continuity: Blum's pledge to work within capitalism, within the exercise of power. He later claimed that he had offered himself as the 'loyal manager' of capitalism; in return he appealed at the outset for 'loyalty' from the capitalist class. The different phases of the Blum experiment were, then, different ways of trying to refloat French capitalism. Blum, who had once criticized Roosevelt's pragmatism, now came to admire it: he told Jouhaux in May 1936 how 'Roosevelt's boldness has enabled him to change his methods when he recognized that the desired ends had not been achieved. Thus nothing is definitive.'[22] This became Blum's model.

There is no doubt that economically the Blum experiment was a failure. The first phase brought to an end the recovery which had started in 1935: between May and September 1936 (the first month of normal production after the strikes and holidays) industrial production fell by 7 per cent, having increased by 4 per cent during the same period of the previous year. The seasonally adjusted index of unemployment rose from 165 to 167: in May 1936 there were 1,100 fewer assisted unemployed than in May 1935; in September 1936 there were 34,000 more than in September 1935. Wholesale prices had increased by 12 per cent and retail prices by 5.5 per cent. The trade deficit had marginally improved, but this, being largely due to a fall in imports of raw materials, was itself a symptom of the industrial downturn: exports of manufactuctures had declined by 2 per cent. The results of the first four months showed, then, the folly of attempting to reflate an economy with an over-valued currency: the increased production costs made French industry yet more uncompetitive.

In the second phase there was a recovery. The index of industrial production rose from 81 in September to 94 in March, its highest level since June 1931. The seasonally adjusted unemployment index fell from 174 in September to 143 in April 1937, when the number of assisted unemployed stood at 368,400; the comparable figure for 1936 was 465,100. The true unemployment figure was probably the lowest since 1933. Paradoxically, devaluation resulted in a deterioriation of the trade deficit. This was not however entirely unhealthy: there was an increase in exports of manufactures (the index rose from 74 in October to 88 in April) but also in imports of industrial raw materials. More ominously, imports of manufactures also rose, indicating that French industry, in spite of its recovery, found it hard to respond to increased domestic demand. There was one black spot: prices continued to rise, threatening the competitive advantage procured by devaluation. The Popular Front had unleashed an inflationary spiral comparable to that of the 1920s.

In the third phase the recovery came to a halt. Industrial production began to decline in March: by July it had fallen to 85, the lowest level since the end of 1935. The seasonally adjusted index of unemployment remained more or less at the level reached in April, rising slightly. A small improvement in the trade deficit only reflected a decline in imports of raw materials and the fact that French prices were rising faster than world prices: in volume, exports of manufactures were falling. Wholesale prices had risen 48 per cent in a year, and retail prices by 27 per cent. Inflation put at risk the wage increases won in June: by May 1938 real wages were roughly at their pre-Matignon levels. This is not to conclude that the Popular Front was ultimately a negative experience for the French working class. In the first place, there was almost certainly an improvement in factory working conditions as well as the winning of paid holidays. Secondly, the Matignon Agreements had also included the readjustment of exceptionally low wages: workers in this category probably did gain overall. Finally, although unemployment began to go up again, there had been a once and for all reduction of 70,000. But these achievements were far short of what had been hoped. The upturn in the economy which took place in the autumn of 1936 was cut short in the spring of 1937: the Popular Front failed to produce a durable recovery.

A number of reasons have been invoked to explain this failure.[23] All commentators would agree that Blum was wrong not to devalue immediately. The first question to answer, therefore, is why he crippled his economic experiment for four months by delaying a measure which was necessary and inevitable, and which would have helped the French economy absorb the increased production costs. Why, instead of boldly announcing a devaluation in June, when the government had public opinion on its side and could blame the measure on its predecessors, was it panicked into one in September? In fact, although on taking office Blum and Auriol both announced their opposition to devaluation, the background to the decision went back to the first days of the government.[24]

On 6 June Auriol was sounded out by the American Financial Attaché, Cochran, over a possible French devaluation. Auriol was not entirely discouraging but insisted that devaluation must be part of an international monetary agreement including other gold block countries; he was not against continuing discussions providing they remained confidential. A few days earlier Blum had independently consulted Emmanuel Monick, French Financial Attaché in London and a longstanding advocate of devaluation within the Finance Ministry.[25] Monick presented the choice before the government: exchange controls and autarchy or devaluation carried out as part of an international monetary agreement which would strengthen French ties with Britain and America. Blum opted for the second alternative and sent Monick to canvas American reactions. Roosevelt was sympathetic but insisted that Britain be brought in. The pressure for immediate action was reduced by the end of June when the conclusion of the strikes halted the capital flight. Monick did not therefore see the British until mid July when he was assured that there would be no retaliation against a reasonable French devaluation. But the British, haunted by the deflationary effects of clinging to an overvalued pound in the 1920s, would make no formal commitments about pegging the sterling exchange rate, as the French desired.

The negotiations, which petered out in August, were resumed in September as the franc again came under speculative pressure. Auriol presented Cochran with a plan for French devaluation accompanied by a joint tripartite agreement guaranteeing fixed new exchange rates and setting as its ultimate goal a restoration of the gold standard. The British found this document 'inconceivably French' and 'even more hopeless' than expected: as in July they would give no guarantees. The Americans were less hostile but suspicious of any mention of the gold standard. When Auriol proposed yet another draft still including mention of the gold standard, Roosevelt saw it as 'a lot of hooey'.[26] Finally, Auriol, under great pressure as speculation against the franc intensified, was obliged to retract his original proposals: the idea of a joint tripartite declaration was dropped in favour of the simultaneous declaration of three separate statements; there were pieties about peace and freedom but no reference to the gold standard; and the British agreed not to retaliate against French devaluation and 'as far as possible' hold the sterling rate. Before this agreement could be published the three governments had to agree on the new parities: the franc was to be devalued by between 24 and 32 per cent (this meant a rate of between 100 and 115f. to the pound). An Exchange Stabilization Fund of 10m was set up to control fluctuations of the franc within its new limits. The Tripartite Declaration was issued on 26 September. This was not a moment too soon since the gold reserves of the Bank of France had fallen perilously close to the 50m considered as a necessary minimum war chest by the French high command.

It is clear, then, that whatever their public statements – and it would have been folly to announce a devaluation before carrying it out – Blum and Auriol had not given up their openmindedness about devaluation: 'we are not children', Blum said later.[27] Some versions of events, including that of Monick, suggest that Blum had his hand forced by the Ministry of Finance officials, most of whom were by this time committed to devaluation. But Blum seems to have needed little pushing although he was hesitant to take the plunge, and possibly flirted during the summer with the idea that devaluation might be avoided. Auriol was even more cautious as his evasive replies to Cochran showed; he told Belin in May that he would never devalue although he had argued for it on the Comité du Rassemblement Populaire in 1935.[28] But for both Blum and Auriol the problem was the same: to present devaluation in a form acceptable to French opinion. Hence the strategy pursued by Monick in June and Auriol in September of using the Americans to push the British into an international agreement. It was this need for an agreement which delayed devaluation: Bullitt remarked only half-facetiously that the French were trying to portray their devaluation as an appreciation of the dollar and sterling 'to make it look as if America and England had finally realised that their currencies were wrongly valued'.[29] The need for Anglo-American approval probably also made the French over-cautious in negotiating the level of devaluation which has been criticized as too moderate in the light of the Matignon wage increases.

It is no doubt true that Blum believed the more highsounding aspirations of the Tripartite Agreement, but its main purpose was to attenuate the political impact of devaluation within France. The reasons for this are clear enough. Four years of hysterical anti-devaluation propaganda had created a situation where even some of its partisans doubted whether it could work in France: prophecies of hyper-inflation could become self-fulfilling if panic occurred. Auriol's warning during the international currency negotiations that the wrong kind of declaration could lead to Communist riots and the fall of the government,[30] was more than just a bargaining counter. In fact, although there was some ritual opposition from the right, the Communists and some Radicals, the sun did not fall out of the sky. It was probably a mistake for the Socialists not to have seized the nettle of devaluation at the outset but if, as Mendès France has said, devaluation was the Socialists' 'inheritance', so too was the psychosis about it. Their caution was only too understandable.

The delay in devaluing is not a sufficient explanation for the failure of the Blum experiment, given that once devaluation did take place there was a shortlived recovery. We need to find other explanations for Blum's failure. To what extent was it attributable to the flaws in the *politique du pouvoir d'achat* theory itself? First, one might consider what could be called 'technical' criticisms of the doctrine. Contemporary critics, such as Charles Rist, claimed that it simply represented a transfer from one section of the population to another, and that its economic effects would be neutral. To this the Socialist answer was, first, that the working-class marginal propensity to consume (the term was not used) was higher than that of the bourgeoisie, and secondly, that some of the increased purchasing power would be distributed by the state (via public works) thereby mopping up hoarded capital. These arguments had validity but the second depended on being able to attract this capital, something which proved less easy than expected. What the Socialists did not argue, since this would have been economically heretical, was that the increase in purchasing power could come about by monetary inflation (advances from the Bank of France): in fact, as we shall see, this is what actually happened.

Two of the economists most critical of the Blum experiment, J.-M. Jeanneney and Alfred Sauvy, claim that the Socialists miscalculated by underestimating labour as a proportion of total production costs.[31] André Philip, *rapporteur* of the bill introducing the 40-hour week, estimated labour costs at 40 per cent of total costs, whereas, according to Jeanneney, probably only 20 to 30 per cent of production costs were totally independent of labour costs: the Socialists had failed to take account of the knock-on effects of increased labour costs incorporated into industrial raw materials. The effect of the Matignon Agreements, the paid holidays and the 40-hour week was to raise labour costs by 44 per cent. Although this was a problem that the Socialists certainly underestimated – even if not so seriously as sometimes alleged[32] – they hoped, over-optimistically, that economic recovery would be underway before these costs were passed on in increased prices. But more effective price controls would have been necessary to prevent industrialists anticipating the increased costs. As for the hope that these costs could be absorbed by increasing production, we shall see below why this was not realized. Close to these technical criticisms is the 'liberal' critique of Blum's economic policies: that although announcing his intention to work within capitalism, Blum failed to respect the logic of the system. Rather than stimulate investment by offering the prospect of increased profit margins (by means of devaluation) he expected employers to invest while rising costs were squeezing their profit margins. This was, says Jeanneney, to require of them 'an act of faith in the success of his policy'.[33] Perhaps this was true about the period up to October, but it does not explain why the industrial recovery which took place at the end of the year was accompanied by an important stock market recovery – the value of French shares in January 1937 was double that of July 1936 – or why a downturn occurred more or less as the government was imposing policies designed to reassure investors in the shape of the 'pause'.

The 'planist' critique of Blum is that the *politique du pouvoir d'achat* was a classic 'redistributional' policy: the economy could not recover without nationalizations. The only measure of this kind carried out was the nationalization of the armaments industry. The reform of the Bank of France, although falling short of nationalization, gave the government effective control over the Bank and ended the days when it could oppose the government's monetary policies. But nothing was done to modify the Bank's mode of operations and the reform had therefore no economic repercussions. Blum's refusal to introduce nationalizations was, we know, a result of his respect for the Popular Front programme and his dependence on Radical support. Whether nationalizations would have substantially aided the government must remain a matter for conjecture. The nationalization of the armaments industry certainly did have beneficial effects on this sector. The increase in aircraft production in 1939 was made possible by the successful modernization of what had been an extremely backward industry. But this reorganization had taken almost three years. And time was an ingredient which, given the financial situation, Blum did not possess. In the short term, 'structural' reforms would only have increased the suspiciousness of financial circles towards the government. Thus it is hard to see how they could have been imposed without exchange controls, and this, we shall see, was something which Blum was reluctant to contemplate.

Exchange controls were seen as desirable by the Polish economist Kalecki who used the Blum experiment in 1937 as a case study for the application of Keynesian economics. His main conclusion was that the Popular Front had reflated the economy insufficiently: more monetary inflation was necessary. And given the existence of what he called 'absurd prejudices' by capitalists on this subject, Kalecki argued the need for exchange controls to allow the experiment to proceed.[34] But he did not consider whether French industry was capable of meeting the increased demand that further reflation would impose on it.

The issue of production is central. Most analysts of Blum's economic policy are united in condemning the effects of the 40-hour week on production; and even those broadly sympathetic to Blum are reduced to pleading politically mitigating circumstances.[35] But it is worth noting that even contemporary opponents of the 40-hour week failed to predict its consequences for production and only attacked its effect on costs.[36] Blindness on this question was evenly distributed. One reason for this was the popularity of so-called 'theories of abundance' which claimed that the problem of production had been solved. By the spring of 1937 the 40-hour week had been applied throughout the economy. And it was in March 1937 that industrial output came up against, as it were, the ceiling imposed by it on production. The intention had been that employers would make up for the lost working hours by taking on unemployed workers, but this failed to take account of the fact that many of them were unskilled and unable to fill the newly created jobs. The number of assisted unemployed fell by about 70,000 in 1937.[37] What remained was largely residual unemployment, that of old or unskilled workers, and required specific re-training policies. The crucial sectors of coalmining, iron, steel and mechanical production all claimed to be unable to meet orders owing to shortages of skilled labour. At the beginning of 1937 the French economy was effectively in a situation of near full employment.

In the words of the historian who has most carefully studied this subject, 'the 40-hour week froze the maximum number of available working hours at about the minimum level of hours actually worked during the deepest moment of the Depression'.[38] Blum's defenders have two not entirely convincing answers to this charge. First, at Riom, Blum himself argued that the 40-hour week did not restrict production since most French factories were not even working forty hours in 1936. Although this statement is incorrect for industrial establishments of over 100 workers (the only ones for which statistics exist), the Socialist Etienne Weill-Raynall has suggested that in smaller factories, which accounted for 60 per cent of the workforce, employers may have been more reluctant during the Depression to lay off workers and more likely to put them on short-time working.[39] Even if this were accurate, it was the larger plants producing capital goods which were most vital to a recovery; and anyway the government ought surely to have based its policies on known statistics rather than guesswork.

Secondly, Mendès France and Moch have pointed out that during a depression the workforce tends not to operate at full capacity: 'slack' could be taken up during a recovery.[40] This also is a plausible hypothesis. Although we have seen that the Depression was in fact characterized by an inténsification of factory discipline, against which there was a reaction after 1936, it is possible that improving working conditions would have had beneficial effects on productivity. But the evidence on productivity is contradictory, and statistics are lacking. Kalecki calculated that given that between April 1936 and April 1937 total hours worked had fallen by 5 per cent and production increased by 3 per cent, productivity had increased by 4 per cent (the statistics only apply to factories employing over 100 workers). But the only reliable figures on productivity, which come from the key mining industry, show a decline of 8.5 per cent by the end of 1937. In the mines of the Nord the economic recovery stimulated increased demand for coal at the beginning of 1937 but they were unable even to maintain the production levels reached before June 1936. Other sources claim that this decline in productivity was replicated in most branches of industry.[41] This picture coincides very well with what we know about the atmosphere in factories and attitudes to work between 1936 and 1938; we have seen how the CGT's productivist rhetoric was ignored by the workforce.

The deleterious effects of the 40-hour law were exacerbated by the way it was applied. An anecdote by Belin illustrates the attitude of the unions: at a meeting between government and CGT in November 1936, Belin proposed a gradual application of the law taking account of the problems of different industries; Blum also favoured this but not Jouhaux who insisted on '40 hours for everyone and at once'. Blum reluctantly agreed. Union intransigence also extended to failure to allow flexible provision for overtime.[42] The result was, as one observer remarked, that the French law became a limitation on work rather than, as in America, a new norm for wages.[43] Most harmful of all was the general adoption of the 5-day week (5×8 hours), which was not actually specified in the law itself, rather than a 6-day week which would have allowed plant to be used more efficiently. Blum himself admitted in 1937 that the 5×8 formula was not the one he preferred. The uncompromising attitude of the unions is comprehensible given their previous experience of how the 8-hour law of 1919 had been by-passed: the 5×8 formula and the difficulties placed in the way of overtime were ways of making the law easily enforceable. But although the 40-hour week came to acquire such symbolic importance among the French working class, various Socialists and union leaders – Spinasse, Jouhaux, Marjolin[44] – had by the middle of 1937 realised the need for its adaptation.

But the 40-hour week was not the only reason for the production difficulties of French industry. Even after November 1938 when Reynaud effectively abolished the 40-hour week and rearmament provided a stimulus to the economy, production again bottomed out at a level not much above the peak of 1937. The Socialists had probably overestimated the productive capacities of French industry. We are well informed about the parlous state of the armaments industries which were taken over by the state in 1936. In some cases the machinery was over thirty years old and almost entirely out of date; the aircraft industry was described in a report in 1940 as artisanal. As for the mining industry, an enquiry in 1936 criticized the mining companies of the Nord for having neglected to invest in new machinery during the early 1930s, even though the low cost of labour had resulted in substantial profits.[45]

Nor did the imposition of the 40-hour week stimulate widespread investment to modernize plant. Various reasons have been suggested for this: the traditionally timid credit policies of the banks; the capital flight (probably not very significant since it affected primarily 'hot money' which would have only been put into short term investments); the hostility of industrialists to the whole Popular Front experiment. We shall examine this last issue more closely in a later chapter but at this stage we can note that the behaviour of industrialists was probably a mixture of genuine alarm and political malice. One Renault official feared in June 1937 that the Popular Front's nationalization of the arms industry was

1 6 February 1934. A burning barricade in the Place de la Concorde just opposite the French Chamber of Deputies. (Photo: H. Roger Viollet)

2 Members of the right-wing Jeunesses Patriotes League of Pierre Taittinger. (Photo: H. Roger Viollet)

3 The left's answer: the demonstration of 12 February 1934 in Paris. The placards read: 'workers unite', 'unity of action', 'fascists . . . you will not pass'. (Photo: Keystone)

PARTI SOCIALISTE

LE POPULAIRE

5 Léon Blum as Socialist leader addressing the 1932 Party Congress in a characteristic attitude of supplication. (Photo: Keystone)

7 Jouhaux speaking in 1928. (Photo: H. Roger Viollet)

4 Léon Blum as Marcel Proust (c. 1900). (Photo: H. Roger Viollet)

6 Thorez addressing the Socialist organized meeting at the Vél d'Hiver stadium, 7 June 1936. Françoise Giroud wrote later: 'Renoir took me to hear Maurice Thorez in 1936. He was captivating: Jean Gabin plus the dialectic'. (Photo: H. Roger Viollet)

8 The speakers' platform in the Place de la Nation, Paris, for the demonstration of 14 July 1936. From left to right Mme Blum, Blum, Daladier, Thorez (wearing, as almost always in this period, a tricolour sash) and Salengro. (Photo: Archive Magnum)

9   Demonstrators carrying the Popular Front oath (*serment*) during the demonstration of 14 July 1935 in Paris. (Photo: H. Roger Viollet)

0   The Mur des Fédérés demonstration of 24 May 1936. Many of the posters were painted by contemporary artists. One of them, Boris Taslitzky, later wrote, 'we carried the museum into the street . . . and returned to the people knowledge of their most precious images, at the same time as Aragon and other writers gave them back Hugo and Anatole France'. (Photo: Archive Magnum. David Seymour)

11　The biggest demonstration of all: 14 July 1936. Demonstrators crossing the Place de la Bastille and heading towards the Place de la Nation. In the background (on the right) can be seen portraits of Diderot, Voltaire and Robespierre. (Photo: H. Roger Viollet)

12　Demonstration as celebration: young Communists, dressed in costumes of the revolutionary period, marching in the demonstration of 14 July 1936. Compare this festive atmosphere with the photograph of the sombre 12 February demonstration in 1934. (Photo: H. Roger Viollet)

13 A procession of young Socialists at the Socialist meeting in the Vél d'Hiver on 7 June 1936. Blum took a break from the Matignon negotiations to address the meeting. The style of the meeting, organized by Pivert, owes much to contemporary fascist political style. The portrait is of Jules Guesde, one of the founders of the party. (Photo: H. Roger Viollet)

15 The anti-war demonstration at the Parc de St Cloud on 9 August 1936. (Photo: Archive Magnum, David Seymour)

14   Renault strikers processing at the Communist organized demonstration in the Buffalo stadium on 14 June 1936. The banner contains the symbols of the Communist, Radical (Phrygian cap) and Socialist (3 arrows) Parties, symbolizing the Popular Front alliance. (Photo: Archive Magnum, David Seymour)

16 Strikes as celebration: dancing workers occupying the shipyards of Bordeaux. (Photo: Keystone)

17 Strikes as defiance: strikers occupy the Sautter–Harlé factory in Paris. The placard shows the boss hanging from a scaffold; at the bottom is written 'one of the robbers'. Note also, as a corrective to excessive political simplification of the strikes, that three different newspapers are being displayed: *L'Humanité* (Communist), *Le Populaire* (Socialist), *Le Libertaire* (anarchist). (Photo: Keystone)

The photograph expresses much of the ambiguity of the experience of occupation: ...... mmerial factory in the Paris suburbs.

19 Employees of the Paris office of Habitations à Bon Marché (cheap housing) occupy their premises for the second time in August 1936.(Photo: H. Roger Viollet)

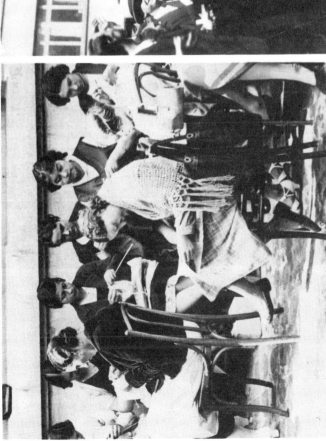

20 'The Army of Sweepers.' Employees of the Trois Quartiers department store occupy their premises and improvize their distractions: the King and Queen of the Sweepers pass under an arch of brooms. (Photo: Keystone)

21　The *congés payés* as seen by the right: Vaillant-Couturier, standing next to Jouhaux (with pipe) says: 'We are transforming Deauville according to the aesthetic of the masses.' (Cartoon first appeared in *Gringoire*)

— Les wagons de troisième classe sont bondés !
— C'est intolérable ! Tous ces gens en congé payé surchargent dangereusement les trains !

— Quelle peste, ces vacances populaires ! Tu sens celle-là comme elle empoisonne la route avec son parfum bon marché ?

— Oh ! Horreur ! Impossible de rester ici ! Ils se baignent dans notre océan, ils respirent notre air et se font brunir par notre soleil !

— Kiki, n'approche pas ces individus, tu vas attraper des puces !

22　The left's view of the right's view of the *congés payés*. The captions read:
Top left: 'The 3rd class carriages are packed'. 'This is intolerable! All these people on paid holidays are dangerously overloading the trains.'
Top right: 'How dreadful these paid holidays are! Can you smell how that girl's cheap perfume poisons the air?'
Bottom left: 'We can't stay here! They're bathing in our ocean, breathing our air and lying in our sun!'
Bottom right: 'Kiki, don't go near those people, you'll catch fleas.'(Photo: H. Roger Viollet)

23 The reality: a Normandy beach in 1938. (Photo: H. Roger Viollet)

24 The *congés payés* as art: a famous Cartier Bresson photograph of 1936.
(Photo: Archive Magnum, H. Cartier Bresson)

25 'I did not often leave my ministerial office during my period of government, but each time that I did and that I crossed the huge Paris suburbs, I saw the roads covered by streams of "old bangers", motorbikes and tandems with working-class couples dressed in matching pullovers. This gave the feeling that, through the organization of work and of leisure, I had . . . brought a ray of beauty, of light, into dark and difficult lives.' (Léon Blum, 1941) (Photo: H. Roger Viollet)

26 A writers' congress in 1936 to celebrate the birthday of Romain Rolland. From right to left: Jules Guéhenno (hand on chair and fist in air), Aragon, Gide (with glasses), Malraux. Guéhenno later wrote of such occasions: 'We held congresses, we held meetings . . . What a gallery of monsters under the glare of the lights with our little brains in a state of exaltation, each with our own illusions, our glasses glinting . . . Although embarrassed, I raised my fist with everyone else.' (Photo: Archive Magnum)

27 Jean Gabin: the worker on the screen. (Photo: H. Roger Viollet)

28 The unfinished Pavilion of Labour decorated by huge murals depicting 'Peace, well-being and Liberty.' (Photo: Keystone)

29 Facing each other across the Seine from the Eiffel tower were the two massive German and Soviet pavilions. Albert Speer, architect of the German pavilion, had seen the plans of the Russian building, and so was able to make his construction even bigger. This photograph is taken from behind the statue in front of the German pavilion looking over to the Russian. Werth commented: 'the aggressively nude Teutons in front of it were an object of loud mirth, especially to the young people who would photograph each other in the shadow of those formidable loins'. They would not be laughing three years later. (Photo: H. Roger Viollet)

only the first stage in the 'complete control of private industry'.[46] An atmosphere in which this could be believed was hardly propitious to investment confidence. It was also the case that the employers were less interested in increasing production than reducing costs. In the mines of the Nord, for example, the employers' strategy (irrespective of the problem of finding skilled labour) was not to take on sufficient new workers to compensate for the introduction of the 40-hour week but to attempt to return to the artificially high levels of output per man obtained during the early 1930s.[47]

The production difficulties of French industry were not only due, then, to the effects of the 40-hour week but also to the responses of both the employers and their workforce. Wherever the responsibility lies, the failure of the French economy to raise output undermined the whole basis of the *politique du pouvoir d'achat*. Inflation was fuelled by rising costs – which were not absorbed by increased output – and by increased demand, which came up against production bottlenecks. This in turn sucked in more imports, deepened the trade deficit and put pressure on the franc which was already being eroded by domestic inflation. It was the resulting exchange crisis, with its repercussions on government finance, which brought Blum down in June. The Socialists had argued that economic recovery would restore financial stability: the fragility of the recovery brought the Popular Front government up against its failure to confront the financial problem before 1936.

The government's financial inheritance had been disastrous.[48] Auriol's first action was to sign a convention with the Bank of France putting an end to the practice of disguised advances to the Treasury: the 13.8m f. of Treasury Bills rediscounted since 1935 were written off and the Treasury given a further credit facility of 10m f. In future these advances were to be direct and open. This was a measure which had already been suggested by Baumgartner, the leading Finance Ministry official, to the previous government. Writing off the 13.8m f. of Treasury Bills still left another 10m f. in circulation; with the ceiling on Treasury Bills at 20m f. this left a margin of 10m f. But the Senate stipulated that these two borrowing facilities – the 10m f. Treasury Bills and the 10m advances from the Bank – could not be combined: the *total* must not exceed 10m f. Given that expenditure for the second half of the year was projected at 17m f. Auriol must have accepted this restriction because ultimately he expected the difference to be funded by a devaluation.

But in the immediate term the government put its faith in the small saver: the Auriol 'Baby Bonds', which raised 4.5m f. between July and September, were aimed directly at this source. In the first flush of optimism, Blum, appealing for lenders, declared that the government could dispense with the 'bad citizens' who exported their capital: 'we appeal to French savings, those which remain, or have returned to, where they ought to be – in France'. But the speculative crisis which hit the franc at the end of August affected the French money markets: Treasury Bills were traded in, and in September the Treasury only survived by 3.4m f. advances from the Bank. The small saver was not enough.

Devaluation had a double repercussion on government finances. The revaluation of the gold reserves resulted in a 17m f. 'windfall' profit, 10m f. of which was earmarked for the Exchange Stabilization fund. The rest was used to reimburse the Bank of France for advances made to the Treasury, thus restoring the initial margin of 10m f. Devaluation was also intended to reverse the flow of capital out of France. In this it was not successful because it was too small and because of a stipulation, intended to prevent speculative profits, that holders of gold had to exchange currency at the old price or pay a penalty equal to the new value. Although in October there was an influx of capital – and for the first time in eighteen months more Treasury Bills were taken out than traded in – this was only a respite. The influx of funds ceased in November, and with a 1.5m f. decline in the circulation of Bills a new Treasury crisis loomed, the immediate situation only being tided over by further Bank advances. Nor was the prognosis for 1937 encouraging: the budget deficit was projected at 4.8m f. and the extra-budgetary deficit (arms and public works) at 16m f. A Minister of Finance memorandum in October concluded: 'to prevent us falling into inextricable difficulties again, the franc must remain in favourable position'.[49]

This was not to be. In January capital exports resumed. On 6 February Blum was warned by Rueff that if present policies continued the government would have to choose between exchange control or further currency depreciation; the only solution was to reduce the 'enormous' Treasury deficit – 'the root of the evil'.[50] Thus the government was trapped in a vicious circle: the large Treasury deficit encouraged the capital exports which made it impossible to fund the deficit. The immediate situation was saved by a British loan and then on 13 February Blum announced the pause.

Le Temps called the pause a 'conversion'. But this was not quite true. The government had passed no social legislation since the summer. On 18 October Blum had told a Radical audience of the need for a 'sufficient period of stability, of normality' to assimilate the government's reforms. This is the period that Lefranc aptly christens the 'implicit pause'. On the other hand, as late as 24 January Blum was still announcing his intention to embark shortly on a second phase of reforms: a national insurance fund and a pension scheme. The pause shelved these for an indefinite future.

What caused the shift in policy? Certainly it was in line with Rueff's advice. But the details of the pause do not seem to have emanated from the Finance Ministry: Rueff, asked to comment, saw it as 'a step down the road of a re-establishment of budgetary equilibrium', but not sufficient to reverse the flow of capital; given the signs of economic recovery, he thought it possible to jettison all public expenditure that had been undertaken with the intention of stimulating the economy. British pressure may have played some role. In early February, the Governor of the Bank of England, Montague Norman, had suggested to Labeyrie that the franc should be allowed to fluctuate, the budget curbed and Auriol replaced. René Girault has attributed considerable importance to British intervention, citing as an example of French subservience to London a letter from Auriol on 17 February assuring the British that the recent budget cuts meant that exchange controls would not be introduced; but a British authority, noting that Auriol's letter blamed the capital flight on lack of fixed exchange rates (that is on the British refusal to stabilize sterling), sees it 'hard to imagine a statement more calculated to enrage Chamberlain'. It all depends which part of the letter one chooses to emphasize. On the other hand, Chamberlain himself had no doubts about his role. After the announcement of the 'pause' he wrote:

the French are being very tiresome about their financial affairs . . . I have had a lot of trouble with them over their loan, the terms of which I did not approve. But I am inclined to think that they really did not appreciate that they were causing me any difficulty and I must say that Blum and his advisers were very ingenious in adopting the suggestions I had made to them, which amounted to a reversal of their previous policy, without involving Vincent Auriol in resignation.[51]

Although the pressure of the Ministry of Finance and the British was no doubt a contributory factor, it was successful because the pause was implicit in the logic of Blum's policy choices and in the financial situation. The crux of the financial situation was the burden of rearmament. The first rearmament programmes had been agreed by Blum's predecessors but it was Blum's government which bore the first financial consequences: rearmament expenditure in the last quarter of 1936 was 110 per cent above the same period of 1935. In September 1936 Blum announced a rearmament programme on a larger scale than any previous government. The financial repercussions of this programme would not be felt until 1937 but it had immediate psychological consequences by rekindling the speculation which finally brought about devaluation.

The reasons why Blum embarked on rearmament will be examined later. Here only the financial implications are relevant. The American Treasury Secretary, Henry Morgenthau, remarked that 'we patch up the French situation every so often but with the constantly increasing proportion of their budget going for war purposes we really cannot help them'.[52] As Blum put it in February 1937: 'it is difficult to combine a bold policy of social reform with an intense rearmament effort. We have attempted both at the same time.' A choice had to be made. This was one of the functions of the pause: to shift expenditure from social to military spending. The final budget accounts for 1937 show that civil expenditure was 2m f. below original estimates and military expenditure 800 million f. higher. As Robert Frank, the historian of rearmament comments, in terms of government spending Blum did more for guns than butter.[53]

There was a means of avoiding this difficult choice: exchange controls and the imposition of some control over the banking system. Although the possibility of exchange controls had been envisaged by the Popular Front programme we have no record of any discussions on the subject and the idea was probably tacked on as a gesture against the 'wall of money'.[54] Labeyrie was in favour of exchange controls and during the devaluation negotiations Auriol used the threat of them as a bargaining counter. But the truth is that both he and Blum had firmly rejected them. There were several reasons for this. First, they would have been unacceptable to the Radicals. Secondly, exchange controls, which existed both in Germany and Italy were seen as a 'fascist' policy involving restrictions on personal liberty, unsuitable for a democratic government dedicated to fighting 'fascism'. Thirdly, exchange controls would have alienated Britain and America, whereas the cornerstone of Blum's foreign policy was to consolidate the unity of the democratic nations against fascism. For Blum the Tripartite Agreement was a diplomatic as much as a monetary policy. He was aware of a potential conflict between his domestic economic experiment and the internationalist posture of his foreign policy but had no doubt that the former should be subordinated to the latter: 'logically our domestic policy would lead to coercive measures against capital exports and speculation . . . But this would be in contradiction with our policy of seeking common action with the great Anglo-Saxon powers.' Blum told Rueff that the domestic consequences of exchange controls did not worry him but they would have the 'fatal effect of straining the ties which unite us to the Anglo-Saxon powers, ties which are essential to the coherent development of our foreign policy'.[55]

Once exchange controls had been rejected, the government needed to win financial confidence. At the end of this road lay the pause. Was this another victory for the 'wall of money'? Was Blum betrayed by the anti-patriotism of French capital? He complained in February 1937 of the 'unfavourable disposition of capital . . . sustained by a press campaign and the intrigues of opponents'.[56] There was some truth in the accusation. The level of Treasury Bills, which in 1935 had been as high as 12m f. (excluding those rediscounted by the Bank of France), had fallen during the first half of 1937 to around 5.3m f., even though bank deposits were rising. Before 1936, on the other hand, the banks had sometimes helped out governments even when deposits were falling. Given that not all the banks' funds were taken up by the abortive economic recovery, the presumption is, as Frank suggests, that they were less willing, for political reasons, to help Blum than they were his predecessors.[57] Some of the capital exports were also no doubt politically motivated. But this is an area where prudential calculation is difficult to separate from political prejudice. Blum's policies, and the continuing labour unrest, did genuinely frighten capital holders, leading to the self-fulfilling belief that the franc could not hold. Whether they acted from malice or prudence is less important than the fact that the need to conciliate capital was implicit in the government's choices from the beginning: 'we cannot carry out both a policy of confidence and constraint', declared Auriol in 1936. The problem is that he pursued neither: the attempt, for instance, to restrict the free market in gold after devaluation did not encourage capital repatriation; its abandonment was part of the pause. But the pause, when it came, was too late. It was born of weakness not conviction and only gave encouragement to Blum's enemies to pursue their advantage to the end.

The financial crisis which brought about Blum's fall was a combination of all the factors considered above: speculative calculation, political hostility ('the wall of money'), and the strains of rearmament. The immediate financial effects of the 'pause' were favourable: the first 5m f. of the new national defence loan was subscribed within a few hours. Most of this money was repatriated French capital. But in April the respite came to an end and the capital exodus resumed. A new Treasury crisis broke in June, partly because of unexpected new armament expenditure. At the same time the money markets were seized by a panic which may in origin have been politically motivated; it was perhaps not entirely a coincidence that, at the start of June, Finaly was ousted from his directorship of Paribas by Emile Moreau, a former governor of the Bank of France and close to circles hostile to Blum.[58] From 8 June the banks began to trade in their Treasury Bills. The capital exodus intensified when the 'experts' resigned on 14 June claiming that the government had rejected their financial proposals. This act of 'treachery', as Cusin describes it, was probably too late to be the 'coup de grace': speculation against the franc had already become unstoppable.

The government asked its advisers to draw up a plan of action. On 7 June Auriol's *cabinet* produced a plan which envisaged some control over the banking system, an increase in direct taxation and a freezing of arms expenditure for three years at 1937 levels; on the same day Rueff drew up proposals for increased indirect taxation, economies in civil expenditure and a freezing of arms expenditure. When the government demanded financial decree powers from parliament on 13 June it inclined to the former plan rather than a further appeal to 'confidence'. But it is difficult to be much more precise about this because the government's intentions remained studiously vague and can only be surmised from explanations provided at the time (and later ones given by Auriol). Exchange control was still ruled out, under pressure from parliament, but 'energetic measures against speculation' were promised. This meant some control over the banks including possibly the compulsory repatriation of non-commercial foreign balances. The fall in the circulation of Treasury Bills unaccompanied by a corresponding increase in banks' commercial port-folios showed, said Auriol, that the banks had deserted the government. In December 1936 Blum claimed that, 'we have pushed economic liberalism as far as any past government, further perhaps than any other government would have done in present circumstances'. In June 1937 it seems that he had decided to go no further (though probably he did not have a clear alternative view). But he was too late: the financial bill was rejected by the Senate. The government resigned.

Blum's failure in economic and financial policy derived from his understandable attempt to evade a number of unpleasant choices. There were various 'left-wing' policies available in 1936: the Communist solution of tax increases, the planist solution of 'structural' reform, the *politique du pouvoir d'achat*. The Popular Front chose the third. Without a relaxation of the 40-hour week it is doubtful if the policy could have worked. By the spring of 1937 there were signs that some Socialists realized this and it is possible that if a Socialist led government had remained in power it could have more smoothly carried out a modification of the 40-hour week than its successors. But without an adequate financial policy the government could not last. In the summer of 1936, Blum, by appealing to the 'good citizen' and calling for 'loyalty', had hoped to elude this problem. Blum the humanist prevailed over Blum the Marxist materialist. The economic system of which he offered himself as the 'loyal manager' had its own financial logic. Blum was excessively optimistic both in his estimation of the regenerative capacities of French capitalism (curious for a Socialist) and of the likely attitude of French financial circles (curious in view of the whole mythology about the 'wall of money'). Blum's choices, however, were not simple, nor ones that he could necessarily have known in advance that he would be obliged to make. He tried as long as possible to preserve the social reforms of 1936, to carry out large-scale rearmament and to consolidate his ties with Britain and America by avoiding exchange controls and respecting economic liberalism. The 'pause' represented a first choice among these policies: further social reform was sacrificed to rearmament and liberalism. The financial bill of June 1937 represented the beginnings of an alternative choice. In the next two years the dilemma was posed in starker terms; its resolution was to bring the end of the Popular Front.

Abandoning the doctrine: from Bonnet to Reynaud

Two interconnected problems dominated economic and financial policy after June 1937: the 40-hour week and the financing of rearmament. For the right, the solution to the latter problem – after an abortive attempt to slow down rearmament – was to win the confidence of the money markets by returning to *laissez-faire* principles and abandoning Popular Front economics; for the Socialists this was an unacceptable price to pay, and they turned to exchange controls as the only way of financing rearmament without renouncing all the social gains of 1936. At the heart of this debate was the 40-hour week which came to be viewed by both sides as *the* symbol of the Popular Front. Of course it was more than a symbol: the restrictions on production that it caused hindered the rearmament programme. But we have already seen that in March 1938 the metalworkers' union did accept the need for a relaxation of the law as long as its principle was not altered, while the employers had objected less to the effects of the law on production than to it as a symbol of the new dispensation on the shopfloor and because they resented paying overtime rates. The end of the 40-hour week represented therefore both a revenge for 1936 and a means of restoring profit margins. This in turn made it more difficult for Popular Front leaders to sell any modification of the 40-hour week to their base. Paradoxically therefore, exchange control, a way of preserving the gains of the Popular Front, could also provide the left with an alibi of political respectability which allowed it to propose a relaxation of the 40-hour week: in April 1938 Blum was both to negotiate a relaxation of the 40-hour week and propose exchange control.

Neither of these problems – the 40-hour week and rearmament – were confronted directly by the Chautemps government. In economic policy as in other areas, the new government represented a transition between the semblance of a Popular Front policy and the economic liberalism imposed by Paul Reynaud. The new spirit was indicated by the abolition of the National Economic Ministry. The choice of Bonnet as Finance Minister was a programme in itself. Bonnet was an able, ambitious but highly conservative Radical known to be unsympathetic to the Popular Front. In 1933, as Finance Minister, he had defended the gold block and deflation.

Although Blum and various Socialists participated in Chautemps' *cabinet*, Blum commented at Riom that the new government had undertaken:

an economic and political programme contrary to that which I had practised and which alarmed me. I had myself at one point, in March, proclaimed the need for a 'pause'. But a 'pause' was not a reversal. I feared the effect of a return to the policy of budget balancing and increased taxation on an economic expansion which was already beginning to manifest itself in a substantial way.

Apart from its dubious final phrase, this statement was largely true. But the new government, still based on a Popular Front majority, could not abandon the former rhetoric overnight: in July 1937 Bonnet had to defend his financial strategy as necessary to consolidate the social gains of 1936.[59] He hoped to achieve the abandonment – or adaptation – of the 40-hour week. But the cabinet would not accept this and instead set up, in August 1937, a Commission of Enquiry on Production. The commission's report, produced in December, proved to be a less damning indictment of the 40-hour week than its sponsors had hoped. It suggested exemptions for certain industries, with safeguards on pay, but it also proposed government aid for the training of skilled labour and the modernization of plant.

As for financial policy, Bonnet accepted the prognosis and remedies offered by Rueff in June. The budget for 1937 was to be balanced by tax increases and the extraordinary budget reduced by cuts in what public works programmes remained. But the main effort was to come in 1938 when borrowing was to be drastically pruned. This could only be done by freezing rearmament below the level requested by the military authorities: thus, as Frank writes, Bonnet 'extended the pause to rearmament'. He also decided that holding the franc within the limits decided in October 1936 was too costly to France's gold reserves; in June 1937 the franc was devalued again. The 'Bonnet franc' was allowed to float freely and not attached to upper and lower limits like the 'elastic' Auriol franc (although initially Bonnet tried to hold the rate at 130 f. to the pound).

In the short term, devaluation again stimulated a recovery although unemployment fell no further. By the end of the year industrial output had almost reached the peak attained in March – but rose no further. At the beginning of 1938 economic activity levelled off once more, and by May had fallen to its lowest level since 1935. This new recession was attributable to the effects of the 40-hour week on productive capacity as well as to the Depression which had started in America in June 1937 and from which France had been protected initially by the depreciation of the franc. Inflation continued: in May 1938 wholesale prices were 75 per cent higher than in May 1936, retail prices 47 per cent higher. In January 1938 the largest banknote was raised from 1,000 f. to 5,000 f.. Inflation stoked labour unrest and this was a further blow to investment.

Bonnet's financial achievement was equally precarious after an encouraging start. The second devaluation had resulted in a return of expatriated capital, encouraged also by the American recession; financial circles took heart from the Rambouillet Declaration, the government's announcement in October that it would deal firmly with strikes and that exchange controls were out of the question. The new flow of funds helped the Treasury: the circulation of Treasury Bills started to rise again (this, given that there was also an industrial recovery which might have been expected to mop up funds, showed that the banks looked more kindly on Bonnet than Auriol).[60] But since Bonnet's budget cutting hardly affected expenditure in 1937, the Treasury had to resort to further advances from the Bank. The weakness of the financial situation was revealed at the start of 1938: the increase in international tension made an intensification of rearmament inevitable; the Goodrich strike undid the effects of the Rambouillet Declaration; and soon afterwards this led to the government's collapse. After a short-lived second Chautemps government Blum returned to head a second Popular Front administration.

Because Blum had no illusions about the durability of this government, its economic plan was drawn up in the certain knowledge that it would not be applied. But the plan is nonetheless important in showing how Socialist thinking on the economy had developed since June 1937. Blum himself took the post of Treasury Minister, aided by Pierre Mendès France as his Under-Secretary of State. The anschluss had made further rearmament unavoidable – though Rueff still hankered for retrenchment[61] – and this was the centrepiece of the government's policy: rearmament was to be the explicit motor of economic recovery. The most original idea was that this expenditure would be financed by a deliberate policy of monetary inflation: contractors were authorized to draw bills on the government which would be rediscountable by the Bank of France. The francs created in this way were then available to be invested in government paper: the state's expenditure would help to create the funds by which it was financed. This 'circuit' was closed by the 'centralization of exchange operations at the Bank of France', a euphemism, as one of the programme's drafters later conceded, for exchange control. There was also to be a capital levy on large fortunes.

Much has been made of the Keynesian inspiration behind this policy – 'the first French government text inspired by Keynes' General Theory, said Mendès France. Although not published in French until 1941, the ideas of the General Theory had begun to filter into French Socialist circles. Georges Boris – among its first readers in France – was Mendès France's chef de cabinet in Blum's second government, and one of the main drafters of the financial proposals. On forming his government Blum was also presented with a set of proposals drawn up by the members of Auriol's former cabinet who had continued to meet and reflect on the failure of Blum's first government. Among these was Jean Saltes, a Finance Inspector and senior official at the Rue de Rivoli, who passed on to his associates pages, as they appeared, of the translation of the *General Theory* being undertaken by his colleague Rioust de Largentaye. Cusin was also kept in touch with developments in British economics by meetings with Gaitskell, Cripps and others at various gatherings of planists and Socialists.[62]

But Blum, in his later references to his 1938 economic plan, never mentioned the name of Keynes. Instead he compared it to the war economy of Schacht in Germany. As Frank points out, although knowledge of Keynes may have given greater sophistication to the government's plans in 1938, the strategy of stimulating the economy by means of government spending was not new, even if the means – rearmament – and method – monetary inflation – were. The major development was acceptance of exchange control. Before 1936 exchange control had been, we have seen, largely absent from economic debate. June 1937 was the end of innocence. For many planists, for the CGT, for the experts of the UTS, for Cusin and the ex-collaborators of Auriol, for many rank-and-file Socialists, exchange controls became the prerequisite of a Socialist economic policy, the only way, in the words of a member of the UTS, 'to save democracy' (in 1936 it had been seen as a 'fascist' policy) and preserve Socialism. The Cusin group had drawn up its first plan for exchange controls in the autumn of 1937. They were the new panacea. In April 1938 Blum explained the reasons for this conversion: 'in June 1937, after having carried out our experiment in total good faith, after having gone to the limits of financial orthodoxy and monetary liberalism, we realised our mistake'. It was necessary to abandon pure liberalism. What made this acceptable in 1938 was that the American government had modified its hostility to French exchange controls because it saw Blum as the most resolute European opponent of Hitler. The policy, therefore, no longer jeopardized relations with America.[63]

The other innovation of Blum's programme in 1938 was the capital levy. According to Cusin this had not been included in an original draft plan drawn up by his collaborators and was added by Blum to ensure defeat in the Senate. Although Cusin's testimony has to be treated with respect this seems implausible: the plan needed little help to be defeated. Frank provides another interpretation which is borne out by Blum's own explanation at the time: capital was required to make a sacrifice to balance that required from labour which was being asked both to reduce consumption in favour of the rearmament effort and to accept longer working hours.

The fall of Blum's government paved the way towards the total abandonment of an economic policy of the left. It fell to Daladier, who defended Popular Front economics in 1936, to bury them in 1938. As such his government falls outside the limits of a study of the Popular Front. But one point must be noted: when Daladier came to power, his views on economic policy were far from fixed, and it was not until October, when he replaced his Radical Finance Minister Marchandeau by Paul Reynaud, that he definitively repudiated Popular Front economics. The pragmatic Daladier hoped to avoid a clear choice between the policy proposed by Blum in March and that demanded by the right. His only inflexible priority was the need to rearm, and he accepted Blum's upwardly revised arms spending estimates. In its financial policy the government embarked on a liberal course: it immediately announced a third devaluation by fixing the minimum value of the franc at 179 f. to the pound; Bonnet's floating franc was replaced by a sterling franc. The purpose of this third devaluation was to attract capital back to France by offering a sizeable profit on exchange transactions. This was highly successful: 18m f. were repatriated in the following months, and in the same period the Treasury was able to raise 16m f.

But on the labour front Daladier did not at once follow through the implications of this appeal to 'confidence'. His initial policy was not to confront the unions but to extend the working week by negotiations on an industry by industry basis. This policy foundered, we have seen, on the intransigence of both the unions, who could not carry their base, and the employers, who were playing for higher stakes. It was the refusal of the Metalworkers' Union which pushed Daladier into a tougher line. The Munich conference finally convinced him that confrontation with labour was both necessary and possible: necessary because it heightened the urgency of rearmament; possible because it increased his political popularity.

The consequences of Munich for financial and monetary policy were more ambiguous. The international crisis had sparked off new speculation against the franc and this convinced even the conservative Marchandeau that exchange control was the only solution; Daladier seems to have come round to the same view. But at the end of October the Radical Congress had formally put an end to the Popular Front alliance. Exchange control was compatible neither with this new political stand nor with the less conciliatory labour policy. The two strands of policy had to be brought into line. In October Reynaud was appointed Finance Minister and embarked on a resolutely liberal policy of which the most spectacular manifestation was the ending of the 40-hour week: exchange control was rejected; the CGT was crushed; confidence was restored.

In the autumn of 1938 the economy at last began to recover: between October 1938 and June 1939 industrial output rose by 20 per cent; the trade deficit was reduced by 26 per cent. But this recovery must not be exaggerated: even at its new peak in June 1939 output did not attain its pre-Depression maximum. The recovery was due largely to the huge levels of arms spending: Reynaud, the arch-liberal, presided over a state-promoted boom. Nor do we need to conclude that Reynaud succeeded where Blum failed. Blum had originally tried to resuscitate the economy by offering the working class a new place in the social order, by taking labour into partnership not, as in Reynaud's case, by driving it back into the ghetto. But in 1936 Blum had lacked, or been unwilling to apply, the financial and monetary policy necessary to protect his economic strategy. The irony is that by 1938, when the Socialists had formulated more coherent financial policies, these would have been applied not to preserve the social gains of 1936 but to provide an alibi for their abandonment. This was a measure of the extent to which the problem had changed between 1935 and 1938: the government elected to preserve peace found itself obliged to prepare for war.

7 ∽ 'Peace': the contradiction

In August 1936 at St Cloud near Paris there took place a grandiose demonstration in favour of peace: the Rassemblement pour la Paix. There were sporting displays organized by the FSGT; music was laid on by the FMP. Speeches by Blum, Duclos and others were interspersed by theatrical presentations. There was a procession of mothers. The festivities ended with the release of hundreds of pigeons and an aeronautical display in which a plane traced the word 'peace' in the sky while an orchestra played a hymn to peace. The mixture of politics, festival, pageant and entertainment made this a quintessentially Popular Front occasion. So too did its theme: peace. Of the motives which impelled people to support the Popular Front in 1934 and 1935, the defence of peace was perhaps the least talked about, but this was because it could most easily be taken for granted: the domestic threat of fascism seemed more immediately threatening; the problems of reviving the economy more immediately complicated. The negotiators of the Popular Front programme did not have any difficulty in drawing up the section relating to foreign policy: there was no difficulty in declaring oneself for peace. The oath of July 1935 offered 'peace for humanity'.

By the time that Blum came to power things seemed less simple. In March 1936 Hitler had reoccupied the Rhineland; in July 1936 civil war broke out in Spain. It was around these two problems of Germany and Spain that the Popular Front's entire foreign policy was to revolve. It is the Spanish Civil War and the issue of non-intervention which has most overshadowed historical discussion but in fact the dilemma posed by non-intervention was only a different version of that posed by Germany: was it worth risking an international war to preserve Spain from 'fascism'? Was it worth risking a conflict with Germany to preserve Europe from the spread of Nazism? In short, the Popular Front, which harboured the dual objectives of fighting fascism and war, defending democracy and peace, discovered that the objectives did not necessarily coincide: choices might have to be made.

The pursuit of peace: June 1936 to June 1937

French foreign policy since 1919 was dominated by the problem of containing Germany. The solutions to the problem had fluctuated between conciliation and intransigence; both postures stemmed from fear. The foundations of French security were the *entente* with Britain and a chain of alliances with a number of Central and East European states. But France was unable to tempt the British into a formal military alliance or to secure from them a guarantee for the frontiers of her Eastern allies. At the Locarno Treaty (1925) she had merely obtained guarantees for her own boundaries. Whether the British would support French action to help her Eastern allies was unknown. Whether France herself could effectively assist these allies was equally uncertain because French military planners had gradually adopted a defensive strategy which ignored the possibly offensive requirements of French diplomacy. The symbol of the strategy was the Maginot line.

During the 1920s, foreign policy had been a major area of conflict between left and right. Broadly speaking the right had favoured military alliances over the League of Nations and preferred to prevent German rearmament rather than pursue the chimera of general disarmament. The left had put its faith in disarmament and collective security via the League of Nations. During the early 1930s the hopes of the left became increasingly unrealistic given the aggression of Hitler and the failure of collective security to prevent the Japanese invasion of Manchuria (1932) or the Italian invasion of Abyssinia (1935). The Abyssinian episode had also caused a deterioration in Anglo–French relations resulting from Laval's attempt to avoid British pressure for sanctions against Italy. Laval was frightened of driving Italy into the arms of Germany. In fact he only alienated Britain without doing enough to satisfy Italy. France's deteriorating diplomatic situation was further undermined by the Rhineland reoccupation to which the French responded only with protests. This event had three consequences: it delivered the *coup de grâce* to collective security, demonstrated the hollowness of Locarno and alarmed France's eastern allies. If France could not even protect her own frontiers, what could she do for her friends in the East?

This 'landscape of ruins', as one historian has described it, was Blum's diplomatic inheritance.[1] The Popular Front programme provided him with no helpful guidance. It called for collective security and general disarmament, repudiated secret diplomacy, and advocated an extension to Eastern and Central Europe of the 'system of pacts open to all' based on the principle of the Franco–Soviet pact. These objectives, pious aspirations even when drawn up, were rendered redundant by the Rhineland invasion. Of the constituent members of the Popular Front alliance, only the Communists had an unambiguous line on foreign policy: the need to resist Germany by strengthening the Franco–Soviet pact.

No French politician had devoted more attention to international relations than Blum. He had long been his party's main spokesman on foreign affairs. As Premier he took enormous personal interest in foreign policy, reading daily all important diplomatic dispatches. In the 1920s Blum was strongly committed to disarmament and collective security: his outlook was internationalist, his abhorrence of war total. Although these were the features of Blum's view which most struck contemporaries, it is clear in retrospect that he never shared the unconditional pacifism of some members of his party. Having as late as 1934 rejected any return to the alliance system which had divided Europe into rival camps before 1914, he came to believe by 1935 that German aggression could only be contained by an *entente* between France, Britain and Russia.[2] And in his second major foreign policy speech as Premier, on 1 July 1936, Blum the peace-lover pronounced the following words:

international agreements are challenged or trampled on if the powers who have subscribed to them are not prepared to defend them up to the hilt. That means accepting the risk of war. It is necessary to accept the eventuality of war to save the peace.

That Blum intended to keep a close watch over foreign policy was clear from the choice of Yvon Delbos as Foreign Minister. Since the principal economic posts had gone to Socialists it was almost inevitable that the Quai d'Orsay would go to a Radical but the appointment of Delbos (after Herriot's refusal) was a surprise. He was not among the leading Radical politicians, although he was liked by, and well-known to, Blum (they inhabited the same apartment block on the Ile St Louis). Delbos was on the moderate left-wing of his party: he was known for his support of collective security and of the Franco–Soviet pact. It may have been these views which recommended him to Blum. More important probably was the fact that he was not likely to dispute Blum's conduct of foreign policy. Delbos should not be excessively belittled – he was no more mediocre than many Third Republic politicians and more honest than most – but he was not a forceful character. Daladier's view was that he was 'no fool, but frightened of his own shadow'.[3] Mention ought also to be made of Aléxis Léger, head of the Quai d'Orsay between 1933 and 1940. Léger, who was a distinguished poet (after the war he won the Nobel prize for literature) as well as a diplomat, was a somewhat shadowy figure. The extent of his influence on policy is unclear. His views on foreign policy were in the Briandist tradition – strong commitment to the *entente* with Britain, and faith in the League and collective security. As Duroselle remarks, Léger does not seem to have questioned whether policies formulated in the

1920s were appropriate to the changed conditions of the 1930s. Although the extent of Léger's influence is not always clear, he could always be relied upon to put – or even to anticipate – the British view: his role in forming the non-intervention policy was important.[4]

For both Blum and Delbos – as for Léger – the cornerstone of French foreign policy was the Franco–British *entente*. We have seen how seriously Blum viewed the Tripartite Agreement as a declaration of solidarity with Britain (and America). This emphasis on the British connexion arose because Britain was vital to French security and because both countries were 'passionately attached to liberty'. Although Blum did not speak English, he admired British culture and constitutional *moeurs*, as he had shown in his *Letters on Government Reform*. Improving Anglo–French relations was seen as especially urgent given their deterioration under Laval. Paradoxically the Rhineland invasion had already begun to repair the damage. There were of course recriminations over the British reluctance to back French resistance to Germany but the main effect of British policy had been to provide the French government with a welcome alibi for the inaction which was favoured, in any case, by most sectors of French opinion. And the Sarraut government had successfully seized upon the crisis as a means of squeezing greater commitment out of the British in the form of staff talks.[5] These began in April, and although they produced nothing substantive in themselves, they were a possible step to closer contacts.

From his first declaration on foreign policy, Blum declared that the British *entente* 'is and remains the primordial condition of European peace', a view which he, Delbos and Daladier reiterated on numerous occasions. In June 1936, the British Ambassador, Sir George Clerk, reported the French government's 'almost pathetic desire to be given the lead by, and to be closely associated with, Her Majesty's government'.[6] Blum had a preliminary meeting with the British Foreign Secretary, Eden, in May, and at French insistence a conference of the French, British and Belgian governments took place in London on 23 July to discuss the consequences of the Rhineland remilitarization. The meeting agreed to send invitations to Germany and Italy for a five-power conference to negotiate a new Locarno. Ideally the French would also have liked to invite the Poles, Czechs and other 'interested powers', but to the British this smelt too like an Eastern Locarno to be acceptable. Nothing came of the idea of a five-power conference because the Germans evaded all invitations. But the London meeting had not been entirely a wasted effort: Blum and Delbos made a favourable impression and succeeded in persuading British ministers that France had not plunged into anarchy (it was by now possible to get bacon and eggs at the Hotel Bristol).

By the end of 1936 Eden was able to assure the British cabinet that Anglo–French relations 'had never been better in recent times'. A year later the new Ambassador, Phipps, mentioned the 'cordiality' existing between the two countries. In a speech at Leamington in November 1936, Eden made a declaration which was greeted with enthusiasm in France: 'our arms may, and if the occasion arose, they would, be used in the defence of France and Belgium against unprovoked aggression in accordance with our existing obligations'. In fact this said nothing which had not been implicitly clear already.

But if Blum and Delbos had succeeded in repairing the damage done to Anglo–French relations by Laval, they had resolved none of the ambiguities of the relationship. In the first place, they failed to entice the British into closer military cooperation or joint military planning.[7] Secondly, in spite of Eden's Leamington speech, the British still refused to provide any guarantees about their reactions to German aggression, resulting from France's fulfilment of her Eastern treaty obligations. In March 1937 Halifax refused to state in advance Britain's attitude to 'hypothetical complications in central Europe'.[8] Could France run the risk of taking independent action in the expectation that Britain would be forced to intervene? Finally, to what extent was French cultivation of British friendship turning into dependence on British policy? On a whole range of foreign policy issues – Russia, the *Petite Entente*, German colonies and Spain – we shall see that the Blum government took significant account of British views. Obviously this was necessary if good relations were to be maintained, but at the end of this path lay Munich.

The French security system in Eastern Europe, out of which Halifax's 'hypothetical complications' might arise, was based on three bilateral treaties with the so-called *Petite Entente* powers – Romania, Yugoslavia and Czechoslovakia – treaties with Poland and a pact with the Soviet Union (1935) which was completed by a Czech–Soviet accord of mutual assistance whose operation was conditional upon that of the Franco–Czech alliance. This patchwork of agreements was less impressive than at first seems the case. Only with Poland was there a full military alliance. The obligations of the other treaties were subject to interpretation. The alliances were riddled with contradictions. The Poles were embroiled with the Czechs in a border dispute, and nervous about the Czech–Soviet alliance. The Poles and Romanians were suspicious of the Soviet Union and unwilling to allow Soviet troops across their borders, thus making it virtually impossible for the Russians to come to the aid of the Czechs. This rendered the Franco–Soviet pact militarily useless given the lack of any Soviet–German border. The shaky structure of alliances was further weakened by the Rhineland occupation which had the paradoxical effect of increasing France's dependence on the Eastern alliances, at the same time as threatening their continuation both because it reduced French capacity to intervene militarily to protect her allies and because it undermined their confidence in her willingness to do so. The overall result of the alliance system, as one Quai official commented, was less to protect France than to implicate her in all possible threats to peace which might arise in Eastern Europe.[9]

In spite of this gloomy prognosis, Blum's government had little alternative but to set about strengthening the alliances. The case of Poland was most immediately worrying. Poland was considered by many in 1936 to be France's most important ally militarily but her most unreliable diplomatically, owing to the tortuous policies of the pro-German Foreign Minister, Beck, who had in 1934 concluded a ten-year non-aggression pact with Germany. The Polish government remained nonetheless wary of Germany and in 1936 it asked the French government for financial aid for rearmament. If this request were granted, could Beck be trusted to abandon his flirtation with Germany? The advice of the French Ambassador in Warsaw, Léon Noël, was that France should build on the known pro-French sentiments of the Polish President, General Smigly-Rydz, and demand Beck's dismissal as the price of French aid. This plan was accepted by Delbos and Blum, Gamelin was sent to Warsaw in August 1936 to meet Smigly-Rydz. But when the Polish President arrived in Paris for a return visit in September, neither Blum nor Delbos pressed the issue of Beck's dismissal and instead accepted verbal assurances about the future course of Polish policy. They were told that in no circumstances would Poland attack Czechoslovakia and that if Czechoslovakia were attacked by Germany, Poland would respect her international obligations to the League of Nations. The agreement signed between France and Poland during Smigly-Rydz's visit granted Poland 2 m.f. of military credits with almost no guarantees in return from the Polish government.

Why was Noël's plan not pursued? Gamelin claimed in his memoirs that Noël had overestimated what could be obtained from Smigly-Rydz. But Noël, who was after all more knowledgeable about Polish internal politics, believed that Gamelin had handled the issue ineptly. It may be that Blum, who was at this time also hopeful of a Franco–German *rapprochement*, at the last moment balked at such an overtly anti-German move; it may be simply that he put too much faith in Smigly-Rydz's promises and exaggerated his influence on policy. But if Blum had failed to secure a more acceptable posture from the Polish government, so too had Barthou in 1934, operating from a much stronger diplomatic position (though it is true that in 1936 the Poles were asking for French assistance). To reconcile Poles and Czechs was, in the words of one historian, to attempt the squaring of the circle.[10]

More feasible theoretically was the prospect of strengthening the *Petite Entente* by consolidating the reciprocal obligations of its members through a mutual assistance pact to operate in case of aggression against one of the members. The main purpose of such a pact would have been a psychological one of reassuring the flagging confidence of France's *Petite Entente* allies. This in itself was of some importance since even Beneš, President of Czechoslovakia, France's closest Eastern ally, was reported in November 1936 to be contemplating overtures to Germany.[11] Possibly this was simply a means of prodding France into action because Czechoslovakia, as the member of the *Petite Entente* most liable to German aggression, had the greatest stake in a mutual assistance pact. And Delbos did need prodding. The idea of a pact was proposed in July 1936 by the Francophile Romanian Foreign Minister, Titulesco. But Delbos, reluctant to embroil France in further commitments, showed no interest at this stage. In October, however, he raised the idea himself – having perhaps heard rumours of Beneš' feelers to the Germans – and the Czechs at once produced a draft proposal. After much delay, Delbos produced a reply containing numerous reservations, ostensibly inspired by the need to win over the other two countries. And the project finally foundered on the reluctance of Romania and Yugoslavia to shoulder France's responsibility to the Czechs at the cost of alienating the Axis powers: in March 1937 the Yugoslav government signed a non-aggression pact with Italy specifying neutrality in case of war with a third party. This break-up of the *Petite Entente* might have been difficult to avoid but Delbos had done little to prevent it. R. J. Young convincingly describes his policy as one of 'wilful negligence'.[12] His lack of ardour was prompted both by the Quai which was reluctant further to extend French commitments and by discreet British disapproval of deeper French involvement in what one British diplomat called the 'irrelevant intricacies' of Balkan politics.[13]

One of the more mysterious – and, to the PCF, disappointing – features of Blum's foreign policy was the failure to strengthen the Franco–Soviet Pact in spite of Soviet attempts to turn it into a full military alliance.[14] The first contacts took place in the autumn of 1936 when the government yielded to Soviet insistence and agreed to preliminary staff talks with the Russian Military Attaché. But few meetings took place. The French negotiators dragged their feet and by the spring of 1937 the talks had petered out. In February 1937 the Soviet Ambassador Potemkin made a direct overture to Blum himself. He promised military aid to France and Czechoslovakia in the event of German aggression. If Poland and Romania refused to open their frontiers, the Soviets would send troops to France by sea, and aircraft to Czechoslovakia. In return Potemkin asked what the French would do to help the Soviet Union. After considerable delay, the French reply politely rebuffed the Soviet advances. A final overture by the Russian Foreign Minister, Litvinov, who saw Delbos in Paris in May 1937, was no more successful. This was the last such effort. In June 1937 the beginning of the Red Army purge ended any French temptation to seek closer military ties with the Soviet Union.

It would be wrong to characterize the attitude of the French government as one of hostility. Staff talks were dragged out rather than refused outright, and in May 1937 Delbos was prepared to offer an exchange of information between Military Attachés. This was a limited bait but enough not to seem entirely negative. It corresponded to the pattern of Franco–Soviet relations throughout Blum's first government: Soviet overtures were met by French prevarication.

Suspicion of the Soviet Union was shared by most of the French military and diplomatic establishment. The attitude of the general staff was especially important given their central role in the conduct of staff talks. Their views were summarized in a pessimistic report by General Schweisguth who had observed the Red Army manoeuvres in 1936. He concluded that the Soviet Union was 'insufficiently prepared for a war against a great European power', and not averse to seeing a war break out in the West, after which it could become 'the arbiter of a drained and exhausted Europe'. Schweisguth's report was only the most influential of numerous similar analyses by the French general staff, all of them hostile to the idea of staff talks.[15] The attitude of the military was shared by Daladier who, we have seen, had never displayed much sympathy towards the Soviet Union. In a letter accompanying the Schweisguth report, he warned Delbos that conversations with the Russians would alarm 'certain friendly powers' and provide Germany with a pretext for aggression. Neither the Quai nor Delbos needed any encouragement in this direction. Léger approved Schweisguth's report, and Delbos, once a partisan of Franco–Soviet *rapprochement*, had become much less favourable. Robert Coulondre, the newly appointed French Ambassador to Moscow, recalled that his instructions from Delbos in the autumn of 1936 were very 'negative' toward the Soviet Union. In the words of a British Embassy observer, Delbos and the Quai made 'no secret of their strong dislike for entering into further engagements with the Soviet Union'.

Numerous arguments – military, diplomatic and political – were marshalled to justify this attitude. At the military level there was little confidence in the Red Army: the French General Staff had greater faith in the Polish forces than the Soviet ones. And as long as Poland and Romania would not agree to the passage of Soviet troops, there was little that they could do to help France. Diplomatically it was feared that closer Franco–Soviet relations might drive Poland and Romania into the arms of Germany or provoke Germany into aggressive action against 'encirclement'. Hitler had already used the ratification of the Franco–Soviet pact in 1936 as a pretext for the Rhineland invasion. Another diplomatic consideration was – again – the British attitude: in the spring of 1937 Eden and Vansittart made their disapproval of a Franco–Soviet military agreement very clear: it might be used by the Germans as a pretext for refusing negotiations over a Western pact.[16] The political arguments against a military alliance were more covertly expressed but no less potent for that. Among the Radicals there was growing alarm about the activities of the Communist Party which they saw as responsible for the continuing labour unrest. Its attacks on the government's policy of non-intervention in Spain raised suspicions that the Soviet Union wanted to push France into war with Germany, a fear which Delbos expressed to Coulondre in the autumn of 1936.

The relative weight of these arguments varied for different individuals, but Daladier and the military were quite capable of using diplomatic and political ones and the Quai of endorsing military ones. More important than any particular argument, is the fact that taken together they combined to create an atmosphere of generalized suspicion towards the Soviet Union. This is not to say, however, that the military and diplomatic establishment 'sabotaged' Popular Front policy, because in this area, as in most others, there was no Popular Front foreign policy. Only the PCF had a consistent line, and it was not represented in the government. Delbos and Daladier had been reserved about the Soviet alliance from the beginning of the government's existence. On the other hand Pierre Cot, Radical Air Minister, was strongly in favour of strengthening the alliance but he was unable to do much on his own. It had been suggested that the decision to accept staff talks in the autumn was a manoeuvre by Gamelin to forestall independent action by Cot.[17] Within the diplomatic hierarchy, Coulondre, in Moscow, also advocated strengthening the pact. But theirs were isolated voices.

What of Blum himself? Since 1935 he had argued for closer cooperation between France, Britain and the Soviet Union. Later he described the idea as a sort of international Popular Front. Blum did not abandon these hopes when he took power. Coulondre noted that his attitude to the Soviet Union in October 1936 was more sympathetic than that of Delbos although he did not actually instruct him to respond to Soviet proposals for a military pact. Blum claimed that he had encouraged the military conversations which began in the autumn of 1936 and this is confirmed by Gamelin. But after the war Blum complained that he met with 'to put it mildly reticence' on the part of the General Staff. They had for instance failed to pass on to him a report on the Red Army manoeuvres of 1935, by General Loizeau, who had been much more impressed by Soviet military capacity than Schweisguth in the following year. The General Staff's attitude to the negotiations with the Soviet Military Attaché at the end of 1936 is revealed by a comment of Schweisguth, one of the chief French negotiators, that his instructions were to 'drag things out'.

Blum's desire to overcome the reticence of the military was much reduced at the end of 1936 when he received a message from Beneš that Czech intelligence reports suggested – incorrectly – that the Soviet General Staff was compromised in 'suspicious relations' with the Germans. But it does not seem that his enthusiasm had ever been all that strong. Already at the beginning of December 1936 – that is, almost certainly before the message from Beneš – Blum had told Clerk that he wished 'to see [the Franco–Soviet Pact] preserved but not grow teeth'. Although Blum, then, was probably more favourable to the Soviet pact than Daladier or Delbos, he too was, no doubt for similar reasons, ultimately reserved in his attitude. In Young's words the Blum government was, 'caught as always between fear of Russia and fear of losing it'. This means that the function of the pact in French eyes was a negative one of preventing German–Soviet *rapprochement*: the Russians who were mistrusted as friends must not be allowed to become enemies.

If the Communists attacked Blum for failing to strengthen the Franco–Soviet pact, by the right he was criticized for failing to improve relations with Italy. A friendly Italy was the most effective insurance against a German anschluss in Austria. In fact Franco–Italian relations deteriorated dramatically during 1936 and Blum's government did not do much to halt the process. It is true that in June 1936 Delbos expressed interest in improving relations with Italy and he was not unfavourable to including the Italians in the London conference of June 1936.[18] And in July the French government followed the British by raising sanctions which no longer had any purpose. But no attempt was made to follow up some informal Italian *démarches*.[19] In October the government announced the replacement of the extremely Italo-phile French Ambassador in Rome, Charles de Chabrun by René de St Quentin. But when Mussolini insisted that the new Ambassador be accredited to the King of Italy and the Emperor of Ethiopia, the French government refused to accept this *de jure* recognition of the conquest of Abyssinia, and France remained without an Ambassador in Italy until May 1938.

André Blumel claims that Blum did make three extra-diplomatic attempts to relaunch a Franco–Italian dialogue – for example in contacts between a French banker and the Italian Finance Minister, Volpi – but we have no further information about this.[20] And when the Italian Ambassador in Paris, Cerutti, conveyed a direct appeal from Mussolini to Blum in January 1937, he met with rebuff. When the British, pursuing a strategy of detaching Italy from Germany, signed a 'gentleman's agreement' over the

Mediterranean with Italy in 1936, the French made no efforts to do the same. By February 1937 French defence planners were assuming a hostile Italy.

Among the reasons for the French attitude, ideological motives can probably be discounted. Certainly Mussolini was detested by the Socialists as the murderer of Matteoti, and this made him sentimentally more antipathetic than Hitler. But in June 1936 Blum explicitly eschewed the idea of an ideological crusade in foreign policy. His own explanation of his attitude, after the war, was that an alliance between the dictators was already inevitable, a view which he expressed to Eden in May 1936. The Austro–German agreement of 11 July 1936 confirmed him in this view. But if Blum was so convinced of Italy's enmity, why the three *démarches* (whose date is unknown) mentioned by Blumel?

Critics of Blum see his Italian policy – or lack of one – as a missed opportunity. It may indeed be that Blum's prophecy about the inevitability of Franco–Italian *rapprochement* was partially self-fulfilling. But Mussolini hardly provided many openings. The crisis over the French Embassy was largely of his making. Although Chabrun was known as an Italo-phile, his replacement does not seem to have been intended as an anti-Italian gesture and his proposed successor was no Popular Front ideologue. The main cause of the deterioration in Franco–Italian relations lay in the outbreak of the Spanish war three days after the French had agreed to lift sanctions against Italy. The Spanish conflict and Italy's violation of non-intervention poisoned Franco–Italian relations beyond repair. When Cerutti made his overture to Blum (for which we only have the latter's account), talking of Mussolini's 'insurmountable repulsion' for Hitler, he offered the prospect of a 'Latin bloc' in return for an end to French aid to the Spanish Republicans. Blum plausibly viewed this as a ruse in Italy's Spanish policy. The French believed that Italian observation of non-intervention provided the best guarantee of Italian intentions towards France. Or should Blum have entirely sacrificed his already tattered Spanish policy to the remote possibility of Italian good will? The British attempt to woo Italy was, after all, hardly successful: the 'gentleman's agreement' which was supposed to settle the Mediterranean was followed by a marked increase in Italian aid to Spain. In short, although Mussolini, who liked to keep his options open was possibly less unshakeably fixed on an anti-French stance than Blum believed, it is hard to believe that a great opportunity was lost.

Blum's attitude to Italy contrasted strikingly with that towards Germany. From his first foreign policy statement on 23 June Blum announced that France would be ready to seek an *entente* with Germany. This was not mere rhetoric. In private, too, Blum expressed himself in conciliatory tones. The first overtures came from the German side during a visit to Paris in August by H. Schacht, Hitler's Economics Minister and President of the Reichsbank. At a private meeting with Blum which took place at Schacht's request, the latter suggested that a European peace settlement might be possible if Germany received some colonies to provide raw materials for the German economy. Blum declared himself interested by the proposal but said that he would need to consult the British. Eden, when informed in September, was startled and extremely discouraging about discussions over colonies, and Blum agreed to pursue the matter no further. By October 1936 Schacht's influence was reported by French envoys to be on the wane.

The issue of colonies seems to have been raised intermittently over the next few months in letters between Blum and Schacht, conversations between Delbos and von Welczeck, the German Ambassador, and between François-Poncet and Schacht. And in a well-publicized speech at Lyon in January 1937 Blum held out the possibility of economic benefits to Germany in return for guarantees of peace. But the French consistently stressed that negotiations over colonies were not possible outside a general European peace settlement. The Germans were not forthcoming, and Franco–German relations were not improved by the Spanish war. When Schacht, who was in Paris for the opening of the German pavilion of the Exposition, met Blum again in May 1937, the tone was much less cordial than in the previous year. Blum was less conciliatory and Schacht had nothing new to offer.

The exact status of Schacht's original proposals is unclear. He may well have acted on his own inspiration, hoping perhaps that the Nazis, of which he was not one, could be diverted from schemes of East European conquest. When informed of Schacht's initiative, Hitler backed the idea, but did not take it very seriously: probably its main function for him was to rock the Franco–British *entente*. Although the British Treasury representative, Leith-Ross, did engage in discussions with Schacht on colonies in February 1937, the official Foreign Office view was resolutely hostile. The Schacht–Blum exchanges were only a minor side-show of German foreign policy but for the student of Blum's foreign policy they are important testimony to his belief in the possibility of conciliation.

Conciliation, however, was only one aspect of Blum's strategy towards Germany. Rearmament was the other. On August 28 Hitler announced the introduction of two-year military service in Germany; on 7 September Blum's government decided on a 14m f. programme of rearmament over four years. The debate about French rearmament has become embroiled in controversy about the defeat of France in 1940. Although this does not concern us here, a few points need to be noted. At the Riom trial the Popular Front was accused of having neglected France's rearmament. In fact, as Frank comments, of the 63m f. of rearmament undertaken between 1936 and 1939, the most important decisions were taken by the two governments of Blum.[21] Furthermore in September 1936 it was the government, prompted by Daladier, which had proposed the figure of 14m f. The military, unused to finding governments so cooperative, had initially suggested only 9m f. Most of the rearmament programme of 1936 was concentrated on land forces with a greater emphasis than in the past on mechanization: 3,200 tanks were to be constructed. But this process of modernization did not go as far as some would have wanted. Daladier and Blum rejected the ideas of de Gaulle about the need to create tank divisions which could act as a mobile attacking force; instead they accepted the views of French military planners who allotted tanks a purely defensive role supporting the infantry and artillery. What this demonstrated was that although Blum's government was more ready to spend money on national defence than any other government of the period, its conception of military strategy did not differ from that of its predecessors.

The same remark could be made of Blum's foreign policy as a whole. There had been no sharp break with the past, only a shift of emphasis; nor had there been noticeably greater success. In Blum's defence it may be said that he had certainly inherited a disastrous situation, but he had definitely failed to improve it. By the middle of 1937 France was, if anything, more isolated than she had been a year earlier: the *Petite Entente* had been weakened, the Soviet Union neglected, Italy alienated. As a further blow, Belgium had declared her neutrality in October 1936. Blum had also failed in his hope of involving America more closely in Europe. This was an idea particularly dear to Monick who offered over-optimistic assessments about what could be expected from Roosevelt.[22] The truth was very little. Blum formed a very close personal relationship with Bullitt but the Ambassador made it repeatedly clear, as he told Roosevelt, that Blum should not base his foreign policy 'or any portion of it' on the belief that France could 'by hook or by crook' get America to accept engagements in Europe. Blum's greatest success was in strengthening the Franco–British *entente* but none of the ambiguities in the relationship had been solved. By May 1937 Blum seems to have been close to despair about his foreign policy. He commented to Bullitt that 'Hitler had the political initiative . . . and he did not see any way to take the initiative out of the hands of Germany . . . the situation was beginning to resemble more and more the situation before 1914'.[23] Was Spain to be the new Sarajevo?

The Spanish imbroglio: the origins of non-intervention

Three days after the Popular Front's apotheosis of 14 July 1936 a military revolt broke out in Spain where a Popular Front government had been elected in February. On 20 July Blum received a direct request for arms and planes from the Spanish Premier Giral. Although Blum's immediate instinct was to respond favourably, within three weeks his government had implemented a non-intervention policy which remained official French policy until Franco's victory in 1939. Spain, Blum later remarked, would be engraved on his heart as Calais on that of Mary Tudor. Cot, the government's most ardent interventionist, claimed that by allowing the defeat of the Spanish Republic, France had lost the first battle of the Second World War. Within France non-intervention threatened the unity of the Popular Front and indeed the continued existence of Blum's government. Non-intervention was, then, the central foreign policy issue of Blum's premiership: its origins must be examined in some detail.[24]

The transition to non-intervention was carried out in three stages each marked by a cabinet meeting. These were, as Blum put it, the cruel stations of his road to the cross – and Spain's.

The first cabinet: 25 July 1936

The decisions to accept Giral's request was taken by Blum after consultation with the three ministers most directly involved: Cot, Delbos and Daladier. The decision was a natural one for several reasons. International law gave any legal government the right to purchase arms to suppress rebellion; and in this case a Franco–Spanish commercial agreement of December 1935 had specified that Spain could purchase up to 20m f. of arms in France. In addition there was sympathy between the French and Spanish Popular Fronts. Finally, Blum's government, dedicated to anti-fascism, had a strategic interest in avoiding another hostile state on its borders.

Knowing that elements of the right would be sympathetic to the military uprising, Blum tried initially to act with a minimum of publicity. Although he must have realized that arms shipments could not be kept secret for long, he may have hoped that the rebellion could be quelled before news of them became public.[25] In fact it was almost immediately leaked to the French opposition press by members of the Spanish Embassy in Paris who were sympathetic to the rebel cause. Newspapers of the right at once revealed and denounced the government's policy.

By this time Blum and Delbos were in London for the three power conference to discuss the implications of the Rhineland occupation. At one time it was believed that Blum's presence on this occasion was due to pressure from the British who wished to discuss Spain.[26] In fact the meeting had been planned long before and no mention of Spain appears in the official record. Informally, however, the British ministers almost certainly expressed reservations about any French involvement in Spain.

According to Blum's testimony in 1947, Eden warned him to 'be cautious' (*soyez prudent*) in the affair. In Paris, meanwhile, the revelations by the right-wing press had had immediate political repercussions: a telegram from the Quai reported to Blum that the powerful Senate Foreign Affairs Commission, alarmed by the press reports, was opposed to involvement in Spain. On his return to Paris on 24 July Blum cannot therefore have been surprised to be met at the airport by Camille Chautemps who informed him of the concern in political circles, especially among the Radicals. Blum consulted Jeanneney and Herriot, respectively Presidents of the Senate and Chamber, both of whom expressed similar fears. In spite of these pressures, on the evening of 24 July, at another meeting between Blum, Cot, Delbos and Daladier, the government's original decision was confirmed. On this occasion, however, Delbos urged caution and refused to allow the French planes to be piloted by Frenchmen. This seemed to indicate a weakening of the government's resolve. But immediately before the first cabinet meeting to discuss Spain, a somewhat distraught Blum told the Spanish government's representative, Rios, that he would stick to his original decision 'at all costs'; Rios had never seen Blum 'so profoundly moved'.[27]

In fact the cabinet marked the first victory of the opponents of involvement in Spain. At the meeting, Chautemps and Delbos were among the most vocal exponents of this view; Daladier, while continuing to support the original policy, was concerned by its possible military repercussions. Blum, whatever his personal convictions, seems to have restricted himself to arbitrating between the different positions. The communiqué issued after the cabinet meeting announced that it had been decided 'in no way to intervene in the internal conflict of Spain'. What this meant in practice was clarified by a Quai d'Orsay circular specifying that arms shipments to Spain were to be suspended, apart from private civil aircraft (which could of course easily be converted to military use). But the anti-interventionists had not won the whole argument: in spite of this public declaration it was privately agreed to continue certain clandestine deliveries via Mexico. Perhaps the most sinister feature of this cabinet meeting for the defenders of Blum's initial policy, was the official use of the word 'intervention' to characterize purchases of French arms by a legal Spanish government: this was to accept the terms of debate proposed by the opposition.

The second cabinet: 1 August 1936

On 30 and 31 July Blum and Delbos informed the Chamber and Senate Foreign Relations Commissions that no deliveries were taking place to Spain. Delbos stated that the French government did not want to furnish

any pretext for interference in Spanish affairs by any other power. But he
and Blum also intimated that if Italy or Germany were tempted to arm the
rebel forces, the French government might reconsider its position. As they
made these statements they had received the first news that two Italian
military aircraft bound for Franco's troops in Morocco had been forced to
land in French territory in North Africa. In 1947 Blum said that this news
had made him feel 'much more at ease' in pursuing his original policy, and
given the recent remarks made by him and Delbos, it might be thought
that the hand of the interventionists – as it is convenient if not strictly
accurate to call them – would have been immeasurably strengthened by
this development. The opposite was true.

At the second cabinet meeting called to consider Spain, Blum now
openly advocated sending aid to Spain, 'whatever the consequences';
Delbos warned of British reservations; Lebrun counselled caution. The
meeting eventually accepted a plan proposed by Delbos but probably
drawn up by Léger, for a general non-intervention agreement to be
submitted to both the British and Italian governments (as the two other
Mediterranean powers). Until this agreement was accepted the French
government would resume deliveries to Spain. Only this final condition
persuaded the partisans of intervention to accept Delbos' proposal. But
they had lost further ground. The implication of the new policy was to
place French deliveries to a legal government and Italian ones to the rebels
on an equal footing. Certainly French deliveries were to be resumed but
they had now become a lever to halt Italian intervention rather than an
end in themselves. Thus, paradoxically, by increasing fears of an inter-
nationalization of the Spanish conflict, the revelation of Italian landings in
North Africa helped the anti-interventionists. When Jules Moch, who had
been in London during this cabinet meeting, returned to Paris, he was
'aghast' at the progress made by the anti-interventionists who had even
won over Socialist ministers such as Spinasse and Rivière.[28]

The third cabinet: 8 August 1936

While the British and Italians were considering the French proposal,
Moch and Cot, the firmest advocates of intervention, were organizing
shipments to Spain, in spite of the warnings of Delbos. Meanwhile, Blum
took the step of sending Admiral Darlan to sound out Chatfield, the First
Sea Lord, at the British Admiralty. Darlan warned the British of the
danger of increased Italian influence in the Mediterranean in the case of a
nationalist victory and he suggested a possible British mediation between
the two sides in the Spanish conflict. Blum's later account that Darlan had
reported back that Franco was seen as 'a good Spanish patriot' at the
Admiralty was a loose interpretation of what took place, but the British

certainly gave Darlan a dusty answer: to the first point Chatfield replied that if the French government had proof of Italian designs, they should transmit them to the Foreign Office; the second he rejected outright.[29] The Darlan mission was a curious episode: Blum seems to have hoped, via the Admiralty, to convert the British towards intervention, at the same time as his government was officially sounding out European opinion for a non-intervention policy.

Meanwhile on 4 August the Foreign Office had responded favourably to the idea of a non-intervention agreement on condition that Germany and Portugal also sign. On 6 August the Quai drew up a non-intervention agreement that it submitted to the governments concerned. Favourable agreements in principle were received from the Soviet Union and Italy. On 7 August, a few hours before the third cabinet, Delbos was visited by Clerk, who, stressing that his initiative was 'entirely personal and on my own responsibility', expressed his fears that the Spanish government was a 'screen for anarchists' and his hope that pending a non-intervention agreement the French would 'limit and retard' deliveries to Spain so as not to 'make more difficult' Franco–British cooperation. At the cabinet meeting Delbos, with Clerk's words no doubt fresh in his mind, argued that given the initially encouraging responses to France's non-intervention proposal, the French government should suspend all shipments, public or private, to Spain. After a stormy debate this idea was adopted with the proviso that if a general non-intervention agreement was not signed quickly, the government would review the position. The government had, in other words, accepted a policy of unilateral non-involvement in Spain even more restrictive than that of 27 July in the hope that other powers would follow.

During the next two weeks five other governments – Britain, Portugal, Italy, the Soviet Union and Germany – signed the non-intervention pact. The delay was used by Italy and Germany to rush arms to Spain in a crucial period for the outcome of the war. On the French side, Moch ensured that those planes assembled in France before 8 August were despatched to Spain before the French embargo came into effect.

The non-intervention policy adopted on 7–8 August remained the official policy of the French government throughout the Spanish Civil War. But its application varied. As proof accumulated that the fascist powers were flouting the agreement, Blum shifted, in the spring of 1937, to a policy of what has been called 'relaxed non-intervention' which involved turning a blind eye to arms shipments to Spain. Auriol, Cot and Moch organized clandestine deliveries with the tacit approval of Blum. In his second government Blum contemplated abandoning non-intervention, and although in the end he drew back from such a step, the policy was 'relaxed' even further. This was too little and too late to save the Spanish

Republic. There are varying estimates of the volume of military aid actually provided by France – Thomas proposes a figure of 200 planes – but there is no doubt that it was substantially inferior to the contribution of the fascist powers.

What can we conclude about the origins of non-intervention? Once the policy had been adopted, Blum defended it consistently, even though after the war he admitted that it had caused 'many disappointments, many vexations'. Zay, who opposed the policy, felt that Blum had personally believed in it.[30] There are conflicting testimonies about the attitude that Blum took at the third cabinet meeting: some suggest that he confined himself to arbitrating between conflicting views, others that he threw his weight behind non-intervention. But no account suggests that he opposed the policy on this occasion. In a famous speech made to a meeting of the SFIO's Seine Federation in Luna Park, Blum, who faced a pro-interventionist audience, assumed full responsibility: 'I talk of the government, but I could equally well speak in the first person, for I assume all the responsibility.' In this and other speeches Blum provided a double justification for non-intervention. First, that it had prevented the escalation of the Spanish conflict into an international war. He later cited four occasions when this might have occurred. Secondly, non-intervention prevented a 'necessarily unequal' European arms race to supply the two sides in the war, a race which would be won by the strongest industrial power, Germany. Blumel neatly summed up this argument by saying that France hoped to prevent others doing what she was incapable of doing herself. Of these two arguments, the first tended from September 1936 to take precedence over the second as it became clear that the fascist powers were infringing the non-intervention agreement on a large scale.

Blum's public defence of non-intervention contrasts with the personal 'anguish' which, according to his son Robert, the policy caused him. In despair and with 'tears in his eyes' he told Jiminez de Asua, one of the emissaries of the Spanish government in Paris, that he preferred to resign rather than desert Spain. But Asua received instructions from Madrid that Blum should be urged to stay in office on the grounds that even with non-intervention the Socialists would be more helpful to the Republican cause in office than out of it. Exactly when this incident occurred is unclear: some accounts place it on 25 July, before the first cabinet meeting, others on 7 August before the third.[31] The date is only important because if the earlier date is correct – and this seems more likely – the incident tells us nothing about Blum's personal attitude to non-intervention which had not yet been conceived. The Darlan mission seems to indicate that Blum was still not reconciled to non-intervention even after the meeting at which it had been agreed in principle. And in some undated notes scribbled during his wartime internment, Blum wrote that he had remained in power because he was 'best able to explain and make accepted this policy which went against my convictions, against my instincts'.[32] These comments, his resignation threat and his anguish (why 'anguish' unless he believed that the policy was harmful to the Spanish Republic?), all suggest that Blum retained many private doubts about the policy which he defended so ardently in public.

Whether, as Colton suggests, Blum, once his conscience had been assuaged by the Spanish government's desire that he should stay in office, convinced himself that the non-intervention policy was the lesser evil, rationalizing for himself a position into which he had been forced, or whether, as Lacouture suggests, he was covering a policy in which he did not believe (hence the 'anguish'), it does seem clear that non-intervention was not a policy that he would have adopted spontaneously or voluntarily. What were the pressures forcing him in this direction? Some opponents of non-intervention, especially Cot, have placed much of the responsibility on the British, and this was a version which gained credence after the Second World War. Strictly speaking the allegation was unfounded. There was at no point any direct official British pressure for a non-intervention agreement (Eden's *soyez prudent* was hardly a prohibition): the policy originated entirely in France. Having said this, however, the French were in no doubt of the British attitude. Blum and Delbos' first visit to London, Darlan's mission to London, and Clerk's *démarche* all made the unsympathetic attitude of the British government only too clear. Moch who had been in London just before Darlan reported a similar impression.[33]

Clerk's *démarche*, the most direct British initiative, has been accorded considerable importance by some historians. Although it was entirely personal the French record states that Clerk, 'unambiguously expressed to M. Delbos his government's preoccupation'. Clerk himself, who had not known that Delbos was about to attend a cabinet meeting commented that his intervention, which Eden retrospectively approved, seemed to 'have been very timely'. Hugh Lloyd Thomas, a British Embassy official, believed that Clerk's words to Delbos might have been the 'decisive factor' in causing the French government to decide finally on non-intervention; on the morning of 7 August he had been told by Bargeton, an official at the Quai, that the position of the anti-interventionists within the government was weakening; the general view of the diplomatic corps was that Clerk's 'counsels of moderation' had tipped the balance in favour of intervention.[34] If this is the case, it is curious that only two of the French participants even mention Clerk's *démarche* as a factor. It is referred to by Blumel, who could not recall when it had occurred, and by Monnet who remembered it as the 'determining element' in causing the cabinet to accept non-intervention (though he wrongly believed that Clerk had seen Blum). But if it was so important, why is it not mentioned by, for example, Cot, who was only too keen to shift responsibility to the British?[35]

The truth would seem to be that Clerk's intervention was important not so much in itself than as yet further evidence of the British attitude. This weighed importantly with the Quai d'Orsay and with Delbos. And we have seen the supreme importance Blum staked on the Franco–British relationship. He told a correspondent in 1942 that if the Spanish conflict had sparked off an international war, Britain would have remained neutral 'and more than neutral'. This became a progressively important factor as the prospect of an escalation of the Spanish war loomed larger. Perhaps the true role of the British in the origins of the non-intervention policy was a negative one. British disapproval left Blum defenceless against government critics of intervention and provided them, especially Delbos, with powerful ammunition. The British did not need to intervene directly if they wanted to influence policy in France.

The decisive, proximate, factor in the adoption of non-intervention was the domestic French political situation. In 1942 Blum claimed that any other policy would have sparked off a civil war in France. Perhaps this was a judgement which owed much to the experience of 1940 and after, although both Moch and Rosenfeld – Socialists who were very close to Blum – believed that the threat of a right-wing uprising was taken seriously at the time by him.[36] What is undeniable is that intervention was opposed by many of the leading personalities of the Republic (Herriot, Jeanneney, Lebrun) as well as by important elements within the Popular Front coalition itself. Although the division in the government was not simply between Radicals and Socialists it was initially from the Radicals that the most vocal opposition came. Chautemps in particular played an important role in transmitting – and stirring up – the hostility of the Radicals, and Delbos in passing on the reservations of the British. Daladier's attitude was characteristically enigmatic leaving different observers with different impressions. He seems to have shifted from support for Blum's original policy on 25 July to support for non-intervention by 7 August (Zay refers to his 'grunts of hostility' during this cabinet meeting). The Radical opponents were joined by an increasing number of pacifist-minded Socialists who feared war above all. The line-up at the cabinet meeting of 7 August was:

For non-intervention		Against non-intervention	
Socialists	Radicals	Socialists	Radicals
Spinasse	Delbos	Auriol	Cot
Faure	Chautemps	Salengro	Zay
Jardillier	Daladier (?)	Dormoy	
Rivière	Bastid	Lebas	
Bedouce		Lagrange	
Blum (?)		Moutet	
		(Moch: not in the cabinet)	
		Violette (Indep. Soc.)	
		Viénot (Indep. Soc.)	

The views of the other cabinet members are unknown. The non-interventionist camp included more political heavyweights – Chautemps, Delbos, Daladier, Faure – and was probably prepared to take its opposition further: it is alleged that Delbos threatened to resign (as indeed did Lebrun).[37]

In short, as his son has pointed out, the choice facing Blum in 1936 was not intervention or non-intervention but non-intervention or the fall of the government. Whether or not Blum should have accepted this is a separate issue. By remaining in power he conferred respectability on a bankrupt policy which helped seal the fate of the Spanish Republic. Although the notion of a universally observed non-intervention policy did have theoretical logic, the unilateral imposition of a French embargo on 8 August was an extraordinary and, as Blum conceded at Luna Park, misplaced act of faith in the good will of Italy and Germany. The intention had been to 'pique the honour' of the other powers; the result had been that 'we had to remain with our hands tied', while the other powers enjoyed total freedom of action. On the other hand, once Blum had become convinced of the onesidedness of non-intervention, he did accept the policy of 'relaxed non-intervention', something which might not have been possible if he had resigned. Defending non-intervention at Luna Park, Blum proclaimed that he would do 'everything to avert the present and future risk of war', and even after 1945 he continued to believe that his policy, whatever its faults, had saved European peace in 1936 and 1937. But at what price – and for how long?

The road to Munich: June 1937 to September 1938

Between June 1936 and June 1937, Blum's government, confronted with the problem of Germany, had pursued complementary strategies of

resistance (rearmament, attempted consolidation of alliances) and conciliation (the Schacht talks). These were hardly novel responses but they
could be accommodated within a Popular Front view of the world as
'standing up to fascism' and 'working for peace'. In Popular Front
vocabulary, Anglo–French cooperation was a union of democracies as
much as a strategic calculation. Although any foreign policy is made up of
the simultaneous pursuit of several approaches to the same end, from the
middle of 1937 the increasing vociferousness of German designs on
central Europe made it gradually less easy to avoid a choice between
conciliation and resistance, between pursuing peace at all costs and
accepting the possibility of war. Munich was to be the time of choices.
Understandably the foreign policy of the next eighteen months tends to be
treated as a prolonged prelude to Munich.[38] For a study of the Popular
Front the interest of the period was that it exposed the contradictions
inherent in the Popular Front's commitment to 'peace' and to 'liberty'. In
the next chapter we shall observe the consequences of this contradiction
on the Popular Front coalition itself; here we are concerned only with the
making of foreign policy. The road to Munich was a sinuous one, made up
as it was of a mixture of cowardice, idealism and prudential calculation.
The moment at which it became possible to think the unthinkable – that
the Czechs should be left to their fate – varied from individual to
individual, and between total abandonment and total commitment there
usually appeared to be a margin of manoeuvre which varied at the last
moment.

The conduct of foreign policy between June 1937 and March 1938,
between the fall of Blum and the anschluss – a period in which Chautemps
was Premier and Delbos remained Foreign Minister – has been viewed
without indulgence by most historians. Duroselle calls the year 1937, 'one
of the most immobile' in the history of French foreign policy; Adamthwaite talks of 'drift'. The only significant French initiative was the Noyon
Conference of September 1937 called at the request of Delbos to discuss
the problem of Italian submarine attacks on neutral shipping in the
Mediterranean. The conference organized joint naval patrols in the Mediterranean and the attacks ceased. Apart from this solitary act of resistance, French policy followed British at a time when, under the guidance of
Chamberlain, British policy was moving decisively towards appeasement.
But dependence did not breed sympathy. The cordiality of the Blum days
was over. Chamberlain was not sympathetic to the French; the British
were exasperated by French ministerial instability, and anxious to be rid
of the Popular Front: one British diplomat bemoaned: 'that terribly
pseudo-Communist government in France, to the coat-tails of which our
Foreign Office is as usual tied, when it would be so much nicer to have it
tied to the good conservative and anti-Communist coat-tails of Hitler'.

French ministers became gradually more pessimistic about the prospects of maintaining the French position in Eastern Europe. And, whether cause or effect, this was the period in which Bonnet was trying to extend the pause to rearmament. In May 1937 Delbos was 'clear that France was no longer strong enough to maintain the status quo in central Europe'; by February 1938 Chautemps thought it 'probable' that Central and Eastern Europe would slip into the hands of Germany without war. We do not need to plot in detail this decline into fatalism. Its progress was not linear, but the trend was clear. The only other solution lay in obtaining British support. But at an important Anglo–French conference in November 1937 Delbos again failed to secure any commitment from the British over Czechoslovakia. More significantly, he did not even try very hard. He presented the alternatives as leaving well alone in Central Europe or taking a 'firm and conciliatory' (sic) line which opened up a vista of possibilities, none very reassuring to the Czechs. This did not of course mean that the French government had decided to renege on its Central European obligations. As if to prove the opposite was true, Delbos went on a tour of France's Eastern allies at the end of 1937. In turn he visited Poland, Romania, Yugoslavia and Czechoslovakia. The object of the journey was to boost morale, but Delbos also took the opportunity to press the Czechs to make concessions to their Sudeten minority. The only substantive result of the tour was to antagonize the Russians whom Delbos had ostentatiously excluded from his itinerary.[39]

In March 1938 came the anschluss. Austria was not linked to France by treaty but her fate seemed a portent of Czechoslovakia's. Although the French military and French governments had been more or less resigned to the anschluss since early 1937, appeals were made to muster British support for Austria, if only for appearances sake. Even this annoyed the Foreign Office who wanted 'to stop the French butting in'. The true French attitude was revealed by Delbos' severe reprimand to the French minister in Vienna who telegraphed to Paris on 7 March that the anschluss might still be prevented if the French could win over Mussolini. Delbos drew the conclusion that the situation did 'not justify panic' but that things would be different if there was any attack on states to which France was linked by treaty; it was necessary to work on the British.[40]

The anschluss occurred during the ministerial crisis in which Blum, having failed to set up a national unity government, formed his second Popular Front government. His first government had taken place in the shadow of the Rhineland reoccupation; his second in the wake of the anschluss. All commentators concur that this second government, short-lived as it was, put an end to the paralysis which had afflicted French policy in the previous nine months. One sign of this was the new rearmament programme. Another was Blum's choice as Foreign Minister, the Independent Socialist, Joseph Paul-Boncour who was known to oppose non-intervention. It was clear that Blum believed that appeasement of Germany should go no further. On 14 March Paul-Boncour assured the Czech Minister, Osusky, that France would fulfill all her obligations to the Czechs.

On the next day, the third of the government's existence, at a meeting of the Council of National Defence, Blum asked the military what direct aid France could provide to the Czechs. Daladier and Gamelin gave negative replies. In that case, said Blum, Russia would have to intervene. Again the military were discouraging: there would be problems regarding Poland and Romania. The meeting also discussed Spain. Blum suggested an ultimatum to Franco: either he should renounce all foreign aid or France would reconsider her position. Possible military intervention in Spain was discussed. Again Gamelin and Daladier provided no support. But after this meeting the government in effect reopened the Spanish frontier and started turning a blind eye to arms deliveries. How the Czechs were to be aided was less clear. On 4 April, Paul-Boncour held a conference of French representatives in Poland, Czechoslovakia and Romania. It emerged that the Czechs could expect little from the Poles or Romanians.[41] Again the key lay in London, and here, as usual, the French received no joy. The British attitude to Blum's second government was expressed in the following way: 'anything we can do to weaken the present French government and precipitate its fall would be in the British interest'.[42] Blum could have been paid no higher compliment.

The Daladier government which followed dropped Paul-Boncour as Foreign Minister. According to Paul-Boncour himself, this was because Daladier disapproved of his strong commitments to Czechoslovakia. The British Ambassador also intervened to express the view that Paul-Boncour would be an 'unfortunate' choice. Instead Daladier took Bonnet who, besides being an anti-Popular Front Radical, was also a convinced partisan of French disengagement from Central Europe. For the PCF such a policy was a betrayal of the Popular Front. But this was a view which depended on a particular conception of the purposes of the Popular Front. There were many who had supported it because above all they supported the cause of peace; this remained in September 1938 their overwhelming priority. Munich therefore did not so much represent a reversal of the Popular Front's foreign policy as the final proof that such a thing had never existed. It was for this reason that, as we shall see in the following chapter, it was around the problem of foreign policy that the coalition was finally to break up in 1938.

PART 4

Coalition and opposition

8 ✤ The mystique of unity

When the Third Estate and the proletariat are united they carry out a 1789, a 1793, and 1848, a September 4 [the date of the overthrow of the Second Empire in 1870]. When they are divided they suffer Thermidor, Brumaire, December 2 [the date of the *coup d'état* which ended the Second Republic in 1851].

(Edouard Daladier, October 1935)

'The theme of this evening's meeting is unity, unity of action, total unity.'[1] These words, spoken by the Socialist Bracke at a meeting in June 1936, could have come from any Popular Front leader at any time. *Unité d'action* was the chant of the demonstrators on 12 February 1934; 'we take the oath to remain united' were the opening words of the oath of July 1935. This persistent, incantatory, invocation of 'unity' was a vital element in the Popular Front mystique. The unity was composed of several strands. First, the unity of intellectuals and working class, as symbolized by the CVIA. Secondly, unity between the two Marxist parties inaugurated by the Unity Pact of July 1934. In 1935 the parties even embarked on negotiations for reunification. Blum wrote that organic unity was the 'decisive step' to be taken in 1936. Although this was never achieved, it illustrates the potency of the idea of unity. Thirdly, there was unity between the 'third estate' and the proletariat, between the Radical and the two Marxist parties.

Could this unity, which had been built around the negative slogan of anti-fascism, survive the experience of power? This was a problem which preoccupied Blum from the beginning. In his speech to the Socialist National Council in May 1936 he raised the issue with habitual frankness: 'I am prepared to confront anything, with one exception: a disagreement (*mésintelligence*) with the party or with the working class as a whole.' The Popular Front should not be asked to surmount a breach of the unity that bound it to the working class.

But if the cost of disunity was failure, what was the price of unity? For many on the extreme left it was too dear. Daniel Guérin writes:

the great anti-fascist movement, essentially composed of workers, which was launched with the strike of 12 February, was our achievement, our treasure, our

215

victory. It reached its apogee in the battle of June 1936 . . . But at the summit, at
the parliamentary level, the Popular Front was less the prolongation of the unity of
action of 1934 than its *distortion* . . . It robbed us of our treasure. It divested us of
our victory.[2]

The extreme left felt themselves to be the spokesmen of the authentic
Popular Front, the Popular Front of neither the organizations nor the
government, but of the street. Not only, then, were there possible tensions
in the unity between the Popular Front organizations and each other, and
between the organizations and the government, but also between the
masses and the organizations which claimed to represent them and
between the masses and the government: in the early stages of the Popular
Front the parties had been impelled towards unity by pressure from the
masses, the base; in June 1936 the masses had taken direct action
independently of government and organizations. It is the evolution of this
triple interrelationship between masses, organizations and government
which forms the subject of this chapter.

Unity and the exercise of power: June 1936 to June 1937

The unity of the Popular Front was expressed institutionally within
parliament by the coalition of Popular Front parties and outside it by the
Comité du Rassemblement Populaire which continued to meet after the
elections. But the uniqueness of the Popular Front, as one of its local
supporters wrote, was that it was not only 'an electoral grouping, the
support of some parliamentary cabal, but a *levée en masse*, a permanent
mobilization of the French people'.[3] One way in which the 'permanent
mobilization' was expressed was through mass demonstrations. We have
already examined these occasions, so central to the Popular Front
experience, as festivals of fraternity; they were also its most palpable
manifestations of unity and strength: André Delmas points out that
although the bourgeoisie was frightened by the factory occupations, it was
at least relieved that they kept the workers off the street.[4] Mass meetings
provided a tangible link between the Popular Front leaders and the masses,
a constant renewal of legitimacy. One striking example of this occurred
when the Matignon negotiations had to be interrupted on the evening of 7
June so that Blum could attend a huge rally at the Vel d'Hiver stadium.
These were the new priorities of Popular Front politics; the lesson was not
lost on the employers' negotiators.

Blum placed great importance on this direct relationship with the
masses. When his Spanish policy came under increasing criticism, he
decided at the last moment to defend himself at a meeting of the Socialist
Seine Federation held at Luna Park. He told the audience that he had come
because he wanted to avoid 'a cruel misunderstanding' between the

government and 'at least a part of the working masses'. By the end of his speech which mixed sentiment ('when I read like you in the press of the agony of the last militias, do you think that my heart was not with them too?'), and argument with consummate skill, Blum had won an ovation from an initially hostile crowd.

Blum's performance at Luna Park was a piece of inspired improvization but many of the Popular Front rallies were highly orchestrated affairs. As time went on the pageantry became more stylized. One spectacular occasion was the Communist Festival of Victory in the Buffalo Stadium on 14 June 1936. The speakers' platform was decorated with a huge portrait of Barbusse; on the left was a band which played revolutionary songs. The proceedings began with processions of victorious strikers' committees down the central arena: the Renault committee carried a banner containing the Socialist, Communist and Radical emblems and proclaiming, 'We won because we were united'. After the processions a giant disc with a hammer and sickle was carried to the platform, followed by members of the Communist Central Committee accompanied by the Socialist, Zyromski. Then suddenly four huge flags were hoisted in the middle of the stadium. As Werth describes the scene:

One realized that each of them was the newly devised flag of Soviet France – a red flag with the Tricolour in a top corner and a golden RF (*République Française*) on the red field, with the Communist hammer and sickle between the two letters. With these flags fluttering in the sun, and these banners, and these processions of the Communist leaders and militants, and the surging crowd of over 100,000 people, one suddenly had a strange vision of a new France in the making.

Werth found the meeting 'in its own way, the most impressive thing I have ever seen in Paris'.[5]

Although it was the Communists who attached most importance to mass meetings[6] they were not the only ones to organize demonstrations of this kind. Pivert, who took in hand the organization of propaganda for the Socialists, laid on hardly less spectacular effects. The Vel d'Hiver meeting of 7 June, at which Thorez and a Radical representative also participated, was one such occasion. There were special lighting effects, huge effigies of Jaurès and Marx, songs and spoken choruses; the climax of the evening was the arrival of Blum. The style of such meetings conformed to the political aesthetic of the age: Werth saw the Communist meeting as 'reminiscent of Moscow, not to say Berlin'. Pivert's ideas on propaganda had been influenced by S. Tchakhotine (alias Flamme), a refugee from Germany, who had studied the propaganda techniques of fascism and believed they could be harnessed to different ends; he wrote a book with the revealing title of *The Rape of the Crowd by Political*

Propaganda. The Popular Front needed to use the weapons of totalitarian politics in its defence of liberty; Blum, the rationalist and classicist, could not dispense with the romantic theatricality of mass politics.[7]

If the mass meeting provided one mode of transmission between government and people, the Popular Front committees provided another. Although French political culture is generally characterized as individualistic – the French do not readily join organizations or form associations – this was not true of the Popular Front period. The Popular Front was born out of, and gave rise to, an extraordinary efflorescence of committees and associations: 'antifascist vigilance committees', 'committees of unemployed', 'recreation committees', 'strike committees', 'Amsterdam– Pleyel Committees' – the list is endless. There seems to have been almost no activity for which a committee was not formed in these years. Each Popular Front demonstration was a gathering of associations: almost every individual marched under a collective banner. At the Mur des Fédérés demonstration on 24 May, among the groups represented were the main political parties, the CVIA, the AEAR, the Maisons de la Culture, the UTS, *Ciné-Liberté*, the FTIF, and innumerable others.

But of all the committees which flourished in those years, we are most ill-informed about the role of the local Popular Front committees. This is partly a reflection of the relative dearth of local studies. But even where these exist, we do not find much reference to the Popular Front committees. One of their main functions was to organize demonstrations – for example, the celebratory demonstrations which occurred throughout France on 14 June. In Marseilles the local committee organized support for the June strikes. In the Vienne, the departmental Popular Front committee, formed of delegates from the local committees, ran a newspaper, arranged meetings and laid on cultural activities. The Menton committee also ran a newspaper. But the political role of these committees was much less than hoped for by the Communists largely because the other political parties, frightened by Communist dynamism, insisted that they should consist only of delegates from the adherent organizations and not allow direct individual membership. In the Hérault and Aude departments, Popular Front committees were set up only after prolonged inter-party discussions in the summer of 1936, but these committees were never more than centres of liaison between the leaders of the respective organizations. In other cases the committees were merely front organizations manipulated by the Communists, their political independence as fictitious as that of the Amsterdam committees.[8] In some places indeed the Communists tried to use the Amsterdam committees to embody their conception of Popular Front committees, but although the appeal of the Amsterdam movement did extend beyond that of the Communist Party, it was never sufficiently broadly based to provide the local Popular Front infrastructure hoped for by the Communists. Institutionally, then, the Popular Front never transcended the organizations of which it was composed. And although some of the Popular Front committees were an unprecedented experiment in political cooperation their existence was dependent on the continued good relations of their constituent organizations.

Representatives from these organizations continued to meet in the Comité du Rassemblement Populaire but this body played no significant political role after the elections. As for the coalition in parliament it displayed throughout its existence a high level of voting discipline. Apart from the abstention of the Communists on 4 December 1936, the only significant defection came from a group of Radicals and various small left of centre groups who voted against the government on selected issues, especially economic policy. But in no sense was there any disintegration of the parliamentary unity of the Popular Front during Blum's government. This dissent was expressed early on – it first surfaced during the devaluation debate – and reflected reservations already perceptible in the statements of the deputies involved before June 1936.[9] Although the number of dissenters fluctuated it did not grow significantly. Blum was throughout sure of his majority in the Chamber.

The existence of a largely homogeneous coalition in parliament disguised the development of growing dissension outside parliament both between the Popular Front organizations and the government and between the organizations themselves.

If one manifestation of politicization in 1936 was to set up committees, another was to join organizations. All the major Popular Front organizations witnessed an extraordinary increase in membership in 1936 as the following figures show:

PCF
1933: 29,000
1934: 42,000
1935: 87,000
1936: Feb. 90,000; Mar. 101,000; Apr. 106,000; May 131,000; June
141,000; July 216,000; Aug. 246,000; Sept. 260,000; Oct.
278,000; Nov. 284,000; Dec. 288,000

Young Communists
1933: 3,500
1934: Dec. 10,000
1935: Dec. 25,000
1936: Jan. 25,000; Feb. 28,000; June 52,000; July 72,000; Aug. 86,000;
Nov. 100,000

SFIO
1933: 131,000
1934: 110,000
1935: 120,083
1936: 202,000

Young Socialists
1934: 11,320
1935: Dec. 16,320
1936: May 20,000; Nov. 40,000
1937: 54,640

CGT
1935: 785,700
1936: 15 June 2.5 million
1937: *c.* 4 million

This increase in membership of Popular Front organizations continued into 1937, though at a decreasing rate: the CGT reached its peak of almost 4 million in the early months of 1937 but there was no significant decline until 1938; membership of the PCF rose to about 302,000 by the end of 1937 and probably reached its maximum of 350,000 in the early months of 1938; Socialist Party membership rose to 241,000 in 1937 and started to decline in 1938.

Of the Socialists and Communists, the latter were the major beneficiary of this expansion: it was in May 1936 that the membership of the Communist Party overtook that of the Socialists. The PCF grew by 331 per cent during 1936. Even more dramatic was the growth of the CGT whose membership increased by at least 1½ million in the month of June 1936 alone. Although membership of all these organizations had started to increase in 1934 and 1935, it is noticeable that the deluge only occurred after the elections and the Matignon Agreement: it was a consequence of victory as much as a cause of it. To join the SFIO, the PCF and especially the CGT in 1936 was less a meditated political decision than an act of allegiance to the mystique of the Popular Front, almost a gesture of conformity. The previous formal political experience of this 'class of Blum' was non-existent. At a Congress of one of the CGT's federations, a seasoned union leader described how many of the new members did not even realize that the CGT was a confederation of unions and could not be joined directly: 'these comrades were amazed but they persevered; it is the CGT that I want to join and nothing else'.[10]

For the CGT this influx offered as many problems as benefits, and it accentuated rivalries between ex-*unitaires* and ex-*confédérés* as both tried to win over the new members; it also provided the organization with unprecedented political influence. The Blum government inaugurated a new stage in the relationship between unions and state in France. One symbol of the change was Salengro's personal visit to the CGT head-quarters on 7 June to invite the leaders to the Matignon meeting: previously, as Delmas remarks, the Minister of the Interior had always been viewed as a 'dangerous enemy' in union circles.[11] The official attitude of the CGT towards Blum's government as expressed by Jouhaux remained broadly sympathetic, although not uncritical, especially of the government's timidity regarding public works. When Blum came under economic difficulty in the autumn, Jouhaux revived the idea of the Plan. There were rumours of a possible Jouhaux government. But as Blum became increasingly beleaguered in the spring Jouhaux strongly affirmed his support for the government. The CGT subscribe to the national defence loan in March. After Clichy, Jouhaux was forced to accept a protest strike but managed to limit it to half a day and to the Paris region alone. But, as we have seen, in the field of labour conflict Jouhaux's willingness to help the government outstripped his capacity to do so.[12]

Even more disquieting for the ultimate fate of the Popular Front was the growth of antagonism between ex-*unitaires* and ex-*confédérés* who had from the beginning viewed each other warily. The influx of new members, which transformed the socio-economic structure of the CGT, had reper-cussions on its political make-up. At the moment of unification the CGT was dominated by tertiary sector unions.

The five largest union federations at the moment of unification

Federation	Numbers	Proportion of unionists to total workforce (per cent)
Railway workers	107,202	22
Post Office	75,841	44
Teachers	73,482	35
Fonctionnaires	59,350	14
Public services	52,534	36

This predominance of the tertiary sector in the newly united CGT had existed in both the old CGT and the CGTU but was more marked in the former than the latter: the metalworkers federation had been the twelfth largest of the CGT and the third largest of the CGTU. This situation, after five years of economic depression, largely reflected the greater job security of the service sector where joining a union was a more established tradition and less exposed to economic fluctuations. In the manufacturing sector, unionization tended to expand rapidly during periods of social conflict and then fall away rapidly. This had already occurred in 1920–1; it occurred on an altogether vaster scale in 1936. Although the explosion of union membership in 1936 occurred in every sector, the largest increase took place in the manufacturing sector. As a result, by 1937 the CGT's centre of gravity had shifted dramatically:

The five largest union federations in 1937

Federation	Numbers	Proportion of unionists to total workforce (per cent)	Proportion in 1935 (per cent)
Metalworkers	832,802	71	4
Railway workers	359,329	73.5	22
Building workers	342,485	63.5	6
Textile workers	342,619	55	7
Mining	268,425	81	13

The ex-*unitaires* were to be much more successful in attracting these new members than were the ex-*confédérés*. By 1938 the Communists were almost certainly numerically preponderant in the CGT, even if the federal structure of the organization meant that they were not in official control. Once they had gained control of a union federation they did not necessarily eliminate all ex-*confédérés* from the leadership but retained them to preserve a façade of unity while diminishing their real influence: in the building federation the two ex-*confédéré* leaders were prevented from seeing mail and excluded from separate meetings of Communists where important decisions were taken. When the Communists took over a union they introduced new constitutional procedures, such as direct voting at mass meetings, which allowed them to impose their policies.[13]

To resist this growing Communist influence, and to provide an alternative to *La Vie ouvrière*, the union newspaper controlled by the ex-*unitaires*, in October 1936 a number of ex-*confédérés* around Belin set up a newspaper, *Syndicats*, dedicated to preserving the political 'independence' of syndicalism. What this meant in practice was the denunciation of Communist manoeuvres and electoral malpractices, or Communist 'colonization' as it described it.[14]

In the conflict between ex-*unitaires* and ex-*confédérés*, Jouhaux's position was difficult. Belin's memoirs portray him as spinelessly going along with the Communist tide. In fact on various occasions he fought a largely futile rearguard action against the Communist advances but his concern to preserve the façade of unity and stand above factions prevented him from becoming associated with *Syndicats*. And his opposition to Blum's Spanish policy brought him closer to the Communists than to *Syndicats* which supported the government. The bitterness of Belin and others against Jouhaux and against 'colonization' was really a reflection of their impotence in the face of Communist dynamism. Communist tactics did often verge on malpractice, but there were more important reasons for the Communist success. The shift in the sociological composition of the CGT would anyway have worked to the advantage of the ex-*unitaires* since they were traditionally stronger in the manufacturing sector than the ex-*confédérés* (at the moment of reunification the former already controlled what were to become in 1937 the three most important federations). The conflict between Communists and ex-*confédérés* was also partly one of generations. Old syndicalist beliefs about the independence of trade-unionists meant little to new recruits with no previous union experience, many of whom were joining the CGT precisely because they identified it with a *political* movement, the Popular Front. In the words of one Communist union leader: 'we perfectly understand . . . how [the] old militants of our federation have retained perhaps a rather particular conception on this question [of political independence] because they were active during a period – before the war – when the working class experienced political betrayal . . . Comrades, we are in 1937.'[15] Where many ex-*confédérés* viewed the new recruits with scepticism – 'have no illusions, many of them will not last' said Jouhaux – the Communists, better adapted to the world of mass unionization, set out to win them over. And their success within the CGT merely paralleled their general political success in the same period.

The growing tensions within the CGT were matched by deteriorating relations between the Communist and Socialist Parties. One root of the trouble was Socialist fear of Communist dynamism. Although the Socialist vote had remained fairly stable in the elections, this had disguised a loss of votes to the Communists compensated by gains from the Radicals. In its areas of traditional strength the party was losing votes to the Communists. This was true also of party membership. In all its most powerful Federations, except the Seine, the party's membership grew less fast than it did overall. In the Bouches du Rhône (Marseilles), one of the three most important Federations, membership grew by 64 per cent between 1935 and 1937 while nationally in the same period it grew by 240 per cent. The Communists in the Bouches du Rhône, on the other hand, expanded faster than at the national level:[16]

Communist membership per 10,000 people

	Bouches du Rhône	France
1933	6 (March)	7
1936	106	69
1937	107	81

In other words, where the Socialists were most powerfully entrenched they were least dynamic and most under threat from the Communists (and it was the big federations which dominated the Party apparatus).

The dynamism of the Communists had implications for the unification negotiations between the two parties. The original initiative had come from the Socialists in March 1935 when an inter-party unification committee was set up. This phase of negotiations came to an end in July 1936 when the CAP rejected proposals highly conciliatory to the Communists that had been drawn up by its own sub-committee. The second phase was started in the autumn of 1936 at the instigation of the Communists. Throughout 1937 any Socialist attempt to raise difficulties was met by a new Communist concession. Finally, in November, the CAP suspended the negotiations. The reversal in the attitudes of the two parties was probably due largely to the change in their respective membership strength in 1936: the Communists could now be accommodating because they hoped to swallow the Socialists; this was precisely what the Socialists feared. As one Socialist wrote in *Le Populaire*, he did not want 'unity like that of the CGT, allowing the deployment of a whole network of colonization'.[17]

Socialist suspicion was not laid to rest by the Communists' attitude to Blum's government. We have seen that Thorez had promised, when rejecting participation, that his party would offer 'loyal support', but that Duclos had also reminded Blum of the 'people beyond the walls of this assembly'. Over the next year Communist policy oscillated between Thorez's promise and Duclos' threat. This involved keeping up a barrage of criticism and exhortation – leading the Ministry of the Masses – while drawing back from outright rupture. During Blum's premiership Duclos and Thorez met him weekly at his home, but their relations remained formal.[18] How much day-to-day autonomy from the Comintern the Communist leaders enjoyed in the making of policy at this time we do not know, since we are ill-informed about the workings of the Comintern after 1935. Fried remained in Paris although after April 1936 he became merely a 'political adviser' rather than head of a college of direction.[19] This may have been a mark of confidence in the French leadership.

Broadly speaking Communist policy towards Blum's government went through three phases. Up to the end of August 1936 the Communists maintained the policy of moderation which they had pursued during the June strikes: strikes harmed the interests of the workers declared Frachon in July. When the Spanish Civil War broke out the Communists immediately spoke out for intervention but in fairly restrained terms. In August they launched the idea of a 'French Front', an extension of the Popular Front coalition to include sections of the right. The purpose of this campaign was to widen as far as possible the union of the French people against fascism, to create a new Sacred Union against Germany. But the idea encountered little support and was abandoned in September.

At the beginning of September there was an abrupt change in policy. After Schacht's visit to Paris Thorez wrote a letter of protest to Blum and a few days later he made a strongly worded speech attacking the idea of a *rapprochement* with Germany and calling on the government to carry out the full Popular Front programme. The strikes which broke out in the metalworking factories of the Paris region and elsewhere in September were directly instigated by the Communists as a protest against non-intervention. The exact reasons for the new Communist line are unclear. It may not be a coincidence that it almost exactly coincided with the Soviet Union's secret decision to intervene in Spain at the end of August.[20]

The tactic of encouraging strikes to force Blum to change his foreign policy was abandoned in October because it gave ammunition to opponents of the Popular Front within the Radical Party. Thorez sent Daladier a sycophantic letter of reassurance on the eve of the Radical Congress, and the order went out that strikes must stop: 'it is necessary in the present period to avoid strikes as much as possible', said Billoux.[21] But the Communists continued their assault on the government. In November Thorez announced that 'the fate of the Popular Front is not restricted to the survival of the cabinet'. Then on 4 December the Communists abstained in a vote of confidence – the first major breach of the Popular Front coalition in parliament. Although Blum decided to ignore it, he had contemplated resignation. This may have been the Communists' objective but it is unclear by whom they wanted him replaced. Brower suggests the name of Daladier whom they incorrectly believed to favour an end to non-intervention. Only two months later, however, they were strongly attacking him for having become the puppet of the general staff.

Having failed to modify Blum's Spanish policy either by strike action or in parliament, the Communists' attitude to his government entered a third phase which lasted until its fall. Criticism of the government did not cease but became less strident. And in the factories the Communists tried to restrain labour unrest. The cautious attitude of the Communists after the Clichy riots is revealing on this score. The Communist-dominated Association of Unions of the Paris region called a half-day general strike of protest on 18 March thus forcing the hand of Jouhaux who would have preferred more restricted action. But according to a Communist union leader the object of this strike was precisely to preserve order by putting an end to the outbreak of uncontrollable protest strikes. It may be that in this period the Communists had become resigned to the impossibility of bringing Blum down or worried about putting too much strain on the coalition. Perhaps Soviet intervention played a part: Coulondre had been charged in November 1936 to warn Stalin of the strain which Communist agitation in France placed on good Franco–Soviet relations. The message may have got back to France via the Comintern.[22]

But the Communists' behaviour can be explained without constant reference to the Soviet Union. The party was torn between retaining its mass support and maintaining the alliance with the Radicals. At meetings of the Central Committee in October and December 1936 and March 1937 there were reports both of discontent among the rank and file at the moderation of the Party's policy and also of the disaffection of the *classes moyennes*. Thorez reminded the party in October that it owed its influence in France not to its size (the KPD had been bigger) but to the alliance with the *classes moyennes*; now, he said, the *classes moyennes* were worried by the strikes and by the Communists' failure to join the government (a change in the party's view since June). The Pc's dilemma was summed up by two interventions at the Central Committee in October: Frachon remarked that the party must not cut itself off from the minority of 'most advanced workers'; conversely, as Thorez put it, the party could 'not move faster than the *classes moyennes*'.[23] The Communists were then simultaneously pursuing three goals: consolidating their mass support; reassuring their Radical allies; and supporting the objectives of Soviet foreign policy. The tactical tergiversations which resulted from the difficulties of reconciling these objectives gave ammunition to opponents of the Popular Front within the SFIO.

The latent divisions within the Socialist Party about the desirability of the Popular Front were accentuated by the manoeuvres of the Communists and by the difficulties of the Blum government.[24] By the beginning of 1936, there were three main *tendances* within the party. The left of the party, which from February 1934 had shown the greatest enthusiasm for an alliance with the Communists, was split into two *tendances* both closely identified with the views of their leading figures – Zyromski of the Bataille Socialiste and Pivert of the Gauche Révolutionnaire. Zyromski had argued ceaselessly for mass action, class war and unity of action with the Communists (he was the most enthusiastic proponent of organic unity). After the signing of the Franco–Soviet pact in May 1935, he abandoned his previous faith in revolutionary defeatism and advocated rearmament and the construction of a full-scale Franco–Soviet alliance: resistance to German fascism had become his major priority. Although this brought Zyromski's position close to that of the Communists, he was suspicious of the tactic of allying with the Radicals; he believed that the Popular Front opened the way to revolution in France. In practice his concern with the international threat to fascism led him to place decreasing emphasis on this.

It was over the issue of revolutionary defeatism that Pivert had split with Zyromski, and formed the Gauche Révolutionnaire which attracted a heterogeneous collection of Socialist dissidents including planists, pacifists and ex-Trotskyists. Like Zyromski, Pivert believed in revolutionary mass action – in 1935 he organized workers' militias – and unity of action with the Communists. But he would not accept the implications of the Franco–Soviet pact: 'on no pretext must the workers let themselves be intoxicated by pernicious capitalist sophistries: no national defence in a capitalist regime'. The development of the Popular Front in 1935 posed problems for Pivert – he was suspicious of any alliance with the Radicals – but he reconciled himself to a 'Popular Front of Combat': once a Popular Front government was formed, the masses would intervene to push it towards revolution.

The majority *tendance* of the party consisted of an uneasy alliance between former centrists – Blum, Auriol, etc. – who had tried to conciliate between right and left over participation, and a number of former anti-participationists – Faure, Lebas, Séverac, – who had originally been allied with the left in the Bataille Socialiste as a means of combatting the participationists on the right. After the secession of the participationists (the future Neo-Socialists) in 1933, this group found itself aligned with the former centrists in a party whose centre of gravity had shifted to the left. Within this majority *tendance*, sometimes known as the centre, there were significant differences of appreciation about the Popular Front. Whereas Blum was in 1934 quickly converted to the necessity of cooperation with the Communists, Faure remained more suspicious. Many Socialists found it difficult suddenly to work with a party which had attacked them for fifteen years. Faure mistrusted the Popular Front committees which he saw as a Communist strategy to suborn Socialist supporters. In the immediate euphoria of victory the divisions between the *tendances* receded into the background. Certainly Pivert argued that Blum should have taken power immediately and that it would not be possible to 'extract a certain number of reforms' from within the capitalist system (as Blum intended), and Zyromski wanted to 'attack the root, the very principle of the structure of capitalism', (the opposite of what Blum intended) but both subscribed to a unanimous motion passed by the 1936

Socialist Congress. Pivert accepted a post in the General Secretariat (with responsibility for propaganda); both he and Zyromski welcomed the Matignon Agreement. Briefly the party was united behind the government.

The existence of a Socialist-led government raised questions about the future role of the Socialist Party: was it to become the government's instrument or its conscience? Blum assured the party that he did not want it to be subsumed by the government but in fact the role of Faure in the cabinet was to transmit the government's views to the party via his control of party bureaucracy. When Pivert attacked the government in April 1937, Faure accused him of treason.[25] The issue of the relationship between party and government arose over the so-called 'Amicales Social-istes'.[26] These were factory-based groups run by Socialist Party members but open to all sympathizers. Originally the Amicales had been an unofficial initiative of the Seine Federation but in December 1936 they were formalized and taken in hand by the party leadership. In the eyes of the leadership their function was to preach the government's message on the factory floor: thus in June 1937 the post office Amicale was told to remind the workers that the Popular Front government must not be judged as a Socialist government.

Another function of the Amicales was to act as a sort of Socialist recruiting agent on the factory floor, and in this role they were viewed with suspicion by the Communists. Although accurate membership figures of the Amicales are not available, they probably reached a peak of about 100,000 in the spring of 1937. They were strongest in the Paris region, especially the metalworking factories and the public service sector. Their effectiveness was limited by the need to avoid hurting the syndicalist susceptibilities of the CGT: thus they were forbidden to take up the material grievances of the workers and had to restrict themselves to 'political' questions. In the end they were no match for the dynamism of the Communists.

By the time that the Amicales had been formed, the honeymoon between the Socialist Party and the government was coming to an end. Blum's government came under attack from both of the left-wing *tendances*. From August 1936, Zyromski waged an unremitting campaign against non-intervention in Spain. He saw the war as another stage of the international fascist offensive against democracy in Europe: victory for Franco would be a fatal blow to France's security. Zyromski set up a Committee of Socialist Action for Spain (CASPE) composed of members of the Bataille Socialiste, the Gauche Révolutionnaire and even some from the centre. Zyromski's campaign had only limited success. Although non-intervention aroused heated debate within the party, most Socialist deputies supported government policy with varying enthusiasm: only three joined the CASPE; and at the National Council of February 1937, where Zyromski brought the issue into the open, his fairly mildly worded motion received only 907 votes with 4,221 against.

Pivert's progressive disillusionment with the government had different origins. On Spain the Gauche Révolutionnaire was deeply divided: some, such as Audry, put international Socialist solidarity before pacifism and condemned the government arms embargo; others supported the government position out of pacifism. Pivert tried to reconcile the two positions by proclaiming solidarity with the 'Spanish revolution' but argued that this should be expressed through international 'class action': he supported non-intervention as a means of preventing war. The Gauche Révolutionnaire was, however, united in its reactions to Blum's domestic policies. It quickly became alienated by Blum's failure to go beyond the 'outmoded' Popular Front programme; the first factory evacuations of occupations it saw as evidence of the government's submissiveness to capital. At a meeting of the National Council in November 1936 the Gauche Révolutionnaire for the first time voted against the official motion. In January 1937 an article written by Pivert for *Le Populaire* was censored by the leadership. At the end of February, Pivert resigned from the government, protesting against its policies of 'social peace' [i.e. the pause] and 'sacred union' [i.e. rearmament]. A few days after the Clichy Affair, a poster denouncing the government appeared in those sectors of Paris controlled by the Gauche Révolutionnaire. In April 1937 the National Council lost patience and voted the dissolution of Pivert's *tendance* which was, however, allowed to retain its organization and merely changed its name to the 'Minority of the CAP.'

The bastion of strength of the Bataille Socialiste and the Gauche Révolutionnaire was the Seine Federation. But they had important local strength as well: at the Socialist Congress of 1937 the Bataille Socialiste acquired one-third of the votes in thirty-six federations and the Gauche Révolutionnaire in twenty-one. They were strongest precisely in those areas where electorally the Socialists were weakest, and least successful in the major Socialist federations of the Nord, Pas de Calais and Bouches du Rhône where the hold of the apparatus was powerful.[27] In federations where party membership grew fastest, so too did support of the Gauche Révolutionnaire. In short, some of the most dynamic federations in the party were attracted to the *tendance* most critical of the government.

At the Socialist Congress of Marseilles in July 1937 this simmering opposition to Blum was able to show its force. After the fall of his government Blum had succeeded in obtaining a substantial majority from the National Council for Socialist participation in Chautemps' government. But at Marseilles the official centre motion asking for loyal collaboration in Chautemps' government was approved by only 54.7 per cent; the Bataille Socialiste motion received 28.7 per cent and the Minority (ex-Gauche Révolutionnaire) 16.6 per cent (in 1936 it had obtained 13.5 per cent). On Spain an acrimonious debate was followed by a unanimously voted motion which avoided the issues by, in effect, criticizing non-intervention without calling for its end. The atmosphere of the Congress was stormy: fights broke out and supporters of Pivert were threatened by stewards recruited from the Marseilles underworld. The party leadership obtained its narrow victory by accepting a few verbal concessions to the opposition – demands for nationalizations and structural reforms were included in the motion of support for Chautemps – and perhaps by massaging of the figures. None of this disguised the real malaise which afflicted the SFIO. As Blum said, the party was experiencing one of 'the most painful moments in its history'.

No less worrying for the future of the Popular Front was the deterioration in relations between the Communists and the Socialists, especially those Socialists close to Faure. In the autumn of 1936 Faure attacked the Communists' 'systematic and hostile criticism' of Blum. It was the campaign against non-intervention which most irritated the Socialists. For Blum non-intervention was a painful necessity which he defended with his head rather than his heart, and many of his close associates, such as Auriol, avoided defending it at all. Faure, on the other hand, had no such inhibitions: the overwhelming priority was to avoid war. The nuances between the views of Faure and Blum, later to develop into a major split, were as yet hardly perceptible to contemporaries – both were defending non-intervention – but they already gave a special edge to Faure's view of the Communists: was the Soviet Union using the Popular Front to push France into war with Germany? This became the suspicion of many Socialists who shared Faure's enthusiasm for non-intervention and it fuelled their mistrust of the Communists: Arnol, deputy for the Isère, urged the government to avoid taking sides between Berlin and Moscow and carry out 'a truly French policy – a policy of peace'. Many others expressed similar sentiments. From this it was but a short step to suggest, as did a Socialist official broadsheet in May 1937, that fascism and Communism were two faces of the same phenomenon. In that case, what was the rationale of the Popular Front?[28]

The Radical Party had even more quickly come round to similar views. For many Radicals the Popular Front was a brief honeymoon followed by rapid desire for divorce.[29] This estrangement was partly due to fears aroused by the government's economic policies – by devaluation and by the 40-hour week which hit the many small employers who formed the backbone of the party. Headlines such as 'The *classes moyennes* must not be proletarianized' became typical in the Radical press. They articulated a profound social panic. In March 1937 the party set up a 'General Confederation of the *Classes Moyennes*' to defend the interests of its members against the twin forces of capital and labour. The Popular Front had been billed as the alliance of the Third Estate and the proletariat – not the swallowing of the former by the latter. A second major cause of Radical disaffection were the strikes. The Radicals had expected the Popular Front to be a traditional left-wing alliance; the social movement of June 1936 transformed it into something which alarmed them. In 1935 the threat of disorder had come from the right; in 1936 it seemed to come from the left. Local Radical committees protested against the factory occupations. As the Radical, Campinchi, said in October 1936: 'the occupation of factories, shops and farms was not in the programme of the Popular Front ... It is not only illegal, it is something worse: a humiliation for the *patron*. The occupations must cease ... today because they make most people abroad believe that our country is bolshevized.' And Campinchi was a supporter of the Popular Front.

The strategy of the right wing of the Radical Party was to focus these fears of the Radical rank and file on to a single target: the Communist Party. The growth of anti-Communism was the most significant feature of Radical politics in the second half of 1936. The Radicals had always rejected Communism ideologically but, as Berstein remarks, this was a theoretical position since 'the political, ideological and social universe of the Radicals was removed from that of the Communists'.[30] In 1935 the Radicals had even found the Communists more accommodating than the Socialists whom they knew better. After May 1936, however, Communism was no longer abstract: it was blamed for the factory occupations, for trying to involve France in a European war, for the Clichy affair.

From the beginning there had been a substantial minority of Radicals hostile to the Popular Front. They included deputies such as Bonnet and Malvy, most Radical senators, and the influential Emile Roche who was President of the party's powerful Nord Federation, editor of its most widely read newspaper, and a confidant of Caillaux. Up to June 1936 these dissenters had been obliged to stifle their views. The growth of the *fronde* at the base allowed them to take the offensive. Radical hostility to the Popular Front surfaced with unexpected violence at the Radicals' Biarritz Congress in October 1936. The right refused to respect the cosy traditions of party unanimity; pro-Popular Front speakers were heckled. On one occasion arms were raised in what seemed like a fascist salute; the left responded with clenched fists. The end of Roche's speech gives a good measure of the atmosphere:

we have had enough and we do not want to capitulate to the orders of Moscow (applause, violent interruptions. Uproar) ... I say to the Radicals: are you going to allow yourselves to be duped any longer? (No! No! Exclamations, Uproar).

The final motion passed by the Congress reaffirmed support for the Popular Front provided that strikes ceased, the Communists ended their campaign against non-intervention and the government considered the interests of the *classes moyennes*. This was merely a reprieve for the Popular Front.

The Biarritz Congress probably gives a distorted picture of the strength of Radical opposition to the Popular Front at this time since the right had successfully packed the assembly with delegates from the more conservative areas. But although it was too early for the right to hope to end the Popular Front, the Congress succeeded in pushing the left on to the defensive; it was the right which had displayed the greater dynamism. This was especially true of the Radical youth movement (different from the Young Turks) which had been founded in 1933. In 1936–7 its membership swelled to perhaps 25,000. The Radical Youth, led by two right-wingers, had been responsible for some of the more extravagant behaviour at Biarritz. Capitalizing on this success they organized a series of meetings in the spring of 1937. The first of these at Carcassonne in April attracted at least 6,000 participants: 30 deputies attended; the tone was hostile to the Popular Front. A few days later, the Radicals of Le Havre decided to leave their local Popular Front committee alleging that it had become 'a permanent enterprise of demagogic sensationalism'.

None of this was lost on Daladier. Surely had been a revelation for him, and, ever attentive to the mood of the base, he began to distance himself from the Popular Front inasmuch as this was possible from within the government. The final stage of this disengagement was a speech in June 1937 which made him sound more like a leader of the opposition than a minister. Two weeks later the government was brought down by the Senate. In the chamber only twenty-two Radicals voted against Blum but many knew that the senators would do their dirty work for them.

The vote of the Radical senators did not signify any evolution on their part: they dared to do in June 1937 what they had not dared to do a year earlier. Partly this was because they knew that they would now have their party behind them. A more important reason was that they no longer feared the reaction of the street: in June 1936 to resist Blum was to court revolution. As late as June 1937 Jouhaux declared that: 'if tomorrow political intrigues brought down the government, the country wouldn't accept it; the era of intrigues is over'. But this assumption that something fundamental had changed in French politics, that the government enjoyed a special relationship with the masses, was disproven only two weeks later when Blum was brought down. One observer commented: 'never has a ministerial fall left the street, the public square, so indifferent. Not a movement. Not even a cry.'[31] Although this was not strictly true – in Paris some 10,000 demonstrators assembled at the appeal of the Seine Federation – the popular reaction to Blum's fall was hardly what it might have been expected to be a year earlier.

Does this mean that the *mésintelligence* feared by Blum had taken place? Were the masses indifferent to the fate of the Popular Front and more specifically the Popular Front government? The seven by-elections which took place during the period of Blum's government all witnessed a slight decline in the Communist vote but none of them were in constituencies where the Communists had done well in May 1936. Lucien Lamoureux, the conservative Radical who fought the Allier by-election in December 1936 detected a change of mood in the electorate: 'the failures of the Popular Front had been felt in the country'. He gained 3,000 more votes than in May, and narrowly won the election. This merely confirms what we already know: that there was a movement away from the Popular Front among the rank and file of the Radical Party. But there is no evidence of major disaffection from the Communist and Socialist parties: at the cantonal elections of October 1937 both parties gained seats. Although the results of these local elections are difficult to interpret, they do not indicate any significant shift in the electoral popularity of the Popular Front since 1936.

But the uniqueness of the Popular Front lay in its capacity to evoke a more activist response than merely an election vote. The membership of all the organizations associated with the Popular Front continued to rise, we have seen, at least into the spring of 1937. The proliferation of meetings and marches which had occurred in the summer of 1936 inevitably diminished somewhat in the following months, but the Popular Front remained capable of mobilizing substantial crowds: a huge cortège accompanied the funeral of the victims of the Clichy riots. In Marseilles the demonstrations of 12 February (25,000 participants) and 1 May (between 35 and 60,000) brought more people into the street in 1937 than in any other year between 1934 and 1939.[32] But these demonstrations were perhaps not too significant: 12 February and 1 May had become somewhat stylized official occasions. As for demonstrating after the Clichy riots, was this a protest against the Croix de Feu or the government – or both?

If in the early days of the Popular Front the mass meeting was the most palpable manifestation of the harmony between political leaders and masses, it could also become the opposite: rare were the meetings after August 1936 where Blum was not greeted with cries of, 'Planes for Spain'. But the impact of the Spanish conflict on the popularity of Blum's government has probably been exaggerated. In the early days of the war, before the Communists had decided upon their full-scale campaign for an end to non-intervention, the CGT in the Renault plant had had to restrain the workers' ardour over Spain, but when the Communists launched their anti-interventionist strike policy in September, they encountered resistance from the rank and file. In Marseilles, meetings on Spain attracted declining audiences over the summer, and the strike over Spain which occurred in the Communist controlled engineering sector was only successful owing to union discipline; the workers were reported to be 'distinctly hostile' to this strike. In Paris the strikes on this issue were only partially successful, again in a sector controlled by the Communists. Thorez admitted to the Central Committee that the protest against non-intervention had left most workers indifferent.[33] This was one reason why this strike tactic was quickly abandoned.

On the other hand, the industrial unrest which surfaced in the autumn of 1936 and the spring of 1937 – against the wishes of the PCF – was a sign of diminishing confidence in Blum's government. The employers were the direct target, but so, increasingly, was the government. The government, by involving itself more closely in industrial relations was forced to accept new responsibilities. This was especially true after the introduction of the new arbitration machinery. When arbitrators awarded wage increases below the rate of inflation – as they often did – the government was doubly blamed: both for the price rises and for the arbitration system which implicated the state in unpopular decisions.[34] One CGT leader warned in March 1937 that restraining strikers in order to protect the government would lead to 'disaffection' from the Popular Front unless the government took active steps to protect the gains won by the workers in 1936.[35]

By June 1937, then, the messianic atmosphere of the previous year no longer existed. Disappointment with Blum was increasing. And no doubt a certain political lassitude had set in. But, on the other hand, no important Popular Front organization called on the workers to demonstrate against the resignation of Blum. Had one done so, there is evidence of a sufficiently high level of political mobilization to assume that large crowds would still have answered the call. In short, in June 1937, the workers who had helped make the Popular Front were disorientated but not quiescent, disillusioned but not passive. Did this mean that at last they would turn to the parties of the extreme left?

The view from the left: unity at what price?

The political dissenters who attacked the Popular Front from the left would today be known as *gauchistes* (leftists). The term was rare in 1936 but not unknown. More popular was the designation 'Trotskyist' – 'filthy Trotskyists', Thorez was heard to mutter after Clichy – or simply 'minorities'. However we choose to describe these groups, they are certainly marginal to the history of the Popular Front but their critique of it is not without interest: they help to define more clearly what it was and suggest what else it might have become.[36]

Among the minority groups, four can be singled out as especially important. First, the group associated with the journal *Révolution prolétarienne* whose guiding principle was fidelity to the tradition of revolutionary syndicalism. Before 1936 *Révolution prolétarienne* had rejected both the reformism of the CGT and the political dependence of the CGTU. It preached the cause of a unified trade union movement free from political attachments: only the workers could carry out their own emancipation. The circulation of *Révolution prolétarienne* was small – 1,200 at the end of 1935 – but its influence was larger than this would suggest owing to the prestige of its editor Pierre Monatte. Monatte had been among the first to oppose the Sacred Union in 1914, and after the war became, as it were, the conscience of French revolutionary syndicalism.

Altogether different were the French followers of Trotsky who centred their hopes for revolution on the political party not the trade union. After a period of growing political influence during 1934 and 1935 when they pursued a policy of 'entryism' into the SFIO, the effectiveness of the Trotskyists had suffered as a result of personal rivalries, sectarian political vocabulary and insufficient implantation among the working class. Having been expelled from the SFIO in 1935, they had split into two organizations each of miniscule size. Their importance derived primarily from the personality of Trotsky himself who bombarded them with instructions from his exile in Norway.

A third group was that associated with the review *Que Faire*, launched in December 1934 with the aim of regenerating the Communist Party from within. Among the leading contributors were the Polish Communist, Georges Kagan, a member of the Comintern's College of Direction in France, and André Ferrat, a member of the PCF's Central Committee. Both were obliged to hide their collaboration on *Que Faire* under pseudonyms. The basic line of the journal was that although the PCF was being strangled by its subservience to the interests of the Soviet bureaucracy, the most 'advanced' section of the working class in France was Communist: any attempt to create a revolutionary movement outside the party was doomed to failure. The solution was to 'renovate [the party] from top to bottom'.[37]

Finally, there was Pivert's Gauche Révolutionnaire. It is debatable whether the Gauche Révolutionnaire should be included among the *gauchiste* groups, at least until it broke with the SPIO in 1938 and formed a separate party. But its outlook was similar in several respects to that of the other groups even if Pivert remained as long as possible loyal to the

SFIO.[38] This is far from an exhaustive survey of the *gauchiste* groups. It omits the anarchists whose main newspaper *Le Libertaire* had a circulation of around 10,000. There was also the *Ecole émancipée*, journal of the Federation of *Instituteurs* who had refused to join the larger union of *Instituteurs* (of which Delmas was head) and formed instead a minority within the CGTU (and later the reunited CGT). But examining the views of all these groups would become repetitious since their analyses often coincided. This did nothing to mitigate their hostility to each other. The Trotskyists despised Monatte's faith in the trade unions and scorned Pivert's cowardice in refusing to break with Blum; *Que Faire* in 1934 accused the Trotskyists of being on the path to Social Democracy.

Before 1935 the *gauchistes* had all deplored the fratricidal division of the French left. Monatte had long argued for trade union unity and Pivert for unity of action between the Socialist and Communist Parties; Ferrat had been the sole member of the PCF Central Committee to refuse to condemn Doriot in January 1934; Trotsky had opposed the tactic of treating social-democrats as 'social fascists'. But when the Popular Front developed during 1935, the unity it offered was not that which the leftists had imagined: having been as it were retrospectively vindicated, they were now by-passed. As Monatte wrote: 'When unity of action occurred, it not only excluded its earliest partisans, but it became dominated by those who had most violently opposed it'.[39]

Trotsky provided in October 1934 the most detailed critique of the emerging Popular Front. He did not deny that winning over the *classes moyennes* was the 'necessary condition' of the defeat of fascism but argued that the Radical Party, which had been the upper bourgeoisie's instrument of control over the *classes moyennes*, was in a state of disintegration: to be tied to the Radicals was to invite the 'contempt' of the *classes moyennes* who were now being attracted to fascism. The *classes moyennes* would only rally to the left if they were offered 'extreme' measures. Ferrat made a similar point in 1936. There were two possible Popular Front tactics: one which involved raising the petit bourgeoisie to the 'revolutionary level' of the proletariat and one which lowered the proletarian struggle to the 'level of the prejudices' of the petit bourgeoisie. The former was the policy which should be followed. The founding manifesto of the Gauche Révolutionnaire similarly claimed that the strategy of the Popular Front's leaders was holding back 'revolutionary possibilities'.[40]

It was Stalin's declaration of May 1935 and the Communists' new attitude to national defence which excited the most alarm on the extreme left: was the Popular Front to be the first step towards Sacred Union? Monatte noted that the 'Communist catechism' had been enriched by a new 'chapter on the *patrie*'. He warned: 'no more than in 1914 will we march in 1935 against Prussian militarism'. *L'Ecole émancipée* attacked the Communists' celebration of Rouget de Lisle, 'the poet of carnage': the Marseillaise spoke only of 'blood, glory and coffins'. This was of course the issue over which Pivert broke with Zyromski.[41]

But there were nuances in the leftists' appreciation of the Popular Front. Pivert and Monatte refused to condemn it totally. Writing in October 1935 of the imminent trade union reunification, Monatte, while conceding that this had not taken place in the form that he would have preferred – it was merely the amalgamation of two 'stale' bureaucracies – nevertheless saw any unity as preferable to none. The chances of a revolution were increased. Rather than working against the Popular Front, it was necessary to support it as long as it acted in the workers' interests.[42]

The strikes of June 1936 were as much of a surprise for the leftists as for the rest of the French political class. Indeed their mood after the elections had tended if anything towards pessimism. The *Ecole émancipée* had 'no illusions in the new Chamber and no confidence in the next government': the weakness of the revolutionary forces would facilitate the victory of fascism. And the leftists played a minimal role in the strikes. But they saw that they had transformed the situation: was this the revolution at last? In *Révolution prolétarienne* Monatte addressed the question in one of the most searching contemporary analyses of the strikes. He admitted that, whatever his reservations about the Popular Front, the strikes would not have occurred without the election victory; for this reason the Popular Front took on a 'less worrying aspect'. But this did not mean that a revolutionary opportunity had been missed: the strikers' gains were in themselves enormous. The problem was whether they could be preserved. Monatte was haunted by the failures of the working-class movement in 1919–20. His analysis was a blend of pessimism – did the workers of 1936 have the political maturity to succeed where those of 1920 had failed? – and faith in the masses who had taken their destiny into their own hands irrespective of their leaders. The ultimate significance of 1936 was that the working class had regained confidence in itself.[43] This analysis was not so far from that of Pivert who also welcomed the results of the strikes.

Trotsky drew very different conclusions. On 9 June he declared: 'the French Revolution has begun'. The strikes of 1936 were 'not corporative strikes . . . but *the* strike: the coming together of the oppressed against the oppressors'. This view did not make Trotsky necessarily optimistic about the future. The gains of June 1936 were important but the laws of capitalism dictated that they would be quickly whittled away. Only then would the decisive struggle for power begin: this second stage would not have the 'pacific, almost debonnaire, springlike atmosphere' of the first.[44]

At the beginning of June, the two Trotskyist parties, in the face of Trotsky's strictures on the need for a revolutionary party, joined forces to form the International Workers Party (POI). The first issue of the new Trotskyist newspaper, *La Lutte ouvrière* was seized by the government on 12 June.

The position of *Que Faire* was somewhere between that of the Trotskyists on one hand, and Pivert and Monatte on the other. Kagan saw the strike committees as 'germs of Soviets'; the task of revolutionaries was to give the strike delegates a sense of their strength so that they could become a second power in the Leninist sense. Ferrat therefore condemned the PCF for having brought the strikes to an end. He did not view the Matignon Agreement as a betrayal but believed that even more could have been obtained. Having been dropped from the PCF's Politburo in January, Ferrat assumed that his cover on *Que Faire* had been blown, and this led him to express his views openly at the Central Committee. In June 1936 he was expelled from the Central Committee for his 'adventurist' policies, and this was followed by his exclusion from the party. This event was a milestone in the party's Stalinization because, unlike Doriot, Ferrat had behaved correctly by expressing his dissent only within the Party (or pseudonymously in *Que Faire*). He riposted by publishing an open letter outlining his opposition to the Popular Front's strategy of 'Sacred Union' and 'class collaboration'. But *Que Faire*, on which Ferrat now partici-pated publicly, retained its objective of renovating the PCF and working for a 'real' Popular Front.[45]

In the months of growing disillusion after June 1936 the leftists provided an acid commentary on the misfortunes of the government in which they had never believed. The devaluation was denounced by the Trotskyists as a swindle: it should be countered by the action of local committees which would bring the speculators to account. *Révolution prolétarienne* attacked the compulsory arbitration law as a step toward fascism since its logical conclusion would be to prohibit strikes: arbitration meant arbitra-riness. The suicide of Salengro excited merely the scorn of the *Ecole émancipée*: by helping to destroy the popular movement of June, Salengro had undermined the popular base on which the government ought to have rested.[46] But the Clichy Affair was, for the leftists, the moment when Blum was definitively unmasked. *La Lutte ouvrière* saw Blum as Noske. For Edouard Berth in *Révolution prolétarienne* Blum now had blood on his hands and would need to be replaced by someone more able to dupe the masses into swallowing the Sacred Union which lay ahead. Blum's fall excited few regrets except from Maurice Chambelland in *Révolution prolétarienne* for whom Blum was, if nothing else, the indirect cause of the *journées* of June.[47]

Analyzing the breach between the masses and the Popular Front was easier than exploiting it. The *gauchiste* groups remained largely ineffective. The Gauche Révolutionnaire, which was the only group to have the popular implantation to make it the viable nucleus of a revolutionary party, still hesitated to break with the SFIO. *Révolution prolétarienne* was increasingly preoccupied with denouncing the Soviet Union and the PCF, especially the growing Communist influence within the CGT. But it was no more favourably disposed to the attempts of the Socialists – 'the rival firm' – to counter this by means of the Amicales Socialistes: it remained hostile to any 'domestication' of syndicalism by political parties.[48] *Que Faire* continued to call for a 'true Popular Front' but the group started to disintegrate as it lost hope of renovating the PCF: some of its members joined the Trotskyists, others the revolutionary syndicalists. The unity of the Trotskyists came to an end in the autumn of 1936 when a split occurred in the POI. The two new Trotskyist parties – the POI and the PCI – wasted much energy in mutual recrimination.

The only exception to this picture of fragmentation was the setting up in January 1937 of the Syndicalist Class Struggle Circle (Cercle Syndicaliste Lutte des Classes) which attempted to bring together all trade unionists who opposed the CGT's 'policy of compromise and successive surrenders'. This initiative was taken by Gustave Galopin, a metal worker who had left the PCF in February 1936. The Cercle's first manifesto proclaimed the need to pursue the class struggle on the factory floor, to defend the gains of June 1936, to oppose compulsory arbitration and to win workers' control. Although, in the syndicalist tradition, it asserted its independence of political parties, the Cercle attracted ex-Communists (many of the *Que Faire* group), members of the Gauche Révolutionnaire, anarchists and Trotskyists. From January 1938 it published a newspaper, *Le Réveil syndicaliste*, which acquired a certain influence, and succeeded in implanting itself on a small scale in certain industrial sectors, especially the Paris engineering industry. It offered the prospect not only of providing a forum of unity for the leftists but also of giving them a genuine popular base.[49]

The recrudescence of industrial unrest at the end of 1937 and during 1938 revealed growing discontent with the Popular Front on the factory floor. In May 1938, *L'Humanité* took the unusual step of publishing a letter from the Communist deputy M. Honel, expressing the 'growing concern, even anguish' among workers tempted to replace the Popular Front by a 'Revolutionary Front'.[50] Although this letter was no doubt a staged opportunity for Thorez to reply at length defending the PCF's policy, it testifies to a real concern by the Party leadership about the threat from the leftists. Had their moment arrived?

Daniel Guérin wrote in February 1938 that June 1936 had been 'a somewhat humiliating lesson' in which the popular movement had taken the organizations by surprise ('we missed the bus' he wrote on another occasion); this should not happen again. And in the strikes of 1938 the leftist groups did play a much greater role than in 1936. The most important development had taken place on the left of the SFIO. In January 1938 the Gauche Révolutionnaire had gained control of the party's Seine Federation. In the process it took over the local Amicales Socialistes which became the responsibility of Guérin who intended to transform them from the 'vulgar theatrical claque' they had hitherto been.[51] The Amicales, together with the Trotskyists played some part in the outbreak of the metalworkers' strikes in March 1938. At the Renault factory the Communist controlled CGT was stung to issue a tract denouncing the 'Trotskyist beast'. When the Communists finally permitted the extension of the strike movement, this may well have been out of genuine alarm at being outflanked by the leftist groups who seemed for the first time to be playing a significant role at the factory level. The Amicalistes ignored instructions from the Socialist leadership to end their support for the strike. Blum's attempt to form a national government in April was denounced by the Seine Federation: 'Alert! The Party is in danger.' In the face of this provocation the CAP dissolved the Federation. The split which Pivert had till the end tried to avoid took place at the Socialist Congress of Royan in June 1938. The Gauche Révolutionnaire left the SFIO to form a new party, the Socialist Party of Peasants and Workers (PSOP).

The PSOP which opted not to join the Comité du Rassemblement Populaire, offered at last a convincing political structure for the leftist groups.[52] Pivert was not followed by all his collaborators but the new party had some 10,000 members, mostly in the Paris region with some important local concentrations in the provinces. Most of the PCI joined it in December 1937 and a minority of the POI in February 1938, following the counsel of Trotsky who remained nonetheless strongly critical of Pivert. The Trotskyists hardly brought large numbers of new recruits – though their influence was increasing among Marseilles dockers as well as Paris metalworkers – but their adherence was a sign of a regrouping of the forces of the left.

At the trade union level too there was a similar concentration of energies. The Cercle Syndical Lutte de Classes had been active in the metalworkers' strikes. According to *Révolution prolétarienne*, often a reliable source, it had offered the main resistance to the Communist line. In 1938 representatives of the *Ecole émancipée* and the Cercle joined together to form a single minority group within the CGT. But the importance of the Cercle must not be exaggerated. In July, at the Congress of the Metalworkers' Union, which had suffered a serious decline in membership after the strikes of the spring, Galopin succeeded in making the voice of his minority heard, but he only received 2,830 votes out of 191,000. The hold of the Communists on the Federation remained strong. In spite of the criticisms of the Trotskyists who accused the Cercle of ignoring the central problem of the struggle for political power, the syndicalists refused to give up their independence of politics, a position respected by the PSOP which, in reaction against Communist 'coloni-zation' of the CGT, rejected the idea of setting up factory based sections. The divide between political and syndical activity remained.

The fact is that the increasing influence of the leftists occurred precisely when the balance of power in the factories had turned against the workers. In 1938, then, they could do little more than rail against the Popular Front in its final stages, and add a touch of futile violence to its death (as in the Renault strike of November 1938). In March 1938, *Le Réveil syndicaliste* wrote what could stand as the *gauchistes'* final judgement on the Popular Front: 'the Popular Front had promised to defend bread, peace and liberty. It has brought the workers misery, subjection and war.'[53]

Perhaps the main interest of the minority groups is, in the words of J.-P. Rioux, to have provided 'a photographic negative of the real militancy of the workers'. As Pivert warned the Socialists in 1938, breaking the thermometer would not cure the fever. The leftists acted, if nothing else, as a thermometer. For many of the strikes of this period the most careful accounts are to be found in the pages *Révolution prolétarienne* or *Le Réveil syndicaliste*. Often these papers resurrect for us conflicts which the official Popular Front press preferred to ignore and they invest the caricatural 'Trotskyists' of the Communist bestiary with flesh and blood reality. But they were better at locating dissent than exploiting it. Their lack of influence derived from a variety of causes – their divisions, the extremism of their rhetoric, their lack of a factory base – but it was also a tribute to the potency of the Popular Front's mystique of unity. In the words of Gilbert Serret to the CGT Congress of November 1938: the Popular Front had been 'a tremendous social fraud which succeeded in making the working class accept what it would never have accepted from a reactionary government'.[54]

From anti-fascist unity to anti-Communist disunity: June 1937 to November 1938

The unity of the Popular Front was built around two latent contra-dictions. The first was sociological: the alliance between the proletariat and the *classes moyennes* – or, in political terms, the Radicals and the Communist Party. The second was ideological: the double commitment to

preserve peace and combat fascism. As long as fighting domestic anti-
fascism remained the first priority both contradictions remained secondary. But, as we have seen, after the elections they began to come into the
open: after the June strikes the Radical electorate became worried about
social disorder; with the outbreak of the Spanish Civil War pacifists on the
left began to worry more about the threat of war than about fascism. The
fears of both began to converge on the PCF. It became gradually
respectable on the left to be anti-Communist: those who feared social
disorder attacked the Communists as fomenters of strikes; those who
feared war attacked them as warmongers – advocates of intervention in
Spain and unqualified resistance to Hitler. Confidence in the Communists
was eroded in other ways as well: many Socialists feared their dynamism;
many intellectuals were shaken by news of the show trials: the rifts
between a Gide and a Guéhenno or a Jeanson and a Renoir were
symptomatic of a transformed political world.

But from the second half of 1937 the foreign policy issue came to
threaten not only the unity of the Popular Front as a coalition but also the
internal unity of its constituent organizations. There was an example of
this as early as June 1936 within the ranks of the CVIA. In November
1934, Michel Alexandre, generally considered to represent the views of
Alain, published a manifesto in *Vigilance*: 'the struggle against fascism is
never a struggle against a supposed external enemy. Fascism is for each
country the enemy from within.' Here in embryo was to be the position of
many pacifists of the left at Munich. For people like Alain fighting an
anti-fascist war was a contradiction in terms since the militarization of
society which war implied was itself a form of fascism. This was obviously
not a position that the Communists could accept. At the CVIA Congress
in November 1935 there had been arguments about the attitude that
should be adopted towards the Franco-Soviet pact and Hitler's repudiation of the Versailles Treaty. The Rhineland invasion increased these
differences. A pacifist brochure entitled *No, war is not inevitable* by Henri
Bouché, a member of the CVIA, was strongly criticized by the Communist
members of the organization. At a special Congress held in June 1936 the
Communists found themselves in a minority and withdrew from the
CVIA's governing bureau. Among these Communist dissidents was Paul
Langevin.[55] The CVIA which had been a precursor of the unity of the
Popular Front in March 1934 became, at the moment of the Popular
Front's greatest triumph, the precursor of its eventual collapse.

Charting the disintegration of the Popular Front coalition does not so
much involve locating a moment of crisis as observing a gradual transformation in the political atmosphere. Central to this change was increasing nervousness about the confusing policies of the PCF and the effects

that this had on the Party's Popular Front's partners. In June 1937 the Communists offered to join Chautemps' government, and although this was refused, up to December the party pursued a conciliatory social policy, even tacitly accepting modifications of the 40-hour week. At the end of the year there was a change of tone and the Communists declared solidarity with the public sector strikers in Paris, and when Chautemps decided to ask for a vote of confidence on his social policy, they announced that they would abstain. In the spring of 1938 the party launched a campaign to resuscitate the Popular Front in the country. It also supported both Blum's attempts at forming national unity governments. Its ambiguous attitude during the strikes in the Paris heavy engineering industry in the spring has already been analyzed. Initially the Communists gave Daladier the benefit of the doubt, voting for his government when it first appeared before parliament. But when Daladier moved on to the offensive against the 40-hour week in August, there was a vigorous Communist response, culminating in strong backing for the general strike in November.

As before the PCF was pursuing three goals: developing its influence in the country (defending the social gains of 1936), maintaining the Popular Front coalition, exerting pressure for a pro-Soviet foreign policy. These goals did not necessarily conflict: strikes could be used to pressurize governments to change their foreign policy and even to try and bring them down. Thus it was no coincidence that the Communists turned against Chautemps after Delbos' snub of the Russians in November 1937, or against Daladier after Munich. But because these attacks on their allies threatened the Popular Front coalition, the Communists were led with increasing desperation to proclaim that the Popular Front was thriving. Thus, in his reply to Honel's letter in *L'Humanité* Thorez asserted that the Socialists and Communists were getting on better and better, even citing the creation of the Amicales Socialistes as proof of this! When the government seemed to offer hope on foreign policy, the Communists were ready to compromise on the social gains of 1936 and try to stop social unrest even at the risk of being outflanked on the left. The prime example of this was the engineering strike in the spring of 1938 which the party brought to an end at considerable risk to its popularity. The balance between alienating the base and supporting the government was always a delicate one: in July 1938 Croizat refused to compromise on the 40-hour week because of a *fronde* at the base. But it was not worth taking many risks for a government that had turned out to show no interest in the Soviet alliance. On the other hand, in the Marseilles dockers' strike of July to September 1938 the Communists advocated a cautious line in the hope that concessions to the spirit of the Popular Front at home would 'stave off concessions to fascists abroad'.[56]

The seeming unreliability of the Communists – actually the only group to pursue constant aims – helped those Radicals who wanted to end the Popular Front. Blum's successor Chautemps was the epitome of the Radical politician: a man of infinite political suppleness, of transitions not solutions. As such he was acceptable, for the moment, to both left and right. The Radical opponents of the Popular Front set their sights on Bonnet. The Radical Congress of September 1937 again witnessed strident criticisms of the Popular Front. There was more airing of the grievances of the *classes moyennes* threatened by the Popular Front's social legislation. As a result the right of the party felt sufficiently confident to mount a challenge to the government. A motion on financial policy, concocted by two conservatives, Potut and Roche, and defended by Bonnet, was passed by the Congress. Its wording implied a total disavowal of Popular Front economics. But Daladier, who had been absent for the vote on this motion, managed to have it rescinded. The right's manoeuvre was thwarted. It is possible that Daladier had been rung by Blum who warned him that the vote would have brought about a Socialist withdrawal from the government. But Daladier did not act out of love of the Popular Front. Aware of the growing dissatisfaction with the Popular Front among the Radical electorate, he had continued to stake out his distance from the coalition. But he wanted its collapse to work to his advantage not Bonnet's.

In January 1938 there was another Radical attempt to reverse alliances, this time in parliament, when Chautemps offered the Communist, Ramette, his 'liberty'. The government fell and Bonnet tried to form a centre–right coalition. This failed because he could not win over enough Radical deputies (most of whom owed their election to the working of the left-wing alliance). The moral for the Radical opponents of the Popular Front was that they needed Daladier to make the necessary reversal of alliance acceptable to the Radical deputies.

Bonnet's abortive government was followed by Blum's proposal for a national unity government, important only because it freed Radicals from the need to pay lip-service to the Popular Front. Although the ministerial crisis was finally ended by a second Chautemps' government, this was clearly recognized to be a stopgap. Chautemps resigned, for obscure reasons, just before the anschluss. As Larmour remarks, the anschluss represented, 'a sort of 6 February for the 1936 legislature'.[57] After it nothing could be the same again. A national union government of some kind was inevitable. The only interest, therefore, that the political class had in Blum's second Popular Front government was the nature of its successor. Even Jacques Kayser, one of the most ardent Radical supporters of the Popular Front – he had helped draft the oath of July 1935 and sat on the Comité du Rassemblement Populaire – now accepted that a new political formula was inevitable.[58] Finally, after Blum's fall, Daladier at last emerged to play the role for which he had been waiting for months. It was not the case at the beginning that Daladier's government of national union need, as in the past, merely have provided camouflage for a return of the right. But whatever direction the government ultimately took its existence clearly signified that as a political coalition the Popular Front was dead.

Far from being able to halt the break-up of the coalition, the Socialist Party itself became increasingly divided. At the Congress of Marseilles there was much recrimination and debate about the reasons for Blum's failure. The Congress instructed the leadership to consider an extension of the Popular Front programme. But nothing had been done about this a year later when the issue was raised again. This time proposals for further nationalizations were put to the Comité du Rassemblement Populaire but the Radical representatives refused even to have them discussed, and given the political climate there was a singular lack of reality about the whole exercise. Another thorn in the side of the party leadership was the opposition of the Pivertists until their exclusion in 1938. The expulsion of Pivert was to be one of the last occasions on which the party experienced an uneasy unity, albeit of a negative kind: Zyromski opposed Pivert's views on foreign policy, Faure resented his indiscipline. Ironically the presence of the Gauche Révolutionnaire in the party would have been extremely beneficial to Faure only a few months later when he found himself opposed to Blum (and Zyromski) on foreign policy.

It was foreign policy which came increasingly to dominate the party's life. The divisions in the party over Spain prefigured those which occurred over the next two years: those most hostile to non-intervention emerged as the more resolute advocates of collective security and resistance to Germany; those most favourable to non-intervention were the most ardent defenders of conciliation. After the Marseilles Congress, Faure started a vigorous pacifist campaign reiterating his opposition to intervention to Spain, opposing war against Germany in any circumstances and rejecting the idea of building an alliance system against her. One of the major mouthpieces of this campaign was *Le Socialiste*, a paper founded by Faure in the summer of 1937. It would be wrong to talk of a Faurist *tendance* at this stage. Faure and his followers remained part of the same majority *tendance* as Blum. Only slowly did it emerge how different their views were. This was because Blum's view on foreign policy had always contained an element of ambiguity. By the time that he came to form his second government, however, Blum had, we have seen, moved in favour of resistance. But it took a certain time before the Faurists realized this. They could present themselves as defending Blum against Bataille Socialiste without seeing – or feigning not to see – that Blum's position was moving closer to Zyromski's. At the Congress of Royan (June 1938) which expelled Pivert, Faure and Blum were still able – just – to agree on a common motion.[59]

The Popular Front became somewhat forgotten in all this except that the Faurists' pacifism stoked their mistrust of the Communist Party. As early as November 1936, Salomon Grumbach, later to be a Blumist, warned the party against being dragged into an anti-bolshevik crusade: the enemy was Berlin not Moscow. By 1938 many Faurists would probably not have agreed. In Spain they attacked the designs of Stalin as much as Franco. On the eve of the Munich agreement one of them wrote: 'a universal massacre for the protection of the Czechs! No, Comrade Thorez.' Among the contributors to *Le Socialiste* were members of the *Syndicats* group for whom pacifism had become an increasingly important theme. Jouhaux continued to try and hold the ring between ex-*unitaires* and ex-*confédérés* but with diminishing success. The view of *Syndicats* before the Munich agreement was that 'an imperfect arrangement is always better than a glorious and victorious war'.[60] Once Faure had finally taken over the *Amicales Socialistes* by the end of 1938 he used them to form further links between pacifists in the SFIO and the CGT. Given that originally *Syndicats* had been founded to resist political interference in trade-unionism, this was a significant example of the way in which foreign policy had come to surpass pre-existing alignments. Another focus of pacifist activity was the Syndicalist Centre for Action against War (CSAG) founded in March 1938 by a number of intellectuals from the CVIA and some members of *Révolution prolétarienne*. Its first manifesto was published by *Syndicats*.

By 1938 the divisions within the Popular Front had started adversely to affect the membership of Popular Front organizations which in all cases began to fall in the early months of the year. Sales of *L'Humanité* started to fall from May 1938. In short, the political world whose boundaries had been defined by the Popular Front was in a state of disintegration. Munich provided the final catalyst. The only organization united in opposition to Munich was the PCF.[61] To be pro-Munich was therefore also to be anti-Communist. Although Blum voted reluctantly for the Munich agreement, he intended to go no further down that path: Faure, on the other hand, was unreservedly enthusiastic. The SFIO moved closer towards open schism at its Montrouge Congress in December 1938. The Faure–Blum axis which had held the party together since 1920 broke up and Faure and Blum supported opposing motions. Zyromski rallied to Blum. Some Faurists such as J.-B. Severac now advocated the abrogation of the Franco-Soviet pact: 'We will capitulate neither to Berlin nor to Moscow', declared *Le Socialiste*. Similarly at the CGT's Nantes Congress (November 1938) the simmering conflict between *Syndicats* and the Communists also came into the open. There were two motions, one on the independence of trade-unionism, the other on foreign policy. In both cases the centrists, the supporters of Jouhaux, sided with the Communists against *Syndicats*. They voted a motion hostile to Munich. Among the supporters of the opposing *Syndicats* motion were Chambelland and Monatte of *Révolution prolétarienne*: revolutionary syndicalists found themselves aligned with reformists in opposition to Communism and war – another reversal of former alignments. The Congress was at least united in opposition to the Reynaud decrees but in fact the main pressure for a general strike of protest came from the Communists who hoped in this way to attack Daladier's government. The supporters of *Syndicats* were less happy to weaken the government responsible for the Munich agreement but were unable to resist pressure for a strike designed to defend the last vestiges of the victories of 1936.

Munich also caused disarray among the leftists. The CSAG called a meeting at the height of the Czech crisis. Some, including Michel Alexandre, were in favour of keeping open channels of communication with the Daladier government in order to encourage it down the path of compromise; the representatives of the Cercle Syndical and the POI refused all contact with Daladier: war should be resisted by class struggle and, if necessary, fraternization with German soldiers. In the end the first view prevailed in the manifesto issued by the CSAG. This was supported by most of the PSOP but criticized by its left wing, including Guérin. The PSOP also supported the general strike of November 1938 while rejecting the anti-Munich interpretation given to it by the PCF. Some leftists, on the other hand, took their pacifism so far as to accept the decrees which effectively terminated the social conquests of the Popular Front. The CVIA split for a second time after Munich. Among those who left were Paul Rivet and François Walter who rejected a totally pacifist position. In the words of Walter: 'We believe that anti-fascism requires certain acts and certain stances . . . and that under the influence of extreme pacifism the action of the CVIA has become so distorted that it can no longer be described as anti-fascist.'

Anti-fascism was also far from the thoughts of the Radical Congress of October 1938. The Munich agreement and the Communist attack on Daladier's government removed the last Radical inhibitions to breaking the Popular Front. The Congress developed, in the words of one historian, into an 'orgy of anti-communism'.[62] Albert Bayet, the only speaker who defended the Popular Front was greeted by shouts of 'To Moscow.' On 10 November 1938 the Radicals formally withdrew from the Comité du Rassemblement Populaire; on the same day *Vendredi* ceased publication.

Only the Communists struggled desperately to keep the Popular Front going. At the beginning of 1939 the Party launched a campaign with the slogan, 'No M. Daladier, the Popular Front is not dead.' But this was pure fantasy. The political alignments of 1939 already prefigured those of Vichy much more than they carried on those of 1936. Nothing demonstrated this fact better than the fact that when war did come in 1939 some contributors to *Syndicats*, having rejected the prospect of an anti-fascist war in 1938, were now willing to accept a conflict that could, since the signing of the German–Soviet non-aggression pact, be presented as an anti-bolshevik crusade.[63]

9 ✖ The view from the right

This atrocious summer

(J. Caillaux to E. Roche, July 1936)

I think of that day as one of the unhappiest memories of my life

(P. Waline on the occupation of his factory in June 1936)

The sky has been dark in France during this month of June

(*Le Pèlerin*, July 1936)

In his novel *Les Ambassades*, Roger Peyrefitte describes the departure of his young hero from Paris in 1937 to take up a diplomatic post in Athens. As the train crosses France, the blinds of the restaurant car are lowered: 'it was only in the last year that the blinds had been lowered in the evenings Previously the diners had enjoyed offering themselves up as a spectacle to the regions that they crossed. In 1937 they were advised to show more discretion.'[1] The quotation admirably reminds us that the Popular Front, which aspired to break down barriers, also created new ones. As the epigraphs to this chapter show, the language of hope in 1936 was paralleled by another language of fear. The Popular Front must be viewed not only as it viewed itself but also as others viewed it anxiously from behind the drawn blind.

The alternative view is all the more important because the Popular Front's propaganda centred around two ideas summed up by the terms Front and Rassemblement: the Front was both an implacable enemy of 'fascism' and a unifier of the French people. The term Rassemblement is one of the favourite words of French political vocabulary on both right and left, signifying the ceaseless quest for consensus in a divided political culture. In the 1930s it expressed the left's aspiration to unite the large majority of the French people against fascism: 'union of the French people' was the slogan of the PCF's 1936 Congress. Thorez stretched out his hand of reconciliation to the Catholics and to members of the Croix de Feu; Blum offered himself as a 'loyal' manager to the capitalist class. How were these offers received?

Politics: rather Hitler than Blum?

In October 1936 the Bishop of Marseilles was reported to have taken preparations for the evacuation of nuns in the case of revolution. Three months earlier Jean Calvet the Dean of Arts at the Institut Catholique in Paris had noted in his diary: 'saw the Abbé D . . . He told me: obviously a revolution is in the making.'[2] Such fears were commonplace in 1936: beliefs on the left that France was on the verge of a fascist coup were mirrored by beliefs on the right that revolution was imminent. Indeed there is a striking symmetry to the politics of the 1930s: on the left 6 February was a plot against the Republic; on the right the strikes of June 1936 were a Communist conspiracy to seize power. No doubt such views were often expressed in a spirit of polemical exaggeration, but in a highly polarised political atmosphere the most wild rumours gained credence: in November 1936, de Wendel received a telegram from a member of the employers' federation informing him that a Communist coup planned for the end of the month had been thwarted by the Ministry of Defence.[3]

The political polarization of 1936 was reflected in the election results. Just as on the left there was a swing to the Communists, so within the parliamentary right there was a shift from the centre–right group, the Alliance Démocratique, to the more conservative Fédération Républicaine. But given the fluctuating boundaries between the right wing groups in parliament, we should not attach too much significance to this. A better indication of the political polarization of 1936 was the extraordinary level of abuse to which certain Popular Front ministers were subjected in the right-wing press. There were three favourite targets of attack: Pierre Cot who was more or less accused of being in the pay of Moscow; Jean Zay, who had when young written a pastiche of pre-1914 anti-militarist rhetoric, which was exhumed by Action Française to demonstrate his anti-patriotism; and Salengro who was driven to suicide by the campaign mounted by the right-wing paper *Gringoire* accusing him of having deserted during the war. But the most constant victim of such attacks was Blum himself.[4] Blum had been no stranger to abuse throughout his political career but in the Popular Front period this reached an unprecedented virulence. 'A man to shoot but in the back' wrote Maurras in April 1935. A year later he repeated the idea: 'It is as a Jew that one must see, conceive, hear, fight and fell Blum' (13 May 1936). The Jewish theme was a favourite one of Action Française:

The Jewish ship adrift (13 June 1936)

The Jewish revolution proclaims its victory (14 June 1936)

Such headlines were the paper's daily staple. Maurras' collaborator Léon Daudet specialized in attacks on 'the cretinistic-talmudist cabinet', the 'circumcized hermaphrodite'. In one fifty-line article Maurras described Blum as a camel sixteen times.[5] It was alleged that Blum had been born Karfunkelstein in Bessarabia. Another common accusation was that he had a massive private collection of silver. *Action Française* was not the only newspaper to indulge in such attacks. In *Gringoire*, Henri Béraud drew up a list of the Jews – 'his tribe' – in the various ministerial cabinets. Such sentiments were even expressed in parliament itself: when Blum presented his government to the Chamber in June 1936, Xavier Vallat of the Fédération Républicaine caused uproar by announcing that for the first time 'this old Gallo-Roman nation' would be governed by a 'subtle talmudist'. A leading member of the party commended this 'courageous' statement.[6]

The anti-semitic theme allowed the right to contrast its Frenchness with the foreignness of its opponents (as it were, an implicit riposte to the 'Coblentzard' accusation). The arrival of refugees from Germany, Spain and central Europe provided further ammunition: 'All the scum of Europe has settled here', wrote Pierre Gaxotte of *Action Française*. The theme of the alien was linked to the fear of public disorder. The demonstrations and strikes which the Popular Front celebrated with such lyricism were seen as manifestations of semi-criminality.

As Socialist, Jew/alien, author of the 'immoral' *Du mariage*, traitor to his class and head of the first government supported by Communists, it is not surprising that right-wing polemic concentrated on the figure of Blum (much less interest was shown in the *person* of Thorez). The genuine hatred which lay behind such abuse was revealed by the physical attack on Blum in February 1936, which won Maurras a short imprisonment for incitement to murder. Although the most scurrilous attacks came from a small number of papers on the extreme right, their circulations were far from insignificant: this was the case of *Gringoire* (640,000 in November 1936), *Candide* (339,500 in March 1936) and *Action Française* (around 100,000). *Vendredi* never exceeded a circulation of 100,000. The cumulative effects of this propaganda had its insidious effects. When Blum was accompanying President Lebrun around the exhibition of French art at the Exposition he stopped before a set of silver from the Louvre and remarked to the President, not known for his sense of humour, 'there is my famous collection of silver'; later Lebrun, who had remained silent, returned to discover if this were true.[7] If the President of the Republic could believe such fantasies what must have been true of the more credulous and less informed. André Maurois tells in his memoirs how he found himself staying at the same hotel as Blum in the south of France: 'if you take in people like that', said an irascible old gentleman, 'we are going to leave'. 'But after all', the manager replied, 'I can't very well refuse the Premier of France.'[8] Such people might have agreed with Jean-Pierre Maxence, friend of the Catholic philosopher Maritain: 'If ever we take power, this is what will happen: at six o'clock, the Socialist press is suppressed; at 7 o'clock, freemasonry is forbidden, at eight o'clock, Blum is shot.'[9]

There is no doubt, then, that during the Popular Front politics reached a level of passion unparalleled since the Dreyfus Affair. How far did this imply that the French right had become radicalized? Was it true, as many on the left believed, that the Popular Front was the last bastion against fascism, or at least that in the 1930s, the right was turning against the Republic? To demonstrate this the left would have looked no further than the events of 6 February which were viewed as a failed *putsch*. The belief in a 'genuine insurrection minutely prepared' was also the conclusion of the Committee of Enquiry set up after the war. But no historian would today accept this verdict. All the different organizations which participated in the demonstration gave different instructions to their members as to where and when to meet.

This dispersal of forces was due not to any carefully hatched plan to converge on the Palais Bourbon from different sides but merely to mutual rivalries and differences of political objectives. Pierre Taittinger, for example, tried to prevent his Jeunesses Patriotes League from mingling with the royalists. When the demonstration turned violent the leaders were as confused as anyone else. Far from plotting the downfall of the Republic, Maurras spent the small hours writing Provençal verse for Daudet's wife. The exact truth about the events of 6 February will probably never be known, but although some circles had no doubt hoped to exploit the riots to overthrow the Republic or at least the government – this seems to be the case of the municipal councillors of Paris – it is hard to disagree with René Rémond that they resembled not so much a failed putsch as the Boulangist street agitation of the 1880s, and that the retrospective importance attributed to them was largely due to their unexpectedly bloody denouement. They were probably no better organized than a similar demonstration on 27 January which, because it ended peacefully, has been largely forgotten.[10]

In the two years after 6 February the various anti-parliamentary Leagues continued their activities. Some, such as the overtly fascist Francistes, founded in 1933, had tiny memberships; others, such as Action Française were vociferous and intellectually influential but hardly posed a political threat to the Republic. The main danger in the eyes of the left was de La Rocque's Croix de Feu which having been relatively small before 6 February (at the most 50,000) grew to about 450,000 members by June 1936. Leaving aside for the moment the nature of the Croix de Feu's ideology, it is worth noting that it did not owe its increasing popularity to any extremism on 6 February. On the contrary, many resented the fact that de La Rocque's men, who had approached the Palais Bourbon from the left bank, avoided any confrontation with the police.

But if the growth of the Croix de Feu was spectacular, it should not lead us to exaggerate the importance of the Leagues before 1936 or the extent of alienation from the Republic which they revealed. The manifestos of right-wing candidates at the 1936 elections displayed little anti-Republican language and if they did mention the Leagues it was usually unfavourably. Presumably this circumspection reflected a view about the opinion of the electorate. One-third of the manifestos, especially those outside the cities, did not even mention the Popular Front.[11] The political polarization of France, at least before June 1936, can be exaggerated. As Emmanuel Leroy Ladurie writes of his Catholic childhood in Normandy, the jubilees of St Theresa were at this time a much more important event in Lisieux than the Popular Front.[12]

But how true did this remain after the strikes of June revealed the Popular Front as a phenomenon which could not be ignored? One of the first actions of the new government was to dissolve the Croix de Feu and two other Leagues. But as far as the Croix de Feu was concerned this was to result in a massive increase of its influence in a new form.[13] Originally the organization had been set up in 1928 as a non-political ex-serviceman's association. When in 1929, de La Rocque, an ex-army officer, became president, he developed its activities in a political direction and set up affiliated organizations open to non-veterans. De La Rocque's independent attitude on 6 February showed that he was not going to allow his movement to be subordinated to any other. By mid-1934 he claimed 150,000 members. Even if the military style parades, the motorcades, the mysterious references to 'H-hour' may have given some of its members a fascist *frisson* – Rémond talks of 'political boy scouting for adults' – de La Rocque's ideology, as summarized in his book *Service Social*, was a collection of all the platitudes of traditional French conservatism: defence of the family, strengthening of the authority of the state, class collaboration, corporatism. None of this was necessarily anti-Republican – although de La Rocque equivocated on the issue – and it was certainly not fascist. The inclusion of corporatism was in the best social-Christian tradition.

After the banning of the Croix de Feu in June 1936, de La Rocque set up the French Social Party (PSF). That the new organization was to be different from the old League was shown both by the disillusioned departure of the more militant members such as Pozzo di Borgo and by the massive increase in membership. The PSF became not only the largest and fastest growing party of the right, but the largest party in France, surpassing the combined totals of the PCF and SFIO. PSF claims of a membership of 3 million by 1938 were exaggerated but the party's historian considers a figure between 700,000 and 1.2 million as plausible. Certainly the rapid growth of the party frightened the parliamentary right: various members of the Federation Républicaine believed that they had little chance of being re-elected in 1940 unless they stood under the banner of the PSF.[14] The Party's main objective was to win over the disaffected *classes moyennes*. In the words of one of the PSF's leaders: 'the Radical–Socialist party has abandoned the defence of the *classes moyennes*; it is the PSF which now has this mission'. And such evidence as exists suggests that the membership indeed consisted of peasants, shopkeepers, clerical workers and so on frightened by the Popular Front.

The party's main themes of propaganda were similar to those of the former League. Its stance on particular issues was predictable: the strikes were a plot, Franco a defender of western civilization, the Matignon Agreement a prelude to the proletarianization of the *classes moyennes*. The party's motto, like Vichy's, was *Travail, Patrie, Famille*, but where de La Rocque had previously cultivated a certain mystery about his attitude to the Republic, he now vowed explicit loyalty to it. De La Rocque's objective was to contest and win the elections of 1940. Even if there was a degree of political opportunism in this rallying to the Republic, the significant point is that de La Rocque achieved his greatest influence when he appeared at his most moderate.

One victim of the PSF's popularity was Jacques Doriot's French People's Party (PPF), also founded in June 1936.[15] There has been debate whether the PPF can be called a truly fascist party. Among its early recruits and sympathizers were various ex-members of Action Française and the Croix de Feu in search of more activist politics, and a number of fascist intellectuals who saw in Doriot a great populist tribune and authentic leader, altogether different from the more genteel de La Rocque. The main inspirer of the Doriot myth was the novelist Drieu la Rochelle: his only disappointment was that his hero wore glasses. For Drieu, Brasillach and other fascist intellectuals, fascism was a mystique, a quest for a spiritual regeneration of humanity. It provided a new aesthetic: 'the poetry of the twentieth century', as Brasillach said. Youth, energy, the countryside and health were the key themes. Drieu compared pot-bellied bourgeois politicians with the muscular youthful generations who represented the future (unfortunately Doriot became very fat). He proclaimed that in Doriot the thousands of young French people who wanted to go skiing and camping had found their champion: 'the France of the camping-site will conquer the France of the aperitif and the party congress'.[16] Much of this could have been said by Lagrange, and it is not so surprising therefore that Brasillach could write later that he did not view the events of May 1936 with hostility.

Despite the elucubrations of his intellectual supporters, up to the war Doriot himself publicly rejected the label of fascist. He certainly was a man of action rather than a thinker, but not exactly of the type hoped for by Drieu. After his exclusion from the PCF in 1934 he had basically become a political adventurer ready to seize his opportunities where he could find them (as leader of the PPF he accepted money from Mussolini and from some French industrialists). Anti-communism became the only consistent thread in his career. His very language mirrored that of the enemy he opposed: 'nationalists of France unite', was one of the slogans of the PPF. By the end of 1938 the love-affair between Doriot and the fascist intellectuals was over, and most of them left the party disillusioned with the inadequacies of their *chef*. But whether we judge the PPF as viewed by Doriot or that constructed by Drieu, there is no doubt that the party displayed many characteristics attributed to fascism: a leadership cult, a taste for political theatricality, a rhetoric of anti-capitalism.

The PPF enjoyed great initial success. By October 1936 Doriot claimed 100,000 members. There was a much higher proportion of working-class membership than in the PSF. According to the party's own statistics, membership reached a peak of 295,000 at the beginning of 1938. This figure may be exaggerated but the trend is probably accurate. Throughout 1938 membership declined; by the end of the year the party was largely a spent force. Its rise and decline paralleled that of the Popular Front against which it was largely a reaction. Its failure indicated the limitations of fascism as a mass movement in France.

That is not to say that the threat to the Republic imagined by the left was totally illusory. Zeev Sternhell has recently shown how during the 1930s a number of individuals from the right and the left converged to produce a radical intellectual critique of bourgeois parliamentary democracy which he describes as 'fascist'. Although the figures considered by Sternhell were often politically marginal, he also argues that their modes of thought had permeated sectors of opinion that were never strictly speaking fascist. The influence of fascism in France should, that is, be sought not in organizations, be they parties or leagues, but in ideas. Sternhell has been justifiably criticized for the excessive looseness of his definition of fascism and he probably overestimates the influence of the groups that he analyses. But there are other indications of the spread, if not of 'fascist' ideas, at least of the new attractions of political extremism on the right. One sign of this was the three loosely linked clandestine terrorist organizations which came to be known popularly as the Cagoule. Among other incidents, the Cagoulards were responsible for the dynamiting of the headquarters of the employers' federation in September 1937, intended to discredit the PCF. The existence of the Cagoule was revealed by the government in December 1937 after the discovery of important caches of arms, but the conspirators had still not stood trial by 1940. One of the three organizations was an anti-Communist network within the army not involved in actual acts of terrorism but there may well have been complicities between certain military officers and the conspirators.

More significant perhaps than the numbers of people involved in the Cagoule was the tendency in right-wing circles to play down the importance of an affair which after all involved a serious attempt to destabilize the Republic. In this context it is striking also how ready a conservative party like the Fédération Républicaine had been to defend the activities of the anti-parliamentary Leagues (even if they were reluctant to admit this in their election manifestos). Philippe Henriot, one of the younger members of the Fédération, became a leading apologist of the Leagues. It is true that after June 1936 relations between the Fédération and PSF quickly deteriorated but this rift was not ideological. It was due to the fact that unlike the Croix de Feu the more moderate PSF was a direct electoral competitor. The latent tension became open at a by-election in Normandy in 1937 when, in a constituency held by the Fédération, the PSF candidate came at the top of the poll in the first round. Although the Fédération candidate grudgingly stood down at the second round, the recriminations between the two parties caused the seat to pass into the hands of the centre. In short, as one historian has written: 'the Fédération saw the PSF not as a threat to French democracy but to its own electoral fortunes'.[17] It was perfectly willing to cooperate with the more extremist PPF which did not offer itself as an electoral rival.

A further sign of the political evolution of the traditional French right in the 1930s was the transformation of its attitude to Nazi Germany. Traditionally the right had mistrusted collective security and put its faith in military alliances as a means of containing German expansionism: it was Barthou who had opened negotiations with the Soviet Union. But when the Franco-Soviet pact came to be ratified in February 1936, 174 members of the right voted against: fear of Russia began to override fear of Germany. The fear was only accentuated by the success of the Communists at the elections of 1936. It became increasingly believed that France was about to be plunged into an international crusade against 'fascism' which would both serve the strategic interests of the Soviet Union and the revolutionary aspirations of the French Communists. One observer wrote of a regional Congress of the Fédération Républicaine at the end of 1938 (after Munich!) that 'one would have thought, to hear the speakers, that France was really being threatened by Russia and that a raid on Paris by Cossacks was imminent'.[18] The celebrated phrase, 'rather Hitler than Blum', may never have been uttered but it did encapsulate an attitude. It did not necessarily imply ideological sympathy with Germany but simply a changed perception of where the immediate danger to peace and order lay. Even such an unyieldingly anti-German conservative as François de Wendel refused to choose between Germany and Russia, hoping for a long time to dissuade Hitler through a *rapprochement* with Italy. Only after the anschluss did he change his view. 'There is at the moment', he wrote during the Munich crisis, 'a domestic Bolshevik danger and an external German danger. In my view the second is greater than the first and I disapprove of those who base their conduct on the opposite view'[19] – as many on the right continued to do. By the time de Wendel wrote these words the right was as divided as the left in its attitude to foreign policy. Pacifist *Munichois* of the left found themselves in agreement with anti-Communist *Munichois* of the right.

To the extent, then, that there was a radicalization of the right after 1936, this was revealed less by the growth of the PSF than by the evolution of the parliamentary right. But did the right's effectiveness match its vociferousness? Can the failures of Blum's government be attributed to the strength of the opposition? Both inside and outside parliament, the right was weakened by its disunity. In theory its full parliamentary strength was 220 but on few occasions did it reach this figure. Because of the strike movement the initial legislation of the Popular Front encountered almost no opposition in the Chamber: there was 1 vote against the *congés payés*, 5 against the collective contracts bill, 77 against the reform of the Bank of France. In the early days of the government only on the Wheat Marketing Board did the right offer effective opposition (26 hours of debate and 215 votes against) possibly because this was an issue unrelated to the strike movement. Even when the right began to recover its nerve, it rarely achieved anything like its full potential voting strength. The Fédération Républicaine was unsuccessful in its attempts to set up a parliamentary intergroup uniting the opposition parties. The deputies of the centre–right – Alliance Démocratique and Parti Démocrate Populaire (a small Christian Democratic party) – hoped, by offering themselves as a constructive opposition, to woo the Radicals away from the Popular Front into a centre–right coalition. As a result the Fédération Républicaine on several occasions found itself isolated in its uncompromising opposition.

The most effective parliamentary opposition was to come therefore from the Senate which was dominated by conservative Radicals opposed to the Popular Front. At the beginning the Senate was too cowed by the strikes but it quickly revealed itself as a formidable restraining influence on the reforming zeal of the government in every area. Any expenditure was seen as suspicious. Zay and Lagrange met with Senate resistance to almost all their efforts in the cultural field; Perrin had to fight to obtain funds for scientific research. In subtle ways the Senate limited the government's margin of manoeuvre, as, for example, in limiting the government's borrowing facilities in the second half of 1936.[20] And of course it was the Senate Finance Commission which brought down Blum in June 1937. The right in the Chamber was to have its moment of posthumous revenge on the Popular Front in March 1938 when it almost unanimously rejected Blum's appeal to join a government of national unity. Among the few who supported the idea were those such as Reynaud who had come to see the German threat as paramount.

The most rapidly expanding and dynamic organization of the right, the PSF, was of course hardly represented in parliament because it had not fought the elections of 1936. But the PSF was bound to be an important force in the elections of 1940, and all attempts to unite the right therefore depended on the cooperation of de La Rocque. In March 1937, Doriot proposed the formation of a 'Front of Liberty' grouping all the parties of the right against the Popular Front.[21] The Fédération Républicaine rallied to Doriot's idea quickly while the Alliance Démocratique refused. But most important was the opposition of de La Rocque who had no intention of allowing his organization to be annexed by any other. De La Rocque's attitude led to violent attacks on him by much of the rest of the right. In July 1937, Pozzo di Borgo, who had defected from the Croix de Feu to become involved in the Cagoule, accused his former chief of having accepted secret funds from the government between 1930 and 1932. The charges were repeated in the press and de la Rocque sued. The year 1937 ended therefore with the unedifying spectacle of the right washing its dirty linen in public. Although there were various points at which the right in the 1930s seemed to offer a symmetrical reflection of the left, unity was not one of these.

The right's most effective weapon of opposition to the government was probably the press. The role of certain newspapers at the beginning of the Spanish conflict was crucial in sabotaging the government's initial hopes of carrying out a discreet policy of aid to the Spanish Republic. And the fact that Blum believed that intervention in Spain might have led to civil war in France was testimony to the febrile political atmosphere created by the press. And yet the success of the essentially conservative PSF makes it questionable how accurately the violence of the press reflected the public mood. The PSF offered the frightened *classes moyennes* not a violent assault on the Republic but a national reconciliation, a *rassemblement* within it. The Popular Front's claim that it represented the true *rassemblement* of the French people was an entirely specious one. The claim was of course largely a rhetorical device, an instrumental political myth. But there were dangers in a simplifying political rhetoric which popularized the notion that the 'enemy' consisted only of a handful of anti-patriotic traitors who barely deserved to be included within the national political community: in 1936 these might be the 'two hundred families' – in 1940 the Jews, Masons and Communists.

Religion: reactions to the *main tendue*

The attitude of the Catholics to the Popular Front deserves special consideration because Thorez's *main tendue* was the most spectacular and original manifestation of the Popular Front's aspiration to be a *rassemblement* of the French people stretching beyond the traditional left. It is also the case that Blum's government, unlike previous left-wing governments in France, displayed no anticlericalism: Blum was the first French Premier to pay a visit to the Papal Nuncio since the separation of Church and state in 1905. Thus the Popular Front offered potential bridges to those Catholics who, taking their inspiration from the christian–democratic tradition of the early twentieth century, hoped to loosen the longstanding association of the Catholics with the right.[22]

Among major representatives of this tradition, which had been powerfully reinvigorated since 1926 by Pius XI's condemnation of Action Française, were two newspapers: *L'Aube*, founded in 1932 by Francisque Gay who had been involved in the Christian Democratic movement since 1924, and *Sept*, founded in March 1934 by the progressive Dominican friars of Juvisy. Both papers shared a common refusal to align Catholicism with either political right or left. More explicitly committed to the left was the Jeune République movement, set up in March 1934 by Marc Sangnier as a successor to his earlier Christian Democratic Sillon movement. Jeune République, which had four deputies elected in 1936, was the only important Catholic organization among the ninety-nine groups affiliated to the Comité de Rassemblement Populaire. Standing slightly apart because it claimed to offer a more radical critique of politics and society than Christian Democracy, was Emmanuel Mounier's *Esprit*, founded in 1932. Mounier was not concerned with reconciling Catholicism with the Republic but on the contrary attacking the 'established disorder' of the Third Republic. He opposed Marxist materialism and crude anti-Marxism, and rejected the categories of right and left. The exact nature of the spiritually reinvigorated politics which he proposed is somewhat elusive but on many issues *Esprit* took a stand which broke decisively with the traditional choices of French Catholicism. Finally, displaying none of the slippery ambiguities of *Esprit*, was *Terre Nouvelle*, whose cover, illustrating a hammer and sickle, summed up its unequivocal advocacy of a synthesis between Marxism and Christianity. The paper was put on the index in June 1936.[23]

L'Aube, Esprit and *Sept* were all founded around the same date: they are further evidence of the intellectual turmoil of the early 1930s – the quest among intellectuals of right and left to overhaul the categories of French politics. These progressive Catholics were not exclusively, or even primarily, concerned with politics, but what Michel Winock has said of *Esprit* would apply to them all: the attempt to assert the 'primacy of the spiritual' had to be provisionally shelved in a decade where political choices became increasingly difficult to avoid.[24]

The main organization of conservative Catholicism, the National Catholic Federation (FNC) took little account of the distinctions between the various currents of progressive Catholic thought: it condemned them all. The FNC had been founded in 1924 to resist the secularizing ambitions of Herriot's government and it retained the embattled mentality of its origins. Its political stance was clear from the fact that its president, General de Castelnau, was a regular contributor to the conservative daily, *L'Echo de Paris*. Much of the FNC's time was spent in polemic with the progressive Catholics. In May 1936 de Castelnau violently attacked a book by a contributor tò *Esprit* who had suggested that Catholics should vote for Bergery rather than Henriot. Castelnau's supporters also intrigued at Rome against the progressive Catholics: in May 1936 both *Esprit* and *L'Aube* came within a hairsbreadth of papal condemnation and were saved thanks to defensive action by Gay. In September 1936 there were rumours that the Pope was contemplating the condemnation of *Sept*.

Finally, within the official Church hierarchy there were also various strands of opinion, although these were less openly expressed. The Cardinal Archbishops of Paris (Verdier) and Lille (Liénart), both of whom owed their promotions to Pius XI, had the reputations of being mildly 'red'. This brief survey should be sufficient to show the heterogeneity of French Catholicism in the early 1930s. One effect of the political polarization of which the Popular Front was a symptom was to accentuate these divisions; another was to restrict the freedom of maneouvre of those Catholics searching for a middle way – a so-called Third Force – between left and right. This became clear as early as 6 February 1934. While most Catholics had defended the right-wing demonstrators – 'they had paid for the salvation of the fatherland with their lives', said Liénart – and *Jeune République* had condemned them unequivocally, *L'Aube*'s attempt to steer a middle course merely resulted in the loss of a number of readers who found its line too favourable to the left.

As the Popular Front developed in 1935, winning the enthusiastic support of *Jeune République* and the sceptical approval of *Esprit*, several of whose contributors wrote articles for *Vendredi*, *L'Aube* continued to argue for a Third Force. At the elections of 1936 Gay, its editor, and Georges Bidault, its leading editorialist, both stood as Third Party candidates against the right (but in seats where the left was very weak). Gay obtained only 412 votes and Bidault 800 (his conservative opponent won 11,000). Their candidatures had only been intended to have symbolic significance but their crushing defeat seemed only to symbolize the limited support for a Catholic centrist position. When *L'Aube* produced a fairly dispassionate article on the strikes of June 1936, it received a letter of protest from the Catholic poet Claudel ending his subscription to a newspaper which 'becomes more and more indistinguishable from the organs of the Popular Front'.

The initial Catholic responses to the Popular Front victory largely reflected pre-existing divisions. The FNC saw simply 'an immense and general fraud'; one influential Catholic journal noted (incorrectly) the presence of twenty-five Masons in Blum's cabinet. Mounier in *Esprit*, while not hiding his 'reservations', offered the new government a 'fraternal greeting'. But perhaps most significant of all, as an implicit recognition from a leading churchman of the need for political change, was Cardinal Verdier's call for 'an atmosphere of peace and fraternity' to allow the 'building of this new order that we all desire'. A possibly propitious omen for Verdier's appeal was the fact that Church–state relations had played no part in the election. But this did not mean that the issue was dead. In the autumn of 1936 there was an outcry when a decree which extended the raising of the school leaving age to Alsace-Lorraine led to local fears that the government planned to call into question the province's special religious status: 'Catholics', thundered the Bishop of Strasbourg, 'they are proposing the lay school . . . the seizure of crucifixes from the school walls'; nuns would be driven out of schools and forced 'to tread the path of exile'. But once the government had given assurances that it intended no such thing, this somewhat artificial controversy fizzled out in March 1937, after having provided temporary ammunition for Catholic anti-semites and other opponents of the Popular Front. Blum, unfortunately for them, was no Combes.[25]

Throughout the course of Blum's government a number of Catholic spokesmen attempted sporadically to calm the political atmosphere. Liénart publicly condemned the press campaign which had driven Salengro to suicide and *L'Aube* published a manifesto of protest signed by leading liberal Catholic personalities (including Mounier, Maritain, Gay, Bidault). In February 1937, *Sept*, with the approval of the Vatican, published a short interview with Blum who talked of a possible collaboration between Catholics and the Popular Front. Blum's declaration was accompanied by a commentary by the editors suggesting that where the Popular Front's reforms fulfilled the aspirations of social Catholicism they should be supported. The consternation caused in Catholic circles by *Sept*'s publication of fifteen lines by Blum illustrates perfectly the dilemmas of liberal Catholics when the general mass of Catholic opinion remained hostile to the left. Liénart received over 160 letters after his repudiation of the campaign against Salengro: two-thirds were hostile, often abusive.[26]

Nothing did more to jeopardize the chances of building bridges between Catholics and the Popular Front than the outbreak of the Spanish Civil War. The right-wing press was quickly full of stories about Republican atrocities against Catholics – burnt churches, massacres of priests, desecrations of graves. In these circumstances Franco was generally depicted as 'defending Christian civilization against Marxist barbarism': the Spanish conflict was a Holy War, a new crusade. Claudel wrote an Ode, 'To the Spanish Martyrs'. Not all French Catholics responded in this manner. For some Catholic intellectuals, most notably the novelists Mauriac and Georges Bernanos, the Spanish War caused agonizing reappraisals and a revaluation of their entire political position. More predictably, for the representatives of the christian democratic tradition the war was a further occasion to refuse simplistic choices between left and right: 'a crusader is not a murderer of children', wrote Bidault after Guernica. *Sept*, which published Claudel's Ode, took a similar line: the appropriate response to the war was pity for the sufferings of all the Spanish people not glorification of the atrocities of either side. But most Catholics were unaffected by these dissenting voices. They saw in the Spanish mirror a bloody reflection of their own conflicts.

It was against this background that the Communists pursued their *main tendue* policy.[27] The reaction of Catholics to the policy was of course theoretically distinct from their response to Blum's government, but in practice the distinction, which was very important to, for example, *Sept*, could easily become blurred. Thorez's appeal was rejected by all shades of Catholic opinion except *Terre Nouvelle*. 'Non Possumus' was the title of *Sept*'s editorial after Thorez's broadcast: 'we say that there is no possibility of, or desirability in, collaboration with the Communists because we agree with them in nothing'. *The Farce of the Main Tendue* was the title of a book by FNC journalist G. Bernonville. Lienart warned the French people in November 1936 against 'the trap which Communism is setting for them'. But this common condemnation of Communism concealed differences of appreciation as to how the Communist appeal should be met. While for the traditionalists of the FNC the 'farce of the main tendue' caused no problems, *La Vie Intellectuelle*, another journal produced by the Dominicans of Juvisy, was 'haunted by the anguishing problem that this strange appeal possesses'. The solution for them was not a simplistic reflex of anti-communism but a 'positive anti-communism' which did not leave to Communists alone the 'honour and privilege' of social progress: it was necessary to distinguish between individual Communists and Communism as an ideology. For Bernonville, on the other hand, these sentiments simply betrayed the 'most demagogic flattery towards the working class'.

The traditionalist camp received powerful support in March 1937 from the Pope's encyclical *Divini Redemptoris* prohibiting any collaboration with Communism. 'A lesson for Francisque Gay, *Sept* and all the proponents of Christian Democracy', declared one paper of the right. And in spite of *Sept*'s attempts to show that Pius had not said anything new, there were signs that the Pope's growing fear of Communism was turning him in an increasingly conservative direction. In August 1937, *Sept*, in the launching of which the Vatican had played a direct role, ceased publication on orders from Rome – a symbolic end to a ten-year period which had opened with the papal condemnation of Action Française.

The Communists continued unabashed to pursue their *main tendue* policy by distinguishing between the 'reactionary' hierarchy and the Catholic workers supposedly flocking to them. An encouraging Christmas message by Verdier in 1937, echoing recent remarks by the Pope, led *L'Humanité* to declare that 'Pius XI accepts the hand outstretched to the Catholics.' But by the end of 1937, with the Popular Front disintegrating, the reiteration of the policy had little contemporary political relevance and had become largely ritualistic. Thorez's assertions that many individual Catholics had responded to his appeal is impossible to substantiate. It would also be interesting to know how far the new pro-Catholic line was followed by rank and file Communists. In 1936 the local Communist paper of Marseilles, which had in 1935 denounced employers for indoctrinating their workers by providing crèches run by nuns, drew favourable attention to the help offered by nuns to strikers! But it seems unlikely that a working class nurtured on anti-clericalism would have altered its outlook quite as easily as the Communist press.[28]

The readership of such papers as *Sept* and *L'Aube* was not inconsiderable but the mass of Catholics voted for the right and no doubt shared the views of the FNC. Among Catholic intellectuals the new challenge posed by the Communists certainly prefigured the Marxist–Christian dialogue of the 1950s, and after dubious beginnings Communists and Catholics were both to play an important role in the resistance, acquiring new claims on national esteem. It may be the case, as some historians have asserted, that the Popular Front was a 'turning-point' for French Catholicism, although, as far as the Catholics were concerned, the roots of post-war Catholic–Communist dialogue lie in the early 1930s. But in the immediate term the polarization of the Popular Front years increased the difficulties of liberal Catholics, although it also speeded up the political radicalization of others. The Communist *main tendue*, by bringing the problem of Communist–Catholic relations to the forefront made it harder for liberal Catholics to differentiate between their hostility to Communism and their measured support for some aspects of the Popular Front, especially Blum's government. Thorez's aim was to include Catholics in the left's attempted *rassemblement* of the French people; paradoxically the *main tendue* may have made this harder to achieve.

Industry: the revenge of the *patrons*

More than any social or political group on the right, it was the attitude of the employers that would prove decisive for the success of the Popular Front. The Matignon Agreement, which enshrined its fundamental social achievements, had been won from the employers at their moment of maximum weakness: how would they react once that moment had passed? Blum, who presented himself as the 'loyal manager' of capitalism, demanded in return 'loyalty' from the capitalist class: did he receive it? We have already examined the attempt to create a *modus vivendi* between capital and labour in the wake of Matignon from the point of view of the workers. It is necessary finally to look at the other side.

The employers' response to the Popular Front is usually described in terms of a reaction against Matignon which set in during the summer of 1936. At the forefront of this reaction, it is claimed, were the small employers who felt they had been sold out to Matignon by the representatives of heavy industry. Within the employers' organization there was a sort of palace revolution: three out of the four employers who negotiated the Matignon Agreement lost their posts. The consequences of this were seen in November 1936 when Gignoux, the new head of the CGPF, broke off talks with the CGT which had been designed to negotiate a second 'Matignon' and effective conciliation procedures. The employers' counter-revolution was underway.

Although in the most general terms this picture is far from inaccurate, the truth is more complex.[29] To understand the reactions of the employers one must begin with the strikes of June 1936. When the first occupations occurred the official position of the CGPF was that negotiations with the strikers could not start until the factories had been evacuated. Nevertheless at the end of May agreements were negotiated for the evacuation of several engineering factories of the Paris region (including the Renault plant) and talks began between the unions and the Parisian metallurgy association (GIM) for a collective contract for the entire Parisian metallurgical industry, at this stage the heart of the strike movement. But these negotiations were broken off by the employers on 3 June when the factory occupations resumed after the Whitsun holiday. This was the situation on the eve of Blum's assumption of power. According to his own account at Riom (and never disputed by any of the other protagonists) the following course of events occurred: on 6 June he was secretly contacted by an old acquaintance from his days at the Conseil d'Etat, Lambert-Ribot, head of the Comité des Forges, the employers' organization of the steel industry, who intimated that the employers, frightened by the extension of the strikes, were now willing to talk to the CGT without prescribing factory evacuations as a prior condition; Blum instructed Salengro to contact the CGT and a meeting took place later that day between Blum and the CGT leaders; finally after this meeting Blum met three representatives of the employers. On the next day the central committee of the CGPF authorized its representatives to negotiate with the CGT. And on 7 June four employers' representatives – Lambert-Ribot, Duchemin (President of the CGPF), P.E. Dalbouze (President of the Paris Chamber of Commerce) and P. Richemond (representing the GIM) – met six representatives of the CGT at the Hotel Matignon. After ten hours of negotiation the Matignon Agreement was signed.

This chronology has recently been questioned by Adrian Rossiter who, using the archives of the Parisian Chamber of Commerce, shows that in fact Blum met the employers' representatives for the first time on the evening of 4 June at the instigation not of Lambert-Ribot personally but the CGPF as a whole. This revised dating – the fact that Blum met the employers before the CGT – contributes to a reinterpretation of the significance of the Matignon Agreement. The agreement comprised three elements: an agreement negotiated between bosses and unions in which the former conceded collective contracts and the election of workers' delegates; a wage arbitration imposed by Blum and reluctantly accepted by the employers; and, finally, a promise by Blum (which did not appear in the text of the Matignon Agreement itself) to pass legislation instituting paid holidays and a 40-hour week, something to which the employers remained implacably opposed. But Rossiter argues that the employers were able to find some compensation in the Matignon Agreement as a whole. First, although collective contracts had been signed on a decreasing scale in the 1920s, there is evidence at least in the Parisian engineering sector, that the employers had begun to reconsider their position just before the elections of 1936 and certainly before the strikes. Secondly, on the 40-hour week the employers were encouraged by private assurances from Blum that the new legislation would be applied gradually and, at least in the engineering sector, flexibly. In this reading of events the context of the Matignon Agreement appears as something other than a total capitulation by the employers.[30]

If this interpretation is correct, why did the CGPF break off negotiations with the CGT in November? The Matignon Agreement had been signed by representatives of heavy industry, and of industries situated in Paris, for whom the new burden of costs it imposed was more easily absorbed than by the mass of small provincial employers, and for whom the factory occupations represented a less personal humiliation than in smaller family enterprises. In the summer of 1936, therefore, there was a campaign of protest against the 'trusts' who were alleged to have sold out the small employers. The Federation of Textile Employers representing the interests of thousands of small employers withdrew from the CGPF. When industrial unrest resumed after the August holidays, the mood of such employers became increasingly bitter. Their grievances centred particularly around the problem of authority. In the words of one liberal industrialist: 'It is not so much the demands of the workforce which have upset industrialists during the last months as the unexpected and peremptory way in which these demands have been presented.' Thus, for example, the plaintive letter addressed to Blum in September 1936 by a leading Lille textile industrialist:

the present conflict lies essentially in the fact that the employers ask your government in vain to give them back their authority. The textile employers of Lille no longer want their factories occupied . . . no longer want to be 'authorized' to enter their own factories. In a word, they do not want to accept the setting up of Soviets in their factories.[31]

Louis Renault complained of the 'increasingly unbreathable atmosphere' in his factory, of the 'continuous strikes, the repeated acts of indiscipline, the systematic resttriction of production.'[32]

During the course of the summer of 1936 the statutes of the CGPF were revised to increase the representation of small employers. And in October Duchemin was ousted from the leadership of the CGPF and replaced by Gignoux, not himself an industrialist but a journalist specializing in industrial matters. But it is too simple to interpret this as a sign that heavy industry had lost its hold over the CGPF: one of the leading members of the restructured organization was Baron Petiet, a right-hand man of Louis Renault.[33]

Similarly Gignoux's decision to break off negotiations with the CGT in October was not simply a response to the *fronde* of the small employers. In fact Gignoux had at first been no less willing than Duchemin to continue the negotiations. The change in his attitude seems to have come about once separate discussions had started in October about the application of the 40-hour week to the metallurgical industry. The employers' representatives found that the concessions previously promised by Blum were not forthcoming: this was the occasion on which Jouhaux, overriding the objections of Belin, insisted on the full application of the 40-hour week at once. The CGT's intransigence on this point has already been examined, and it was no doubt fuelled by the belligerent statements emanating from many small industrialists and the increasing evidence of an employers' counter-offensive at factory floor level. But if the CGT was not willing to compromise on the 40-hour week, the representatives of heavy industry who dominated the CGPF were unwilling to restrain the aggressiveness of their rank and file any longer.[34]

Within the factory the employers' offensive against the Popular Front took various forms. The Grenoble Chamber of Commerce, for example, advised its members in 1937 not to apply collective contracts or at least to do so only partially, thereby either winning back ground lost in June 1936 or provoking the workforce into a strike which would be met by a lockout. In the same region employers also founded 'yellow' company unions: the first appeared in June 1936, by March 1937 there were twenty-three. These unions preached capital–labour collaboration and engineered incidents during strikes as a way of discrediting the CGT.[35] At the Renault factory the management encouraged yellow unions by recruiting workers through extremist right-wing organizations; from the winter of 1937/8 the collective contract was flouted by moving union activists and workers' delegates arbitrarily from workshop to workshop. Another development was the creation of so-called 'professional unions' from the summer of 1936 under the aegis of the PSF. The exact membership of these organizations is unknown – they claimed 500,000 members in 1936 and 1 million in 1938 – but in certain sectors, especially the department stores, they were undoubtedly successful. Although distinguishing themselves from employer sponsored company unions they advocated an identical doctrine of class collaboration.[36]

One important result of the Popular Front was to develop a new sense of class self-identity on the part of the employers. Significant in this respect was the change in the name of the CGPF (the initials remained identical) from General Confederation of French Production to General Confederation of French Employers. Gignoux published a pamphlet entitled *Bosses Act Like Bosses*.[37] This emergence of a clearer class identity occurred also among the ranks of factory managers, technicians and engineers, or, as they came to be known, *cadres*. This was an important development to some extent promoted by the employers' organizations as part of their search for allies in their counter-offensive. Previously they had devoted little specific attention to the intermediary class between the workers and themselves. As a result in June 1936 many technicians and engineers had joined the strikers and formed a union which affiliated to the CGT. After June 1936 the employers' organizations begun to propagate the idea that the *cadres* were the employers' 'collaborators' and representatives on the factory floor. The *cadres* were encouraged to join their own unions and challenge the monopoly of the CGT. What this shows is that the employers were capable of a certain flexibility and subtlety in their response to the Popular Front. The days of the employer as absolute dictator in the factory were over. Louis Renault, who had before 1936

rejected the idea of selling company shares to cadres or workers who had
worked in his factory for over ten years, was now persuaded to appoint a
new 'director of social relations' who was instructed to show 'greater
suppleness and skill towards the workers'.[38]

The months after June 1936 also saw the creation of new organizations
which improved the efficiency of the employers' struggle against the CGT.
The most vociferous and stridently anti-Communist of these was the
CPAS presided over by the former Finance Minister of Doumergue and
Flandin, Louis Germain-Martin. The CPAS became in effect the propaganda wing of the CGPF producing a barrage of brochures and posters, as
well as providing employers with improved documentation. It also
attempted the organization of popular leisure and tourism – a further
indication that the employers' response to the Popular Front did not
simply take the form of crude repression: some lessons had been learned.
Another new organization was the Central Committee of Professional
Organization (CCOP) and its offshoot the Centre for Young Employers
(CJP), grouping employers of under forty years old who shared corpora-
tist and technocratic views. This list is far from exhaustive but it is
sufficient to demonstrate the extent to which the Popular Front had
stimulated a regrouping of forces and a process of self-examination in the
world of the employer.

In June 1936 the employers had been overwhelmed by a movement of
social protest which took them by surprise: they were frightened, discontented and disunited. Two years later they had regained confidence in
themselves as a class, acquired new organizations to defend their interests
politically, and started to organize their revenge on the factory floor. The
working-class defeat of November 1938 had been long prepared.

PART 5

The end of the Popular Front

10 ∾ Post-mortem

At the end of 1936 Blum addressed the nation optimistically about the achievements of his government: 'Hope has returned; once again there is a zest for work, a zest for life. France has a new face, a new appearance. New social relations are being established. A new order is emerging.' But six months later in the early hours of the morning of 21 June, Blum announced his resignation after the Senate had twice rejected his demand for financial decree powers. Whether the Senate enjoyed the right to bring down a government had always remained a grey area of the constitution. In theory Chamber and Senate enjoyed equal legislative power (except that financial bills had to be introduced in the Chamber first), but in the first years of the Republic the accepted convention was that because the Senate could not be dissolved it should not bring down a government. The first government to resign as a result of a hostile Senate vote was that of Léon Bourgeois in 1897 and this created an important constitutional precedent. In the inter-war years, before the fall of Blum, the Senate had brought down governments in 1925 (Herriot), 1930 (Tardieu) and 1932 (Laval). Blum had already considered the problem of the Senate in his *Letters on Government Reform*. He suggested that the Senate should be obliged to vote on proposed legislation within a limited timescale so as to eliminate its powers of obstruction by means of systematic adjournment. He did not contest its *de facto* power of veto because, 'I do not believe that it would ever use this right against a resolute agreement of the Chamber and the government.'[1] In June 1937, then, in spite of Blum's optimism of six months earlier and in spite of the fact that his government was fully supported by the Chamber, Blum no longer displayed this 'resolute' attitude. What had happened to weaken its resolution?

The resignation of Blum disappointed many of his supporters and has perplexed historians. The episode is worth exploring in some detail as a way of examining Blum's own estimation of the achievement of the Popular Front. Was the resignation an admission of failure? Or was it, as it were, the logical political consequence of the acceptance of the 'pause' in February – a reflection of the belief that significant reforms had been carried out but that a period of respite and consolidation was necessary for them to be incorporated into French society. Starting from these questions we can finally attempt a sort of post-mortem on the Popular Front – an assessment of its achievement, and of its impact on French society and history.

The resignation of Blum

Resignation was not the only option open to Blum after his defeat in the Senate. The defeat itself did not come as a total surprise. The Senate, dominated as it was by conservative Radicals, had made little secret of its hostility to Blum's government. But at the beginning it was forced to bow to the popular will as expressed in the strikes. This did not stop the Senators from sniping at the government from time to time. For example, in July 1936, Bienvenu-Martin, a leading Radical Senator, cornered Salengro into announcing that the government would not tolerate further factory occupations, a declaration which caused irritation from the Communists and some Socialists. This had been the purpose of the manoeuvre. If at first the Senate dared not confront the government directly on any major issues of policy we have seen that on many subsidiary issues – colonial policy, cultural policy, aspects of financial policy, and so on – it did as much as possible to hinder the government's task. By the spring of 1937 such obliqueness was no longer necessary once it no longer seemed likely that a parliamentary defeat for the government would result in street violence. In the financial crisis of June 1937 the Senate could at last move in for the kill.

The bill demanding decree powers passed the Chamber in June by 346 votes to 247 (20 Radicals voted against). By 220 votes to 54 the Senate proposed a much more restrictive text limiting the use to which the decree powers could be put. On 19 June the Chamber, with the agreement of the government, voted a compromise text. But for a second time the Senate reaffirmed its support for a text almost identical to its first one. Part of the difficulty of understanding the significance of this crisis lies in a certain ambiguity about the nature of the financial bill proposed by the government.[2]

There was nothing novel about a government demanding decree powers to deal with a financial crisis – these had been granted to Poincaré in 1926, Doumergue in 1934, Laval in 1935 – but the government was required to give some idea how it would use them. The view of the Socialist Party in 1937 was that Blum's radical economic proposals had been finally sabotaged by the reactionary Senate: the government had fallen on the left. This was certainly true of the fall of Blum's second government – although no one had ever had any illusions about its survival anyway – but the situation in 1937 was more complicated: the government, as we have seen, was far from clear what it intended to use the financial powers for. Taxes were to be increased to help reduce the deficit of the railways and post office; banks were to be required to maintain a proportion of their reserves in state securities. The government however agreed not to impose exchange controls and accepted an amendment to this effect. The revised bill proposed on 19 June also accepted further restrictions imposed by the Senate: the decrees could not be used to impose any new expenditure, nationalizations or limitations on the free movement of currency in and out of France. But the government gibbed at prohibitions on the reorganization of the Bank of France or on movements of specie. These measures certainly represented a shift away from the government's initial optimism that its programme could be carried out with the minimum of economic controls – 'we have pushed economic liberalism as far as any past government', said Blum – but on the other hand they did not represent a repudiation of the pause: rather they were a means of allowing it to be carried on. If the measures of June 1937 stand somewhere between the pause and those of March 1938, they are certainly nearer the former than the latter.

Although Blum was perfectly entitled to ask the Chamber to pass his bill a third time there was in fact no constitutional means of forcing the Senate to submit. One possibility was to threaten to appeal for street demonstrations if it persisted in its refusal, to call upon the masses to frighten it into compliance as they had in June 1936. Another was to dissolve the Chamber and obtain a new popular mandate in elections. But the Chamber could only be dissolved with the agreement of the President of the Republic and the Senate. If this agreement were withheld – a highly probable eventuality – the only alternative was for the Popular Front deputies to resign their seats and offer themselves for reelection in the hope that triumphant electoral success would force the Senate to climb down. Instead of chosing any of these options Blum chose to resign.

On at least four previous occasions Blum had contemplated resignation. The first, we have seen, was at the time of the application of non-intervention. The second was in December 1936 when the Communists abstained in a vote of confidence on foreign policy. According to Jules Moch, Auriol, Cot, Dormoy and Violette (all against non-intervention) were in favour of resignation; the Radical members of the government were for staying on. The third occasion, so Blum himself later said, was when the government was forced to implement the pause. The fourth was after the Clichy incident when Blum told Monnet that he could no longer carry on but was argued out of his depression by various colleagues.[3] In June 1937 the roles were reversed. Zyromski and Pivert (not in the cabinet of course) argued for an appeal to the masses; Auriol was in favour of dissolving the Chamber or, if this proved impossible, of the Popular Front deputies resigning their seats and standing for reelection. But the Radical ministers, having held a separate deliberation, refused to contemplate this. At the Socialist Congress of Marseilles a few weeks later Blum attempted to justify his decision to resign. Disappointment of the party rank and file. He argued that although it would have been possible to force the Senate into submission by appealing to the population to demonstrate in the streets, he had opposed this for three reasons. First, France was in the middle of a financial crisis which would only be aggravated by prolonged political uncertainty. Secondly, the international situation was menacing. On 19 June the German cruiser Leipzig had been torpedoed by submarines of the Spanish Republican forces. Hitler and Mussolini had at once withdrawn from the naval part of the non-intervention pact. At such a time, Blum claimed, France needed firm government. Thirdly, there was a risk – especially irresponsible at such a time – of plunging France into prolonged social conflict, even a 'revolutionary struggle', with the likely consequence of alienating the Radicals from the Popular Front.[4] Moch recounts that at the cabinet meeting called to decide upon how to respond to the Senate, Blum was passed a note informing him that Pivert and Zyromski were proposing to call a mass demonstration outside the Senate. Reading the note Blum cried out in horror: 'No! In no circumstances.'[5] He was not willing to risk another Clichy.

The Congress of Marseilles witnessed a revealing exchange between Blum and the Socialist, Pierre Brossolette. Brossolette expressed his disappointment at Blum's resignation: 'our faith in the Party came above all from the fact that we thought it was not a party *like the others*, that its leader was not a man *like the others* and that it could not fall like the others'. But now Blum had fallen like Herriot in 1925. Blum took up the point. His government was indeed not 'altogether identical to the others' because it rested on an unprecedented popular will. But it was a 'legitimate government, relying on legality' and subject to all the constitutional rules: 'essentially it was not as different as you believed'. This for Blum was the heart of the matter. His critics were guilty of 'the fateful confusion' between the conquest and the exercise of power – the exercise of power by a coalition Popular Front government.[6]

Blum, then, was not willing to commit the *escroquerie* that he had denounced many years before. But did his resignation imply an admission that the exercise of power itself had failed and could be carried on no longer? On the eve of taking office he had (in the same speech in which he analysed his capacities of leadership) considered with typical frankness, the possibilities of failure,

if it so happened that we failed, if there was insurmountable opposition that forced us to conclude that it is impossible to reform society from within . . . I would be the first to come and say to you: it was a chimera, it was a vain dream. There is nothing to do with this society as it is; we can expect nothing from it; the power of tradition and self-interest is insurmountable. And I would be the first, then, to tell you why and how we failed, and the consequences that you should draw from our failure.

On 6 June 1937 a few days before the final crisis he spoke in similar terms. But this was not the conclusion that Blum drew at the Congress of Marseilles. Within the limitations of the exercise of power his government had not, he said, been a failure: the reforms carried out represented a 'profound modification of the nation's life'. A year later he still saw them as having been, 'a veritable revolution in the individual, moral and material conditions of the workers of this country' (defining revolution, as he had many years before, as a change which speeded up the normal course of history).[7] The exercise of power had not, then, been a chimera. Blum remained faithful to his earlier analysis. He retained his objection to planist demands for structural reforms – 'a notion to which I have never reconciled myself'. But to assimilate the reforms already carried out under the exercise of power there was need for a 'period of adaptation'.

Blum was a man whose public explanations for his actions always deserve serious consideration. But there were nonetheless good reasons why he should have presented these arguments to a Socialist Congress which needed to be persuaded to ratify Socialist participation in a Popular Front government headed by Chautemps. Historians have therefore sought deeper reasons for his resignation. At least three different theories have been suggested. For Georges Dupeux, if the will had been there Blum could easily have overcome the Senate.[8] Blum resigned because, whatever his protestations to the contrary, he had in fact lost faith in what could be achieved by the exercise of power. He had hoped that his moderately reformist programme would meet with a responsible and cooperative response from enlightened sectors of the bourgeoisie; instead he had encountered obstruction and hostility. Dupeux points to Blum's comprehensive indictment of the French bourgeoisie in his little book *A L'Échelle humaine* written in 1941. There Blum described how his government, although its programme did 'not include a very profound social transformation' (compare this with what he said in 1937!) was based on 'a sort of political lie' since a 'hostile bourgeoise continued to occupy solid and powerful positions of power'. This was a more meditated version of this comment to Bullitt a few days after his resignation: 'I've had enough. All I have tried to do has been sabotaged.'[9] Dupeux's argument has some plausibility although he underestimates the problems in overcoming the Senate, especially given Blum's visceral fear of violence. As for Blum's estimate of the bourgeoisie, there were good reasons why a book written in 1941 should be particularly pessimistic.

Irwin Wall had argued that the political crisis of June 1937 was engineered by Blum.[10] Given that Blum was not intending to use the decree powers to introduce substantial new reforms – implicitly the pause was to be continued – it would have been possible to reach an accommodation with the Senate. The points on which Blum refused to budge were comparatively trivial ones. He resigned therefore to stave off the growing dissent among the rank and file of the Socialist Party and avoid the danger that at the forthcoming party Congress the government would come under pressure from the party to modify its Spanish policy and its financial policy. There are two objections to this argument. In the first place, far from engineering a crisis with the Senate, Blum tried hard to reach a compromise. Secondly, the opposition to Blum at the Congress was likely to be much greater after he had resigned without putting up a fight than if he remained in government. It would have been reasonable to expect more difficulty in persuading the party to support unpopular policies when carried out by a government headed by Chautemps than by one headed by Blum. As Brossolette himself said, he would have voted the Bataille Socialiste motion even if Blum's government had remained, there was all the more reason after its fall. Indeed Blum only just succeeded in persuading the Congress to ratify the participation of the Socialists' Chautemps government.

René Girault has posed the question of Blum's resignation in somewhat different terms. He asks not why Blum resigned in June but why he didn't do so in March rather than implement the pause.[11] His answer is that Blum was willing to compromise his domestic financial policy because he retained hopes of being able to carry out certain foreign policy aims. By June, however, these hopes had vanished. The Schacht talks had broken down; the break-up of the *Petite Entente* (the signing of the Italy–Yugoslav pact) and the news of the Red Army purges reduced the prospect of reinforcing France's Eastern alliances; the replacement of Baldwin by Chamberlain in May 1937 was a blow to any Franco-British policy of firmness towards Hitler. Given this combination of unfavourable circumstances Blum saw no point in carrying on. While Girault is correct in believing that foreign policy had come to take an increasing significance in Blum's mind, the details of his argument are not convincing. The resignation of Baldwin did not at the time have the significance it has since acquired; the government had hardly been enthusiastic about the Soviet alliance before June; serious hopes of obtaining concessions from Schacht had dissipated well before May 1937. Also if Blum believed that the outlook for foreign policy had deteriorated, it would perhaps have been logical to stay on rather than let responsibility for it fall into less reliable hands.

What, finally, are we to conclude about the reasons for Blum's resignation? There is no doubt some truth in the motives considered above. Blum's decision was the result of a combination of circumstances. Sheer exhaustion was a contributory factor (possibly aggravated by the strain caused by the illness of his second wife who was to die in January 1938). At Marseilles, Blum described his thirteen months of office in the following terms: 'days without relief and nights without sleep in which it seemed that . . . by some malign twist of fate every possible trial and difficulty that could be predicted, and those also that could not be predicted, converged at the same moment.'

But Blum's resignation was not only an act of personal lassitude. There is one aspect of the question that has received inadequate attention. By resigning the premiership Blum was contributing to holding together the Popular Front as a coalition. One of Blum's leading biographers, Joel Colton, has criticized him for being too constrained by his own distinctions between the exercise and conquest of power: he artificially restricted his freedom of manoeuvre by imposing severe limitations on what could be achieved during the exercise of power. Thus, in June 1937, Blum could conceive of no middle way between capitulating to the Senate or a 'revolutionary struggle' against the Senate. Colton contrasts this with the pragmatism of Roosevelt in overcoming the opposition of the Supreme Court or Lloyd George the House of Lords (an example which Blum himself invoked at Marseilles.)[12] But it is hard to see how Blum could have resisted the Senate without breaking up the Popular Front coalition. The Radicals in the cabinet opposed such action; in the Chamber many Radicals had only voted for the government secure in the knowledge that the Senate would oppose it and their support would certainly not have survived an appeal by Blum for popular demonstrations. Once defeated in the Chamber owing to the defection of the Radicals, Blum would anyway have been forced to resign – but this time at the cost of breaking the Popular Front alliance. By allowing his government to fall Blum preserved the Popular Front as a coalition, even if for some he betrayed it as a mass movement. Why did Blum feel it so important to preserve the coalition even when he had come to believe that for the moment no further economic and social reforms were possible? He had initially viewed the Popular Front primarily as a defence against the threat of fascism in France. We have seen that by the beginning of 1938 he had come to view the German threat as the most serious. By June 1937 his thoughts were possibly already moving in this direction. Nothing therefore must be done to undermine the unity of the left – or indeed the unity of the French people as a whole. The irony, of course, is that this was precisely the issue upon which, as 1938 would demonstrate, the left was most divided.

The Popular Front: a summing up

Looking back in the 1970s on the CVIA, which he had helped to create in 1934, Francis Walter judged it as a disaster: 'we had wanted to fight fascism and war, and we had both – with defeat as a bonus'.[13] If this statement is extended to a judgement of the Popular Front as a whole, we might add that it failed also to bring 'bread', to overcome the Depression. Accepting, for the moment, this premise that the Popular Front was a failure, where do the causes of the failure lie? The obvious place to begin is with the government of Blum which assumed the responsibility in 1936 of transforming the Popular Front's aspirations into policy. One line of criticism directed against Blum is that, although modelling himself partly on Roosevelt, he lacked the necessary pragmatism for the role: having prepared his party psychologically for the 'exercise of power', his ideological inflexibility prevented him from making it work. He undertook to manage capitalism while theoretically committed to the position that this was in fact impossible. This dilemma was not unique to the French Socialists. It was classically expressed by the German trade-unionist Fritz Tarnow in 1931:

> Are we sitting at the sickbed of capitalism, not only as doctors who want to cure the patient, but as prospective heirs who cannot wait for the end and would like to hasten it with poison? . . . We are condemned to be doctors who seriously desire a cure, and yet we maintain the feeling that we are heirs who wish to receive the entire legacy today rather than tomorrow. This double role, doctor and heir, is a damned difficult task.[14]

Planism, which some French Socialists saw as a means of resolving this conflict by offering a 'middle way' – an 'intermediary regime' in contemporary jargon – between capitalism and socialism, was rejected by Blum.

But this criticism of Blum is more telling in theory than in practice. Although from the very beginning of his premiership he did – with that famed frankness which was meant to disarm his opponents but sometimes backfired against its practitioner – envisage the possibility of failure, he was in fact much more committed to the position that he could make capitalism work – or at least that he could make it work better than could its avowed defenders – than were, say, such Socialists as Müller in Germany or MacDonald in Britain both of whom were taken unawares by the Depression. The French Socialists, on the other hand, had had six years to prepare their response to the Depression; they arrived in office with a doctrine (*la politique du pouvoir d'achat*) and a set of proposals specifically designed to combat it. In this sense Blum's theoretical rejection of planism recedes into insignificance; in practice he was in 1936 a planist in spite of himself.

The planists did not however merely claim that it was possible to manage capitalism, they also argued that only their solution – the Plan – would achieve this. The planist critique of Blum's government is therefore that its programme – the Popular Front programme – did not go far enough. But here again Blum was, in practice, not so far from the planist position. Partly under their influence, he had come to believe by 1935 that nationalizations were necessary, although he rejected their argument that they represented a 'structural' transformation of capitalism. In other words he took on board some of their proposals without accepting the theory that underlay them: the Socialists tried hard to include nationalizations in the Popular Front programme. If Blum's government carried out no nationalizations – except for the special case of the armaments industry – this was not because it rejected planist solutions but because Blum felt bound by the Popular Front programme.

This leads to a different charge against Blum – not that he was an excessively doctrinaire Socialist who lacked a view of how to run capitalism but that, although he did have such a view, he timidly allowed himself to be hemmed in by the Popular Front programme. 'Scrupulousness' and 'caution' are words commonly used about Blum. All commentators stress his 'legalism'. But Georges Dupeux makes the perfectly valid observation that there was a margin of manoeuvre between legalism and strict observance of the Popular Front programme.[15] There are two points to be made here. First, the Popular Front government was a coalition: Blum's restricted interpretation of his mandate was not only self imposed but also politically imposed. And if, secondly, it be said that the strikes of June 1936 had transformed the situation and given Blum the power to go farther than the Popular Front programme, it should be noted that this is precisely what occurred. There was much disingenuousness in Blum's assertion that his hands were tied by the Popular Front programme since in fact none of the measures agreed at Matignon had been included in it (similarly in the pause Blum announced the effective abandonment of those reforms in the programme which still remained to be carried out). In fact Blum's economic experiment was hampered less by the inadequacies of the Popular Front economics – of the *politique du pouvoir d'achat* – than by the form in which they were implemented as a result of the strikes: this applies especially to the 40-hour week which emerged as one of the central demands of the strikers in 1936 although the Socialist Party had itself only recently abandoned the idea. The 40-hour week was not, as Sauvy and others have portrayed it, the sole cause of the difficulties of the French economy in 1937, but its economic effects (on costs and production) were certainly detrimental; and by becoming for both capital and labour the symbol of the Popular Front's economic policy, it undermined Blum's attempts to transform the Matignon Agreement into a more durable pattern of industrial relations, through which industrial conflicts could be settled consensually by national negotiation between the CGT and CGPF, thereby preserving for the CGT the central role that it had won for itself, in very special circumstances, in June 1936. The 40-hour week poisoned industrial relations and blocked any prospect that, once the employers had recovered their strength, they would accept anything less than an almost total reversal of Matignon.[16]

If, then, the strikes of 1936 opened up possibilities to the incoming government, they also closed off others. Blum's failures must be considered in the context of the immensely complicated situation which he faced when taking office. Apart from very slight signs of economic recovery at the beginning of 1936, Pierre Renouvin's phrase 'a landscape of ruins' admirably describes Blum's inheritance in 1936. Renouvin himself applied these words to France's international position after Laval's disastrous period in office. And it was indeed the international situation which weighed most heavily on Blum's government: it tied his hands in domestic economic policy (by excluding exchange control in order to retain British approval) and undermined government finances (by requiring rearmament); in addition, the Spanish Civil War embittered political conflict in France and threatened the unity of the Popular Front. As Guéhenno wrote many years later: 'it was an illusion to believe that France could create her modest ration of happiness in the middle of a world devastated by violence'.[17] The threat from Nazi Germany gradually transformed Blum's conception of the primary objective of the Popular Front. But he failed to express his new view with sufficient clarity. The fact that, as late as the summer of 1938, the Faurists could believe that Blum shared their views on foreign policy was partly a result of Blum's efforts to hold the party together by not stating his case too brutally; it was also due to his hesitation in finally throwing off the language of pacifism that the left had employed since 1918.

Blum's failure to give a clear lead on this issue could be extended to a more general criticism that he lacked the qualities of a genuine leader. His very awareness of the complexities of any situation reduced his capacity to make the necessary simplifications. Blum, in this view, was too rationalist a figure in an era which demanded not reasons but slogans. Formulated slightly differently, the charge does contain some truth. Although in theory a Marxist and materialist, Blum in fact viewed politics in primarily moral terms. He lived politics as a personal moral drama – the agony of Spain was transformed into the agony of Blum – and expected the same from others: 'loyalty' and 'fidelity' were favourite words. He asked for loyalty from the working class (to raise production), loyalty from the employers (to invest), loyalty from the British (to back French foreign policy), loyalty even from Hitler and Mussolini (to respect non-intervention). In return he got strikes, a flight of capital, Neville Chamberlain and Guernica. By June 1937 Blum seems to have been close to despair. Whatever the reasons for his resignation, there seems little doubt that his heart had partly gone out of the fight.

For Colette Audry and others, Blum's mistake was to have failed to exploit sufficiently the mass support enjoyed by the Popular Front and failed to perceive that the Popular Front was a qualitatively new kind of political movement. Audry sees Blum, not without reason, as someone who was always slightly suspicious of the masses: as a Third Republic politician with a long memory, he saw every street crowd as a potential Boulangist rabble.[18] There are two possible lines of attack here. The first is that Blum missed the opportunity to carry out a revolution in 1936. It is certainly true that the festive atmosphere of the strikes of June has often been overplayed but it is quite wrong to believe that the institutions of the state were so weakened in 1936 as to create a 'revolutionary situation'. There is simply no comparison with Russia in 1917, Germany in 1919 (when there was no revolution, after all), Spain in September 1936 or even France in 1944. And in France in 1936 the Communists of course had no intention, if they could prevent it, of allowing a revolution to occur. A second line of attack blames Blum, not so much for failing to carry out a revolution, as for neglecting to use the popular movement to bolster his government and carry out more radical policies – a criticism levelled at Blum both by the leftists and by the Communists, although they share very different views as to what policies should have been carried out.

This question usefully directs our examination of the failure of the Popular Front away from the person of Blum, and the action of his government, to an examination of the Popular Front as a whole – as political coalition and mass movement. One of the Communists' own later explanations for the weakness of the Popular Front was that they were never able to give the political coalition an effective base of mass popular support. This was the function that they had hoped to give the Popular Front committees, which would ideally have consolidated the links between the mass movement and the political parties, providing the mass movement with, as it were, a formal political structure of its own. What this really meant was directing the popular movement – especially those people who were not members of any political party – in the direction desired by the PCF: opposition to non-intervention, support for the Soviet alliance, and so on. The Communists blamed their coalition allies for refusing to allow the Popular Front committees to become at best more than local replicas of the Comité du Rassemblement Populaire. But this did not stop them trying to use the Amsterdam Committees and other front organizations for the role they had ascribed to the Popular Front committees. We therefore need to look more closely at the Communists' failure: it cannot merely be attributed to their allies.

The paradox of the PCF's situation was that between 1934 and 1936, acting from an almost non-existent parliamentary base, it held most of the initiative on the left: the other parties were obliged to react to it. But after

1936, although now a sizeable parliamentary force and the largest party of the left (in terms of members), the PCF lost the initiative and found itself responding to events. Partly this was the result of a tactical error which the Party understood too late: the Communists were less effective as 'ministers of the masses' than they might have been as ministers of Blum. The popular movement which the Communists aspired both to articulate and control was not always susceptible to their influence. One problem was that there was not one popular movement but two, and only briefly did they mesh – around negative slogans. First, there was the anti-fascist movement which, in 1934 and 1935, united the working class and elements of the *classes moyennes*. Secondly there was, in 1936, a strike movement of social protest. Although there is some anecdotal evidence – small shopkeepers supplying occupied factories and so on – to suggest that in the early days of the strikes the workers benefited from the sympathy of the *classes moyennes*, this situation did not last. As with the students' and workers' movements in 1968, so too in 1936 the two protest movements diverged. The PCF, which tried to hold them together – this was the essence of its Popular Front strategy – found itself in an increasingly difficult position.

But quite irrespective of this dilemma, there were also tensions between the Communists and their natural working-class constituency. Between 1934 and 1936 the Communists had exploited and developed the nascent anti-fascist movement among the working class more successfully than any other party. The Communists' success was due to the fact that they were the most fervent partisan of left-wing unity (they had nothing to lose and much to gain) and were viewed as a party of active, new, men uncontaminated by previous implication in parliamentary manoeuvrings (and not hidebound by distinctions between syndical and political activity which seemed irrelevant in 1936). In this way the 'purity' of their class against class line might up to a point have retrospectively benefited the Communists once they had adopted a less sectarian political stance. This second condition was essential: although the PCF's *tournant* was chronologically a slightly more complex affair than is sometimes supposed (as the AEAR, the Amsterdam–Pleyel movement, the overtures to the Socialists in March 1933 and the doctrine of *revendications partielles*, all demonstrate), June 1934 remains a crucial date. But there is another curious paradox here: at the national level this appears as a period in which the PCF become more 'moderate' – for example, in the negotiations over the Popular Front programme – but at the local level it was precisely the Communists' dynamism and energy which attracted members. The thousands of new members who joined the Party in 1936 certainly did so because the *tournant* had made it seem at last a realistic political force; they also did so because, locally, it appeared more radical than its Socialist rivals. This was the source of future confusion: many of those who flocked to the PCF – or supported the Communists in the CGT – did not do so because they necessarily accepted or understood the Communist line. This confusion can be illustrated by two examples central to the PCF's Popular Front strategy. First, the productivist appeals of the Communists – and the CGT – were largely ignored in the factories: the workers who struck in 1936 had not done so to find themselves working as hard as they had done previously. 'Leisure' was seen as one of the great conquests of 1936, the *chronométreur* as the great enemy. And one reason why the workers were deaf to productivist rhetoric highlights a second failure of the Communists: it is far from the case that the party's newly acquired Jacobin vocabulary – its advocacy of national defence – was swallowed by its supporters. The campaign against non-intervention received only lukewarm working-class support; in Marseilles, the working class shared the general sense of relief after Munich.[19] There is no reason to suppose that this attitude was not fairly widespread. The rhetoric of Coblentz resulted in a Munich not a Valmy. It may also be, as we have suggested, that the Popular Front's cultural policies contributed to a process of depoliticization which militated against the Communists' hopes of building up anti-fascism and anti-Nazi sentiment: possibly the very ecumenicalism and apoliticism of the Popular Front's cultural line was ultimately self-defeating. But there was little the Communists could have done to resolve the two latent contradictions which finally destroyed the Popular Front: the sociological contradiction of a coalition uniting working class and *petite bourgeoisie*, and the ideological contradiction between commitments to 'peace' and 'liberty'. And after the first show trials even the PCF espousal of liberty come to seem a little sour: Gide was not alone in having his doubts.

The PCF's problem in presenting a clear line on national defence was complicated by its attempt also to defend the 40-hour week, which had in many people's eyes become the main obstacle to such a policy. This was the view of, for example, Robert Marjolin who mounted from 1937 a sustained personal campaign against the 40-hour week. As he wrote in May 1938:

these parties and unions do not understand that, if they behave simply like one faction among others, defending interests which are no doubt respectable but which are nonetheless particular interests, the nation's recovery will occur without them and against them. If there is one moral to draw from the victory of fascism and national socialism it is that the working class is lost when, during a period of crisis, it abandons to others the responsibility of representing the interests of the nation.[20]

These words were only too prescient. Marjolin was no Communist but his words expressed one of the central objectives of the Communists' Popular

Front strategy and were eloquent testimony to the Communists' failure to make the Popular Front an instrument of national unity against the threat from Germany.

It would be wrong, however, to view the Popular Front, as we have done so far, entirely as a failure. In the first place, the Matignon Agreement represented a significant shift of wealth and power to the working class. It is true that most of these gains had been lost by 1938. But the *congés payés* remained, and even the crushing of the labour movement in 1938 did not signify a total return to the old order in the factory: the *patrons* had learnt something from 1936. Did it, however, require a movement on the scale of 1936 to produce such meagre results? Almost certainly it did. The political scientist, Stanley Hoffmann, has on many occasions noted that as a result of the weakness of voluntary associations in France, of the strength of the state bureaucracy, of the blocking power of the Senate (in the Third Republic) and of the fragmentation of political parties, the 'French body politic lacked adequate institutional channels for the expression and redress of grievance'.[21] The result is that political change in France often requires a movement of direct action: it did take a social upheaval of the dimensions of 1936 to bring France's labour legislation more or less in line with that of other industrial countries.

Did the Popular Front contribute in any way to ending that alienation of the working class from the state, of which such movements of protest were a partial symptom. This is less sure. Certainly the Popular Front had shown that the Prefect, even the Minister of the Interior, was not necessarily an enemy of the working class. And Levy concludes his study of Marseilles by suggesting that the Popular Front helped to integrate the Marseilles working class into national politics: ethnic and local identities were transcended in favour of class and national identities. But the Popular Front's more durable legacy was perhaps less to integrate the working class into the nation than to turn the PCF into the privileged defender of its interests *against* the state, creating what Annie Kriegel has called a 'counter-society'.[22] The Popular Front was the making of the French Communist Party as a mass movement.

Secondly, as a movement of Republican defence, the Popular Front was not as catastrophic a failure as the opening quotation by Walter suggests. Indeed Walter himself went on to qualify the remark by pointing out that as a result of the Popular Front the French people did reject 'fascism' in the 1930s, and that the destruction of French democracy in 1940 came about through external defeat in war. Put in this crude form Walter's qualification cannot stand: the only successful fascist movement in France – Doriot's PPF – grew up as a direct reaction to the Popular Front, and died with it. But that is not to say that there was no threat to French democracy in 1934 and 1935. There may not have been an abortive *coup* on

6 February but, more insidiously, anti-parliamentarianism had become respectable. The Popular Front mounted a successful counter-attack. In March 1934, Guéhenno, hearing of Walter's proposals for the CVIA, wrote to Romain Rolland: 'my feeling is that if the line of resistance to fascism is to be effective, it must be more Dreyfusard than Communist'.[23] And this is precisely what it became. The Popular Front successfully turned anti-fascism into a great Republican crusade which echoed in many ways the Dreyfusard campaign of the 1900s. There were continuities of personnel as well. Victor Basch, one of the founder members of the League of the Rights of Man in 1896, was one of the most active members of the Comité du Rassemblement Populaire in 1935. At the Buffalo Stadium on 14 July 1935 he spoke in the following terms:

We all sense that this day will take its place among the memorable dates of the history of democratic France and that it recalls the celebrated *journées* of 14 July 1789 and 14 July 1790. As on 14 July 1789, when the people demolished the royal dungeon stone by stone, on this 14 July 1935, the People are determined to storm the remaining Bastilles.[24]

Although this was the language of a particular French tradition, the Popular Front was at the same time a movement absolutely characteristic of European politics in the 1930s. Many of its themes – youth, health, sport, mass participation – and its style – the theatrical politics of mass demonstrations – were not so different from those of fascism. But that was part of the point: to provide a new mystique for republican democracy, to romanticize again the shabby realities of Third Republic politics. And the comparison with the fascist style of politics must not be exaggerated. Certainly mass demonstrations and meetings did play an important part in Popular Front politics, but, as we have seen, each of the great Popular Front demonstrations was made up of a heterogeneous collection of committees and associations. They represented, not the subsuming of the individual in an unstructured atomized mass, but precisely an assertion of the vitality of French democracy as articulated in a dense tissue of independent organizations. This was the exact opposite of Nazi *gleichschaltung*. In the area especially of culture and leisure one of the strengths of the Popular Front was precisely the contribution of the independent organizations which collaborated with, supplemented, and inspired the efforts of the government. This significantly distinguished Popular Front cultural policies from those of fascist Italy or Nazi Germany.

In its defence of democracy the Popular Front was not unsuccessful: for a while at least, the Third Republic did seem worth supporting again. But given that much *was* wrong with the Third Republic in the 1930s, was a defence of the constitutional status quo necessarily the best means of defending democracy? It is possible in this view – and this is to some extent the perspective of Lefranc – to see the Popular Front not as a renewal of French politics but rather as a return to tradition. It is indeed the case that many critics of the prevailing state of politics in the early 1930s – among whom were those who have been christened the 'non-conformists of the 1930s' – found themselves marginalized by the Popular Front. Among these 'losers' could be placed planists disappointed by the Popular Front programme, *gauchistes* disappointed that left-wing unity had occurred around reformist platforms, liberal Catholics whose hopes of building bridges to the left were set back (in spite of the *main tendue*) by a return to political bi-polarisation. To this list could be added such cultural dissidents as the Surrealists and the October group. But it would be wrong to overplay this 'traditional' aspect of the Popular Front. In the first place, Blum's government, even if committed to a defence of the constitutional status quo, did represent a brief attempt to overhaul France's system of government. Blum's government was less an abortive experiment in Socialism than a sketchy prefiguration of postwar modernization: the General Secretariat, the National Economic Ministry, the attempt to set up a National School of Administration, the setting up of the CNRS, the increased funding for science – all these were attempts to increase the efficiency of government and extend its sphere of influence beyond the limited role it was generally ascribed in the liberal order of the Third Republic. Secondly, the Popular Front was a movement diverse enough to incorporate many of those who had been by-passed by it: planists played a key role in government economic policy; the Popular Front's cultural eclecticism allowed it to embrace much of the avant-garde – to celebrate Le Corbusier *and* the medieval heritage; the October group may have broken up, but its members contributed to those quintessentially Popular Front products, *The Crime of M. Lange* and *La Vie est à nous.*

Thirdly, in the words of Manès Sperber, a participant and observer, the Popular Front 'transformed a defensive movement of anti-fascism into an authentic movement of liberation'.[25] It represented an attempt to 'break down the barriers' (a recurrent theme) of a compartmentalized and formal society –, the barriers between worker and worker, intellectual and masses, culture and people, science and art, theatre and politics. The words that one writer has used to characterize May 1968 are reminiscent also of 1936; as in 1968, so also in 1936 there was a 'rush towards community', 'a sudden joyous release from silence and isolation', 'a holiday from the boredom of everyday life'.[26] One of the central symbolic moments of the events of May 1968 was the students' occupation of the state Odeon Theatre. In 1936 also, we have seen that theatrical imagery came readily to participants in the Popular Front. Guéhenno watched himself 'playacting the Revolution'; Jamet saw himself as a character in a historical epic; theatrical groups mounted plays in occupied factories; strikers mimed the funerals of their bosses; demonstrators dressed up in costumes of the Revolution. The Popular Front may have had its shadowy *metteurs en scène* – Fried/Clément, Gerôme/Walter, Münzenberg, Tchakhotine/Flamme – but it lived its politics as a public spectacle. The workers who danced in factory courtyards danced for themselves and for the cameras; Cartier-Bresson transfigured the *congés payés* into art. The French Popular Front defused the bloody conflicts of the 1930s into a confrontation (not entirely bloodless) of symbols.[27]

If theatre cannot change the world, it can at least enrich it. The Popular Front too did not fundamentally change the world but it briefly and deeply illuminated the lives of many who had participated in it. Even when disillusioned by its failures they retained nonetheless a memory of the hopes it had aroused – which were real enough – and of the unique experience it had briefly represented, which was no myth. Sperber, who was not sentimental, writes that he had never before or since experienced such fraternity; Guéhenno, who was sentimental, used similar language. Let us end with the words of another participant who was not like Sperber or Guéhenno, based in Paris, but in Chambéry, where he was a young *professeur* in 1936. Looking back forty years later he wrote: 'for the people on the left of my age, 1936 will remain the light of their life. I know the joy which today forbids me to despair completely of mankind.'[28] This, as well as disappointment and failure, was the legacy of the Popular Front.

Epilogue: The Popular Front in history

Seule la mémoire est révolutionnaire

(François Mitterrand, 1979)

It is not for its achievements that one remembers 1848 but for the promise and the immense hopes to which it gave birth.

(Léon Blum, 1948)

In the rich mythology of the French left nothing succeeds like failure. The left has lovingly licked the wounds of its disasters and nursed its defeats with an exclusive pride. During the 1930s – and indeed until quite recently – one of the major dates in the calendar of the French left was the anniversary march to the Mur des Fédérés. The Mur des Fédérés demonstration of 1936 was one of the most impressive of the Popular Front period. As in previous years, poignancy was added by the presence of survivors from the Commune. Among the speakers was Blum: 'the vanquished of 1871 were in fact the victors. Today we have the right to invoke the memory of these glorious dead in proclaiming to them: our victory is yours. Long live the Commune. Long live the Popular Front'. Very quickly the Popular Front started to celebrate its own anniversaries. As early as March 1934 Thorez could talk of the 'historic *journées* of 9 and 12 February'. To what extent has this judgement been vindicated by history? To what extent have the failures of the Popular Front, like those of 1871 or those of 1848, been transfigured into legend? What vision remains of the Popular Front, and the hopes it aroused, in the years following its demise? This book opened with François Mitterrand's invocation of the Popular Front in 1981. It seems appropriate to end the study of a movement which was obsessed with the myths of the past, by examining the myths that it bequeathed to the future. No doubt this investigation could be pursued outside the borders of France but for present purposes we shall confine it to France alone.

The debate on the Popular Front began almost immediately after the fall of France. The Vichy regime was largely a reaction against the revolution that the Popular Front had represented in the eyes of much of the French bourgeoisie. Laval, whom the Popular Front had defeated in 1936, savoured his revenge in 1940; many veterans of 6 February reappeared on the fringes of the new regime; Zay and Basch were assassinated. When Blum, Daladier, Gamelin and others were tried at Riom in 1942 it was the Popular Front that was on trial for its supposed responsibility in France's defeat. And the myth that the Popular Front failed to rearm adequately remains widely believed.

If the Popular Front was attacked by Vichy, this did not mean that it was warmly embraced by the resistance. Many resisters rejected any return to the Third Republic with which the Popular Front was closely associated.[1] This was not true of all resistance groups, however. In January 1941 the Communist paper *La Vie ouvrière* called for workers to unify against Vichy 'under the flag of June 1936'.[2] And once the Communists entered the resistance wholeheartedly in June 1941 they quickly resumed the language of Republican patriotism that they had first discovered during the Popular Front. They adopted the label 'National Front,' reminiscent of the abortive 'French Front' idea in August 1936.

The political atmosphere of the Liberation was in many respects similar to that of 1936. The left had rediscovered its unity; Communists and Socialists sat in government together. At the municipal elections of April 1945 – the first elections to be held since the Liberation – the left triumphed. *Le Populaire's* headline proclaimed: 'after the municipal elections of 1945, 1936 is confirmed'.[3] A march to the Place de la République in February 1945 to commemorate 12 February 1934 attracted some 250,000 participants; in 1947 the march still attracted sufficient people to last five hours, according to *Le Monde*.[4] In 1944/5 there was the same feeling as in 1936 that a new world was about to be constructed; there was a similar cultural and intellectual effervescence, a renewed interest in popular education directly inspired by the precedent of 1936. Among the organizations set up was Peuple et Culture whose motto was, in the words of Benigo Cacérès, one of its founders, 'bring the people to culture and culture to the people'.[5] The Ministry of Education set up a section responsible for popular education and sport with Guéhenno as its first head.

The unity of the left collapsed in 1947 with the ousting of the Communists from government in May and the beginning of the cold war in September. The Communists retreated into the ghetto. When Blum, whose health had never totally recovered from his wartime incarceration, died in March 1950, *L'Humanité* reported the event in a few lines. It referred to him as 'the object of the greatest praise from the extreme right', 'the man responsible for the rupture of working-class unity at Tours', the man of non-'intervention' and of the 'pause'.[6] Annie Kriegel tells the story of hearing a Communist bus-conductor whistling merrily one morning. When asked why he was so happy, he replied 'because Léon Blum has died'.[7]

During the period of the Fourth Republic (1945–58), it was, however, largely the Communists who kept alive the memory of the Popular Front by their annual celebration of the *journée* of 12 February. The treatment of this event by *L'Humanité* has been analyzed by Jacques Ozouf.[8] Up to 1945 5 per cent of the newspaper on the relevant day was devoted to 12 February. Between 1949 and 1954 the level of coverage declined only slightly. For the Communists, celebrating 12 February always had contemporary political purposes. Parallels were drawn between past and present, with different morals being drawn in different years. The aim was always didactic. 'The lesson of February has lost none of its force,' declared *L'Humanité* in January 1961. Between 1948 and 1955 the occasion was used to remind the working class of the duplicity of the Socialists; after 1956, when the PCF was again building bridges towards the Socialists, the slogan became: 'Long live the unity of the working class and the Popular Front.' *L'Humanité* constantly reminded its readers that the men of 6 February were still present in different incarnations (conveniently forgetting that Communists had been among them). The Gaullists of 1947 were compared with the fascists of 1934. The fact that a dramatic demonstration by Algerian colonists in 1956 occurred fortuitously on 6 February only encouraged such analogies.

But in spite of the best efforts of the PCF, participation in the 12 February demonstrations declined sharply, and in recognition of this fact the amount of space devoted to them in *L'Humanité* also decreased after 1955. Between 1945 and 1951 the celebration took the form of a procession ending in the Place de la République. Between 1953 and 1955 there were meetings in the Vel d'Hiver (whose maximum capacity was 25,000). This became too big a venue and in 1956 the meeting was held at the Mutualité hall (maximum capacity 5,000). In 1957 it moved to an even smaller hall (maximum capacity, 1,000). After 1959 the meetings ceased. What this seemed to indicate was a decreasing knowledge of, and interest in, the Popular Front among the French working class. This was confirmed by a study of working-class culture carried out by R. Kaes between 1958 and 1961. He found a low level of awareness of the history of the labour movement: 'a large number of young workers know hardly anything about 1936'.[9] But for those with a historical memory the Popular Front remained potent. According to a survey carried out by Sartre's *Temps Modernes* in 1955, the Popular Front was the historical period to which people on the left referred most readily. By a large majority of those placing themselves on the left it was judged positively, particularly for its social reforms. The survey had no scientific statistical validity but probably reflected the truth fairly accurately.[10]

The Socialists were less keen during this period to summon up the ghosts of the Popular Front than were the Communists. Some Socialists like Moch, many times a minister during the Fourth Republic, remained faithful to the memory of Léon Blum. Blum's government was also an inspiration to younger Socialists such as Pierre Mauroy (8 years old in 1936) who in 1951 helped to set up the Léo Lagrange Federation, a people's education movement which organized a network of local clubs based on the idea of the Clubs des Loisirs proposed by Lagrange in 1936. But in such cases the point of reference was not to the Popular Front as a whole but specifically to Blum's government. In Mauroy's vision of the period the Communists hardly figure at all[11] (conversely the Communists commemorated February 1934 not June 1936). An issue of the Socialist journal *La Revue socialiste* devoted to the twentieth anniversary of 1936 was headed not 'Popular Front' but 'Twenty Years Ago, the first socialist led government.' It rejected any notion of reviving a Popular Front alliance: 'there is nothing comparable between the situations in 1936 and 1956'. It was fear of being swallowed up by the Communists which accounted for the SFIO's general tendency to play down the memory of the Popular Front. In 1958 there was a military revolt in Algeria. The Republic was on the verge of collapse and de Gaulle was waiting in the wings to assume power. Many Socialists saw the situation as a replay of 6 February 1934. But the leader of the party, Guy Mollet, saw the alternatives as follows: 'if the choice is de Gaulle or the Republic we have won, if it is de Gaulle or the Communists we have lost'. He preferred to lose with de Gaulle than win with the Communists, accepting the fall of the Republic rather than the revived Popular Front which many on the left were demanding.

On the afternoon of 28 May, the day on which the last government of the Republic resigned to make way for de Gaulle, there was a large anti-fascist demonstration from the Bastille to the Place de la Nation. Some 300,000 people marched to the slogan 'fascism will not pass'. Among them were Mendès France, François Mitterrand . . . and Edouard Daladier. But all accounts of the demonstration describe it as a somewhat lacklustre and unconvinced affair – not so much a replay of 12 February as a funeral cortège for a Republic that had already died. It was difficult to be enthusiastic about the Fourth Republic or to see de Gaulle as a fascist especially when it was known that the leader of the SFIO was secretly negotiating with him.

During the Fifth Republic the Popular Front seemed to become an increasingly 'safe' memory, emptied of much of its class content – a subject for nostalgic television documentaries in the new consumer society. The left-wing *Nouvel Observateur* relegated its commemoration of the Popular Front's fortieth anniversary in June 1976 to its arts section.[12] In 1964 *L'Humanité* devoted one article to 12 February; in the following year the date passed without mention. The fortieth anniversary of the Popular Front generally attracted much less attention than the centenary of the Commune in 1971 or the thirtieth anniversary of the Liberation in 1974. In the events of May 1968 there were almost no explicit references to the Popular Front – though for Daniel Guérin and others they were another missed opportunity and another example of the perfidy of the Communist Party.

But politically the relevance of the Popular Front had if anything increased in the Fifth Republic. The major reason for this was the fact that the new constitution and electoral system militated in favour of political bi-polarization, especially in the presidential election. If the left was to stand any chance of a return to power it had to be united. The Communists were the first to recognize this, and from 1962 they began to court the Socialists actively. This process had begun while Thorez was still leader but in 1964 he died (on holiday in the Soviet Union) and the pace of *rapprochement* was speeded up by his successor Waldeck Rochet. In 1965 the Communists agreed not to present a presidential candidate and rallied instead behind Mitterrand as the single candidate of the left. As a result Mitterrand managed to force de Gaulle to a second round. In March 1966 Rochet wrote to Mitterrand proposing cooperation at the legislative elections in the following year. He cited the example of 1936 to show that a unified left could win. The Communist analysis of the Popular Front at this stage was that it had been a partial success. It had prevented the triumph of fascism and carried through important social reforms. Its failures were due partly to Blum and more importantly to the non-existence of local Popular Front committees as demanded at the time by the Communists. As a result it had lacked an adequate popular base to withstand the attacks of the trusts. But still the Popular Front's achievement was judged by Duclos in 1966 to be 'positive overall'. The moral for the present was that the left must draw up a common programme.[13]

The Socialists were slower to grasp the necessity for unity in the new political system – perhaps because they recalled that unity in both 1936 and 1944 had worked to the advantage of the Communists. In 1965 the Socialist, Gaston Defferre, had hoped to draw the SFIO into a centre–left alliance at the Presidential election – against both de Gaulle and the PCF. Only when Defferre's attempt failed did the left rally around Mitterrand who was not yet a member of the Socialist Party. It was Mitterrand who most quickly perceived the necessity for left-wing unity and realized moreover that it would be turned to the advantage of the non-Communist left. The demise of the old SFIO and the founding of a new Socialist party in 1971 with Mitterrand at its head led in 1972 to the signing of the famous Common Programme of the left. This was the first time since 1936 that the Socialists and Communists had signed a joint programme. At the PCF's Twentieth Congress in December the party's new leader Georges Marchais reminded delegates that the Popular Front had been an early stage on the road to unity. He called for a Popular Union around the Common Programme. This was to be even wider than that of 1936, embracing artists, peasants, *lycéens*, Christians, and so on: a *main tendue* for the 1970s. For the Communists, then, 1936 remained a crucial point of reference, from which they drew fatefully erroneous conclusions.[14]

The Socialists also made comparisons with 1936. In 1976 the Socialist Party paper *L'Unité* saw the Common Programme of 1972 as a double improvement on the Popular Front programme. First, because it committed the Communists and Socialists to govern together: the refusal of the Communists to assume ministerial responsibilities in 1936 had fatally weakened Blum's position. Secondly, the Common Programme contained essential structural reforms, notably nationalizations, which had had to be omitted by the Popular Front programme. But in spite of its weaknesses, *L'Unité* saw the Popular Front as providing the example of a legal and pluralistic route to power for Socialism – an alternative to the Leninist model.[15] The left wing of the Socialist Party – the so-called CERES group of J-P. Chevènement – was resolutely unsentimental about 1936. The Popular Front had been an unmitigated failure, content with a legalistic management of the capitalist economy. It fell because it failed to carry out the necessary structural economic transformation. The Socialist Party needed to have clear strategy for the transition to Socialism based on nationalizations, state planning and alliance with the PCF.[16]

References to the Popular Front and the example of Blum were increasingly frequent during the 1970s. But this was due less to the contemporary parallel of Socialist–Communist unity, which was becoming increasingly frayed, than to the Socialists' need, as a newly founded party, to establish themselves in the French Socialist tradition. This was especially true of Mitterrand himself who had a far from Socialist past. In 1969 Mitterrand told of his memory of the joyful election night of 1936 when he 'discovered that there were still causes for which to live and to die', when he 'glimpsed where right and justice lay'.[17] This was total myth-making. The truth is that in 1936 his sympathies had lain more with the Croix de Feu than the Popular Front.[18] At the Socialist Congress of Metz in 1979, when Mitterrand, vulnerable after the left's defeat in the legislative elections a year earlier, came under attack from Michel Rocard on the right of the party, he appealed to the memory of Blum to justify his advocacy of a 'break' between capitalism and Socialism. Like Blum, Mitterrand proposed a synthesis between the Socialism of Marx and

Jaurès.[19] At the Presidential election of 1981 Mitterrand's election posters pictured him in front of a small country church; underneath were written the words: 'La Force Tranquille.' How many electors in 1983 realized that this was the phrase that Blum had used in his radio broadcast to the nation on 5 June 1936? One of Mitterrand's first acts as President was to place a rose on the tomb of Jaurès in the Pantheon. Pierre Mauroy, Mitterrand's first Prime Minister, went to visit the tomb of Blum at Jouy-en-Josas near Paris.

This renewed political interest in the Popular Front does not seem to have penetrated deeply among the population as a whole. An oral history study in the mid-1970s discovered that without special prompting few people referred to the Popular Front when recalling their memories of the 1930s. The Popular Front was not one of those moments in history when private memory meshes inextricably with national memory, the private with the public.[20] At a political level, however, it was with the Socialist victory of 1981 that contemporary comparisons with the Popular Front reached their peak. In fact the situations could hardly have been more different. The victory of 1981 did not occur as a result of left-wing unity since Socialist–Communist relations had deteriorated sharply after 1977 when the Communists had realized that unity did not necessarily work to their benefit. They had correspondingly modified their assessment of the Popular Front. A Party Conference in 1980 judged the results of unity in 1936 to have been negative.[21] Nor did the victory of 1981 result from, or give rise to, any great social or cultural upheaval: the intellectuals had never been more silent or the factories quieter. In truth 1981 was almost an electoral accident, a freak result with momentous consequences. Another difference from 1936 was the fact that in the legislative elections which followed Mitterrand's victory, the Socialists gained an overall majority: Mitterrand did not, unlike Blum, have to take account of reluctant allies. Nonetheless the left's sudden return to power after twenty-three years of right-wing dominance did result in genuine popular enthusiasm which revived memories of 1936.[22] This was especially true of Mauroy for whom, more than any other politician, the Popular Front government represented an inspiring example not just a rhetorical device. On the evening of the victory he bumped in to Lagrange's widow at a television studio: 'Madeleine's emotion was equal to my own.' The joy of May 1981 reminded Mauroy of 1936 and 1944: 'the two moments when the working class celebrated the rediscovery of its dignity and the recovery of its liberty. Two occasions of France's reconciliation with herself.'[23]

The memory of 1936 was more than purely sentimental. In practical ways also Blum's government provided Mauroy with a precedent. One of the first acts of the incoming government was to set up a Commission, presided over by François Bloch-Lainé, to report on the state of France.

The Commission commented: 'in 1981 as in 1936 the link between economic crisis and political change is quite clear'.[24] Raymond Barre was cast in the role of Pierre Laval. Like Blum in 1936, Mauroy in 1981 proposed a policy of economic expansion – conquering unemployment was the predominant objective – and although his government had at its disposal sophisticated Keynesian techniques unavailable to Blum, some of the measures proposed were directly inspired by the precedent of 1936. The 12 per cent wage rises of the Matignon Agreement were paralleled in 1981 by a 10 per cent increase in the statutory minimum wage. Blum had reduced the working week to forty hours; Mauroy's government set itself the task of reducing it to thirty-five hours. Blum had introduced the first two weeks of paid holidays; Mauroy introduced a fifth week (a third had been granted by Mollet in 1956 and a fourth had become general during the 1960s). One big difference of economic policy, however, was that the Mauroy government carried out a vast programme of nationalizations.

The Popular Front was present in 1981 not only as an inspiration but also as a warning. The speed with which the government acted owed much to the memory of 1936. As Mitterrand said: 'there is a risk that what is not achieved at the beginning of the parliament will never be achieved'.[25] The government also learnt from the mistakes of 1936 by acting very cautiously on its pledge regarding the shorter working week. In 1982 it reduced it to thirty-nine hours without any reduction in wages. And the ultimate objective of thirty-five hours (in fact never attained) was postponed until 1985 for negotiation between unions and employers on an industry by industry basis. But the government did not learn from all the mistakes of its predecessor. The results of reflation in 1981, as in 1936, were to stoke inflation and increase the trade deficit. Like Auriol and Blum in 1936, Mitterrand had come to power announcing that he would not devalue; like them he was forced to eat his words. There were three devaluations while Mauroy remained Prime Minister as there were three in the Popular Front period: September 1936, October 1981; June 1937, June 1982; May 1938, March 1983. The extraordinary similarity in timing almost suggests that a sort of fatality hangs over the experience of the French left in government. In November 1981 the Finance Minister, Jacques Delors, mooted the idea of a 'pause' in the implementation of reforms. The word, charged with historical resonance, caused rumblings on the left. And when the government was forced to introduce economically restrictive measures in April 1982, 'rigour' not 'pause' was the description used. When further measures had to be introduced in March 1983 the preferred term was 'austerity'. March 1983 was indeed the turning point of Mauroy's government. The choice was between accentuating the policy of austerity or leaving the European monetary system and adopting a protectionist and isolationist policy, as proposed by Chevènement and other members of CERES. Exactly the same alternatives had faced Blum in 1936. In 1983 the Socialists chose the former policy and a year later Mauroy was replaced as Prime Minister by the technocratic figure of Laurent Fabius, much less steeped in historical nostalgia than his predecessor. The left had lost its final illusions.

This was perhaps the most poignant difference between 1936 and 1981. The political weakness of Blum's government prevented him from having to preside over the gradual drift to the right; as a result it was possible to retain the memory of a noble attempt cut short by circumstances. The political strength of the Socialists in 1981 – partly a result of the new institutions bequeathed by de Gaulle – allowed them to preside over a u-turn in economic policy. Talk of a rupture with capitalism had been abandoned; the Socialists had become a party of government. In the process they had lost their mystique. Providing the possibility of political durability was de Gaulle's most poisoned legacy to the legend of the left in France. The alibis had gone; the sweet romance of failure had disappeared.

During the legislative elections of 1986 the Popular Front was hardly mentioned. 'Whatever happened to 36' ran a headline in *Le Monde* in March 1986.[26] And the fiftieth anniversary of the Popular Front coincided with the return of the right to power. But the Popular Front has not entirely lost its power to stir passions. In 1985 Mitterrand commissioned a series of statues to be put up in Paris. One of the proposed subjects was Alfred Dreyfus, in defence of whose innocence Blum had entered the political fray for the first time. A minor controversy ensued as to whether or not the statue could be put in the courtyard of the War Ministry. Controversy also broke out over the location of a second statue – of Léon Blum himself. The government hoped that it could be sited in the Place Léon Blum in the eleventh *arrondissement* of Paris, once the heart of working-class Paris. Jacques Chirac, the Gaullist Mayor of Paris, refused on the pretext that plans for the redevelopment of the square were in progress. The statue was therefore consigned, at least provisionally, to the Tuileries garden which falls under the control of the government.[27] A petition was quickly drawn up demanding that the statue be moved to the Place Léon Blum:

At the moment that the country is preparing to celebrate the fiftieth anniversary of the Popular Front to which his name will always remain attached, the whole people of France, and especially those of Paris, wish to pay tribute to the statesman, man of letters and jurist, in a word the humanist and man of conviction who wrote such a great chapter in the history of the universal Republic'.

For the moment, however, the statue remains consigned to the imperial alleyways of the Tuileries. The controversy, minor though it may be, demonstrates that the memory of Blum, and of the government he led has, not yet at least, been altogether sanitized by history. *Affaire à suivre* perhaps . . .

Appendices

Programme of the Popular Front (published 11 January 1936)

The programme of immediate demands that the Rassemblement Populaire publishes to-day is the result of a unanimous agreement between the ten organizations represented on the National Committee of the Rassemblement: the League of the Rights of Man, the Vigilance Committee of Anti-fascist Intellectuals, the Amsterdam–Pleyel Movement, the Mouvement d'Action Combattante, the Radical Party, the Socialist Party, the Communist Party, the Socialist–Republican Union, the CGT, and CGTU. The programme is directly inspired by the watchwords of 14 July. These parties and organizations, representing millions of human beings who have sworn to remain united, in accordance with their oath, 'to defend democratic freedom, to give bread to the workers, work to the young and a great human peace to the world', have together sought the practical means of a common immediate and continuous action.

This programme is voluntarily limited to measures that can be immediately applied. The National Committee wishes every party and organization belonging to the Rassemblement Populaire to join in this common action without abandoning either their own principles, doctrines, or ultimate objectives. It has assigned itself the task of offering positive solutions to the essential problems facing French democracy today.

Thus in the political arena it defines those measures indispensable to ensure the respect of national sovereignty as expressed through universal suffrage, and to guarantee essential freedoms (freedom of opinion and expression, trade union freedoms, freedom of conscience and *laïcité*); in the international arena it lays down the conditions necessary to safeguard and organize peace according to the principles of the League of Nations; and in the economic and financial arena it aims to struggle for the interests of the mass of working people and savers, against the crisis and against the fascist organizations who exploit them on behalf of financial powers.

The Rassemblement Populaire refuses to treat these financial and economic problems separately: it wants to attack the causes of the fall in tax revenues by acting against the economic crisis, and to complete its action against the crisis by improving the availability of credit, both public and private.

The Rassemblement Populaire emphasizes that a great many of the demands that it presents here already figure in plans and programmes worked out by the trade union organizations of the working class.

It adds that even if these urgent, and therefore necessarily limited, measures provide an initial modification of the present economic system, they will have to be followed up by more profound measures to liberate the State definitively from the grip of the financial and industrial feudalities.

To all these problems the Rassemblement has sought just solutions which alone conform to the principles of democracy: equality of treatment for all in the application of penal laws, fiscal justice, justice for the natives of the colonies, international justice within the framework and spirit of the League of Nations.

If it has been possible for the National Committee of the Rassemblement Populaire to produce unanimous proposals, this is because the parties and organizations which it represents have collaborated amicably in a spirit of conciliation and with a desire to reach a synthesis.

Now it is for the masses to support these demands and see that they prevail!

When this programme has become reality a great change will have occurred: freedom will have been better defended, bread more certainly ensured, peace better preserved. These aims are precious enough for everything to be subordinated to the attempt to achieve them.

It is for the achievement of these objectives that the Rassemblement Populaire appeals. This requires close co-operation to carry on the fraternity of 14 July [1935] and show everyone, inside and outside France, that democracy is invincible once it rediscovers its creative force and power to attract.

I Defence of freedom

1 *A general amnesty*
2 *Measures against the Fascist Leagues:*
   (a) The effective disarmament and dissolution of all semi-military formations, in accordance with the law.
   (b) The enforcement of legal measures in cases of incitement to murder or any attempt against the safety of the State.
3 *Measures for the cleansing of public life*, especially by forbidding Deputies to combine their parliamentary functions with certain other forms of activity.
4 *The Press:*
   (a) The repeal of the laws and decrees restricting freedom of opinion.
   (b) Reform of the Press by the following legislative measures:
      (i) Measures effectively repressing libel and blackmail.
      (ii) Measures which will guarantee the normal means of existence to newspapers, and compel publication of their financial resources. Measures ending the private monopoly of commercial advertising and the scandals of financial advertising, and preventing the formation of newspaper trusts.
   (c) Organization by the State of wireless broadcasts with a view to assuring the accuracy of wireless news and the equality of political and social organizations in relation to radio.
5 *Trade freedoms:*
   (a) Application and observance of trade union freedom for everyone.
   (b) Recognition of women's labour rights.
6 *Education and freedom of conscience:*
   (a) Measures to safeguard the development of public education, by the

necessary grants and by reforms such as the raising of the school leaving age from thirteen to fourteen and, in secondary education, the proper selection of pupils as an essential accompaniment of grants.

(b) Measures guaranteeing to all concerned, pupils and teachers, perfect freedom of conscience, particularly by ensuring the neutrality of education, its non-religious character, and the civic rights of teachers.

7 *Colonies:*

Formation of a Parliamentary committee of inquiry into the political, economic and cultural situation in France's territories overseas, especially French North Africa and Indo-China.

II Defence of peace

1 Appeal to the people, and especially the working classes, for collaboration in the maintenance and organization of peace.

2 International collaboration within the framework of the League of Nations for collective security, by defining the aggressor and by joint application of sanctions in cases of aggression.

3 Ceaseless endeavour to pass from armed peace to disarmed peace, first by a convention of limitation, and then by the general, simultaneous and effectively controlled reduction of armaments.

4 Nationalization of war industries and suppression of private trade in armaments.

5 Repudiation of secret diplomacy; international action and public negotiation to bring back to Geneva the states which have left it, without weakening the essential principles of the League of Nations, which are the principles of collective security and indivisible peace.

6 Greater flexibility in the procedure provided by the League of Nations' Covenant for the peaceful adjustment of treaties dangerous for the peace of the world.

7 Extension of the system of pacts open to all nations, particularly in Eastern Europe, on the lines of the Franco–Soviet Pact.

III Economic demands

1 Restoration of purchasing power destroyed or reduced by the crisis:
Against unemployment and the crisis in industry.
(a) Establishment of a national unemployment fund.
(b) Reduction of the working week without reduction of the weekly wage.
(c) Bringing young workers into employment by establishing a system of adequate pensions for aged workers.
(d) Rapid execution of a public works programme, both urban and rural, linking local investments with schemes financed by the State and local authorities and investors.
Against the agricultural and commercial crisis.
(a) Revaluation of agricultural produce, combined with measures against

speculation and high prices, in order to reduce the gap between wholesale and retail prices.

(b) Establishment of a National Wheat Marketing Board to abolish the tribute levied by speculators against both the producer and the consumer.

(c) Support for agricultural co-operatives, and supply of fertilizers at cost prices by the National Boards for Nitrogen and Potash.
Control and certification of sales of superphosphates and other fertilizers, extension of agricultural credits, reduction of leasehold rents.

(d) Suspension of distraints and adjustment of debt repayments.

(e) Pending the complete and earliest possible removal of all unjust measures imposed by the economy decree laws, immediate abolition of measures affecting those groups whose conditions of life have been most severely endangered by these decrees.

2 *Against the robbery of investors and for the better organization of credit:*
(a) Regulation of banking business. Regulation of balance sheets issued by banks and joint-stock companies. Further regulation of the powers of directors of joint-stock companies.

(b) State officials who have retired or are on the reserve-list to be prohibited from joining the board of directors of a joint-stock company

(c) In order to remove credit and investment from the control of the economic oligarchy, the Bank of France must cease to be a private concern, and 'The Bank of France' must become 'France's Bank.' The Council of Regents of the Bank of France must be abolished; the powers of the Governor of the Bank of France must be increased, under the permanent control of a council composed of representatives of Parliament, of the executive authority, and of the main organized forces of labour and of industrial commercial and agricultural activity. The capital of the Bank must be converted into debentures, with measures to safeguard the interests of small shareholders.

3 *Financial purification:*
(a) Control of the trade in armaments, in conjunction with the nationalization of armaments industries. Prevention of waste in the civil and military departments.

(b) Establishment of a War Pensions Fund.

(c) Democratic reform of the system of taxation so as to relax the fiscal burden blocking economic recovery, and raise revenue by measures against large fortunes. Rapid progressive increase in income tax on incomes above 75,000 f. a year; re-organization of death duties; special taxes on monopoly profits, but without affecting retail prices. Measures against tax evasions, in connexion with transferable ('bearer') securities.

(d) Control of export of capital, and punishment of evasion by rigorous measures, including confiscation of property concealed abroad or of its equivalent value in France.

The government of Léon Blum (formed on 4 June 1936)

(The government was supposedly grouped into seven main departments or committees; the first name in each group was the minister at its head.)

Premiership and Ministers of State
Léon Blum (Socialist) – Président du Conseil
Camille Chautemps (Radical) – Minister of State
Paul Faure (Socialist) – Minister of State
Maurice Violette (Republican-Socialist) – Minister of State
Marx Dormoy (Socialist) – Undersecretary of State for the Premier's Office
François de Tessan (Radical) – Undersecretary of State for the Premier's Office

National Defence
Edouard Daladier (Radical)   Minister of Defence and of War; Vice-Premier
Alphonse Garnier-Duparc (Radical) – Navy Minister
Pierre Cot (Radical) – Air Minister
François Blancho (Socialist) – Undersecretary of State for the Navy

General Administration
Roger Salengro (Socialist) – Minister of the Interior
Raoul Aubaud (Radical) – Undersecretary of State for the Interior
Marc Rucart (Radical) – Minister of Justice
Jean Zay (Radical) – Minister of National Education
Cécile Brunschvicg (Radical) – Undersecretary of State for National Education
Jules Julien (Radical) – Undersecretary of State for Technical Education
Irène Joliot-Curie (Socialist) – Undersecretary of State for Scientific Research

Foreign Relations and France overseas
Yvon Delbos (Radical) – Minister of Foreign Affairs
Pierre Viénot (Republican Socialist) – Undersecretary of State
Marius Moutet (Socialist) – Colonial Minister

Finances and National Debt
Vincent Auriol (Socialist) – Minister of Finances
André Rivière (Socialist) – Minister of Pensions

National Economy
Charles Spinasse (Socialist) – Minister of the National Economy
Paul Ramadier (Republican Socialist) – Undersecretary of State for mines, electricity and liquid fuel.
Albert Bedouce (Socialist) – Minister of Public Works
Henri Tasso (Socialist) – Undersecretary of State for the Merchant Marine
Paul Bastid (Radical) – Minister of Commerce
Georges Monnet (Socialist) – Minister of Agriculture
André Liautey (Radical) – Undersecretary of State for Agriculture
Robert Jardillier (Socialist) – Minister of Posts and Telegraphs

Social Solidarity
Jean-Baptiste Lebas (Socialist) – Minister of Labour
Henri Sellier (Socialist) – Minister of Public Health
Pierre Dezarnaulds (Radical) – Undersecretary of State for Physical Education
Léo Lagrange (Socialist) – Undersecretary of State for the Organization of Sport and Leisure
Suzanne Lacore – Undersecretary of State for the protection of children

Jules Moch, defeated in the elections of 1936, became head of the General Secretariat. After his election to the Chamber in May 1937 this post was given to his former deputy Yves Chataigneau.

In September 1936 Joliot-Curie resigned and was replaced by Jean Perrin, and in November, after the suicide of Salengro, Marx Dormoy became Minister of the Interior.

After the fall of Blum's government on 21 June 1937 there were three more governments that could more or less accurately be described as Popular Front governments:
Camille Chautemps: 22 June 1937 – 1 January 1938
Camille Chautemps: 18 January 1938 – 10 March 1938
Léon Blum: 13 March 1938 – 10 April 1938

The Matignon Agreement

Article 1: The employers' delegation allows the immediate establishment of collective labour contracts.

Article 2: These contracts will include the following provisions (articles 3 to 5).

Article 3: Since all citizens are required to observe the law, the employers recognize their employees' freedom of opinion, and the right of the workers freely to join a trade union constituted according to the terms of the labour code.

The employers agree to take no account of the fact that a worker might belong to a union when taking decisions relating to the hiring of labour, the allocation of jobs, the imposition of disciplinary action or the dismissal of employees.

If one of the contracting parties claims that the dismissal of a worker had occurred in violation of the trade union rights mentioned above, the two parties agree to establish the facts and reach an equitable solution to the question at issue.

This, however, does not prevent the parties from attempting to obtain legal redress for any injury caused.

The exercise of trade union rights must not result in actions contrary to the law.

Article 4: From the day on which work resumes, all real wages, as they stood on 25 May 1936, shall be increased on a sliding scale ranging from 15 per cent for the lowest wages to 7 per cent for the highest. In no factory (*établissement*) shall the total increase in wages exceed 12 per cent.

Any increases in wages granted since the above-mentioned date shall be included in the readjustments in wages mentioned in the previous paragraph. But to the extent that these increases exceed the pre-mentioned readjustments they will be paid.

In the negotiations which will commence immediately to establish collective contracts prescribing a minimum wage by region and by category, special attention must be paid to the necessary readjustments of abnormally low wages.

The representatives of the employers agree to carry out the adjustments necessary to maintain a normal relationship between wages and white-collar salaries.

Article 5: Except in special cases already covered by the law, every factory employing more than 10 workers will create two or several (depending on the size of the factory) workers' delegates after agreement between the union organizations or, if there is no union, between the interested parties. These delegates will present to the management individual claims which have not been satisfied, relating to the application of laws, decrees and regulations contained in the labour code, to wage levels and to measures concerning hygiene and safety.

The delegates will be elected by all workers, male and female, over eighteen, providing that they have been in the factory at least three months and have not been deprived of their civic rights.

Workers over 25, of French nationality, who have worked in the factory without interruption for a year (or less if this provision reduces the number of eligible candidates to less than five) are eligible for election as delegates.

Workers holding a retail business of whatever kind, either themselves or through their spouses, are not eligible for election.

Article 6: The employers' delegation undertakes not to take any reprisal against the strikers.

Article 7: The CGT delegation requests the workers on strike to resume work as soon as the management of their factory has accepted this general agreement, and as soon as conversations concerning its application have begun between workers and management.

Paris, 7 June 1936

For the CGT	For the CGPF
Léon Jouhaux	René-Paul Duchemin
René Belin	P-E. Dalbouze
Benoît Frachon	Pierre Richemond
Henri Cordier	Alfred Lambert-Ribot
Pierre Milan	

During the Matignon negotiations Blum passed Jouhaux the following note: '7th June, Midnight. My dear friend, I here confirm in writing the undertakings I have given. Bills concerning the 40-hour week, the paid holidays and collective contracts will be presented to parliament the day after tomorrow. Tuesday.'

Popular Front Paris

Much has been made in this book of the importance of mass demonstrations as a vital part of the Popular Front experience. The Popular Front was born in the street, and in the street it lived its most glorious moments. Demonstrations were both a manifestation of political strength – a reply to the Leagues which had descended into the street on 6 February – and an expression of fraternity. In his book *La Vie quotidienne sous le Front populaire*, Henri Noguères, who had as a young man participated in Popular Front demonstrations, describes how carefully planned such occasions were. The days before the demonstration were ones of feverish preparation and excitement for the participants. Several days in advance *Le Populaire* and *L'Humanité* would carry instructions and print maps indicating the different assembly times and places: 'demo. 14th. in front of Café *A la Parisienne*, 24 Av. de la République'. These demonstrations, however, were significant not only for the events that gave rise to them – commemorating 14 July, protesting against the attack on Blum or the death of Salengro – but also for the places in which they occurred. Streets, especially in France, are no more neutral than dates. It may be useful, therefore, for the reader unfamiliar with Paris, to provide a short note on the topography of Popular Front Paris, the city in which the most massive and celebrated demonstrations took place.

Halls and stadia

The Popular Front met not only in the street but also in political halls and sports stadia. One way of measuring the movement's growing strength is to see how stadia increasingly replaced traditional political halls, as these became too small to contain the crowds that the Popular Front could attract (just as, in the Epilogue, we have charted the declining importance of the memory of the Popular Front, as the PCF's commemoration of the 'February days' moved from the street to the stadium to the political hall). Of the political halls, the two most important were the Salle Bullier (originally opened as a dance hall in 1843) on the northern edge of Montparnasse, and the Mutualité (constructed in 1931) near the quiet eastern end of the Boulevard St Germain. It was at the Mutualité ('Mutu'), which could hold up to 5,000, that Thorez launched the idea of the Rassemblement Populaire in October 1934, that Daladier first appeared on a public platform with Blum and Thorez (8 June 1935), that the Communists organized their Congress of Writers in June 1935. At the somewhat larger Salle Bullier the Socialist federation of the Seine organized its meeting with the Communists on 2 July 1934. The crowds were so large that an overspill meeting had to be held at the Hughyens Hall. Another important meeting at the Salle Bullier was held on 18 January 1935 when representatives of most of the leading organizations of the left met under the chairmanship of Victor Basch, President of the League of the Rights of Man, the first occasion on which this organization officially associated itself with the emerging Popular Front.

These meetings were more important for the fact of their taking place than for the numbers participating. Where larger numbers were involved the meetings would take place in sports stadia, especially the Vélodrome d'Hiver ('Vel d'Hiver') and the Buffalo Stadium, so called because it was built on the site of Buffalo Bill's circus (there are shades of Lange's Arizona Jim here). The Buffalo Stadium was situated in the southern suburb of Montrouge and the Vel d'Hiver just off the Rue de Grenelle, very near the Citroën plant on the Quai Javel. Both were founded during the craze for *vélodromes* – cycle tracks – which hit France at the end of the nineteenth century, but they were also the scene of various other forms of popular mass entertainment. Thus the holding of ostensibly political meetings in these two stadia, besides being a practical necessity if large numbers were to be accommodated, perfectly symbolized the Popular Front's fusion of politics and celebration. (It was also democracy's riposte to the huge rallies held by the Nazis in the Nuremberg stadium.) The Vel d'Hiver was the venue for the Socialist meeting organized by Pivert on 7 June 1936. Although it could hold up to 25,000 people it proved too small on this occasion and the crowds spilled into the neighbouring streets. On the other hand, for the performance of Bloch's *Naissance d'une cité* in October 1937 (supposedly symbolizing the new marriage between the People and the Art) the stadium proved somewhat too large. The Buffalo Stadium was the scene both of the swearing of the Oath on the morning of 14 July 1935 and of the spectacular PCF demonstration of 14 June 1936.

The Street

For the very biggest Popular Front demonstrations stadia were too small – as would have been even the colossal stadium projected by Le Corbusier for his Centre de Loisirs in 1937. It was in the street that the Popular Front showed its full strength.

Almost all the major demonstrations took place in the east of Paris in the triangle of streets connecting three great squares: the Place de la Bastille, the Place de la Nation and the Place de la République. This area was one of the centres of working-class Paris, and, no less importantly, each of the squares was a symbol of the republican and revolutionary tradition.

In the Place de la Bastille stands the July Column (or Column of Liberty) erected in the 1830s to the martyrs of the Revolution of 1830. (Although neither the event which the square calls to mind – the taking of the Bastille in 1789 – or the monument erected in it – commemorating an Orleanist revolution – have, strictly speaking, republican associations, this did not worry the Popular Front whose Oath of 14 July referred to 'this day on which we relive the first victory of the Republic'.) The Place de la Bastille is linked to the Place de la Nation by the Rue du Faubourg St Antoine, one the centres of Parisian radicalism during the Revolution and the nineteenth century. In the Place de la Nation, which lies almost at the eastern boundary of Paris, stands Dalou's statue the 'Triumph of the Republic', inaugurated on 19 November 1899 at the moment that the Republic seemed finally to have triumphed over the anti-Dreyfusards. Finally, nearer to the centre of the city, lies the Place de la République, linked to the Place de la Nation by the Boulevard Voltaire (which passes through what is now the Place Léon Blum). In the Place de la République is the sober Statue of the Republic (by the brothers Morice), inaugurated on 14 July 1883 during the early years of the Third Republic. At the base of the Statue are twelve bas reliefs (by Dalou) depicting the history of the Republic from the Tennis Court Oath of 1789 to 1880 when 14 July became a national holiday. (Ironically one municipal councillor in 1879 had proposed that the statue be placed in the Place de la Concorde, which would be renamed for the occasion. This was of course the site of the riots which sparked off the Popular Front in 1934! In the end the more 'popular' site in the east was chosen.)

This, then, was the Republican heartland to which the Popular Front demonstrations laid claim. The growing importance of the movement can also be illustrated by the itineraries chosen for marches. The Communist demonstration of 9 February 1934 was banned by the Doumergue government. The Place de la République, the intended site of the demonstration, was sealed off by the police and the demonstrators instead found themselves scattered in the neighbouring streets in some of which they erected barricades. Some demonstrators penetrated into the Gare de l'Est. The occasion descended into a bloody affray between police and demonstrators. The demonstration of 12 February was authorized by the government but confined to the eastern edge of Paris. It marched from the Porte de Vincennes, one of the eastern gates of Paris, down the wide Cours de Vincennes, to the Place de la Nation. All avenues leading from the Place to the centre of Paris were blocked off by the police. Although the demonstration of 14 July 1935 reached nearer to the centre of the city, marching from the Place de la Bastille to the Place de la Nation, it moved from west to east, from centre to periphery. At the same time the Croix de Feu was marching up the Champs Elysées towards the Place de l'Etoile, also from centre to periphery but in the other direction. Finally, the massive demonstration of 14 July 1936 started in two different places. One column assembled in the Place de la République and Avenue de la République in the east, the other, however, assembled in the very centre of Paris near the Louvre, and marched down the Rue de Rivoli to the Place de la Bastille where it met the other column which had marched down the Boulevard Beaumarchais. The two processions then proceeded by different routes – one by the Boulevard Diderot, the other by the Rue du Faubourg St Antoine – to the Place de la Nation. The demonstration was so huge that while the first marchers were listening to speeches in the Place de la Nation, others were still at the points of departure.

From the demonstration of 12 February, confined to the very fringes of Paris, or that of 9 February, denied even the space on which to demonstrate, to that of 14 July 1936, which inhabited the very heart of the city, there is not only a difference of size and mood but also a kind of geographical progression, an occupation of even larger tracts of Parisian space.

Some Popular Front demonstrations took somewhat different itineraries from those described above. The protest demonstration against the attack on Blum marched from the Pantheon on the left bank across the river to the Place de la Bastille. This was partly because the attack on Blum had occurred on the left bank, at the western end of the Boulevard St Germain, when Blum, who was leaving the parliament building to return to his apartment on the Ile St Louis, had the misfortune to come across the funeral cortège of the Action Française historian Jacques Bainville. It was also the case that the Latin Quarter, where the Pantheon stands, was an area in which Action Française activists, especially students, were particularly in evidence. By choosing this district as the starting point of its demonstration the Popular Front was issuing a direct challenge to its enemies. The focus of the Mur des Fédérés demonstration of 24 May 1936 was of course the Père Lachaise cemetery somewhat to the north east of the symbolic Republican squares mentioned above. But although this occasion, to commemorate the dead of the Commune, was one of the largest demonstrations of the period, it was technically not a *Popular Front* march since the Radicals did not officially participate.

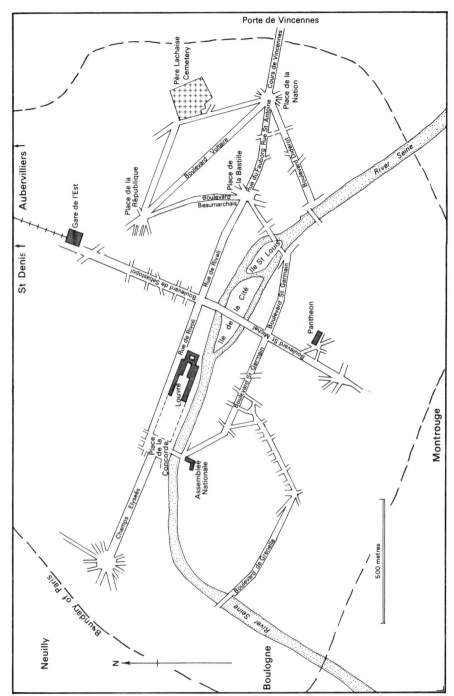

Popular Front Paris

Glossary

Cabinet	the name given to ministers' private staff who could be drawn from the civil service or from politics. The head was known as the *chef de cabinet*. Blum's *chef de cabinet* was the Socialist lawyer André Blumel, Lagrange's was the labour historian Edouard Dolléans
Camelots du roi	literally 'hawkers of the king'. The name was applied to streetsellers of *Action Française*, and, more generally, to Action Française activists
Cartel	the *cartel des gauches* was the Socialist–Radical coalition which won the elections of 1924. Thus the term cartel majority was generally used to describe revivals of this coalition
Coblentz	the place where in 1791 the French émigrés formed a counter-revolutionary army. Hence under the Popular Front 'coblentzard' was used by the left to attack the right, especially the Leagues
confédéré	a member of the pre-1936 CGT (see also *unitaire*)
Dreyfusard	a supporter of the innocence of Alfred Dreyfus, and hence a Republican opponent of the nationalist right in the 1900s
Instituteur	a primary school teacher
Jemappes	a French revolutionary victory over the Austrians in 1792, and hence a symbolic event of Republican patriotism
normalien	a graduate of the Ecole Normale Supérieure, one of France's most exclusive educational institutions, providing a literary and liberal education. Jaurès and Herriot were *normaliens*, so was Jean-Paul Sartre; Blum left after one year
polytechnicien	a graduate of the Ecole Polytechnique, a military school founded in 1795 and giving a general scientific education. It provided the top places in the technical corps of the civil service
président du conseil	the president of the council of ministers and thus the Prime Minister
Riom	the name of the town at which Blum, Daladier, Gamelin and others were put on trial by the Vichy regime in 1942

Sacred Union	the name given to France's coalition government, including Socialists, during the First World War
unitaire	a member of the CGTU
Valmy	a French revolutionary victory over the Prussians in 1792, and hence a symbolic event of Republican patriotism

Notes

The following abbreviations have been used:

CHIMT   *Cahiers d'histoire de l'Institut Maurice Thorez*
CIRM   *Cahiers d'histoire de l'Institut de recherches marxistes*
MS   *Mouvement social*
EDC   R. Rémond and J. Bourdin (eds.), *Edouard Daladier. Chef de gouvernement* (Paris, 1977)
LBC   P. Renouvin and R. Rémond (eds.), *Léon Blum. Chef de gouvernement* (Paris, 1981, 2nd edition)

The first mention in each chapter of a book or article of which full details have been given in a previous chapter will be followed by the chapter and note number specifying where those details can be found.

Preface

1 See D. Bell and B. Criddle, *The French Socialist Party: Resurgence and Victory* (Oxford, 1984).
2 J. Guéhenno quoted in H. Lottman, *The Left Bank: Writers in Paris from Popular Front to Cold War* (London, 1982), p. v.
3 All these books have, however, been updated and reissued. The most recent synthesis, from a mildly leftist angle, is J. Kergoat, *La France du Front populaire* (Paris, 1986).
4 See also J. Barrot *et al.*, *La Légende de la gauche au pouvoir: Le Front populaire* (Paris, 1973).
5 R. Bourderon, J. Burles *et al.*, *Le PCF: Etapes et problèmes* (Paris, 1981). For a Communist view of Popular Front historiography see B. Chambaz, 'Petite bibliothèque critique sur le Front Populaire', CHIMT, 4 (1973), pp. 186–91.
6 J-V. Le Gallou, 'Le Vrai bilan du Front populaire', *Contrepoint*, 52–53 (1986), pp. 15–18. It should be noted that this poll is mentioned in an article resolutely hostile to the Popular Front, in a special issue of *Contrepoint* entitled 'Rompre avec 50 ans de socialisme 1936–1986'.
7 D. Thomson, *Democracy in France* (London, 1964), p. 200.

Introduction

1 Léon Blum writing in *Le Populaire*, 12 February 1950. The article is reproduced in *L'Oeuvre de Léon Blum III-1 (1914–1928)* (Paris, 1964), pp. 16–17. The

314

bulk of Blum's writings are contained in the nine volumes of his collected works: *L'Oeuvre de Léon Blum 1891–1950* (Paris, 1954–72). All the quotations from Blum contained in this book come from the *Oeuvre*. Many of them are very familiar, and I have therefore given references only when quoting somewhat less well-known passages.

2 Lucie Mazauric quoted in Lottman, *The Left Bank* (Preface, 2). Mazauric was the wife of the novelist and Popular Front activist, André Chamson.

1 The origins of the Popular Front

1 A. Delmas, *Mémoires d'un instituteur syndicaliste* (Paris, 1979), pp. 225–6. L. Mazauric, *Vive le Front populaire* (Paris, 1976), p. 38.

2 On these groups see J. Loubet del Bayle, *Les Non-Conformistes des années trente* (Paris, 1969), and J. Touchard, 'L'esprit des années trente' in G. Michaud, ed., *Tendances politiques dans la vie française depuis 1789* (Paris, 1960), pp. 90–120.

3 The latest account is to be found in CIRM, 18 (1984) which contains an article by R. Martelli, 'Le PCF, l'Internationale et la France', pp. 5–23, and a number of previously unpublished texts from the PCF archives, with commentaries by D. Tartakowsky, pp. 25–83. The quotation about Thorez comes from p. 20. For the older view see G. Cogniot's contribution to J. Chambaz *et al.*, *Le Front Populaire: La France de 1934 à 1939* (Paris, 1972), pp. 98–139: he attacks 'anti-Communist' historians who claim that the Popular Front was invented in 1934; in a similar vein, D. Blumé, R. Bourderon *et al.*, *Histoire du réformisme en France depuis 1920* (Vol. 1) (Paris, 1976), p. 122, views the main change in 1934 as having come from the Socialists. In between these two approaches – but nearer the former than the latter – lies Bourderon, Burles *et al.*, *Le PCF* (Pref. 5), pp. 129–51. Of non-Communist historians, the book which most strongly emphasizes the importance of Soviet foreign policy requirements is D. Brower, *The New Jacobins* (Ithaca, NY, 1968).

4 The two most balanced recent accounts are J. Santore, 'The Comintern's United Front initiative of May 1934: French or Soviet inspiration?', *Canadian Journal of History*, XVI, 3 (1981), pp. 405–21 and J. Haslam, 'The Comintern and the Origins of the Popular Front', *Historical Journal*, 22, 3 (1979), pp. 673–91. A recent article by P. Burrin, 'Diplomatie soviétique, internationale communiste et PCF au tournant du Front populaire (1934–5)', *Relations Internationales*, no. 45, Spring 1986, pp. 19–34, which appeared too late to be consulted for this book, lays considerably more emphasis than either of the preceding articles on the importance of Soviet diplomacy. Unless further Soviet archives are released, the *exact* contribution of the Comintern, the Kremlin and the PCF in the *tournant* of 1934/5 must remain ultimately a matter for speculation.

5 On the Comintern in this period see E.H. Carr, *The Twilight of Comintern, 1930–1935* (London, 1982); F. Gaudin, *La Crise du mouvement communiste: du komintern au kominform* (Paris, 1972) stresses the Comintern's subservience to Soviet foreign policy; A. Agosti, 'L'Historiographie de la Troisième Internationale', CIRM, 2 (1980) pp. 7–59, is a survey of the historiography of

the Comintern. On the origins of the class against class tactics see W. Hoisington, 'Class against Class: the French Communist Party and the Comintern, a study of election tactics in 1928', *International Review of Social History*, 15, 1 (1970) pp. 19–42, and T. Draper, 'The Strange Case of the Comintern', *Survey*, 18, 3 (1972), pp. 91–137, who argues that there were 'two left-turns – a Bukharinist and a Stalinist'.

6 Bourderon, Burles *et al.*, *Le PCF* (Preface, 5), pp. 65–6. See also C. Willard, *Socialisme et Communisme Français* (Paris, 1978), pp. 138–9.

7 The point is made in an interesting review article by T. Judt, 'Une historiographie pas comme les autres: the French Communists and their history', *European Studies Review*, 12, 4 (1982), pp. 445–77.

8 I. Wall, *French Communism in the Era of Stalin* (London, 1983), p. 12. P. Robrieux points out in volume one of his *Histoire intérieure du Partie Communiste* (Paris, 1980), p. 355, that three of the members of the Politburo in 1931 were still there on Stalin's death in 1953. On the significance of the Barbé–Célor affair, see J.-P. Brunet, 'Une Crise au Parti communiste français', *Revue d'histoire moderne et contemporaine*, XVI (1969), pp. 438–61.

9 D. Levy, 'The Marseilles Working-Class Movement, 1936–1938', unpublished Oxford D.Phil. thesis, 1983, p. 128.

10 On the Amsterdam movement see Carr, *Twilight of Comintern*, pp. 387–94; Robrieux, *Histoire Intérieure*, vol. 1, pp. 419–21; and J. Prézeau, 'Le Mouvement Amsterdam–Pleyel', CIRM, 18 (1984), pp. 85–99. All these studies give somewhat different figures of membership. But the orders of magnitude are comparable.

11 B. Badie, *Stratégie de la grève. Pour une approche fonctionaliste du parti communiste français* (Paris, 1976).

12 A. Fourcaut, 'La Conquête d'une municipalité au moment du Front populaire: les élections municipales de 1935 à Bagneux', CHIMT, 19 (1976), pp. 93–107.

13 J. Jackson, *The Politics of Depression in France* (Cambridge, 1985), pp. 45–6.

14 On the reasons why the KPD was reluctant to give up the 'social fascist' line even after 1934, see E. Rosenhaft, 'Looking Back from the Front: Was Antifascist Unity Possible before 1935', a paper presented to the Conference on Popular Fronts in Spain and France held at Southampton in April 1986. Most of the papers are due to published in shortened form as a book.

15 J. Berlioz and R. Jean cited in CIRM, 18 (1984), pp. 61, 78.

16 *Ibid.* p. 63. See also the comments of Arrachard and Croizat cited in *ibid.* p. 62.

17 The possible role of Kirov and intervention by Moscow is mentioned by Martelli (based on a Soviet source) in *ibid.* p. 11. It was Vassart who claimed that Fried's intervention was the key factor, and this is followed by Brower, *New Jacobins*, p. 36. Lefranc, who talks of a telegram from Moscow, *Histoire du Front populaire* (Paris, 1974), p. 28, is probably confusing this with the telegram sent in June. See below p. 33.

18 See A. Prost, 'Les Manifestations du 12 Février 1934 en province', MS, 54 (1966), pp. 6–26.

19 Fried quoted in CIRM, 18 (1984), p. 59, fn. 1. Part of Gitton's report is printed

in CIRM, 18 (1984), pp. 56–61: the Socialists were 'more strongly than ever the part of social-fascism' but the 'principal enemy' was now 'fascism'.

20 See his comments to Barbé and Ferrat reported by Robrieux, *Histoire Intérieure*, vol. 1, pp. 355, 449: the leaders were 'bastards', the Comintern 'rotten'.

21 Much is made of this factor by Martelli and Tartakowsky in CIRM, 18 (1984), pp. 10, 38. In fact, as Communist historians delight in pointing out (see Tartakowsky in *ibid.*, p. 40) the policy advocated by Doriot in January was different from that adopted by the PCF in June; Doriot presented his proposals for negotiations with the SFIO as a means of unmasking their Socialist leaders to the followers rather than as a genuine attempt to attain unity 'at the summit'. But this was almost certainly, as Doriot's own actions in St Denis show, a matter of tactics: only presented in this way did his ideas have any chance of being accepted in the party.

22 On the CVIA see N. Racine-Furland, 'Le Comité de vigilance des intellectuels anti-fascistes, 1934–1939', MS, 101 (1977), pp. 88–114. There is a vivid account of the first meeting in Delmas, *Mémoires*, pp. 238–9. Useful information on the organization is to be found in its monthly bulletin *Vigilance* which appeared from April 1934.

23 R. Abellio, *Les Militants* (Paris, 1975), p. 230.

24 D. Lemaire, 'Le Mouvement Amsterdam–Pleyel dans le Loir-et-Cher', CIRM, 18 (1984), pp. 101–21.

25 Brower, *New Jacobins*, p. 41, fn. 19, counted 40 committees in which Communists participated between February and May; Doriot's open letter spoke of 86. For the Languedoc see M. Caron, 'Le Front Populaire dans le Bas-Languedoc et le Roussillon', unpub. *3ème Cycle* thesis, Montpellier, 1972, pp. 201–14. See also Kergoat, *La France* (Pref. 3), p. 45. Further information on the committee movement can be found in *Vigilance* and in the F7 series of prefects' reports in the Archives Nationales.

26 See Prost, 'Les Manifestations'.

27 Santore, 'The Comintern's United Front Initiative', p. 415 Fn. 40.

28 F7 13024, report of May 14.

29 On the attitude of the Amsterdam–Pleyel movement at this time, see Bourderon *et al.*, *Le PCF* (Pref. 5), pp. 134–6.

30 The suggestion comes from the memoirs of Vassart and Barbé. Ferrat thought the same but D. Wolf, *Doriot*, pp. 127–9, is sceptical. In the view of Doriot's most recent biographer, J.-P. Brunet, *Jacques Doriot* (Paris, 1986), p. 160, it is impossible to know but irrelevant because Doriot had already decided to break with the Party.

31 Vassart in C. and A. Vassart, 'The Moscow Origins of the French Popular Front' in M. Drachkovitch and B. Lazitch, *The Comintern: Historical Highlights* (New York, 1966), p. 245. Vassart's account of this period, which perhaps tends to overplay his personal influence, is nonetheless a very important source. It was all the more so when it first appeared at a time when none of this information was available from official communist sources.

32 Cited in CIRM, 18 (1984), pp. 73–4.

33 *Ibid.*, p. 45. Originally the only source for the telegram was C. and A. Vassart,

'The Moscow Origins', pp. 248–9, who went as far as to say that it contained a draft of the non-aggression pact that was to be addressed to the Socialists. Until recently Vassart's testimony has been accepted by most historians but ignored by French Communist ones: Bourderon, Burles *et al.*, *Le PCF* (Preface 5) has no mention of a telegram. But CIRM, 18 (1984), p. 46, fn. 33, reveals that on 30 June Thorez told the Politburo of a telegram from the Comintern without, however, specifying when it arrived. This seems to clinch the matter.

34 CIRM, 18 (1984), p. 76.

35 C. and A. Vassart, 'The Moscow Origins', p. 249.

36 S. Wolikow in R. Bourderon *et al.*, p. 136, suggests that there was a 'slight' increase in Communist influence and membership before June 1934, but this was too small to be of any significance.

37 CIRM, 18 (1984). On the Socialists' attitude in this period see J.T. Marcus, *French Socialism in the Crisis Years, 1933–1936* (New York, 1958).

38 Haslam, 'Comintern', p. 689. On Soviet foreign policy in this period see Haslam, *The Soviet Union and the Struggle for Collective Security in Europe 1933–9* (London, 1984).

39 For this paragraph see especially Santore, 'The Comintern's United Front Initiative'.

40 See also André Blumel's account to Blum of a meeting of the CAP in January 1935 where the unity pact was criticized by Faure, Séverac, Grumbach and Dormoy ('On tue, on assasine notre parti par l'unité d'action'). But only Frossard wanted to end it. Blum Papers 2BL 1 Dr. 2.

41 For these developments see R. Tiedrich 'Le Comintern et le Front populaire', *Contrepoint*, No. 3 (1971), pp. 120–45. The article is based on Comintern sources revealed by Soviet historians. See also Carr, *Twilight of Comintern*.

42 The delegation consisted of Togliatti, Gottwald and Fried; Stepanov, originally included, was ill. The most detailed account of the meeting is by G. Ceretti, *A L'Ombre des deux T: Quarante ans avec Maurice Thorez et Palmiro Togliatti* (Paris, 1973), pp. 158–62. It is also referred to by M. Thorez, *Fils du peuple* (Paris, 1960), p. 102 and J. Duclos, *Mémoires I, 1896–1934* (Paris, 1968), p. 421, who refer only to the 'leader of a sister party'. Togliatti's role is a little unclear. According to Ceretti, an Italian member of the PCF, Togliatti told him that he personally backed the French initiatives but that Stalin was hesitant. But his letter to Manuilsky, dated 19 November 1934, shows no sign of this. The main burden of his criticism was that the PCF had failed to seize the political initiative from the Socialists and develop the Popular Front as a mass movement – see P. Togliatti, *Opere*, III, 1 (Rome, 1973), pp. cxci–cxcii. There is no doubt that doubts were being expressed at this time in the Comintern: these surfaced at a meeting of its Presidium on 15 October.

43 This is the view of Brower, *New Jacobins*, pp. 75–6.

44 The visit to Herriot is mentioned by Duclos, *Mémoires I*, pp. 419–20, and that to Daladier by S. Berstein, *Histoire du Parti Radical* Vol II (Paris, 1982), p. 364.

45 Brower, *New Jacobins*, pp. 80–2.

46 *Ibid.*, pp. 82–5.

47 In towns with a population of over 5,000 the number of Communist controlled councils rose from 38 to 90. The success was especially great in the Paris region.
48 Haslam, *The Soviet Union*, p. 51.
49 F7 13028 Seine, 17 November 1934.
50 Cited in CIRM, 18 (1984), p. 44.
51 Brower, *New Jacobins*, p. 78.
52 Berstein, *Parti Radical*, p. 368–9.
53 See, for example, Caron 'Front Populaire' p. 432. For a dossier of police reports on the demonstration see F7 13305.
54 Lemaire, 'Mouvement Amsterdam–Pleyel', p. 106; F7 13024, Aude, 23 October 1934.
55 G. Lefranc, *Histoire*, pp. 56–7.
56 *Qu'est que le fascisme? Le Fascisme et la France* (CVIA, 1935).
57 Lemaire, 'Mouvement Amsterdam–Pleyel', p. 107; F7 13024, Ardèche, report of June 14 1934.
58 C. Jamet, *Notre Front Populaire: Journal d'un militant 1934–9* (Paris, 1977), p. 62.
59 Lemaire, 'Mouvement Amsterdam–Pleyel'; F7 13024 report of 30 July 1934.
60 F7 13028, Seine Inférieure. There is no date; it was almost certainly September 1934.
61 Caron, 'Front Populaire', p. 259; *Vigilance*, 5 November 1934; F7 13025, Eure et Loir, gives a similar impression after July 1934; see also F7 13024, Basses Alpes, 5 November 1934.
62 For preceding paragraphs see Jackson, *Politics of Depression*, pp. 84–6, 131–3.
63 Caron, 'Front Populaire', p. 484.
64 On the drawing up of the programme see Jackson, *Politics of Depression*, Chapter 5. An eye-witness account was provided by J. Kayser, one of the Radical delegates, in 'Le Parti radical–socialiste et le Rassemblement populaire 1935–1938', *Bulletin de la Société d'histoire de la III République*, April–July 1955, pp. 271–84.
65 See M. Anderson, 'The Myth of the Two Hundred Families', *Political Studies*, XIII, 2 (1965), pp. 162–78; J.-N. Jeanneney, *L'Argent caché* (Paris, 1984), pp. 17–19; P. Birnbaum, *Le Peuple et les Gros: Histoire d'un mythe* (Paris, 1979).
66 G. Cudenet, 'La Ruée sur l'or' in *Paix et Liberté*, December 1935. Cudenet was a dissident ex-Radical; *Paix et Liberté* was the journal of the Amsterdam movement. Such quotations could be easily duplicated. See for example, F. Bonte, 'Fascisme et Patrie' in *ibid.*, January 1936.
67 The fullest study of the election is G. Dupeux, *Le Front Populaire et les élections de 1936* (Paris, 1959).
68 LBC, pp. 50, 95.
69 A. Werth, *The Destiny of France* (London, 1937), pp. 240–70.
70 For all details concerning the Radicals and the elections see Berstein *Parti Radical*, pp. 422–45.
71 This point is often noted but it should be remembered that the swing is

measured against what had already been a substantial left-wing election victory in 1932.

72 For details on the Socialist results see N. Greene, *Crisis and Decline. The French Socialist Party in the Popular Front Era* (New York, 1969), pp. 64–70.

2 The leaders

1 The best general biographies of Blum are J. Lacouture, *Léon Blum* (Paris, 1977) and J. Colton, *Léon Blum* (1966, New York). (My references are to the translation of Colton). G. Ziebura, *Léon Blum et le parti socialiste 1872–1934* (Paris, 1967) is the best study of Blum and the Socialist Party but unfortunately it stops just before the Popular Front.

2 Ziebura, *Léon Blum*, p. 92.

3 R. Belin, *Du Secrétariat de la CGT au Gouvernement de Vichy* (Paris, 1978), p. 107.

4 See, for example, the unfavourable impression made on M. Jaquier, a member of the extreme left of the SFIO: M. Jaquier, *Simple militant* (Paris, 1974, p. 123.

5 Belin, *Secrétariat*, p. 107–8; Delmas, *Mémoires*, (1, 1), pp. 335–6.

6 C. Audry, *Léon Blum ou la politique du juste* (Paris, 1955).

7 See Blum's lecture on Jaurès, delivered in 1917 and republished in Blum, *L'Oeuvre 1914–1928*, III-1 (Intro, 1), pp. 3–21.

8 The passage comes from his pamphlet *Pour être socialiste*, first published in 1919 and many times reissued. It is reproduced in *ibid.*, pp. 22–12.

9 Ziebura, *Léon Blum*, p. 106.

10 The point is clearly made by T. Judt, *Marxism and the French Left* (Oxford, 1986), p. 144. See also T. Judt, *La Réconstruction du parti socialiste 1921–1926* (Paris, 1976).

11 J. Touchard, *La Gauche en France depuis 1900* (Paris, 1977), p. 169.

12 See Judt, *Marxism*, p. 148.

13 J. Joll, *Intellectuals in Politics* (London, 1960), p. 21.

14 R. Abellio, *Les Militants* (1, 23), p. 243.

15 See the testimony of Blumel in LBC, p. 38.

16 J. Zay, *Souvenirs et solitude* (Paris, 1946), pp. 284. Moch makes a similar observation and gives further examples in LBC, p. 41.

17 All the biographical information in this section comes from P. Robrieux's excellent biography of Thorez, *Maurice Thorez. Vie sécrète et vie publique* (Paris, 1975).

18 J. Bruhat, *Il n'est jamais trop tard* (Paris, 1983), pp. 92–5.

19 This was the view of Maurice Thorez junior who wrote about Fried in a letter to *Le Monde*, 11/12 May, 1969.

20 See A. Kriegel, 'Un phénomène de haine fratricide: Léon Blum vu par les communistes' in *Le Pain et les roses* (Paris, 1968), pp. 391–433.

21 On the Communists' attitude to political power see generally R. Tiersky, *Le Mouvement communiste en France* (Paris, 1973); and J.-J. Becker, *Le Parti communiste veut-il prendre le pouvoir?* (Paris, 1981). On the specific issue of participation in 1936, see S. Wolikow, 'Le Parti communiste et la question de

sa participation au gouvernement du Front populaire', CHIMT, 34 (1980), pp. 55–110; A. Kriegel, 'Léon Blum et le Parti communiste' in LBC, pp. 125–35. An expanded version of this essay is contained in M. Perrot and A. Kriegel, *Le Socialisme français et le pouvoir* (Paris, 1966).

22 The statement comes from Duclos' report to the Latin Secretariat of the Comintern on 5 January 1936. It is published in CHIMT, 12–13 (1975), pp. 289–306.

23 See Wolikow, 'Le Parti communiste'.

24 Brower, *New Jacobins* (1, 3), p. 134.

25 M. Thorez, *Oeuvres de M. Thorez*, vol. 12 (Paris, 1953), p. 329.

26 See Ceretti, *A l'Ombre des deux T* (1, 42), p. 163, A. Lecoeur, *Le Partisan* (Paris, 1963), p. 52; Duclos, CHIMT, 2 (1966), p. 19 and *Démocratie nouvelle*, 5 (1966), p. 43, claimed that Thorez favoured participation while others, Duclos included, had doubts, but he had a few years earlier told Jacques Fauvet that the issue was not discussed; F. Billoux, *Quand nous étions ministres* (Paris, 1972), pp. 17–18, alleged that Thorez raised the issue informally with members of the Politburo but that, meeting with an unfavourable response, he went no further and the issue was not officially discussed by the Politburo.

27 This is essentially the view of Wolikow, 'Le Parti communiste'.

28 Dimitrov's report is contained as an annex to *ibid.*

29 Brower, *New Jacobins*, p. 134.

30 Quoted in CIRM 24 (1986), p. 38. This issue contains a number of previously published texts by Thorez, presented by D. Tartakowsky.

31 This no doubt also had the secondary advantage of leaving open the long-term revolutionary option. Thus in January 1936 Duclos described the Popular Front committees, to which the Communists attached such importance, as 'an element of our revolutionary policy'. See his intervention to the Presidium of the Comintern on 9 January 1936, published in CHIMT, 12–13 (1975).

32 Berstein, *Parti Radical* (1, 44), p. 288. There is no serious biography of Daladier, and the biographical information in this section comes from Berstein, unless otherwise stated.

33 *Ibid.*, p. 151.

34 Jackson, *Politics of Depression* (1, 13), p. 70.

35 See, for instance, the comments of L. Lamoureux, his budget minister in 1933, quoted in *ibid.*, p. 75.

36 Belin, *Secrétariat*, p. 77.

37 Brower, *New Jacobins*, pp. 93–4, 131, 141.

38 C. Campinchi cited in Berstein, *Parti Radical*, p. 378.

39 For Jouhaux's life see the two volume biography by B. Georges and D. Tintant: *Léon Jouhaux: Cinquante ans de syndicalisme: Des origines à 1921*, vol. 1 (Paris, 1962), and *Léon Jouhaux dans le mouvement syndical français*, vol. 2 (Paris, 1979).

40 For Belin's views of Jouhaux see Belin, *Secrétariat*, pp. 31–42.

41 Delmas, *Mémoires*, p. 323.

42 Georges and Tintant, *Léon Jouhaux*, vol. II, p. 140.

43 On planism see Jackson, *Politics of Depression*, p. 137–66 and the biblio-

graphical references provided there. In addition there is a new biography of de Man: H. Brelaz, *Henri de Man: Une autre idée du socialisme* (Geneva, 1985).
44 See below pp. 164–6.
45 Belin, *Secrétariat*, pp. 83–4.
46 The memorandum is published in Georges and Tintant, *Léon Jouhaux*, vol. II, pp. 409–11.

3 The social explosion

1 J. Coutrot, *Les Leçons de Juin 1936. L'Humanisme économique* (Paris, 1936), p. 13; Werth, *Destiny of France* (1, 69), p. 305.
2 There is a substantial literature on the strikes. The most useful general accounts are: J. Danos and M. Gibelin, *Juin 1936* (Paris, 1952); H. Proteau, *Les Occupations d'usines en Italie et en France (1920–1936)* (Paris, 1938); S. Schwartz, 'Les Occupations d'usines en France de mai et juin 1936', *International Review of Social History*, II, (1937), pp. 50–104; G. Lefranc, *Juin 36, l'explosion sociale du front populaire* (Paris, 1966) and his article 'Problématique des grèves françaises de mai–juin 1936' in *Essais sur les problèmes socialistes et syndicalistes* (Paris, 1970), pp. 127–40; and A. Prost, 'Les Grèves de juin 1936, essai d'interprétation', LBC, pp. 69–87: the debate which follows this, pp. 88–107, is also interesting.
3 See G. Lemarchand, 'Juin 1936 à Caen', MS, 55 (1966), pp. 75–85.
4 PRO FO 371, 10857, Clerk to Vansittart, 11 June 1936.
5 On the Nord see M. Gillet and Y.-M. Hilaire (eds.), *De Blum à Daladier, le Nord–Pas-de-Calais 1936–1939* (Lille, 1979).
6 J. Bardoux, *Les Soviets contre la France* (Paris, 1936).
7 Proteau, *Les Occupations*, pp. 136–7.
8 Prost, 'Les Grèves', p. 73. In the Ardennes, the strike started in the north where unionization was low, and not in Rheims where it was higher. See D. Candille, 'Le Front populaire dans la vallée de la Meuse', memoir, University of Paris-I, 1973.
9 See F. Cahier, 'La Classe ouvrière havraise et le Front populaire, 1934–1938', unpublished memoir, University of Paris-I, 1972; and L. Eudier, 'Bréguet–Le Havre: première grève-occupation en 1936', CHIMT, 29 (1972), pp. 67–70. All future references to this strike come from these sources.
10 B. Badie, 'Les Grèves du Front populaire aux usines Renault', MS, 81 (1972), pp. 69–109. There is a considerable literature on the Renault factory. See also J.-P. Depretto and S. Schweitzer, *Le Communisme à l'usine* (Paris, 1984), which incorporates Badie's findings; R. Francotte, 'A l'Usine Renault: Souvenirs', CHIMT, 30 (1973), pp. 136–48; J. Durand, *La Lutte des travailleurs de chez Renault* (Paris, 1971).
11 Werth, *Destiny of France* (1, 69), p. 299.
12 On these see R. Hainsworth, 'Les Grèves du Front populaire de mai et juin 1936', MS, 96 (1976), pp. 3–45.
13 Levy, 'Marseilles Working-Class Movement' (1, 9), pp. 226ff.
14 Quoted in CIRM, 24 (1986), p. 41, fn. 24.

15 See Thorez's remarks to the Central Committee in April 1936, quoted in CIRM, 24 (1986), p. 37.
16 Levy, 'Marseilles Working-Class Movement' (1, 9), p. 263.
17 Badie, 'Les Grèves', p. 80.
18 J.-P. Brunet, *St Denis, la ville rouge, 1890–1939* (Paris, 1980), p. 406.
19 A. Prost, *La CGT à l'époque du Front populaire* (Paris, 1964), pp. 36–7.
20 Lefranc, *Juin 1936*, p. 200.
21 Lefranc, 'Problématique', p. 137.
22 Lefranc, *Juin 1936*, p. 211. All future references to this strike come from Brient's testimony in *ibid.*, pp. 208–22.
23 LBC, p. 100.
24 Testimony of Madeleine Colliette in Lefranc, *Histoire* (1, 17), pp. 489–93. All future references to this strike come from this source.
25 M. Collinet, *L'Ouvrier français: esprit du syndicalisme* (Paris, 1951), pp. 114–16.
26 J. Moch, *Rencontres avec Léon Blum* (Paris, 1970), pp. 156–7. A. Delmas, *A Gauche de la barricade* (Paris, 1950), pp. 95–6 gives a somewhat different account of this incident; see also Belin, *Secrétariat* (2, 3), p. 98.
27 See Badie, 'Les Grèves', pp. 98–9; Hainsworth, 'Les Grèves', pp. 27–30.
28 F7 13040 report of 25 June 1936.
29 Levy, 'Marseilles Working-Class Movement' p. 262.
30 Audry, *Léon Blum* (2, 6), D. Guérin, *Front populaire, révolution manquée* (Paris, 1963); Jaquier, *Simple militant*, (2, 4).
31 J.-P. Joubert, *Révolutionnaires de la SFIO* (Paris, 1977), pp. 102–3.
32 Lefranc, *Histoire*, p. 148, fn. 1.
33 Kriegel, 'Léon Blum' (2, 21), pp. 126–7.
34 Collinet, *L'Ouvrier français*, pp. 106–9. This is very much the interpretation offered by Prost, 'Les Grèves'.
35 Weil's article was republished in S. Weil, *La Condition ouvrière* (Paris, 1951), pp. 230–2.
36 For statistics on the social effects of the Depression see A. Sauvy, *Histoire économique de la France entre les deux guerres*, Vol. II (Paris, 1967), pp. 278–96; Dupeux, *Le Front Populaire* (1, 67), p. 124.
37 O. Hardy-Hémery, 'Rationalisation aux mines d'Anzin, 1927–1938', MS, 72 (1970), p. 31. On rationalization in the Nord mining industry, see also A. Moutet, 'La Rationalisation dans les mines du Nord à l'épreuve du Front Populaire', MS, 135 (1986), pp. 61–99.
38 See especially Depretto and Schweitzer, *Le Communisme à l'usine*, pp. 20–46.
39 G. Navel, *Man at Work* (London, 1949), pp. 58–9.
40 Weil, *La Condition ouvrière*, pp. 25–6, 28, 50, 68, 100, 110.
41 See M. Couteaux, 'Les Femmes et les grèves de 1936, l'exemple des grands magasins', unpub. memoir, University of Paris–VII 1975.
42 See the enquiry undertaken by Jamet for *Vigilance* into the conditions of textile workers near Rouen. Reprinted in Jamet, *Notre Front populaire* (1, 58), pp. 77–81.
43 Hardy-Hémery, 'Rationalisation', p. 34.
44 See his testimony in Lefranc, *Juin 1936*, pp. 196–8.

45 S. Schweitzer, *Des engrenages à la chaine: les usines Citroën 1915–1935* (Lyon, 1982), p. 102 (the first epigraph to this chapter comes from p. 91).

46 Hardy-Hémery, 'Rationalisation', pp. 32–5; Hainsworth, 'Les Grèves', pp. 12–13.

47 Werth, *Destiny of France* (1, 69), p. 296; Lime, quoted in Lefranc, *Juin 1936*, p. 190.

48 Quoted in Lacouture, *Léon Blum*, p. 283.

49 Such cases are reported to Lefranc in *Juin 1936*, passim.

50 Jaquier, *Simple militant*, pp. 96–7.

51 On this and subsequent meetings of the strike delegates of the Paris engineering sector see Danos and Gibelin, *Juin 1936*, pp. 95–100.

52 The most detailed account is in Gillet and Hilaire, *De Blum à Daladier* (3, 5), pp. 135–40.

53 Hainsworth, 'Les Grèves', p. 15.

54 Quoted in Lefranc, *Juin 1936*, p. 183.

55 *Ibid.*, p. 184; Badie, 'Les Grèves', p. 89.

56 Lemarchand, 'Juin 1936 à Caen', pp. 82–3.

57 The problem of boredom was also mentioned by H. Vieilledent who confided his memories of a strike in a factory to Lefranc: *Juin 1936*, pp. 203–8.

58 Schweitzer, *Des engrenages à la chaine*, p. 120.

59 See M. Seidman, 'Work and Revolution: Bourgeoisie and working classes in Paris and Barcelona in the 1930s', unpublished Ph.D., Amsterdam, 1982, p. 135. Some of the conclusions of this thesis are summarized in M. Seidman, 'The Birth of the Weekend and the Revolts against Work. the workers of the Paris region during the Popular Front', *French Historical Studies*, 112, 2 (1981), pp. 249–76.

60 Hardy-Hémery, 'Rationalisation', pp. 37–8; Lefranc, *Juin 1936*, p. 215.

61 Coutrot, *Les Leçons*, p. 15.

62 The phrase comes from A. Prost, 'Le Climat social', in EDC, pp. 99–111. This piece provides a good overview of the period after June 1936. Very useful also is G. Bourdé, *La Défaite du Front populaire* (Paris, 1977).

63 Lefranc, *Juin 1936*, pp. 263–7.

64 See J. Colton, *Compulsory Labour Arbitration in France* (New York, 1951), pp. 81–5.

65 See below Chapter 10, section 3.

66 The formulation is M. Seidman's: see note 59 above.

67 Gillet and Hilaire, *De Blum à Daladier* (3, 5), pp. 146–8.

68 Seidman, 'Birth of the Weekend', pp. 258–60.

69 Weil, *La Condition ouvrière*, p. 277.

70 Prost, 'Le Climat', p. 102.

71 Moutet, 'La Rationalisation', pp. 83–96.

72 For the first approach see P. Broué and N. Dorey, 'Critiques de gauche et opposition révolutionnaire', MS, 54 (1960), pp. 91–133. For the second, Lefranc, *Histoire*, p. 276, n. 3.

73 My description of the strike is pieced together from the accounts by Brower, *New Jacobins* (1, 3), pp. 211–17; Bourdé, *La Défaite*, pp. 33–7; and Broué and Dorey, 'Critiques de gauche', pp. 122–5.

74 See below p. 233.

75 On the compulsory labour arbitration legislation the best study is Colton cited in note 64 above. See also J.-P. Rioux, 'La Conciliation et l'arbitrage obligatoire des conflits du travail' in EDC, pp. 112–28.

76 On the reaction to the decrees, see Bourdé, *La Défaite*, pp. 128–49.

77 P. Fridenson, *Histoire des usines Renault* (Paris, 1972), p. 271.

78 Bourdé, *La Défaite*, p. 148.

4 The cultural explosion

1 H.-R. Lenormand, *Confessions d'un auteur dramatique*, Vol. 2 (Paris, 1953), p. 349.

2 G. Dimitrov, *Selected Articles and Speeches* (London, 1951), p. 100.

3 *L'Art musical populaire*, No. 1, 1 May 1937. This was the journal of the FMP.

4 See D. Tartakowsky, 'Stratégies de la rue 1934–1936, MS, 135 (1986), pp. 31–62.

5 On the contribution of painters, B. Taslitzky, 'Le Front populaire et les intellectuels', *Nouvelle Critique*, 70 (December 1955), pp. 11–16. This issue also contains three pages of reminiscence by the film-maker J.-P. Le Chanois, 'Le Front populaire et les intellectuels', pp. 17–21, from which the first epigraph to this chapter comes.

6 Caron, 'Le Front populaire' (1, 25), pp. 632–3; Lemaire, 'Le Mouvement' (1, 24), pp. 112–3.

7 *Vendredi*, 17 July 1936 quoted in L. Bodin and L. Touchard, *Front populaire 1936* (Paris, 1972); pp. 121–4; J. Pary *L'Amour des camarades* (Paris, n.d.), p. 11; *Combat Social*, 20 July 1935, quoted by Caron, 'Le Front populaire', p. 433.

8 Jamet, *Notre Front populaire* (1, 58), pp. 26–9; Mazauric, p. 46.

9 Quotations respectively from J. Guéhenno, *La Foi difficile* (Paris, 1957), pp. 152, 156 (these are his memoirs); *Caliban Parle* (Paris, 1928), p. 35; *Journal d'une 'Révolution'* (Paris, 1939), pp. 165–6. On *Vendredi* see also C. Estier, *La Gauche Hebdomadaire 1914–62* (Paris, 1962), pp. 57–74.

10 On the Gide–Guéhenno controversy see Appendix 1 to *Journal d'une 'Révolution'* which reprints the correspondence, and A. Gide, *Literature engagée* (Paris, 1950), pp. 200–10. Appendix 2 of *Journal d'une 'Révolution'* contains Guéhenno's two articles criticizing the Moscow trials. For Communist criticisms of these, see G. Sadoul in *Commune*, February 1937. For Sperber's views see M. Sperber, *Au delà de l'oubli* (Paris, 1979), p. 110.

11 On the PCF's attitude to intellectuals see J.-P. Bernard, *Le Parti communiste et la question littéraire 1921–1939* (Grenoble, 1972); D. Caute, *Communism and the French Intellectuals 1914–1960* (London, 1964); 'Le Parti communiste française et les intellectuels 1920–1939', *Revue française de science politique*, XVII, 3 (1967), pp. 468–833.

12 On the AEAR see N. Racine, 'L'Association des Ecrivains et Artistes révolutionnaires. La revue *Commune* et la lutte idéologique contre le fascisme', MS, 54 (1966), pp. 29–49. On *Commune* see W. Klein, *Schriftsteller in der*

französischen Volksfront. Die Zeitschrift Commune (Berlin, 1978), shortly to appear in French.

13 Vaillant-Couturier, *Commune*, January/February 1934.

14 Quoted by P. Ory, 'Le Front Populaire et la creation artistique', *Bulletin de la Société d'histoire moderne*, 8 (1974), p. 7.

15 There is a vivid account of this congress in H. Lottman, (Pref. 2), pp. 83–98.

16 Ory, 'Le Front populaire', p. 7.

17 B. Chambaz, 'La politique culturelle du PCF', CHIMT, 12–13 (1975), pp. 66–87.

18 *Commune*, January 1936.

19 P. Vaillant-Couturier, *Vers des lendemains qui chantent* (Paris, 1962), pp. 263–85 (a posthumous collection of his texts). J. Duclos, *Les Droits de l'intelligence* (Paris, 1938), p. 58.

20 On the Communists' attitude to French history in this period see N. Buzon, 'Le PCF et l'histoire nationale (1933–1939)' unpublished memoir, University of Paris-VIII, 1979.

21 P. Ory, 'La Commémoration révolutionnaire en 1939' in R. Rémond (ed.), *La France et les Français 1938–1939* (Paris, 1978), pp. 115–36. Duclos, *Mémoires*, Vol. II (Paris, 1969), pp. 364–410.

22 The figures come from contemporary Communist sources and are probably somewhat inflated.

23 For example, R. Blech, *Commune*, April 1937.

24 On the October Group see M. Poch, 'Le Groupe Octobre', unpublished memoir, University of Paris-I, 1970, M. Faure, *Le Groupe Octobre* (Paris, 1977); 'Théâtre de l'agitation: le Groupe "Octobre"', MS, 91 (1975), pp. 109–19. For a study of another FTOF group, L.-D. Cortes, 'Une Expérience de théâtre populaire: la compagnie Proscénium (1929–1939)', Unpublished memoir, University of Paris 1972. See also the general reflexions of M. Rebérioux, 'Culture et Militantisme', MS, 91 (1975), pp. 3–12.

25 See M. de Vetch, 'La Politique culturelle des syndicats ouvriers pendant les entre-deux guerres', unpublished thesis, Institut français of Utrecht, 1981 (a copy exists at the Centre de Recherches d'Histoire du Syndicalisme, Paris).

26 See, for example, D. Fisher, 'The Origins of the French Popular Theatre', *Journal of Contemporary History*, 12 (1977), pp. 461–97.

27 The fundamental article is P. Ory 'La Politique culturelle du première gouvernement Blum', *Nouvelle revue socialiste*, 10–11 (1975), pp. 75–93. Also important – although slightly overlapping – is Ory's article cited in Note 14 above. See also G. Cogniot, 'La Politique scolaire et culturelle du gouvernement Blum vue par un parlementaire de l'époque', *Nouvelle revue socialiste*, No. 10–11, 1975, pp. 94–9.

28 J. Zay, *Souvenirs* (2, 16), p. 54. The politician was de Monzie – about as cynical as they came even in the Third Republic. These memoirs, written during Zay's wartime incarceration, contain much on his activity in this period. Also useful, though in a somewhat hagiographical mode, are M. Chavardès, *Un Ministre éducateur: Jean Zay* (Paris, 1965) and M. Ruby, *La Vie et l'oeuvre de Jean Zay* (Paris, n.d.).

29 J. Soustelle, *Vendredi*, 26 June 1936; J. Berlioz in his report on the budget of

the Beaux Arts Ministry, *Journal Officiel, Documents parlementaires* (Chamber), 1936, No. 1285, p. 405.

30 *Le Musée vivant*, May 1937. This was the journal of APAM (first issue February 1937).

31 Ory, 'Le Front Populaire', p. 13.

32 *Ibid.*, p. 12.

33 See C. Halphen-Istel, *Le Club–Bibliothèque du centre Kellermann à l'Exposition de 1937* (Paris, 1938).

34 *Commune*, July 1936. For the activities of the FMP, see generally *L'Art musical populaire* and the musical rubric of *Commune*.

35 Both quoted in Bodin and Touchard, *Front populaire*, pp. 146–8. *La Lumière* was a Radical weekly sympathetic to the Popular Front.

36 Paz's review in *Le Populaire*, 14 July 1936: the audience's attitude was 'so clear, so unanimous, that it was tangible, visible, it had consistency'.

37 Thus in July 1937 when the political fervour of the previous year had subsided, *Syndicats* (on which see Chapter 8 Section I) described the production of *Juillet 14* as follows: it was 'badly directed [and] degenerated more than once into a sort of grotesque masquerade . . . into such chaos that each actor seemed to be wondering what he was doing on the stage and Marie Bell what she was doing in a theatre'. L. Sauvage, *Syndicats*, 8 July 1937 (*Syndicats* was of course unlikely to approve of anything staged by a Maison de Culture).

38 C. Koechlin, *L'Art musical populaire*, No. 1, 1 May 1937. See also Koechlin, *La Musique et le peuple* (Paris, 1936) for a more extended discussion of this problem.

39 On the visual arts in this period see P. Gaudibert, 'Front populaire et arts plastiques', *Politique aujourd'hui*, October/December 1974, pp. 105–21; *Action culturelle: intégration et/ou subversion* (Paris, 1972), especially pp. 68–82; and on Le Corbusier's Pavilion see, Le Corbusier, *Des Canons, des munitions? Merci! Des Logis S.V.P.* (Paris, 1938).

40 *La Quérelle du réalisme* (Paris, 1936). I have not been able to find a copy of this book. But the debate over realism can be followed in the May and June 1935 issues of *Commune* which ran a series entitled, 'Où va la peinture?'; L'Aragon, Pour un réalisme socialiste (Paris, 1935), 'Le Réalisme socialiste à l'ordre du jour', *Commune*, September 1936; and 'Réalisme socialiste et réalisme français', *Europe*, March 1938, pp. 289–303.

41 *Commune*, May 1935.

42 In *L'Art musical populaire*, August/September 1937.

43 In *ibid.* For the previous quotation see *Peuple et culture* 20 January 1937. (This was the journal of the Marseilles Maison de Culture.)

44 Quoted by Gaudibert, 'Front populaire', p. 100.

45 R. Brasillach, *Notre avant-guerre* (Paris, 1941), p. 183. On the performance of *Naissance d'une cité* see W. Klein, 'L'Espoir naïf' in *Europe*, no. 683 (March, 1986), pp. 107–113. The text has been recently republished in J. Albertini, *Avez-vous lu Jean-Richard Bloch?* (Paris, 1981).

46 H. Sauveplane in *L'Humanité*, 19 July 1936.

47 See the account by Lenormand, one of the authors, in Lenormand, *Confessions*, pp. 223–4, or the account in *Syndicats*, 8 July 1937.

48 In *Le Musée vivant*, June 1937.
49 *Le Peuple*, 2 April 1937.
50 G. Vidalenc, 'Le Problème de l'orientation des loisirs' in *Le Droit au savoir* (publication of the CCEO, Paris 1938), p. 18.
51 Kergoat, *La France* (Pref. 3), pp. 357–60.
52 Quoted in G. Cogniot *et al.*, *L'Avenir de la culture* (Paris, 1937), p. 13.
53 R. Holt, *Sport and Society in Modern France* (London, 1981), p. 85.
54 There was a large contemporary literature on leisure from which much of what follows is taken. See especially: J.-V. Parant, *Le Problème du tourisme populaire* (Paris, 1939); F. Bloch-Lainé, *L'Emploi des loisirs ouvriers et l'éducation populaire* (Paris, 1936); G. and E. Lefranc, *Le syndicalisme devant le problème des loisirs* (Paris, 1937?).
55 On Lagrange there is an informative, though hagiographical biography: J.-L. Chappat, *Les Chemins de l'espoir ou les combats de Léo Lagrange* (Paris, 1983). His speeches and articles are collected in E. Raude and G. Proteau, *Le Message de Léo Lagrange* (Paris, 1950) and *1936 Léo Lagrange* (Editions Temps Libres 1980).
56 Chappat, *Les Chemins*, p. 175.
57 Depretto and Schweitzer, *Le Communisme* (3, 10), p. 131.
58 All quotations from *Le Cri des Auberges de jeunesse*. See also Kergoat, La France (Pref. 3), pp. 312–15, based on L. Heller, 'Histoire des Auberges de jeunesse', Doctorat d'Etat, Nice 1984. Chamson's article in *Vendredi* is quoted by Bodin and Touchard, *Front populaire*, pp. 152–3.
59 See F. Havret, 'Un Sport rouge au sport populaire en France', Mémoir, Paris 1972; S. Paolo, 'Le Sport travailliste en France sous le Front populaire', Memoir, Paris 1984.
60 On the Bureau of Tourism see *Syndicats*, 10 April 1937; *Vendredi*, 7 May 1937; P. Daniel, 'La CGT et les loisirs ouvriers', *Dossiers de l'action populaire*, 10 June 1937.
61 *Syndicats*, 10 April 1937.
62 Bruhat, *Jamais trop tard* (2, 18), pp. 79, 102.
63 See F. Cribier, *La Grande migration de l'été* (Paris, 1967).
64 Quoted in Depretto and Schweitzer, *Le Communisme* (3, 10), pp. 210–12.
65 On *Dopolavoro* see V. de Grazia, *The Culture of Consent: The Mass Organisation of Leisure in Fascist Italy* (Cambridge, 1981).
66 R. Halls, *The Youth of Vichy France* (Oxford, 1981), p. 9.
67 G. and E. Lefranc, *Le Syndicalisme*, pp. 38–9.
68 J. Martin, *The Golden Age of French Cinema, 1929–1939* (Boston, 1983). The pioneering article on the cinema of the Popular Front was G. Fofi, 'The Cinema of the Popular Front, 1934–1938', *Screen*, Vol. 13, No. 4 (1972/3), pp. 5–57. (First published in Italian in 1966.) There is now a fairly substantial literature. A good bibliography of this is provided in G. Vincendeau and K. Reader, *La Vie est à nous: French Cinema of the Popular Front* (London, 1986). Two especially useful books are J.-P. Jeancolas, *15 ans d'années trente. Le cinéma des français 1929–1944* (Paris, 1983) and E. Strebel, *French Social Cinema of the 1930s: A Cinematic Expression of Popular Front Consciousness* (New York, 1980).

69 E. Strebel, 'French Social Cinema and the Popular Front', *Journal of Contemporary History*, 12, 3, pp. 499–515, especially p. 501.
70 Vincendeau and Reader, *La Vie est à nous*, p. 60.
71 Fofi, 'Cinema', pp. 12–13.
72 See E. Strebel, 'Renoir and the Popular Front', *Sight and Sound*, Vol. 49, No. 1 (Winter 1979/80), pp. 36–41; J. Renoir, *Ma Vie et mes films* (Paris, 1974), pp. 142–3.
73 The film, at one time unobtainable, is now readily available. A video cassette of it exists in the library of the Centre Beaubourg in Paris. See also, 'La Vie est à nous, film militant', *Cahiers du Cinéma*, No. 218 (1970), pp. 44–51.
74 On Ciné-Liberté, and on its major production *La Marseillaise* see P. Ory, 'De "Ciné-Liberté" à La Marseillaise', MS, 91, (1975), pp. 153–75. (The article has been reprinted in translation in Vincendeau and Reader, *La Vie est à nous*).
75 Jeancolas, *15 ans*, pp. 220, 271.
76 Quoted in Strebel, 'French Social Cinema', p. 511.
77 R. Chirat, *Le Cinéma des années 30* (Paris, 1983), pp. 41–8.
78 F. Garçon, *De Blum à Pétain* (Paris, 1985), pp. 53–8.
79 On Renoir's political views in this period see C. Gauteur, *Jean Renoir: La double méprise 1925–1939* (Paris, 1980).
80 Jeancolas, *15 ans*, p. 272.

5 'Liberty': defending democracy

1 Blum, *Le Populaire*, 2 January 1935, reprinted in *Oeuvre de Léon Blum IV–2* p. 448.
2 The *Letters* are to be found in *Oeuvre 1914–1928*, III-1 (Intro., 1), p. 1. For admiring references to Britain, see pp. 516, 522, 525, 532.
3 For a general survey of Blum's attitude to administrative problems in 1936 see 'Léon Blum et l'Etat', a conference organized by the CNRS in June 1973. The unpublished contributions are available in typed form. Especially relevant is J. Marchal, 'Léon Blum et l'exercice de pouvoir 1936–1938', pp. 43–77. There is useful material scattered in LBC. See also J. Moch. 'Léon Blum et l'équipe de 1936' in *Le Vétéran socialiste* (March 1960).
4 G. Lefranc, *Histoire* (1, 17), p. 150.
5 C. de Gaulle, *Mémoires de guerre*, Vol. I, p. 29.
6 A. Delmas, *A gauche de la barricade* (Paris, 1950), pp. 85–6.
7 On the Socialist Party's desire for a purge as well as the actual measures taken by the government, see I. Wall, 'Socialists and Bureaucrats: the Blum Government and the French Administration', *International Review of Social History*, 19, Pt. 3 (1974), pp. 325–46.
8 On the Socialists see *ibid.*; on the CVIA, Lefranc, *Histoire*, pp. 289–90.
9 On the attitude of the army see M. Alexander, 'Hommes prêts à tout accepter? The French Officer Corps and the Acceptance of Leftist Governance, 1935–37', paper presented to the Southampton Conference 1986 (1, 14).
10 W. Cohen, 'The Colonial Policy of the Popular Front', *French Historical*

Studies, VII, 3 (1972), pp. 368–94 provides a useful introduction. So also does C.-A. Julien, 'Léon Blum et les pays d'outre-mer', LBC, pp. 377–90.

11 On the Socialists and the colonies see M. Semedei, 'Les Socialistes français et le problème colonial entre les deux guerres', *Revue française de science politique*, XVII, No. 6, 1968, pp. 1115–53; on the Communists, T.-A. Schweitzer, 'Le Parti communiste français, le Comintern et l'Algérie dans les années 1930', MS, 78 (1972), pp. 115–36.

12 Julien, LBC, p. 378.

13 G. Oved, *La Gauche française et le nationalisme marocain 1905–1954*, Vol. II (Paris, 1984), p. 98.

14 The quotation comes from a memorandum emanating from Moutet's *cabinet*. It is quoted by D. Hémery, 'Aux Origines des guerres d'indépendance vietnamiennes: pouvoir colonial et phenomène communiste en Indochine avant la Seconde Guerre Mondiale', MS, 101 (1977), pp. 3–35 (p. 28). On Moutet's views see also J. Marseille, 'La Conférence des gouvernements généraux des colonies (November 1936)' in *ibid.*, pp. 61–84. (This article contains an annex reproducing a policy statement by Moutet.)

15 Marseille, 'La Conférence', p. 84.

16 Cohen, 'Colonial Policy', p. 379; D. Hémery, *Révolutionnaires vietnamiens et pouvoir colonial en Indo-chine* (Paris, 1975), p. 282; Oved, *La Gauche française*, p. 94.

17 On Senegal see Y. Person, 'Le Front populaire au Sénégal (Mai 1936–Octobre 1938)', MS, 107 (1979), pp. 77–102.

18 On India, China and Hémery, *Révolutionnaires*, and 'Origines'.

19 Hémery, 'Origines', p. 84; Marseille, 'La Conférence', reaches similar conclusions which he slightly tones down in his *Empire colonial et capitalisme français* (Paris, 1984), p. 337.

20 Oved, *La Gauche française*, p. 147.

21 Hémery, *Révolutionnaires*, pp. 301–11.

22 For the case of Morocco see Oved, *La Gauche française*, pp. 93–189.

6 'Bread': the Blum New Deal

1 Quoted by J. Colton, 'Politics and Economics in the 1930s: the Balance Sheet of the "Blum New Deal"' in C.K. Warner (ed.), *From the Ancien Regime to the Popular Front* (New York and London, 1969), pp. 181–208. The article is a useful introduction to Blum's economic policy.

2 On Socialist economic policy see Jackson, *Politics of Depression* (1, 13), pp. 35–41, 112–16. Also M. Margairaz, 'Les Propositions de politique économique, financière et monétaire de la SFIO de 1934 à 1936' (memoir, University of Paris-VII, 1972).

3 For a more complex appreciation of the ideology and background of the Finance Inspectors see N. Carré de Malberg 'Le Recrutement des Inspecteurs des Finances de 1892 à 1946', *Vingtième Siècle*, 8 (1985), pp. 67–91, and 'Les Limites du Libéralisme chez les Inspecteurs des Finances de la IIIe République', *Bulletin du Centre d'histoire de la France contemporaine*: No. 6. See also the remarks of J.-B. Duroselle, 'Notes de lecture; Inspecteurs des Finances et

politique etrangère dans les années trente', *Relations Internationales*, 13 (1978), pp. 117–22.

4 G. Cusin, LBC, p. 294.

5 Jackson, *Politics of Depression*, passim.

6 G. Cusin, LBC, p. 292–3.

7 On Boris see M. Nouschi, 'Georges Boris, analyste de la crise économique', MS, 115 (1981), pp. 51–75; and M.-F. Toinet, 'Georges Boris (1888-1960), Un Socialiste humaniste' (*3e cycle* thesis, University of Paris-X, 1969).

8 F. Bloch-Lainé, *Profession fonctionnaire* (Paris, 1976), p. 50. Labeyrie he considered to be an 'absurd' figure.

9 Belin, *Secrétariat* (2, 3), p. 103.

10 On the previous two paragraphs see Jackson, *Politics of Depression*, pp. 145–50, 191–3.

11 Z. Sternhell, *Ni droite ni gauche* (Paris, 1983), pp. 160–233.

12 Georges Politzer, who acted as one of the PCF's leading spokesmen on economic affairs, quoted in M. Margairaz, 'Le Parti communiste, l'économie, les finances et la monnaie en 1935–1936', CIRM, 24 (1986), pp. 6–35. This article is a useful examination of the Communists' view of economic policy in 1935–6.

13 Delmas, *A gauche* (5, 6), p. 78.

14 A. Sauvy, *De Paul Reynaud à Charles de Gaulle* (Tournai, 1972), p. 46.

15 Lefranc, *Histoire* (1, 17), pp. 325–6. He gives no further details of this plan.

16 R. Abellio, *Les Militants* (1, 23), pp. 262–75.

17 In LBC, p. 283.

18 A useful overview is provided by J.-M. Jeanneney, 'La Politique économique de Léon Blum' in LBC, pp. 208–32. See also M. Wolfe, *The French Franc Between the Wars, 1919–1939* (New York, 1951) and Colton, 'Politics and Economics', in note 1 above.

19 Blum, *Oeuvres* IV-1 (Intro. 1), p. 316.

20 Georges and Tintant, *Léon Jouhaux* (2, 39), Vol. II, p. 160.

21 P. Saly, *La Politique des grands travaux en France 1929–1939* (New York, 1977).

22 See also Blum's homage to Roosevelt's pragmatism in a speech to the Chamber in September 1936, quoted in Colton, Léon Blum (2, 1), p. 196.

23 For an excellent general discussion see M. Magairaz, 'Les Socialistes face à l'économie et à la société en juin 1936', MS, 93 (1975), pp. 87–108. See also the debate between J.-M. Jeanneney, P. Mendès France and others, 'L'Experience économique du Front populaire' (this debate took place at the Ecole Normale Supérieure in 1965: a typed version is available), and the comments on it by J. Bouvier, 'Un Débat toujours ouvert: la politique économique du Front populaire', MS, 54 (1966), pp. 175–81.

24 On the devaluation negotiations see J.-P. Cuvillier, *Vincent Auriol et les finances publiques du Front populaire ou l'alternative du contrôle et de la liberté* (Paris, 1978), pp. 11–25; R. Girault, 'Léon Blum, la dévaluation de 1936 et la conduite de la politique extérieure de la France', *Relations internationales*, 13 (1978), pp. 91–109; S. Clarke, *Exchange-rate Stabilization in the mid-1930s: Negotiating the Tripartite Agreement* (Princeton, NJ,

1977); I. Drummond, *The Floating Pound and the Sterling Area, 1931–1939* (Cambridge, 1981), pp. 201–22. Some points remain obscure but perhaps the recent opening of the Auriol papers will cast further light.

25 For Monick's own account of his role see E. Monick, *Pour mémoire* (n.p., 1970).

26 Clarke, *Exchange-Rate Stabilization*, p. 39.

27 He made the remark at the Socialist Congress in 1938, quoted by Colton, *Léon Blum*, p. 195.

28 W. Baumgartner, the leading Finance Ministry official, claimed that Blum was resigned to devaluation on taking office, LBC, pp. 281–2; for Auriol's remark to Belin, see Belin, *Secrétariat*, pp. 109–10.

29 Clarke, *Exchange-Rate Stabilization*, p. 39.

30 Drummond, *Floating Pound*, p. 209.

31 Sauvy, *Histoire* (3, 36), Vol. II, p. 194–6.

32 See Margairaz, 'Les Socialistes face à l'économie', pp. 94–5.

33 In LBC, p. 228.

34 M. Kalecki, 'The Lesson of the Blum Experiment', *The Economic Journal*, XLVIII, 189 (1938), pp. 26–41.

35 The debate on this issue still goes on. The most balanced examination of the 40-hour week is by J.-C. Asselain, 'Une Erreur de politique économique; la loi des quarante heures de 1936', *Révue économique*, 25, 4 (April–June 1974), pp. 672–705. The most relentless critic is A. Sauvy, *Histoire économique* (3, 36), especially Vol. II, pp. 191–201, 297–305. Also very critical is R. Marjolin, 'Réflexions sur l'expérience Blum experiment', *Economica*, V, 18 (1938), pp. 177–91. On the other hand, H. Ehrmann, 'The Blum Experiment and the Fall of France', *Foreign Affairs* (October, 1941), pp. 152–64, concluded that 'the decay of the French economy can be explained without even mentioning the 40-hour week'.

36 Asselain, 'Une Erreur', p. 678.

37 In factories employing over 100 workers some 160,000 jobs were created in the year after October 1936. The difference between this figure and the reduction in unemployment is to be explained by the fact that many of the new jobs were taken up by peasants, immigrants or non-registered unemployed.

38 J.-C. Asselain, *Histoire économique de la France*, Vol. II (Paris, 1984), p. 64.

39 E. Weill-Raynal, 'Les Obstacles économiques à l'expérience Léon Blum', *La Revue Socialiste* (June, 1956), pp. 49–56.

40 Mendès France, LBC, p. 237; Moch, quoted by Margairaz, 'Les Socialistes face à l'économie', p. 90, calculated that if workers employed at 90 per cent of full capacity for 44 hours, worked at full strength for 40, there would have been a 30 per cent increase in production.

41 Kalecki, 'Blum Experiment', p. 27; Moutet, 'La Rationalisation' (3, 37), pp. 84–7.

42 Belin, *Secrétariat*, p. 106.

43 Colton, *Léon Blum*, p. 171.

44 On Jouhaux see Ehrmann, *French Labour*, p. 91; on Spinasse, Lefranc, *Histoire*, p. 320, and Sauvy, *De Paul Reynaud*, p. 51; on Marjolin, note 35 above: Marjolin wrote a whole series of articles for *L'Europe nouvelle* in 1937

and 1938 attacking the 40-hour law: in an article of 28 June 1938 he called it a 'loi de trahison nationale'.

45 See respectively R. Frank, *Le Prix du réarmament français* (Paris, 1982), pp. 238–9, Moutet, 'La Rationalisation', p. 98.

46 Quoted by J. Clarke, 'The Nationalisation of War Industries in France, 1936–1937: a Case Study', *Journal of Modern History*, 49, 3 (1977), p. 427.

47 Moutet, 'La Rationalisation', pp. 85–6.

48 On the financial management of the Blum government the most useful book is R. Frank, *Le Prix*, pp. 128–62 on which the following account is based. On monetary policy and the problems of the franc see I. Drummond, *London, Washington and the Management of the Franc 1936–1939* (London, 1979).

49 Ministry of Finance Archives: B 33 194, No. 47.

50 For Rueff's account of this period see *De l'Aube au crépuscule: autobiographie* (Paris, 1977), pp. 131–7.

51 Quoted in Drummond, *London, Washington*, p. 14. On the different interpretations of Auriol's letter see Drummond, p. 12, from whom the quotation in the text comes, and R. Girault, 'The Impact of the Economic Situation on the Foreign Policy of France, 1936–9' in W. Mommsen and L. Kettenacker, *The Fascist Challenge and the Policy of Appeasement* (London, 1983), pp. 209–26, especially p. 219.

52 Colton, *Léon Blum*, p. 192.

53 Frank, *Le Prix*, p. 33.

54 For the debate over exchange controls see D. Lecomte and D. Pavy, 'Le Front populaire face au mur d'argent: le problème du contrôle des changes dans les années 1936–1938', memoir, University of Paris-VIII, 1975, and Cuvillier, *Vincent Auriol.*

55 See Rueff's note drawn up after seeing Blum on 6 February and reproduced in Rueff, *De l'Aube*, p. 130.

56 Blum, *Oeuvres 1934–1937*, IV-1 (Intro., 1), p. 483.

57 Frank, *Le Prix*, pp. 100, 142, 155.

58 The ousting of Finaly was revealed at the time by R. Louzon in *Révolution prolétarienne* (on which, see below Chapter 8, Section 2). The real significance of the event is unclear but it is taken seriously enough by Frank, *Le Prix*, p. 158.

59 Wolfe, *The French Franc*, p. 173.

60 Frank, *Le Prix*, p. 173.

61 *Ibid.*, p. 152.

62 Mendès France, LBC, pp. 239–40; Cusin, *ibid.*, p. 294.

63 Cuvillier, *Vincent Auriol*, pp. 64–5; Frank, *Le Prix*, pp. 156–7; Lecomte and Pavy, 'Le Front populaire'. For the new obsession with exchange controls see *Etudes socialistes*, a journal founded by the UTS in 1938.

7 'Peace': the contradiction

1 The quotation comes from P. Renouvin, 'La Politique extérieure du premier gouvernement Léon Blum', in LBC, pp. 329–53. This piece provides a useful overview of Blum's foreign policy. The fullest study of the foreign policy of the

Popular Front is J. Dreifort, *Yvon Delbos at the Quai d'Orsay: French Foreign Policy during the Popular Front* (Lawrence, 1973). Also very useful are the following general books on French foreign policy in the period: R.J. Young, *In Command of France: French Foreign Policy and Military Planning 1933–40* (London, 1978); A. Adamthwaite, *France and the Coming of the Second World War* (London, 1977), and J.-B. Duroselle, *La Décadence* (Paris, 1979). There is also a good chapter in Colton's biography of Blum.

2 For Blum's views on foreign policy see, besides his major biographers, N. Greene, *Crisis and Decline: The French Socialist Party in the Popular Front* (New York, 1969), pp. 13–34; M. Bilis, *Socialistes et pacifistes* (Paris, 1970), pp. 37–79.

3 Daladier quoted in Berstein, (I, 44) p. 452. For biographical details on Delbos see Dreifort, *Yvon Delbos*.

4 On Léger see E. Cameron, 'Alexis Saint-Léger' in F. Gilbert and G. Craig (eds.), *The Diplomats* (Princeton, 1953), pp. 378–405.

5 This is the interpretation followed by Young, *In Command of France*, p. 131 and Adamthwaite, *France*, p. 40. On Franco–British relations in this period see also P. Renouvin, 'Les Relations franco-anglaises, 1935–1939. Esquisse provisoire', in *Les Relations franco-britanniques de 1935 à 1939* (Editions du CNRS, Paris, 1975), pp. 16–51. This volume contains the proceedings of two colloquia held in 1971 and 1972.

6 Dreifort, *Yvon Delbos*, p. 218, n. 24.

7 Young, *In Command of France*, pp. 160–1; Adamthwaite, *France*, p. 51.

8 Renouvin, 'La Politique extérieure', p. 316.

9 Duroselle, *La Décadence*, p. 298.

10 *Ibid.*, p. 322. On the Polish issue see G. Gamelin, *Servir Vol. II: Le Prologue du drame* (Paris, 1946), pp. 224–38; L. Noël, *L'Agression allemande contre la Pologne* (Paris, 1946), pp. 139–48.

11 Lacroix to Delbos, *Documents diplomatiques français, 2 Serie*, Vol. III, no. 448.

12 Young, *In Command of France*, p. 145.

13 Dreifort, *Yvon Delbos*, p. 137; Duroselle, *La Décadence*, p. 322.

14 See especially J. Dreifort, 'The French Popular Front and the Franco–Soviet Pact, 1936–1937: A Dilemma in Foreign Policy', *Journal of Contemporary History*, 9 (1976), pp. 217–36; Young, *In Command of France*, pp. 145–50; H. Michel, 'Le Front populaire et l'URSS', in *Les Relations franco-britanniques*, pp. 215–21.

15 For example, General Gauché, head of military intelligence, believed that staff talks would push Poland into the arms of Germany: Young, *In Command of France*, p. 146. See also the comments by Generals Le Goys and Giraud cited in Dreifort, 'French Popular Front', p. 232, fn. 15.

16 Adamthwaite, *France*, p. 49. The British even disapproved of an exchange of military information: Dreifort, *Yvon Delbos*, pp. 14–15.

17 Young, *In Command of France*, p. 148. This is allegedly what Gamelin had said himself.

18 *Ibid.*, p. 285, fn. 8; Dreifort, *Yvon Delbos*, p. 218, fn. 28.

19 These were made through the Radical Senator Malvy and through Hubert Lagardelle, at this time an attaché at the French Embassy in Rome.

20 See his remarks in LBC, p. 360.

21 See Frank, *Le Prix*, (VI, 45), p. 91.

22 R. Girault's notion of a grand Anglo-American design to associate France in a plan to offer Hitler economic concessions in return for political guarantees is not borne out by British or American sources. It may have existed in the mind of Monick – but nowhere else. See R. Girault, 'Léon Blum, La dévaluation et la conduite de la politique extérieure de la France', *Relations internationales*, 13 (1978), pp. 91–109, and Duroselle's comments in *La Décadence*, pp. 311–14.

23 Adamthwaite, *France*, p. 56.

24 Non-intervention has stimulated a considerable literature. Besides the works on foreign policy already mentioned, see the useful collection of material in *Cahiers Léon Blum*, No. 2 and 3, 1978 ('Contribution à l'histoire de la politique de la non-intervention: documents présentés par Daniel Blumé'); D. Carlton, 'Eden, Blum and the Origins of Non-Intervention', *Journal of Contemporary History*, 6, 3 (1971), pp. 40–55 (the most vigorous demolition of the theory of British influence); M. Gallagher, 'Léon Blum and the Spanish Civil War', *Journal of Contemporary History*, 6, 3 (1971), pp. 56–64; G. Warner, 'France and Non-Intervention in Spain, July–August 1936', *International Affairs*, 38, 2 (April, 1962), pp. 203–20; J. Bowyer Bell, 'French Reaction to the Spanish Civil War' in L.P. Wallace and W.C. Askew (eds.), *Power, Public Opinion and Diplomacy* (Durham, North Carolina, 1959), pp. 266–96; there are also good chapters in Colton's and Lacouture's biographies of Blum.

25 This is what Moch said in LBC, p. 370.

26 The only evidence for this was a despatch to Cordell Hull, the American Secretary of State, from Straus, the American Ambassador in Paris.

27 See the letter from Los Rios to Giral printed in LBC, pp. 407–9.

28 Moch's account of the Spanish Civil War is contained in J. Moch, *Le Front populaire, grand espérance* (Paris, 1971), pp. 230–48; and Moch, *Rencontres avec Léon Blum* (Paris, 1970), pp. 189–217.

29 For the French account of this meeting see *Documents diplomatiques français*, 2 Série, Vol. III, no. 87; Carlton, 'Eden, Blum', gives the British account.

30 Zay, *Souvenirs* (2, 16), p. 114.

31 The first date seems to be the one suggested by the testimony of Jiminez de Asua in LBC pp. 409–11, as Renouvin, 'La Politique extérieure', p. 340, and Lacouture, *Léon Blum* (2, 1), p. 337, also believe. But Colton, *Léon Blum* (2, 1), pp. 258–9, Lefranc *Histoire* (1, 17), p. 190, and Dreifort, *Yvon Delbos*, p. 48, prefer the later date. In this they are supported by Blum's own remarks to the parliamentary commission of enquiry in 1947, *Les Evènements survenus en France de 1933 à 1945*, I, pp. 218–19. But it is quite probable that Blum himself had confused the dates.

32 These notes are in the Blum papers at the Fondation Nationale des Sciences Politiques, and cited by Lacouture, *Léon Blum* (2, 1) p. 385.

33 Moch, LBC, p. 371. Jimenez de Asua claims that Blum told him that Baldwin

had appealed directly to Lebrun: LBC, p. 410. There is no other evidence for this statement.

34 Quoted in *Cahiers Léon Blum*, No. 2 and 3. Thomas also claimed to have heard from Viénot that Clerk's 'opportune words' had been very useful. But this is odd because Viénot is usually believed to be one of those who opposed non-intervention.

35 Blumel, LBC, p. 358, talks of two *démarches*; Monnet, LBC, p. 360. Cot in fact told Bell, 'French Reaction', p. 281, fn. 21, that he knew nothing of Clerk's intervention.

36 Colton, *Léon Blum* (2, 1), p. 274; Greene, *Crisis and Decline*, p. 86, fn. 35.

37 Lacouture, *Léon Blum*, p. 353, based on the memories of Monnet, Cot and Moch. Dreifort gives an identical line-up except that he includes Monnet among opponents of non-intervention, probably wrongly (see LBC, p. 360), and has no mention of Dormoy. On Delbos' resignation threat see *ibid.*, p. 48, on Lebrun's, Greene, *Crisis and Decline*, p. 84, fn. 30.

38 But it ought to be remembered that for much of the period French governments were more immediately concerned about the prospect of a conflict with Italy than Germany. Adamthwaite, *France*, p. 87; Young, *In Command of France*, pp. 192–3.

39 On previous two paragraphs see Adamthwaite, *France*, pp. 58–76.

40 On the anschluss, Duroselle, *La Décadence*, pp. 326–8; Adamthwaite, *France*, pp. 77–84; Renouvin, 'Les Relations', pp. 35–9.

41 *Documents diplomatiques français*, 2 Série, Vol. VIII, no. 446.

42 Ormo Sargent cited in Adamthwaite, *France*, p. 84.

8 The mystique of unity

1 *Le Populaire*, 8 June 1936. He was speaking at the meeting organized by the Socialists at the Vel d'Hiver on 7 June.

2 Guérin, *Front populaire* (3, 30), p. 65.

3 C. Jamet in *Le Front populaire de la Vienne*, 11 January 1936. Note that this statement was made before the explosion of June.

4 Delmas, *A Gauche* (1, 6), p. 92.

5 Werth, *Destiny* (1, 69), pp. 310–14.

6 Thus the Buffalo meeting had been held because the Comité du Rassemblement Populaire decided, owing to the situation caused by the strikes, not to hold in Paris a victory celebration of the kind that it had organized throughout France on that day.

7 Werth, *Destiny*, p. 312. On the style of political propaganda in France at this time see P. Burrin, 'Poings levés et bras tendus: la contagion des symboles au temps du Front populaire', *Vingtième siècle*, 11 (1986), pp. 5–26. On Tchakhotine see also Guérin, *Front populaire* (3, 30), p. 113.

8 Levy, 'Marseilles Working-Class Movement' (1, 9), p. 255; *Le Front populaire de la Vienne* and *Le Front populaire de Menton* are both conserved in the Bibliothèque nationale: in both cases the Popular Front committees seem to have functioned fairly effectively, at first, but only as bringing together

representatives from the major parties; Caron, 'Le Front populaire' (1, 25); Guérin, 'Front populaire' (3, 30), pp. 102–3.

9 For a computer analysis of the Popular Front coalition in parliament see P. Warwick, *The French Popular Front: a Legislative Analysis* (Chicago, 1977); A. Prost, 'L'Eclatement du Front populaire. Analyse factorielle des scrutins de la Chambre des députés', in EDC, pp. 25–44, also G. Dupeux, 'Léon Blum et la majorité parlementaire', LBC, pp. 109–24.

10 Prost, *La CGT* (3, 19), p. 39.

11 Delmas, *Mémoires* (1, 1), p. 288.

12 On Jouhaux and Blum's government, see B. Georges, 'La CGT et le gouvernement Léon Blum', MS, 54 (1966), pp. 49–68.

13 All statistics relating to the CGT come from Prost, *La CGT*, passim.

14 On *Syndicats* see M.-F. Rogliano, 'L'Anti-Communisme dans la CGT: Syndicats', MS, 87 (1974), pp. 63–84; also Belin's comments in MS 90 (1975), pp. 151–2.

15 Prost, *La CGT*, p. 157.

16 Levy, 'Marseilles Working-Class Movement', pp. 126–7.

17 On the reunification negotiations there is an unpublished memoir by J.-F. Gelly, 'Recherches sur les problèmes de l'unité organique du PCF et de la SFIO (1934–1937)', Paris-I, 1974, whose conclusions are summarized in Gelly, 'A la recherche de l'unité organique: la démarche du Parti communiste, 1934–1938', MS, 121 (1982), pp. 97–116.

18 These meetings are referred to by Blumel in LBC, p. 163. According to Thorez they in fact became rarer and decreasingly productive: see CIRM, 24 (1986), p. 21.

19 Robrieux, *Maurice Thorez* (2, 17), p. 210.

20 Brower, *New Jacobins* (1, 3), pp. 162–8. Brower provides the most detailed day to day analysis of the PCF's attitude in this period. His account always stresses the role of Soviet foreign policy.

21 Levy, 'Marseilles Working-Class Movement', p. 278.

22 Brower, *New Jacobins* (1, 3), p. 182.

23 For reports of dissent at the base see the extracts from the Central Committee debate printed in CIRM, 24 (1986), especially pp. 42, fn. 32, 46, fn. 40, 48 (L. Mauvais talked of 'the development of sectarianism and anti-socialism which could become anti-Popular Front and anti-governmental'), 51 fn. 49. For Thorez's speech to the central committee see *ibid.*, pp. 43–8.

24 For the Socialists and the Popular Front government see I. Wall, 'French Socialism and the Popular Front', *Journal of Contemporary History*, 5, 3 (1970), pp. 3–20; N. Greene, *Crisis and Decline* (7, 2). D. Baker, 'The Politics of Socialist Protest in France: the left-wing of the Socialist Party, 1921–1939', *Journal of Modern History*, Vol. 43, No. 1 (1971), pp. 2–41; G. Lefranc, *Le Mouvement socialiste sous la Troisième république* (Paris, 1963).

25 Greene, *Crisis and Decline*, p. 109, fn. 6.

26 On the Amicales see D. Baker, 'The Socialists and the Workers of Paris: the Amicales Socialistes 1936–1940', *International Review of Social History*, XXIV, 1 (1979), pp. 1–34; J.-P. Rioux, 'Les Socialistes dans l'entreprise au temps du Front populaire: quelques remarques sur les amicales socialistes',

MS, 106 (1979), pp. 3–24. Their interpretations do not differ significantly.

27 Joubert, *Révolutionnaires* (3, 31) pp. 134–5; Greene, *Crisis and Decline*, pp. 165–7.

28 Greene, *Crisis and Decline*, pp. 107–84; Bilis, *Socialistes* (7, 2), pp. 189–95.

29 On the Radicals in this period see Berstein, *Histoire* (1, 44), pp. 445–502; P. Larmour, *The French Radical Party in the 1930s* (Stanford, 1964), pp. 197–226.

30 Berstein, *Histoire* (1, 44), p. 458.

31 Quoted in A. Mitzman, 'The French Working Class and the Blum Government (1936–37)', *International Review of Social History* XI (1964), pp. 363–90. This article provides a useful general survey of the government's relations with the working class.

32 Levy, 'Marseilles Working-Class Movement'.

33 *Ibid.*, pp. 275–8; Thorez in CIRM, 24 (1986), pp. 45–6. On reactions to the Spanish Civil War see S. Schweitzer, 'Les Ouvriers des usines Renault de Billancourt et la guerre civile espagnole', MS, 103 (1978), pp. 111–21; J. Girault, 'Le Syndicat national des instituteurs et les débuts de la guerre d'Espagne 1936–7', MS, 103 (1978), pp. 87–109. For a more general study of public opinion (in effect, newspaper opinion) and the war see D. Pike, *Les Français et la guerre d'Espagne 1936–1939* (Paris, 1975).

34 Levy, 'Marseilles Working-Class Movement'.

35 Savoir, an ex-*confédéré*, quoted by Broué and Dorey, 'Critique de gauche' (3, 73), p. 117. The communists' analysis was no different: see note 23 above.

36 On the leftists the pioneering study is Broué and Dorey 'Critique de gauche' (3, 73); J. Rabaut, *Tout est possible* (Paris, 1974) is a useful general survey; J.-P. Rioux, *Révolutionnaires du Front Populaire: choix de documents, 1935–38* (Paris, 1973), provides an excellent selection of texts with a commentary.

37 Quoted in Rioux, *Révolutionnaires*, pp. 90–7.

38 Joubert, *Révolutionnaires* (3, 31), is a history of the Gauche Révolutionnaire.

39 Quoted in Rioux, *Révolutionnaires*, pp. 171–2.

40 'Où va la France?' in L. Trotsky, *Le Mouvement communiste en France 1919–1939* (Paris, 1967), pp. 448–75. This is a collection of texts edited by Broué. See also J.-P. Joubert, 'Trotsky et le Front populaire', *Cahiers Léon Trotsky*, 9 (1982), pp. 27–51. On Ferrat see Rioux, *Révolutionnaires*, pp. 216–7.

41 Rioux, *Révolutionnaires*, pp. 45–7, 197–201.

42 *Ibid.*, pp. 77–80.

43 *Ibid.*, pp. 135–40, 166–78.

44 L. Trotsky, *Le Mouvement communiste*, pp. 578–83.

45 *Ibid.*, pp. 202–7; Broué and Dorey, 'Critiques de gauche' (3, 73), p. 107.

46 Rioux, *Révolutionnaires*, pp. 292–5.

47 *Révolution prolétarienne*, 10 July 1937.

48 *Révolution prolétarienne*, 10 January 1937. The same issue contained articles on the Soviet legal system, the new constitution of the Soviet Union, the Stalinists in Spain, and so on. This was a fairly typical selection.

49 On the Cercle see Rabaut, *Tout est possible*, pp. 288–90; Broué and Dorey,

pp. 131–2; Joubert, 'Trotsky', pp. 168–9. Rioux, *Révolutionnaires*, pp. 288–91 reprints its founding manifesto which was published at the time by *Commune*, journal of the PCI, and *Révolution prolétarienne* – a good indication of the widespread interest excited by the Cercle.

50 Rioux, *Révolutionnaires*, pp. 361–1.
51 *Ibid.*, pp. 322–4.
52 On the PSOP see Joubert, *Révolutionnaires*, pp. 153ff.
53 Rioux, *Révolutionnaires*, p. 379.
54 Quoted in Broué and Dorey, p. 133.
55 See N. Racine, 'Le Comité de vigilance' (1, 22).
56 Levy, 'Marseilles Working-Class Movement', p. 319.
57 Larmour, *The French Radical Party*, p. 239.
58 Berstein, *Histoire*, p. 532.
59 Bilis, (7, 22), Greene, *Crisis and Decline* (1, 72) and R. Gombin, *Les Socialistes et la guerre* (Paris, 1970), all examine in detail the conflict over foreign policy within the SFIO.
60 Echoed by the Socialist J.-B. Severac: 'the heaviest concessions are better than the most victorious wars'.
61 For Munich and the French intellectuals see M. Winock, 'Les Intellectuels français et l'esprit de Munich', in A. Roche and C. Tarting, eds., *Des Années trente: groupes et ruptures* (Paris, 1985), pp. 147–57.
62 Larmour, *The French Radical Party*, p. 245.
63 Rogliano, 'L'Anti-Communisme', p. 81.

9 The view from the right

1 R. Peyrefitte, *Les Ambassades* (Paris, 1951), pp. 7–8.
2 Levy, 'Marseilles Working-Class Movement' (1, 9), p. 365, fn. 3; P. Christophe, *1936: les Catholiques et le Front populaire* (Paris, 1979), p. 88.
3 J.-N. Jeanneney, *François de Wendel en république: l'argent et le pouvoir* (Paris, 1976), p. 565.
4 See J. Droz, 'L'Image de Léon Blum dans la presse d'extrême-droite des années 30', *Nouvelle revue socialiste*, 10/11 (1975), pp. 67–74. On the attitude of the right to the Popular Front there are some general remarks in S. Osgood, 'The Front Populaire: Views from the Right', *International Review of Social History*, Vol. IX, No. 2 (1964), pp. 189–201.
5 E. Weber, *Action française* (Stanford, 1962), p. 374.
6 W. Irvine, *French Conservatism in Crisis* (Baton Rouge, 1979), p. 93.
7 The anecdote is told by Zay, *Souvenirs* (2, 16), pp. 352–3.
8 A. Maurois, *Call No Man Happy* (London, 1944), p. 232.
9 Droz, 'L'Image', pp. 70–1.
10 The best book is S. Berstein, *Le Six février* (Paris, 1975). See also M. Beloff, 'The Sixth of February', in J. Joll (ed.), *The Decline of the Third Republic* (London, 1959), pp. 9–35; R. Rémond, *Les Droites en France* (Paris, 1982), pp. 195–230.
11 A. Shennan, 'The Parliamentary Opposition to the Front Populaire and the Elections of 1936', *Historical Journal*, 27, 3 (1984), pp. 677–95.

12 E. Leroy-Ladurie, *Paris–Montpellier* (Paris, 1982), p. 13.
13 We still await a full length study of the Croix de Feu and PSF. For the moment see P. Machefer, 'Les Croix de Feu 1927–1936', *Information historique*, No. 1 (1972), pp. 28–33; and 'Le Parti social français en 1936–1937', *ibid.*, 2 (1972), pp. 74–80.
14 J.-N. Jeanneney, 'La Fédération républicaine', in *La France et les Français en 1938–1939*, p. 351.
15 On Doriot and the PPF see D. Wolf, *Doriot* (I, 30); J.-P. Brunet, *Jacques Doriot* (I, 30), and 'Un Fascisme français: le Parti populaire français de Doriot (1936–1939)', *Revue française de science politique*, 33, 2 (1983), pp. 255–80; G. Allardyce, 'Jacques Doriot et l'esprit fasciste en France', *Revue d'histoire de la deuxième guerre mondiale* 25, 97 (1975), pp. 31–44.
16 Quoted by R. Girardet, 'Notes sur l'esprit d'un fascisme français 1934–1939', *Revue française de science politique*, 3, 3 (1955), p. 533, fn. 10. The study of inter-war fascism in France is a rapidly expanding field. For thorough bibliographies and divergent interpretations – see Sternhell, *Ni droite, ni gauche* (6, 11) and R. Soucy, *French Fascism: the First Wave* (New Haven and London, 1986).
17 Irvine, *French Conservatism*, p. 157.
18 *Ibid.*, p. 179.
19 Jeanneney, *François de Wendel*, p. 583.
20 See above p. 177.
21 See P. Machefer, 'L'Union des droites, le PSF et le Front de la Liberté, 1936–1937', *Revue d'histoire moderne et contemporaine*, (Vol. 1 / (1970), pp. 112–26.
22 The best general study of Catholics and the Popular Front is Cristophe, *1936.* See also R. Rémond, *Les Catholiques, le Communisme et les crises 1936–1939* (Paris, 1960), and 'Les Catholiques et le Front populaire', *Archives de Sociologie des Religions*, No. 10 (1960), pp. 63–9; O. Arnal, 'Catholic Roots of Collaboration and Resistance', *Canadian Journal of History*, XVII, I (1982), pp. 87–110, and 'Alternatives to the Third Republic among Catholic Leftists in the 1930s', *Historical Reflections*, V, 2 (1978), pp. 177–95.
23 On *Sept* see A. Coutrot, *Un Courant de la pensée catholique. L'Hebdomadaire 'Sept', Mars 1934 – Août 1937* (Paris, 1961); on *L'Aube*, F. Mayeur, *L'Aube: Etude d'un journal d'opinion* (Paris, 1966); on *Esprit*, M. Winock, *Histoire politique de la revue 'Esprit'* (Paris, 1975), J. Hellman, 'The Opening to the left in French Catholicism: the role of the Personalists', *Journal of the History of Ideas*, 34, 3 (1973), pp. 381–90: R. Rauch, *Politics and Belief in Contemporary France: Emmanuel Mounier and Christian Democracy, 1932–1950* (The Hague, 1972).
24 Winock, *Histoire politique*, p. 103.
25 On this controversy, see J.-M. Mayeur, 'Une Bataille scolaire: les catholiques alsaciens et la politique scolaire du gouvernement du Front populaire', *Cahiers de l'association interuniversitaire de l'Est*, 1962, pp. 85–101.
26 Cristophe, *1936*, pp. 162–7.
27 For the reactions to the *main tendue* see, besides the general studies already cited, J. Hellman, 'French Left Catholics and Communism in the Nineteen-Thirties', *Church History*, 45, 4 (1976), pp. 507–23; F. Murphy, *La Main*

tendue: Prelude to Christian–Marxist dialogue in France, 1936–1939', *Catholic History Review*, 60, 2 (1974), pp. 255–70; E. Rice-Maximin, *The Main tendue:* Catholics and communists during the Popular Front in France', *Contemporary French Civilization,.* IV, 2 (1980), pp. 194–210.

28 Levy, 'Marseilles Working-Class Movement' (I, 9), pp. 364–5.
29 A useful overview is provided by P. Fridenson, 'Le Patronat français', in R. Rémond and J. Bourdin (ed.), *La France et les Français en 1938 et 1939*, pp. 139–58. On the employers' organizations see G. Lefranc, *Les Organisations patronales en France* (Paris, 1976), and H. Ehrmann, *La Politique du patronat français* (Paris, 1957). An important recent study, not used here, is I. Kolboom, *Frankreichs Unternehmer in der Periode der Volksfront* (1983).
30 See Rossiter's contribution to the Southampton conference, 'Popular Front Economic Policy and the Matignon Negotiations', based on his forthcoming Oxford D.Phil. thesis.
31 The first quotation comes from Jacques Barnaud, cited in Lefranc, *Juin 36*, p. 273; the second is cited in *ibid.*, p. 289.
32 Fridenson, *Histoire* (3, 77), p. 271.
33 *Ibid.*, p. 143.
34 The interpretation in this paragraph follows Rossiter, 'Popular Front Economic Policy' (see n. 30).
35 P. Guillen, 'La Situation sociale en province: l'Isère', EDC, pp. 156–9; Bourdé, *La Défaite* (3, 62), pp. 26–31.
36 See P. Machefer, 'Les Syndicats professionels français (1936–1939), MS (1982), pp. 90–112.
37 Gignoux, *Patrons soyez des patrons* (Paris, 1937).
38 See I. Kolboom, 'Patronat et cadres: la contribution patronale à la formation du groupe des cadres (1936–1938)', MS, 121 (1982), pp. 71–95.

The Post-mortem

1 L. Blum, *Oeuvres*, III-2 (1914–1928), p. 560.
2 On the details of the conflict with the Senate, see B. Minot, 'La Chute du premier gouvernement Blum et l'action des commissions des finances', *Revue d'économie politique*, 1 (1982), pp. 35–51.
3 G. Lefranc, *Histoire* (1, 17), p. 237.
4 L. Blum, *Oeuvres 1937–1940*, IV-2 (Intro., 1), pp. 42–64.
5 J. Moch, *Rencontres avec Léon Blum* (Paris, 1970), p. 235.
6 Parti Socialiste SFIO, XXXIVe congrès national (Paris, 1937), especially pp. 326–29, 451ff.
7 *Oeuvres 1937–1940*, IV-2 (Intro., 1), p. 137.
8 G. Dupeux, 'L'Echec du premier gouvernment Léon Blum', *Revue d'histoire moderne et contemporaine*, X (1963), pp. 35–44.
9 Quoted in Colton, *Léon Blum* (2, 1), p. 282.
10 I. Wall, 'The Resignation of the First Popular Front Government of Léon Blum, June 1937', *French Historical Studies*, VI, 4 (1970), pp. 538–54.
11 'Les Relations internationales et l'exercice du pouvoir pendant le Front populaire', *Cahiers Léon Blum*, 1 (1977), pp. 20–46.

12 Colton, *Léon Blum*, pp. 284, 292–3.
13 See his contribution to Roche and Tarting, *Des Années trente* (8, 61), pp. 69–72.
14 Quoted in A. Sturmthal, *The Tragedy of European Labour* (London, 1944), p. 71.
15 In LBC, p. 169.
16 See Rossiter, 'Popular Front Economic Policy' (9, 30).
17 Guéhenno, *La Foi*, (4, 7), p. 218.
18 Audry, *Léon Blum*, (2, 6), p. 49.
19 See D. Levy's contribution to the Southampton Conference, 'Economy and Society, Politics and the Working Class: Factors in the Organisation and Mobilisation of the Marseilles Working Class'.
20 Marjolin, *Europe nouvelle*, 14 May 1938.
21 S. Hoffmann, *Decline or Renewal* (New York, 1974), especially pp. 118–21.
22 See Judt, 'Une historiographe' (1, 7), p. 466.
23 Letter of 28 March 1934 in *Cahiers Romain Rolland 23. L'Indépendance de l'Esprit* (Paris, 1975).
24 *Cahiers des droits de l'homme*, 10 August 1935.
25 Sperber, *Au-delà de l'oubli* (4, 10), p. 122.
26 Hoffmann, *Decline*, p. 150.
27 This view of the Popular Front as a conflict of symbols is suggested by S. Berstein, 'L'Affrontement simulé des années 1930', *Vingtième Siècle*, no. 5, January/March 1985, pp. 39–53.
28 Roger Gouze, later to be brother-in-law of François Mitterrand, quoted in C. Nay, *Le Noir et le rouge* (Paris, 1984), p. 107.

Epilogue

1 H. Michel, *Les Courants de pensée de la Résistance* (Paris, 1968), pp. 352–5.
2 H.R. Kedward, *Resistance in Vichy France* (Oxford, 1978), p. 108.
3 J. Touchard, *La Gauche* (2, 11), p. 291.
4 J. Ozouf, 'L'Humanité et les journées de février 1934 (1945–1964)', MS, 1966, pp. 151–71, especially pp. 168–71.
5 *Le Monde*, 25/26 May 1986.
6 J. Lacouture, Léon Blum (2, 1), pp. 558–9.
7 A. Kriegel, *Un phénomène de haine* (2, 20), pp. 391–2.
8 Ozouf, 'L'Humanité'.
9 R. Kaes, *Les Ouvriers français et la culture: Enquête 1958–1961* (Paris, 1962), p. 208.
10 *Les Temps modernes*, X (1955), pp. 1576–625.
11 P. Mauroy, *Héritiers de l'avenir* (Paris, 1977), pp. 42–3.
12 On the treatment of the 40th anniversary of the Popular Front see J.-P. Rioux, 'Le Front populaire 40 ans après ou le cadavre dans le placard', *Esprit*, 6 (1977), pp. 93–102.
13 'Le Front populaire 1936 et l'unité aujourd'hui', *Cahiers du communisme*, 9 (September 1966).
14 *20e Congrès du Parti Communiste français* (1972), pp. 59, 65.

15 *L'Unité*, 14–20 May 1976.
16 'Front populaire: 1936–7; l'Echec des socialistes', *Repères*, June 1976; M. Charzat and J.-P. Chevènement, *Le CERES, un combat pour le socialisme* (Paris, 1975), pp. 7–10.
17 Quoted from Mitterrand's *Ma part de la verité* in C. Manceron, *François Mitterrand: l'homme, les idées, le programme* (Paris, 1981), p. 10. Or see Mitterrand's preface to P. Joxe, *Le Parti socialiste* (Paris, 1973): the PS 'a reçu en héritage la plus grande et la plus belle tradition socialiste. Il reste le parti de Jaurès, de Guesde, de Léon Blum'.
18 C. Nay, (10, 28), pp. 62–77.
19 *Le Monde*, 8/9 April 1979.
20 P. Joutard, *Ces voix qui nous viennent du passé* (Paris, 1983), pp. 174–5.
21 *Le Nouvel Observateur*, 28 September 1984.
22 See the articles of Meyer and Rioux in *Nouvelle revue socialiste* July/August 1981.
23 P. Mauroy, *C'est ici le chemin* (Paris, 1982), pp. 13, 21.
24 For an interesting comparison of the two experiments see R. Frank, 'La Gauche sait-elle gérer la France? (1936–1937/1981–1984)', *Vingtième siècle*, p. 3–21. See also T. Chafer and B. Jenkins, 'Ideological Parallels: 1936 and 1981', in S. Williams ed., *Socialism in France from Jaurès to Mitterrand* (London, 1983), pp. 35–56.
25 Cited in Frank, 'La Gauche', p. 5.
26 *Le Monde*, 16/17 March 1986.
27 *Libération*, 7 August 1985.

Bibliographical note

The notes provide a full bibliography of the historical literature on the Popular Front. This note will simply provide a selective guide to some of the more useful studies already mentioned in the notes as well as mentioning one or two others. When a book or article has already been listed in the notes, I will only give the name of the author followed in brackets by the chapter and note reference where full details can be found.

1 General studies

There is no general study in English. James Joll, 'The Front Populaire After 30 Years', *Journal of Contemporary History*, I, 2 (1966), pp. 27–42, is a brief introduction. Also H Johnson, 'Léon Blum and the Popular Front', *History* (1970), pp. 199–206. Otherwise Werth's contemporary journalism (1, 69) is as good a start as any, and highly readable. In French the best book remains Lefranc (1, 17), although Kergoat (Pref. 3) is now the most up to date. Bodin and Touchard (4, 7) is excellent on the atmosphere of 1936. The 1965 Sciences Po. Colloquium remains essential for a study of Blum's government. There are also a number of dependable narratives, strong on atmosphere weak on analysis: M. Chavardès, *Eté 1936. La Victoire du Front populaire* (Paris, 1966); J. Grandmougin, *Histoire vivante du Front populaire* (Paris, 1966); J. Delperrie de Bayac, *Le Front populaire* (Paris, 1972); A. Rossel, *Eté 36, 100 jours du Front populaire* (Paris, 1976) reproduces facsimiles of contemporary newspapers.

2 Films and photographs

For such a visual and theatrical experience as the Popular Front photographs are a vital source. A fascinating collection of photographs has been published: R. Capa, D. Seymour and G. Elgey, *Front populaire* (Paris, 1976). There are also many good photographs in R. Bordier, *36 le fête* (Paris, 1985). There are four documentary films: *Léon Blum ou la fidelité* by J.-N. Jeanneney; *Le Front populaire ou la mémoire du peuple* by C. Santelli and F. Verney; *Le Grand tourant* by Henri de Turenne and *Un Gout de bonheur* by Y. de Durandeau; and also important is Renoir's *La Vie est à nous* of which a video now exists at the Centre Pompidou, Paris.

344

3 Periodicals

There are frequent articles on the Popular Front in *Mouvement Social*. Issue No. 185 (1986) provides a nearly exhaustive list of previous articles appearing on the subject in the journal. Very important also are the PCF's *Cahiers d'histoire de l'institut de recherches marxistes*. In its previous incarnation as the *Cahiers d'histoire de l'Institut Maurice Thorez* the periodical was primarily useful as a guide to the latest official party line (there were few references to non-communist historians); in its new incarnation it has become much more open to the rest of the world and often publishes interesting extracts from the party archives which are available nowhere else: especially useful are issues No. 18 (1984) and No. 24 (1986), both devoted almost exclusively to the Popular Front.

4 Memoirs

Delmas (1, 1) and Belin (2, 3) are good on the *confédéré*, and later the *Syndicats*, points of view, without indulgence for the Communists or anyone else. Zay (2, 16) is interesting on the activities of an energetic minister. Duclos (1, 42) is no more revealing than most memoirs of Communists, while Bruhat (2, 18), although only briefly treating the Popular Front, is unusually open for a Communist. Among intellectuals, Guéhenno (4, 9) and Sperber (4, 10) are mainly Paris centred, and Jamet (1, 58) is local. For the right L. Rebatet, *Les Décombres* (Paris, 1976), is even more rancorous than Brasillach (4, 45). Abellio (1, 23) is interesting on the planist wing of the SFIO and on the Gauche Révolutionnaire; so also, on the latter, is Guérin (3, 30) whose book is as much a memoir as a history. J. Moch, *Rencontres avec Léon Blum* (Paris, 1970) is adulatory.

Of the four 'leaders', Thorez (1, 42) tells us nothing, Daladier never got beyond some preparatory notes for his memoirs which can be found in his papers at the Fondation Nationale des Sciences Politiques, and Jouhaux wrote nothing. Blum's collected works are an important source: Volume IV covers the Popular Front years and Volume V contains short memoirs and his defence at the Riom trial.

5 Biographies

Blum is well served by Lacouture (2, 1), Colton (2, 1) and Ziebura (2, 1); Joll (2, 13) provides a penetrating essay; Audry an intelligent critique (2, 6), Robrieux (2, 17) is excellent on Thorez, Georges and Tintant (2, 39) is the only study of Jouhaux, and there is nothing serious on Daladier. Chappat (4, 55) has lots of information on Lagrange, Brunet (1, 30) is definitive on Doriot. There is much of interest in J. Lacouture, *Malraux, un vie dans le siècle* (Paris, 1973).

6 Particular aspects

(i) *Local studies:* Levy (1, 9) on Marseilles is easily the best; Caron (1, 25) on the Languedoc stops in 1936; there is something in Gillet (3, 5) on the Nord. There are a large number of *mémoires de maîtrise* (masters' dissertations) on the Popular Front. Among these, which are of variable quality, there are several local studies.

Most of these *mémoires* have been very conveniently assembled at the Centre de Recherches d'Histoire du Syndicalisme in Paris. A pretty exhaustive list of them is provided by Kergoat (Pref. 3) in his bibliography. (Unfortunately one or two of those on the Popular Front are missing.)

(ii) *Origins:* James Joll, 'The Making of the Popular Front', in James Joll (ed.), *The Decline of the Third Republic* (London, 1959), pp. 36–66, is a good introduction. On the question of the role of Soviet foreign policy and Comintern's influence Santore (1, 4) and Haslam (1, 4) are especially useful; Vassart (1, 31) is still worth reading, though now incorporated in most versions.

(iii) *Strikes:* Danos and Gibelin (3, 2) remains the best overall study of the strike movement, from a 'leftist' perspective. It has been reissued in France in 1986 and also translated as, *June '36: class struggle and the Popular Front in France* (London, 1986). It must be supplemented by some case studies, especially Badie (3, 10) on Renault, Hainsworth (3, 12) on the mines of the Nord and Levy (1, 9) on Marseilles. For the degradation of the social climate after June 1936 see Bourdé (3, 62).

(iv) *Culture and Art:* There is lots of information in B. Cacérès, *Allons au devant de la vie. La Naissance du temps des loisirs en 1936* (Paris, 1981) and H. Noguéres, *La Vie quotidienne au temps du Front populaire* (Paris, 1977). But for analytical rigour the Ory articles (4: 14, 27, 74) are indispensable. His imminent Doctorat d'Etat on the Popular Front and culture promises to be a major work. Also interesting, with a strong *parti pris,* is Gaudibert (4, 39). To get a full appreciation of the cultural atmosphere of the period nothing is better than reading some contemporary periodicals, especially *Vendredi, Commune* and *Regards* (a popular magazine produced by the PCF); for the CVIA see *Vigilance,* for Amsterdam–Pleyel in the Popular Front period, *Paix-et-Liberté.* More esoteric, but also interesting, are *Le Musée vivant* (APAM), and *L'Art musical populaire* (FMP).

(v) *Economic policy:* Jeanneney (6, 18) although highly critical, remains a good introduction; Colton (6, 1) is judicious. For the 40-week Asselain (6, 35) is essential. Frank on rearmament (6, 45) is the best study of Popular Front finances.

(vi) *Foreign policy:* Dreifort (7, 1) is the most detailed study but he fails to convince that Delbos was a significant figure; Renouvin (7, 11) provides an excellent short introduction. On Spain, there are good chapters in Colton and Lacouture's biographies of Blum, and a useful collection of materials in Cahiers, Léon Blum (7, 24).

(vii) *The Popular Front organizations:* On the day to day politics of the PCF, Brower (1, 3) remains best but overplays the importance of Soviet diplomacy and needs to be supplemented by various recent issues of CIRM. Berstein (1, 44) is definitive on the Radicals, though his conclusions are not so different from Larmour's (8, 29). There is nothing as substantial on the Socialists: Greene (1, 72) is the weightiest study but, like Bilis (8, 2) and Gombin (8, 59), it concentrates almost exclusively on the foreign policy issue; Lefranc (8, 24) remains helpful. On the CGT, Prost (3, 19) is more than merely a statistical study, and Georges and Tintant (2, 39) are best on day to day evolution of policy. See also G. Lefranc, *Le Mouvement syndical sous la IIIe République* (Paris, 1967). Rogliano (8, 14) sets out the position of *Syndicats*.

(viii) *The Right:* There is no overall study but Rémond is the best introduction. For the Catholics see Cristophe (9, 22) and the employers Kolboom (9, 29).

7 Literature

It has been observed that, with the possible exception of Malraux's *L'Espoir*, the Popular Front produced no major work of literature. It has however figured in a number of works of fiction from J. Rémy, *La Grande lutte* (Paris, 1937) to J.-P. Chabrol, *L'Embellie* (Paris, 1968). For an exhaustive treatment of this issue see G. Leroy and A. Roche, *Les Ecrivains et le Front populaire* (Paris, 1986).

Index